D1222248

WARSHIP
VOLUME VII

Edited by John Roberts

Conway Maritime Press

Naval Institute Press

WARSHIP Volume VII

Managing Editor Robert Gardiner
Editor John Roberts
Art Editor Mark Stevens

Frontispiece: Apart from the Greek *Averoff*,
the Japanese *Mikasa* (shown here) is the only
remaining example of a predreadnought
battleship, a type that is covered in detail in
this volume.
CPL

© **Conway Maritime Press Ltd 1983**

**All articles published in WARSHIP are
strictly copyright and may not be reproduced
without the written consent of the publisher**

Published in the UK by
Conway Maritime Press Limited
24 Bride Lane
Fleet Street
London EC4Y 8DR

**Published and distributed in the
United States of America and Canada by**
the Naval Institute Press
Annapolis Maryland 21402

Library of Congress Catalog Card No 78-55455
UK ISBN 0 85177 309 5
USA ISBN 0-87021-982-0

Manufactured in the United Kingdom

Contents

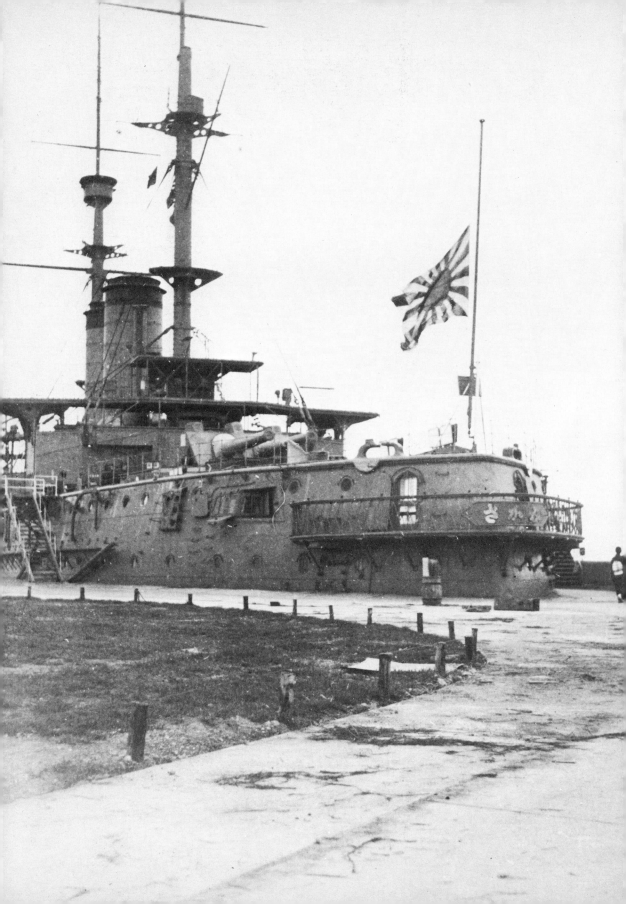

EDITORIAL John Roberts

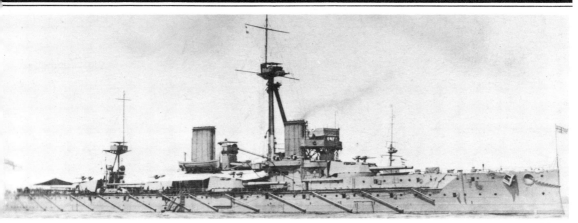

HMS *Dreadnought*
Marius Bar

In this issue of *Warship* we begin a four part series on the British predreadnoughts of the *Majestic* class. The first two parts, written by Karl Lautenschläger provide the background to the development of the type, details the circumstances which brought the predreadnought into existence and the reasons for its success. The final two parts, by R A Burt, will cover the technical details and history of the ships of the class in some detail. The approaches are different but equally of value to the naval historian and warship enthusiast.

The former, 'analytical', approach provides a broad picture from which can be viewed not just the ships in question but the whole period to which they belong. To be successful such a study requires detailed background research from which accurate conclusions can be made – no easy task as the omission of but one vital aspect of the whole can distort the resultant picture. Historians all too often over simplify the complex factors which produce major technological change, tending to seek one event or person upon which a new development hinged.

With the major change brought about by the battleship *Dreadnought*, for example, much, if not all, of the credit is often given to Admiral Fisher. In fact he was the catalyst which added the final impetus to the introduction of a type which, given a little time, would have appeared anyway. Fisher's particular brilliance was in realising that this was the case. In his view, in order to maintain the Royal Navy's supreme position it was necessary to take the first step, despite the effect it would have on Britain's considerable capital investment in pre-dreadnoughts, rather than risk a period of vulnerability which was likely to follow the introduction of the type by a foreign power. Whether he was right or not is debatable as Britain given its financial and industrial power, would have had little difficulty in recovering its position if such an event had occurred. A couple of dreadnoughts in a foreign fleet, would not, given the numerical advantage enjoyed by the Royal Navy, have brought about a defeat at sea. However, it must be admitted that *Dreadnought* did gain Britain a considerable advantage in time over the production of a German dreadnought fleet.

In fact the *Dreadnought* type, like the majority of major changes in warship development, was the result of improvements in technology, allowing the enhancement of ship design to an extent which required a reconsideration of their technical employment and the best configuration to meet it. In other words much the same circumstances as brought about the introduction of the predreadnought as so ably described herein by Karl Lautenschläger.

That Fisher did not entirely understand this natural chain of cause and effect can be seen in his continuous attempts to produce ever more powerful ships, which was likely to cause a continuous cycle of expensive obsolescence. The production of, for example, a larger and more powerful gun did not make possible the production of a ship, which would give one country the ultimate naval weapon, because the length of time required to build a fleet of such ships, and the certainty that other countries would quickly produce similar vessels, made such an attempt impracticable. Eventually the new weapon would simply be balanced by either improved protection, increased battle ranges or both. However, one such attempt can be described as coming close to succeeding. With the *Yamato* class 18in gun battleships the Japanese tried hard for a qualitative superiority by maintaining a degree of secrecy which was intended to ensure a long period of advantage for their battlefleet. Unfortunately for the Japanese the superbattleship was overtaken by events, never being produced in sufficient numbers and rendered obsolete by yet another technological change – the coming of the age of naval air power.

Northern Patrol Part 1

By Donald L Kindell

The battlecruiser *Hood* in 1939.

Tom Molland

In early August 1939, the old light cruisers that were to form the Northern Patrol's 7th and 12th Cruiser Squadrons were units of the reserve fleet. Those that would become the 7th Cruiser Squadron were *Diomede* and *Calypso* at Devonport; *Caledon* and *Dragon* at the Nore; *Effingham, Dunedin* and *Enterprise* at Portsmouth; and *Cardiff, Ceres* and *Colombo* at Devonport; while *Delhi* and *Emerald*, at the Nore, would form the 12th Cruiser Squadron.

Some 15,000 Naval Reservists had been ordered to their respective manning stations on 26 May 1939 and helped to provide crews for the reserve fleet ships which were brought forward to readiness for service on 15 June. The reserve fleet, with other units totalling 133 ships, were brought to Weymouth Bay where they were inspected and reviewed by King George VI on 9 August prior to being put on active service. Dispersal to their assigned stations began that night.

The 7th and 17th Cruiser Squadrons were based at Scapa Flow, but only *Diomede* and *Dragon* were completely operational by 31 August and both departed Scapa Flow on this date to patrol in the North Atlantic with the Home Fleet. When war was declared, four days later, the 7th Cruiser Squadron comprised *Diomede* (flying the flag of Captain Edward B C Dicken, OBE, DSC, Commodore Second Class), *Dragon, Caledon* and *Calypso*. The 12th Cruiser Squadron consisted of *Effingham* (Vice Admiral Commanding Northern Patrol, Vice Admiral Sir Max K Horton, KCB, DSO; formerly commanding the reserve fleet), *Dunedin, Emerald* and *Cardiff*.

The Northern Patrol was formed to enforce the blockade of Germany and exercise contraband control. It had been intended to maintain patrols between North Rona and the Faroe Islands, between the Faroe Islands and Iceland, and in the Denmark Strait, but due to the overage condition of the cruisers assigned to the duty and the arduous weather of the North Atlantic, an average of only two cruisers could be kept south of the Faroes and three between the Faroes and Iceland. This amounted to some five cruisers stationed in the 450-mile sealane between the north of Scotland and Iceland. The situation was not relieved until the middle of October when armed merchant cruisers (AMCs) began to be assigned to take up this shortage.

Without radar, these cruisers had a particularly difficult task. They were stationed some 20 miles apart and ordered to steam eastbound during night hours at a speed about equal to that of a merchant ship. Then at daybreak, they would steam westward combing a belt of some 200 miles during the day. While weather and the ever shortening days of the late autumn complicated an already difficult task, this system *did* prove itself to be effective.

To support the Patrol, a contraband control station

The battleship *Rodney* shortly before the outbreak of war.
Tom Molland

was located at Kirkwall. There eastbound merchant ships suspected of carrying contraband were taken for inspection.

EARLY OPERATIONS

Patrol activities began on 6 September. The *Caledon*, *Calypso*, *Cardiff* and *Dunedin* had already departed

The cruiser *Sheffield*, seen here entering Valetta harbour, Malta, on 17 July 1946, served with the Home Fleet during the early years of the war and was often employed in support of the Northern Patrol.
A & J Pavia

Scapa Flow on 5 September, while *Diomede* followed on the 9th as did *Effingham* and *Emerald* on the 10th.

To reinforce the Patrol and the blockade, Admiral Forbes (C-in-C Home Fleet) sortied from Scapa Flow at 0600 on 7 September with the battleships *Nelson* and *Rodney*, the battlecruiser *Repulse*, the aircraft carrier *Ark Royal*, the cruisers *Aurora* and *Sheffield*, and the destroyers *Faulknor, Firedrake, Fortune, Fury, Somali, Ashanti, Tartar, Bedouin, Mashona* and *Punjabi*. After patrolling off the Norwegian coast from 61° to 63° north, the ships returned at 18.15 on 10 September. Extremely poor visibility was the principal reason for the lack of contact on this patrol.

At dawn on 8 September, Rear Admiral Whitworth departed Scapa Flow with the battlecruisers *Hood* and

The destroyer *Foxhound*, as completed.
MoD

Renown, the cruisers *Belfast* and *Edinburgh*, and the destroyers *Fearless, Forester* and *Fame* to patrol between Iceland and the Faroes. The destroyer *Fury*, which had sailed the day before, joined the *Hood* force at sea. At noon on 12 September, Whitworth, like Forbes, returned empty-handed to Scapa Flow.

Reinforcements for the 12th Cruiser Squadron arrived at Scapa Flow on 11 and 13 September in the form of the light cruisers *Enterprise* and *Delhi* respectively. By 28 September, 108 ships had been sighted by the Patrol of which 28 were sent into Kirkwall for inspection. However, Kirkwall's first German prize was not captured by the Northern Patrol; during the first day's operation the German merchant ship *Hannah Boge* (2377 tons) arrived after being captured by the *Somali* in the North Atlantic on 3 September.

The Patrol was not without political complications beyond the obvious ones with neutral European nations. On 14 September, the American merchant ship *Warrior* (7551 tons) was sent into Kirkwall where her 5900-ton cargo of phosphates was seized as contraband. Despit protests from the United States, by 11 November 4. American ships had been inspected, of which 6 wer 'investigated as suspicious'. The issue came to a head o 3 January 1940 when the American merchant shi *Mormacsun* was intercepted and brought to Kirkwal Protests from the United States resulted in the practic of halting American ships being abandoned.

CAP NORTE

The light cruisers of the 18th Cruiser Squadron of th Home Fleet were also employed on Northern Patro duties. The *Belfast*, after sailing from Scapa Flow on October, achieved the Patrol's greatest single success On 9 October, 50 miles northwest of the Faroes, sh intercepted and captured the German liner *Cap Nort* (13,615 tons) carrying German Reservists from Sout America. *Belfast* also stopped two other merchant ship on the 9th and sent them into Kirkwall for inspectio before returning to Scapa Flow that evening. From 2 September to 12 October, 64 ships were sighted by th Northern Patrol and 20 were sent into Kirkwall but *Ca Norte* was the only German ship intercepted during th period.

In early October, with the German pocket battleship

at large in the Atlantic, priorities for convoy escorts required that *Effingham, Enterprise* and *Emerald* with their excellent endurance and seakeeping qualities, be sent to the convoy routes. The *Ceres* and *Colombo*, detached from other commands, replaced them in the 12th Squadron. When Vice Admiral Horton transferred his flag to *Colombo,* the Squadron was redesignated as the 11th.

Of the merchant ocean liners being converted to AMCs, the *Alaunia* and *Scotstoun* were ready by the end of September and in the next month, *Ascania, Asturias, Aurania, California, Chitral, Cicilia, Laurentic, Letitia, Maloga, Montclare, Rawalpindi, Salopian* and *Transylvania* were commissioned and entered duty assigned to the Northern Patrol.

In the period from 13 October to 26 October, 112 ships were sighted by the Northern Patrol and 53, including 6 German, sent in for inspection.

After the loss of the battleship *Royal Oak* in Scapa Flow on 14 October, the Northern Patrol cruisers were ordered to use Sullom Voe in the Shetlands as their new temporary base, although that base's only defences were anti-submarine nets.

Admiral Forbes, on report of the German armoured ship *Deutschland* attempting to break out into the Atlantic, took his fleet to sea to support the Northern Patrol cruisers and sweep for the enemy vessel. He sailed from Loch Ewe on 15 October with *Nelson, Rodney, Hood,* the aircraft carrier *Furious*, the cruisers *Aurora* and *Belfast* and the destroyers *Bedouin, Fearless, Foxhound* and *Fury*. The destroyer *Matabele* departed Aberdeen and later joined Forbes at sea, as did *Mashona* and

The destroyer leader *Faulknor* on 15 July 1935.
MoD

Firedrake from Scapa Flow. The *Repulse* departed Rosyth on 18 October with the destroyers *Jervis, Jersey, Cossack* and *Maori*. *Cossack* and *Maori* returned to Rosyth the next day and *Repulse* with *Jervis* and *Jersey* joined Forbes at sea on 20 October. This sortie which took the fleet 150 miles into the Arctic Circle north of Iceland ended without success on 21 October when the Fleet arrived back at Loch Ewe.

OCTOBER INTERCEPTIONS

Meanwhile, the Northern Patrol cruisers were doing well. British agents at Teneriffe reported that the German tanker *Biskaya* (6386 tons) had arrived off Las Palmas at 0200 on 7 October. *Biskaya* then steamed away and remained at large until she was intercepted and captured in the Denmark Strait by *Scotstoun* on 19 October. *Biskaya* was taken to Leith and later entered service under the British flag.

Also on the 19th, the German tanker *Gonzenheim* (4574 tons) which had left Rio Plata before the war began, scuttled herself when stopped by *Rawalpindi* who picked up the crew.

The German merchant ship *Bianca* (1375 tons) had departed Rotterdam before the war began for Lisbon. Disguised as the Finnish *Bian* she was challenged by a British destroyer 300 miles west of the Faroes and forced to seek refuge at Reykjavik. She attempted to escape back to Germany on 18 October, but two days later, at 11.50 on the 20th, in the Denmark Strait north of Iceland, she was captured by *Transylvania*.

On the following day the German merchant ship *Gloria* (5896 tons) was captured by *Sheffield* and taken to Kirkwall. En route, three of the German crew escaped in a lifeboat and were later picked up and taken to Methil, arriving 6½ days later. *Gloria,* herself, later sailed from Kirkwall and arrived at Leith for British service on 17 November.

Also on the 21 October, *Scotstoun* intercepted the German merchant ship *Poseidon* (5864 tons) in the Denmark Strait North of Iceland. She escorted *Poseidon* for 29 hours, but in thick snow the German crew abandoned ship and *Scotstoun* lost touch with the enemy vessel. *Transylvania* relocated *Poseidon* early on the 25th and found her incapable of steaming, so took her in tow and proceeded towards Reykjavik with *Sheffield* in company. When Icelandic waters were reached, *Sheffield* returned to Sullom Voe. However, before reaching Reykjavik, the tow parted in a gale and *Transylvania* was forced to sink *Poseidon* with gunfire on 27 October.

On 26 October, the German merchant ship *Rheingold* (5055 tons) was captured by *Delhi* on Northern Patrol. *Rheingold* went to Kirkwall, then Greenock arriving 20 November.

Seventy-nine ships were sighted by the Northern Patrol from 27 October to 9 November and 20 were sent into Kirkwall for inspection.

The *Javelin*, leading another *J* class destroyer.
IWM

NOVEMBER INTERCEPTIONS

Another wave of German merchant ships attempting to return to Germany resulted in 8 German ships being intercepted from 10 November to 23 November. In all, the Northern Patrol during this period sighted 93 ships and sent 50 into Kirkwall for inspection.

The German merchant ship *Mecklenburg* (7892 tons) had left Pernambuco on 14 October disguised as the Dutch ship *Hoogkerk*. On 12 November, she was intercepted by *Delhi* northwest of the Faroes and scuttled herself. On the following day the German merchant ship *Parana* (6038 tons) also scuttled herself when intercepted by *Newcastle* west of Iceland in the Denmark Strait.

The German merchant ship *Borkum* (3670 tons) was captured by *California* on 18 November in the Denmark Strait and, under a prize crew, she set off towards Greenock but en route she was torpedoed by the German submarine *U33*. The crew was able to run *Borkum* aground to prevent her sinking but she became a total loss.

On 20 November, *Punjabi* sailed from Greenock to join *Scotstoun* in escorting the German merchant ship *Eilbeck* (2185 tons), which had been captured earlier by the AMC in the Iceland-Faroes Channel, to the Clyde where all three arrived on 21 November. Also on 20th the German merchant ship *Berta Fisser* (4110 tons) was intercepted by *Chitral* southeast of Iceland. Much earlier on her voyage, she had the good fortune to be challenged in mid-Atlantic but not identified as German and allowed to proceed. This time, *Berta Fisser* scuttled herself; her crew of thirty two being picked up by *Chitral*. On 21 November, another German ship – *Tenerife* (2436 tons) – scuttled herself when intercepted by *Transylvania* west of Iceland (her crew of twelve officers and sixty one ratings were taken aboard) and, on the following day, a third vessel, the German *Antiochia* (3106 tons) also scuttled herself when intercepted by *Laurentis* west of Ireland.

On 23 November the German merchant ship *Konsul Hendrik Fisser* (4458 tons) was captured by *Calypso* north of the Faroes and taken to Leith for British service.

To be continued

The destroyer *Tartar* on 3 November 1941.
IWM

Warship Wings No4 FAIREY FLYCATCHER

By Roger Chesneau

Air-to-air shot of a Flycatcher from 403 Flight, HMS *Hermes*, showing the 'cranked' profile of the fuselage and uncowled Jaguar engine.

By courtesy of Ian Huntley

The Fairey Flycatcher is an aeroplane recalled with much affection by those associated with it, not only for its brisk yet docile flying characteristics but also for its legendary achievements at the public air displays of the 1920s and early 1930s. However, it was a remarkable aircraft for other reasons, not least because it was the first successful British fleet fighter designed from the outset for deployment aboard carriers. Requirements for flight deck operations were by no stretch of the imagination as taxing to the designer 60 years ago as they are today, indeed the aircraft deployed at sea in the early years of carrier aviation were essentially land-based types and made the transition with relative ease. Even so, the peculiar needs of carrier-based aircraft were already being understood, and the basics – compact stowage dimensions, short take-off runs, good stopping characteristics and general all-round ruggedness – were specifically designed into the Flycatcher.

Air Ministry Specification 6/22 invited manufacturers to produce a fleet fighter powered either by a 400hp Jupiter or a 400hp Jaguar engine, with a view to embarking new, standard equipment on board the carriers *Hermes* and *Eagle*, which were due to complete early in 1923. Both competitors, the Flycatcher and the Parnall-designed Plover, were accepted into Fleet Air Arm service, although in the event the latter was quickly phased out in favour of its demonstrably superior rival.

VARIABLE CAMBER WING

Fairey's long association with floatplanes enabled the firm to incorporate in the Flycatcher a device which lent itself admirably to shipboard operation. One of the major problems in flying from water had been the marked reluctance of the craft to become airborne: even before the actual take-off, the flying surfaces were tasked with the more difficult job of pulling the machine out of its partially immersed state. Maximum lift (in association with high forward speed – restricted by the drag imposed by the water) was therefore an essential prerequisite of such an operation. Such could be obtained by increasing the camber of the aircraft's wings, but the penalty would be an unacceptable drop in

Peaceful scene at Gibraltar, c1929: a Flycatcher floatplane from one of the FAA's Catapult Flights overflies the harbour, with *Argus* in the foreground. Alongside the quay are *Renown, Repulse* and *Tiger*; beyond them, a *Hawkins* class cruiser, HMS *Adventure*, a C class cruiser and two V & W class destroyers.

By courtesy of Ian Huntley

maximum achievable speed. Fairey had overcome the problem by introducing their 'patent camber-changing gear': in essence, this was the forerunner of the modern trailing-edge flap, wherein the cross-sectional geometry of an aircraft's wing is made variable in order to provide the increased curvature required and therefore greater lift, at the same time retaining the optimum aerofoil section for maximum speed in the conventional attitude. It is to Fairey's credit that they managed to incorporate the mechanisms for this device with a wholly acceptable weight penalty.

The relevance of such a device to flight-deck take-offs and landings is readily apparent since it contributes significantly to a lowering of an aircraft's stalling speed and hence reduces the length of flight deck required to be used, and the gear was to be a feature of Fairey designs through to the 1930s. It was incorporated in the Flycatcher, and was one of the reasons why that aircraft was able to 'slip-fly' straight out of the forward hangar on *Furious, Glorious* and *Courageous* via their auxiliary bow take-off decks and was the last British aircraft capable of flying off from turret platforms.

DECK HANDLING

Short-distance landings are another vital requirement of carrier-based aircraft, and in this respect, with the aid of its 'flaps', the Flycatcher could stop in 50yds with zero wind-over-deck: with a stalling speed of some 45kts, it may be appreciated how suited this performance was to a carrier steaming flat-out into a head wind!

A notable Flycatcher 'first' was the provision, in later

Superb study of the second Flycatcher amphibian, probably in 1925. The fixed wheels can just be distinguished in the chines of the floats. Note that this aircraft has a faired propeller, and that the fin is of larger area than that fitted to the landplane version. The fabric and metal areas of the fuselage can readily be identified.

By courtesy of Ian Huntley

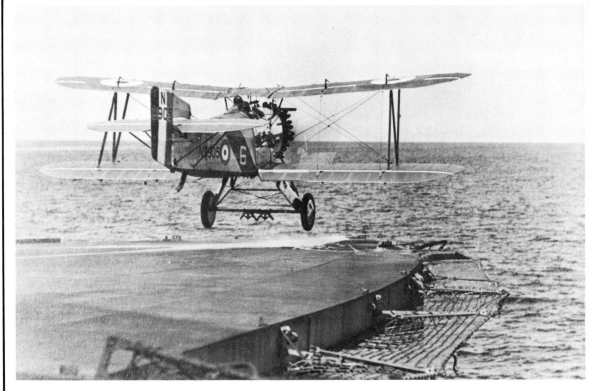

'Slip-flying' from a carrier – probably *Courageous* in this instance – was routine for Flycatchers in the 1920s, whereby the short forward deck permitted take-offs without interfering with main flight-deck operations. The photo shows well the Flycatcher's full-span 'flaps' and the Bryer axle hooks referred to in the text.

All photos: Fleet Air Arm Museum, via author

batches of aircraft, of hydraulic wheelbrakes. It should be noted that these did not reduce the landing run *per se*, but were fitted in response to one of the original (and somewhat fundamental) problems experienced by carrier pilots, namely keeping their mounts on the flight deck once touch-down had been achieved. Such was the frailty of early carrier-based aeroplanes, a frailty exacerbated by wind buffeting and pitching in any conditions other than a flat calm, that directing them along anything approaching a straight line on contact with the deck was a rare art, and one not mastered by many. It was for this reason that longitudinal wires were fitted along about half the flight deck length (generally just abaft amidships), to be engaged by Bryer hooks mounted on the aeroplane's undercarriage axle, thereby keeping the landing more or less parallel with the carrier's centreline. The Flycatcher was initially so fitted, but after the fore-and-aft wire system was abandoned about 1926, the wheel-brakes were utilised to the same end.

The Flycatcher did not have folding wings – its diminutive airframe posed no problems for carrier lifts – but it was capable of being disassembled into sections each measuring not more than 13ft 6in along its maximum dimension for the purposes of below-decks stowage; this was a stipulation of S.6/22. Further, it had to be capable of ready conversion into floatplane or amphibian configuration, versions which were not widely used, although the floatplane was employed as a spotter on board cruisers, stressed for catapult launches and the first FAA machine to be so.

In terms of longevity of service, the Flycatcher had few peers: deck-flying trials took place aboard *Argus* early in 1923, the type entering service later the same year, and the last FAA Flycatcher Flights converted to Ospreys in the summer of 1934. Testimony to its ruggedness is the fact that in its bombing role it could be dived vertically at full power; it was, indeed, the first FAA aeroplane to be subjected to official trials in this respect.

FAIREY FLYCATCHER, SPECIFICATIONS

Overall length:	23ft
Span:	29ft 0in
Max height:	12ft 0in
Wing area:	288ft²
Engine:	1 × 400hp Armstrong Siddeley Jaguar III/IV 14-cylinder 2-row radial
Max speed:	134mph (sea level)
Combat radius:	300nm at 80kts (10,000ft)*
Weight:	3000lb max loaded
Weapons:	2 × 0.303in Vickers machine-guns, 4 × 20lb bombs

*In practice, the endurance figure of about 3 hours is of more relevance to carrier-based Flycatchers, since on fighter missions they would not often have ventured outside visual range of the parent ship. No radio equipment was carried, signals from aircraft to base being communicated via flares or flags.

Askold Part 1

By Andrzej M Jaskuła
Translated by Adam Smigielski

After early delays in the construction of protected cruisers, Russia undertook the building of many such ships in the 1890s. Shortly after ordering the three protected cruisers of the *Diana* class from St Petersburg (now Leningrad) shipyards, the Russian Admiralty prepared specifications for a protected cruiser considered best suited to Russian needs. Such a cruiser was to displace no more than 6000 tons, to be armed with twelve 152mm QF guns, have a range of 5000nm, and be a fast twin screw ship capable of 23kts. The *Morskoj Techničeskij Komitet* (MTK – Maritime Technical Committee) received many tenders from foreign shipyards and one from a Russian yard. After careful examination, it was concluded that the two best designs were from the German shipyards Krupp-Germania Werft, of Kiel and Vulkan, of Stettin and in the spring of 1898 both were offered contracts.[1].

Thus on 16 August 1898[2] Krupp-Germania Werft received an order to build the first class protected cruiser *Askold* for the Russian Navy. Finance was provided from the 1898 Naval Programme in the same way as it had earlier with the cruiser *Varyag* built in the USA (see *Warship* 11). The ship was to be built in 23 months and the cost (without armament) was calculated as 8.2m Marks (3.9m gold Rubel). The new contract was a prestige one for the shipyard. According to captain, first class, N K von Reitzenstein, who was to be the future commander of the ship, and was overseeing the progress of building, the Germans were making every effort to 'make the cruiser the best, and the first to be completed, of all Russian ships ordered in foreign shipyards'.

BUILDING HISTORY

To obtain the specified high (for the time) speed of 23kts the German designers chose an excessively long and narrow hull, which was to be built with very light scantlings. *Askold* was 130m long and had a beam of 15.0m compared with *Varyag* at 127.9m long and 15.8m beam and *Bogatyr* even shorter at 126m length and 16.46m beam.

Askold differed in many respects from the, earlier, *Varyag*. She was fitted with, as it turned out, very reliable Thornycroft-Schulz watertube boilers, had a three shaft machinery arrangement, five very characteristic long thin funnels and her main guns were protected by small splinter shields. Three shaft machinery was

The hull before launching – present are members of the church and officers.

J Miciński collection

included contrary to the initial Russian specification but as the shipyard already had experience with this arrangement (in the cruiser *Kaiserin Augusta* for the German Navy) it was approved.

For no known reason there was no mention in the contract of the required metacentric height. Only in 1900 was this important parameter guaranteed by an additional clause specifying 0.96m GM with normal coal supply and 0.86m GM with full coal supply. Calculated maximum tensional stress was double that normally adopted in Russian shipbuilding practice. Subsequently, following trials, the ship's hull had to be strengthened.

Askold's keel was laid on 20 July 1899 and she was launched on 15 March the following year. As the shipyard was, for the first time, undertaking the construction of both the ship and her machinery it could not keep to the schedule and completion was a little late. There were many defects resulting from the haste and these were put

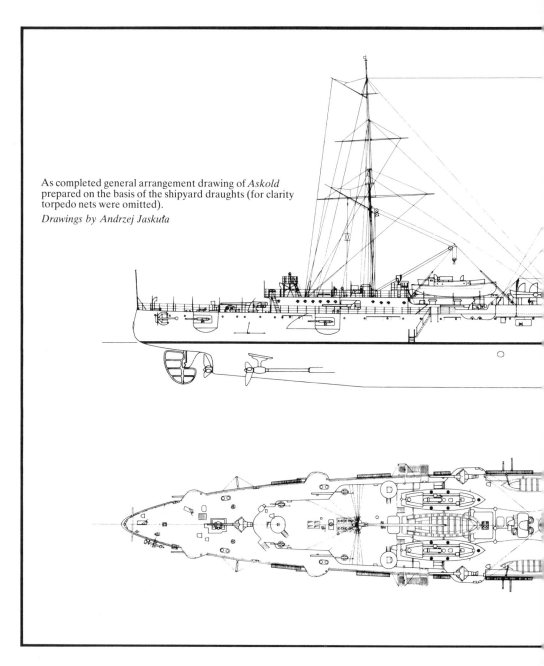

As completed general arrangement drawing of *Askold* prepared on the basis of the shipyard draughts (for clarity torpedo nets were omitted).

Drawings by Andrzej Jaskuła

right only after they were located by the Russians, especially by engineer E R de Grofe.

CAREER OF THE ASKOLD

The cruiser was delivered to the Russians on 2 October 1901 after the trials programme was complete. The rest of the crew arrived in Germany on 1 December 1901 – 300 officers and men from Kronstadt. *Askold* was officially commissioned on 25 January 1902 at Kiel and a few days later was sent to her Russian home port. During the summer of 1902 she was assigned to the Trial Ships division and on 16 September 1902 to the Pacific Fleet, sailing via the Suez Canal for the Far East, although officially she still belonged to the Baltic Fleet. On the way from Kiel to Alger engineer colonel A N Krylov took measurements of the tensional stress in the hull in a seaway. *Askold* visited some Persian Gulf ports[3] and later went to Yokohama where she arrived on 4 February 1903. On 26 February, together with the two battleships *Peresvet* and *Petropavlovsk* she arrived at Port Arthur.

The journey from the Baltic to the Far East took 3 months and 13 days – much less time than taken by other Russian ships sent earlier. Her commanding officer captain N K von Reitzenstein and his chief engineer, I I PoklevskiKozell, took good care of the ship. Shortly

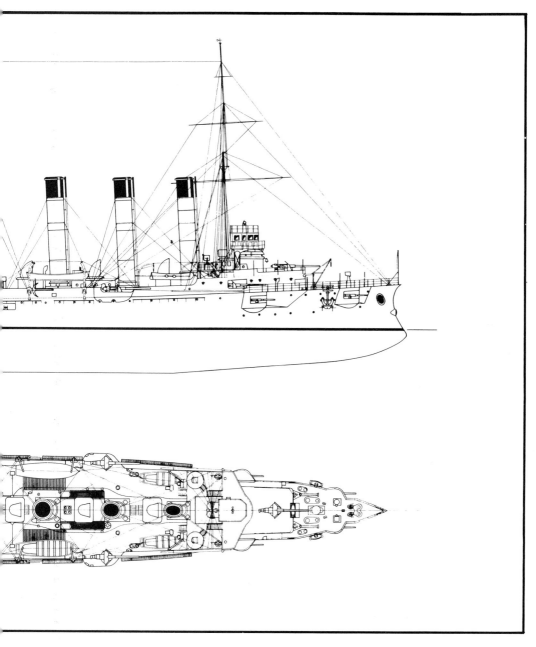

after arrival, *Askold* went out for trials, and although the Thornycroft-Schulz boilers were at the time considered by some as useless, she attained with ease the designed indicated horsepower and a mean speed of 20kts. It is worth noting that she went on trial without preparation or docking shortly after a trip half way round the world, a feat made possible by the good work of her crew and because the boilers were fired with high quality Cardiff coal. Feed water was supplied from the ship's evaporators. Some of the officers considered the black gang too few to maintain high speed for long periods but *Askold* had one of the best trained crews in the Russian Far Eastern Fleet. She made many trips between Japan-

ese and Chinese ports. According to the ship's log she was painted grey and olive green on 9 October 1903, together with most of the other ships in Port Arthur.

THE RUSSO-JAPANESE WAR

Askold proved her worth in the early days of the Russo-Japanese war. At that time she was commanded by captain first class K A Grammatĉikov. The war had begun with a surprise attack by Japanese destroyers on the Russian fleet anchored in the roadstead of Port Arthur. *Askold* was not damaged and survived the terrible night of 8–9 February 1904 intact but on the next

Askold on trial in 1901; note the thinner forward funnel.

Askold before the Russo-Japanese war; the pilot house was already mounted on the top of the conning tower and the topmasts fitted; note the peace-time white paint scheme.

J Miciński collection

The damaged *Askold* arrives at Shanghai in 1905

J Miciński collection

day, after successfully operating in support of Russian destroyers, she was slightly damaged by Japanese cruisers.

On 8 March Vice Admiral S O Makarov arrived at Port Arthur and took overall command of the Far Eastern Fleet, hoisting his flag in *Askold*. He was an able and courageous commander and took the Fleet to sea many times to fight the Japanese, believing that offense was the best form of defence.

When on 10 March 1904 the Russian destroyer *Stereguŝĉij* was overwhelmed by the Japanese, he sailed in the scout cruiser *Novik*, because *Askold* could not raise steam quickly enough. However, the Japanese under Admiral Dewa,7with a more powerful force, necessitated a return to Port Arthur (*Novik* had only 120mm QF guns) where he transferced back to *Askold* and sailed once more, this time preventing the Japanese capturing the sinking Russian destroyer.

On the night of 21/22 March Japanese destroyers attacked the Russian base and Makarov pursued them in *Askold* accompanied by a squadron of battleships and cruisers but he returned to port when the main Japanese force was sighted. Early on the morning of the 27 March the fleet, under Makarov, sailed to intercept a Japanese attempt to block the entrance of Port Arthur but the Japanese withdrew.

On 12 April Makarov put to sea with battleships *Petropavlovsk, Poltava* and *Pobieda* escorted by four cruisers, including *Askold*, to help the armoured cruiser *Bajan* which had been surprised by the Japanese Third Cruiser Division when rescuing survivors from the destroyers *Straŝnyj*. All went well, but on the return trip *Petropavlovsk* hit a mine, there was a magazine explosion and the ship, together with Admiral Makarov, was lost. After the death of Makarov the Port Arthur fleet nearly ceased operations and only a direct order from Tsar Nikola II to the new commander, Rear Admiral Vitthoft, forced him to try, on 10 August 1904, to escape to Valdivistok.

TSUSHIMA

During this attempt the Russian fleet was intercepted by Japanese forces under Vice Admiral Togo near Cap Shantung. The leading Russian battleship was hit twice by 305mm shells and Rear Admiral Vitthoft and his staff were killed. The ship left the line causing confusion among the Russian fleet and the commander of the cruiser division Rear Admiral von Reitzenstein (a former commanding officer of *Askold*) on seeing this decided to break off the action and go directly to Vladivostok. In his flagship, *Askold*, a signal was hoisted which read 'Follow me' and the cruisers turned to a southern course where they had to pass four enemy cruisers and many destroyers. *Askold* was followed only by *Diana* and *Novik*, the other Russian cruisers choosing to remain with the battleships.

In the meantime the number of Japanese cruisers opposing the Russian ships had risen to seven but, due to the coming of dusk, and their high speed of about 20kts *Askold* and *Novik* escaped.

According to Admiral Sir C Bridge (The Russo-Japanese Naval Campaign of 1904, published in Brassey's Naval Annual 1905) 'The condition in which *Askold* emerged from the fight deserves attention. In the earlier part of the action, when the cruisers were but little engaged, she was hit twice. A 12in shell, believed to have been fired by the *Shikishima*, burst close above the upper deck near the foremost funnel. It killed the officer who was working the rangefinder on the starboard side of the bridge, which was shattered. The lower plating of the funnel was torn. This lead to the blocking of the uptakes from the foremost boilers, which had to be disconnected as already mentioned. A shot on ricochet passed through the outer skin about 4.5ft above water, and ignited some ready use 3in QF ammunition. The fire burnt itself out without any damage. It may be observed that of the fires which occurred on board Russian ships in action, more than one was due to the ignition of their own ammunition where it had been allowed to accumulate ready for supply to the guns. In the latter part of the fight when the *Askold* broke through the Japanese Fleet, she is stated to have been exposed to the concentrated fire of seven Japanese ships – principally unarmoured cruisers, but one cruiser of the *Asama* type, most likely the *Yakumo*, was amongst them. The *Askold* closed in the hope of being able to discharge a torpedo at a Japanese armoured cruiser but the chance did not occur, or the torpedo missed, for, if discharged at all, it did no harm.

'The ship, in this latter part of the battle, was hit, mostly abaft the beam, by shot in ricochet, by 14 large and great number of smaller projectiles and fragments of shells. Two of her funnels were shot away. Her boats were riddled by small shot and flying fragments and were rendered unserviceable. A heavy shell made a hole about a foot square in the breastwork of the upper deck but the explosive effect was slight. About five 8in and three 6in shell hit her, besides two small-calibre, probably 3in, shell, which did visible damage, one having gone through the upper deck, and burst in a cabin, whilst the other put a shot-hoist out of action. The other striking shots of which the effects could be traced were believed to be of large calibre. A 6in shot struck the ship near the waterline but its explosive effect was small, and it was specially noted that the armoured deck was uninjured. An 8in shell struck her exactly on the waterline, and tore a hole about 2.5ft square in the outer skin, but did no further mischief. At last three 8in shell made holes in the ship's side, and wrecked officers' cabins. In one case an insignificant fire was started. When she arrived at Shanghai the *Askold* was found to be without her two midship 6in guns. She had been five times in action, and each of her 6in guns had been damaged, but were replaced by others before 10 August. The absence of the two guns above mentioned may have been due to insufficient reserve at Port Arthur to replace damaged pieces, or because guns had been landed from the Russian fleet to supplement the armament of the land defences. It is to be noted that no 6in gun-shield was perforated or considerably bent. The *Askold*, during the whole action, fired 200 6in and 300 3in QF shells'.

On the morning of 11 August 1904 it was found that, because of the damaged funnels, coal consumption rose

Askold in the First World War; she was painted grey; forward casemates were plated over and the torpedo nets were removed.

J Miciński collection

to such a level that there was insufficient fuel to get the ship safely to Vladivostok. *Novik* went alone to that base where she went aground off Sachalin Island and was destroyed by her own crew to prevent capture by Japanese cruisers. *Askold* arrived at neutral Shanghai where she was docked and interned for the rest of the war. There was also the destroyer *Grozovoj* in Shanghai.

THE FIRST WORLD WAR

After the war *Askold* was released and served with the Siberian Flotilla in the Far East. When the First World War broke out she was in the Ochotsk Sea. Together with *Zemchug* she was detached to Hong Kong and served under the orders of Vice Admiral T Jerram – commander of the British Eastern Fleet. They were the only Russian ships which took part in the hunt for the German East Asiatic squadron commanded by Vice Admiral Graf von Spee, *Askold* patrolling the waters around the Marianas, Caroline and Marshall Islands. At the beginning of September 1914 both Russian cruisers were sent to the Indian Ocean where they escorted convoys between Calcutta and Suez. Later *Askold* patrolled the Calcutta-Colombo route against possible attack by the German raider *Emden*. After Turkey joined the war she was sent to the Mediterranean on 11 December 1914 and served there under the orders of British Admiral Peirse, but she still officially belonged to the Siberian Flotilla.

Many times *Askold* conducted shore bombardments She shelled Urla on 7 December and Beirut on 16 December where she sank the German transport *Pete Rickmers* (1913, 5162 grt) and the hulk of the old Turkish gunboat *Kilid el Bahr* (ex *Sed el Bahr* 1894, 632 tons). On 15 December she took a prize – the Turkish steamer *Haife* (1790 grt).

Askold was the only Russian ship to take part in the Anglo-French action against the Dardanelles and she distinguished herself shelling Turkish shore positions. At one time she was sighted by Kptl Hersing, commanding *U-21* but she was spared, despite a good firing position for the U-boat, as her sinking would have alerted the nearby British forces to the U-boat's presence. This was on the 25 May 1915 and on the following day *U-21* returned to sink *Askold* but did not find her.

In 1916 *Askold* was assigned to the Northern Flotilla, which was formed in February. Duty on *Askold* was very hard for the crew because of the lack of contact with their families and the long stays at sea. During 18 months of war she sailed nearly 55,000nm. In 1914 alone she steamed 2653 hours and covered 27,460nm, consuming over 16,000 tons of coal. Leaking boilers and machinery in grave need of overhaul made it necessary to put the ship under repair.

REFITS

Before going north she was sent, on 3 February 1916, to Toulon in France for an overhaul. Work proceeded very slowly and there was some crew unrest caused by revolutionaries, inspired by Russian emigrants and radical French workers. Four crew members were shot and another 100 were sent to prisons and forced labour camps in Russia.

On 26 December 1916 *Askold* was sent to Gibraltar for a work-up lasting two weeks. In January 1917 she arrived in Great Britain for further repairs at Devonport. Where, after receiving news of the February revolution in Russia, some officers were removed from their duty at the crew's request.

Between January and June the ship was docked, her condensers were repaired and she was fitted with depth charge launching gear. *Askold* arrived at Murmansk on

17 June 1917 where she was used to screen convoys between Arkangielsk and Bodo in Norway, against the reported presence of German U-boats.

On 14 July 1918 the ship together with other Russian warships of the North Flotilla was captured by the British, preventing the crews plan to scuttle their ship. The crew did not want to serve under foreign officers and left the ship. Part of the armament was removed and installed on the armoured train Admiral Kolcak which was later captured by the Red Army.

From 3 August 1918 until 1921 *Askold* was listed as the British ship *Glory IV*, moored in the Garelock, Scotland, as an auxiliary ship.

In 1921 the British Government agreed to return the old cruiser to Russia. The ship was carefully examined by a soviet commission under engineer A N Krylov (mentioned earlier in this article) and it was decided to pay the British for the upkeep of the ship for two years and then take it over. As *Askold* was by this time old and surplus to the new Soviet Navy's requirements she was sold to German breakers in 1922. The money received in payment for her and other old, ex tsarist, warships sent to the breakers, was used to buy locomotives for Russia's heavily devastated railways.

To be continued

Footnotes

1 The design of *Bogatyr*, prepared by Vulcan , was better than that of *Askold* but was submitted later.

2 All dates in this article are given according to the Georgian calendar (new style – vice old style ie Julian calendar used in old Russia).

3 As the only five funnelled warship in the world, *Askold* made a great impression on the Persians – it was a time when laymen in this area judged the power of a ship by the number of her funnels. Shortly after *Askold*'s visit, the British protected cruiser *Amphitrite* visited the Persian Gulf area on her way to the China station. She was twice the size of *Askold* but had one serious drawback – she only had four funnels. To save the prestige of the Royal Navy her commanding officer ordered his crew to rig two dummy wooden funnels bringing the total number of funnels to six – one more than in the Russian ship. To make the deception more realistic, steam pipes were placed inside the dummy funnels.

The Development of the British Escort Carrier

By D K Brown RCNC

Britain's first escort carrier, the *Audacity* in 1941
IWM. All photographs courtesy of R A Burt

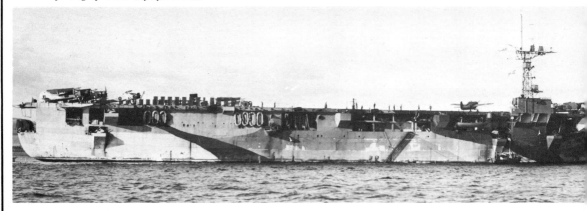

HMS *Campania* in June 1944.
IWM

The *Activity* in 1944.   *IWM*

The earliest ideas for carrying aircraft to sea in defence of trade were put forward by the Admiralty to the Air Ministry in 1926. It seems likely that the intention was to use seaplanes, launched by catapult, and recover them by crane as was actually done in a few Second World War armed merchant cruisers. By 1931 plans had advanced further and it was suggested that the catapult should be capable of launching aircraft of up to 7000lbs in weight and that a landing deck, with arrester wires, be fitted abaft the funnel. At this stage the ideas for carriers were at a very informal stage; there was no Staff Requirement and no sketch design was prepared.

In November 1932, the Director of Naval Construction (Sir A W Johns RCNC) was asked to investigate the possibility of modifying a merchant ship into a small aircraft carrier but, due to other commitments for his small staff, it was not until 1934 that the first studies were forwarded to the Controller together with a request that further work be deferred until 1936. The 1934 studies covered a range of merchant ships from 14,000 to 20,000 gross tons and from 15 to 20kts. In all these studies a hangar and a single lift were provided together with three arrester wires. The deck varied in size from 285ft × 65ft to 300ft × 80ft and it was estimated that the conversion work would take about 9–12 months.

It was then realised that a landing deck abaft a funnel and superstructure was not really practicable as had been demonstrated in HMS *Furious*. Further studies concentrated on diesel engined ships where it would be easier to divert the uptakes to the sides of the ship with either an island or flush deck configuration.[1]

TRADE PROTECTION CARRIERS

In 1935 the Naval Staff agreed on firm requirements for the type of ship needed for conversion to trade protection: **a** Gross tonnage between 10,000 and 20,000 tons; **b** Diesel machinery, with as high a speed as possible; **c** Endurance of at least 600nm at 14kts; **d** A flight deck, with a minimum width of 70ft, fitted with arresting gear and aircraft lifts; **e** Hangar stowage for 12–18 aircraft; **f** HA/LA armament of 4.7in guns and close-range weapons.

By February 1936 outline arrangements to meet these requirements had been prepared for two typical ships: the MV *Winchester Castle*, a twin screw diesel ship of 20,000 tons gross and 631ft overall length; and MV *Waipawa*, also a twin screw diesel ship but of 12,500 tons gross and 516ft overall length. The Controller approved these plans in April and asked for the conversion of four more liners to be investigated to a Naval Air Department requirement issued in March 1937. The DNC suggested that approval be sought for suitable merchant ships to be earmarked for conversion to aircraft carriers in the event of war. It was also suggested that the structural plans of the selected ships should be obtained so that the conversion could be worked out thoroughly in advance of the war. In 1937 five ships were selected as suitable – *Winchester Castle, Warwick Castle, Dunvegan Castle, Dunottar Castle* and *Reina del Pacifico* – it was decided that *Waipawa* was too small to be suitable). No

staff were available to pursue the work and it was shelved entirely until after the Munich crisis. Even then, the project was given very low priority since there were seven carriers complete and six were building or planned. It did not seem worth diverting the attention of scarce staff to add to this number. Money was still limited and the aircraft industry would have had difficulty in producing the planes needed for these five ships in addition to other requirements.

AUDACITY

When war broke out no action was taken to complete the plans or to reserve the chosen ships. The two smaller 'Castles' became armed merchant cruisers and the others were used as troop ships.

In 1940 the need to provide fighter and anti-submarine protection to convoys became acute and outline plans were prepared for a range of conversions known as Types 'A', 'B' and 'C'.

It is interesting that the description in Table 1 seems to be the first RN acceptance of a deck park, used by the USN for many years, and proposed by the DNC (Johns) in the early 1930s. The specification was seen as an elastic one which could be varied to match the characteristics of the actual ships requisitioned.

Towards the end of 1940 the Director of Air Material proposed that a small merchant ship should be given a very limited conversion as a trade protection carrier and a Staff Requirement was issued on the 12 December. The captured German merchant ship *Empire Audacity* (ex-*Hannover*) was allocated on the 2 January 1941 for conversion to a carrier – it *had* been intended that she become an armed boarding vessel. Advance information was supplied to the Blyth Shipbuilding Yard on the 17 January and final information completed by 7 March. HMS *Audacity* completed on 26 June followed by 10 days of trials and a month for working-up.

The minimum possible amount of work was carried out in order to get her into service quickly: superstructure, masts, derricks, etc above the shelter deck were removed and a flight deck built to a height of 60ft above the keel. In order to preserve stability it was necessary to stow 3000 tons of ballast. The shelter deck remained as the strength deck and, in order to prevent the flight deck, and hangar sides, from taking unwanted loads, three expansion joints were fitted. The deck, which was 435ft × 60ft was supported by deep beams and longitudinal girders, with pillars to the shelter deck. The ship's side was plated-in up to the flight deck with openings for boats and the embarkation of stores.

There was no island; the diesel exhaust was led out through the starboard side and platforms were built both sides, 4ft 6in below the flight deck, for navigation and signalling. There were two arrester wires designed for 9000lb aircraft giving a pull out of 120ft for an entry speed of 55kts. There was no accelerator and no hangar, the six aircraft being parked on the flight deck. *Audacity* retained much of her merchant ship character below the flight deck. The original passenger cabins were used by the air crew. All the engine room personnel together with many seamen were Merchant Navy personnel with

TABLE 1: PARTICULARS OF ESCORT CARRIER DESIGNS

	A	B	C
Max speed (kts)	20	18	16½
Endurance (nm)	15,000	15,000	As much as possible
Aircraft	25	15	10
Aircraft in hangar	16	12	4
Lifts	2–45ft × 34ft, 15,000lbs	1–45ft × 34ft, 15,000lbs	1–42ft × 20ft, 10,000lbs
Flight deck min (ft)	550ft × 75ft	500ft × 70ft	450ft × 60ft
Arrester wires	6	6	4–5
Barriers	2	2	1
Petrol stowage min (gallons)	75,000	50,000	33,000
Armament	2 twin 4in HA/LA 4-M pom-poms, Oerlikons	2 twin 4in HA/LA 4-M pom-poms, Oerlikons	1 twin 4in HA/LA 4-M pom-poms, Oerlikons

Notes: All these ships were to have had an island bridge and one accelerator (catapult). They were also to have had asdics and a crane.

The largest of the British escort carriers, the 17,000 ton *Pretoria Castle*, was employed only on training duties after her conversion from an AMC in 1943.

MoD

T124X articles.[2] *Audacity* quickly proved her value in operations against both submarines and long-range aircraft but was sunk on 21 December 1941, on her fourth convoy. Because of the severe shortage of British ships suitable for conversion, the US Navy was asked, on 20 January 1941, to act as agents for the building of six modified *Audacitys* in American yards. Drawings were forwarded on 4 February but the programme was dropped in favour of US designs, as was a later plan (1 April) for six larger vessels based on the *Winchester Castle* plans. The availability of US built Escort Carriers to the

RN combined with shortage of suitable merchant ships meant that the British programme of conversions had low priority.

IMPROVED CONVERSIONS

Experience with *Audacity* showed the need for a hangar and a new design was prepared and approved in November 1941. Lifts, and other long-lead equipment were ordered in December and on 10 January 1942 the *Telemachus* – then building at the Caledon Shipbuilding Co, Dundee – was requisitioned.

This ship was launched on 5 May 1942 as HMS *Activity* and completed on 14 October that year. She was intended to comply with the Type 'C' design, modified in the light of experience with the *Audacity*. The *Telemachus* was not stripped down to the upper deck and

TABLE 2: ESCORT CARRIER PARTICULARS

	Audacity	Activity	Pretoria Castle	Nairana, Vindex	Campania
Length (oa)	467-3	513	594-7	525-6	538
Breadth (mean)	56	66	76	68	70
Draught (ft-in)	21-7	25-2	29-1	25-8	22-10
Displacement (deep/ light) (tons)	10,200/8600	14,250/10,870	23,450/19,000	17,200/14,500	15,970/13,000
Horsepower (bhp)	5200	12,000	16,000	10,700	13,250
Speed (kts)	14½	18	18	16	18
Endurance (at speed)	12,000 (14½)	15,000 (16)	16,000m (16)	13,000 (16)	17,000 (17)
Ship fuel (tons)	649	2015	2430	1655	2229
Complement	210	375	666	639	639
Armament	1-4in 4-20mm 2 single pom-poms	1-twin 4in 4-20in (single) 10-twin 20mm	2 twin 4in 2 quad pom poms 10 twin 20mm	1 twin 4in 4 quad pom-poms 8 twin 20mm	1 twin 4in 4 quad pom-poms 8 twin 20mm
Aircraft hangar/deck	–/6	6/6	15/6	19/7 (total 20 in service)	19/7 (total 20 in service)
Lifts, dimensions (ft)/ weight capacity (lbs)	–	42×20/10,000	45×39/15,000	45×34/15,000	45×34/15,000
Flight deck (ft)	453 × 60	498 × 66	560 × 76	502 × 66	515 × 70
Arrester wires	2	4	6	8 (N) 6 (V)	4
Barriers	–	1	2	2 (N) 1 (V)	1
Petrol stowage (gallons)	10,000	20,000	74,000	52,000	52,000
GM deep/light (ft)	3.3/2.7	4.3/3.9	3.8/1.97	4.8/2.75	4.95/3.85
GZ deep/light (ft)	4.2/4.1	3.4/3.8	5.4/4.54	5.8/4.38	5.6/4.6

TABLE 3: CONSTRUCTION PARTICULARS

	Builders	Laid Down	Launched	Completed
Nairana	John Brown	6 November 1941	20 May 1943	12 December 1943
Vindex	Swan Hunter (Flight deck by Smiths dock)	1 July 1942	4 May 1943	3 December 1943
Campania	Harland & Wolff	12 August 1941	17 June 1943	7 March 1944

Vindex on 5 January 1944.

MoD

hence the only space on which to build a hangar was the after well deck. This hangar was 87ft long and 66ft (59ft clear) wide, just big enough for six folded Swordfish aircraft. Initially, she carried six other aircraft on deck but by 1944 her complement was reduced to three Swordfish and seven Wildcat fighters. There was a single lift, 42ft × 20ft, to the flight deck at the after end of the hangar which could carry 10,000lb aircraft. The flight deck was 498ft long and 66ft wide with four arrester wires for 15,500lb aircraft, two with a pull out of 145ft at 60kts entry speed and the other two with 120ft pull out at 55kts entry speed. In addition a safety wire, with a very short pull out, and a crash barrier were fitted.

The minimum stability requirement was for a metacentric height of at least 3ft in any undamaged conditions and 1600 tons of ballast was required to reach this standard. The crew was a mixture of RN and Merchant Navy (T124X) and hence there were two standards of accommodation. A small island superstructure was fitted on the starboard side.

PRETORIA CASTLE

On 24 March 1942 it was decided to convert HMS *Pretoria Castle*, then serving as an armed merchant cruiser, into a Type 'B' escort carrier. It was also intended to convert the *Dunnotar Castle, Carnarvon Castle* and the *Georgic* but the Ministry of War Transport would not agree to release the three latter ships. Three diesel engined cargo ships, then under construction were allocated in their place and will be discussed later.

Pretoria Castle was then in hand by Swan Hunter's in July 1942 and completed twelve months later. The superstructure was stripped down to 'C' deck which was extended to become the strength deck. A hangar and flight deck were built on top with expansion joints. The hangar was 354ft long, 46ft wide and 17ft high and could accommodate fifteen aircraft – a deck park for a further six planes was also provided. The lift was fitted at the forward end. A very useful feature of *Pretoria Castle*'s equipment was a cordite operated catapult (Mk CII) which could launch any plane in service up to the end of the war.

She had 40lb protective plating over her bomb rooms, magazines and steering gear together with a similar thickness on the sides; 2500 tons of ballast was needed. Like the other ships, she had a mixture of RN and Merchant Navy in her crew.

The three fast cargo ships allocated by the Ministry of War Transport for conversion into escort carriers became HMS *Nairana*, *Vindex* and *Campania* and were taken over on 29 June, 20 October and 29 July 1942. They differed in dimensions (Table 2) and in the details, which were left to the builders.

All three ships were already under construction when requisitioned – *Campania* had been on the stocks for almost a year and *Vindex* the least, at 3½ months. Some dismantling of existing structure was needed before the conversion could begin. The original, merchant ship structural design was followed except in the region of the upper and second decks where the thickness of the shell was slightly reduced. Internal decks were made watertight and additional transverse bulkheads built near the bow and stern to improve subdivision. The gallery and flight decks were built above the upper deck with the shell plating carried up to the flight deck. The hangar and flight deck were worked structurally –ie no expansion joints were fitted. This new structure was mainly welded.

The hangar extended the full width of the ship and was 231ft × 61ft × 17ft 6in (*Campania* 198ft × 63ft 6in). One lift was fitted at the after end of the hangar and this slowed aircraft operation to such an extent that this class never carried more than twenty planes for operational work.

The aviation fuel tanks were surrounded by void spaces as were bomb rooms and magazines. One-inch protective plating was fitted over the latter compartments and empty oil drums were used for torpedo protection. No bomb lifts were fitted. Accommodation was all to RN standards.

These three ships were used entirely for Arctic operations and were fitted for night flying operations and for fighter direction. Little was known in 1944 concerning the low temperature brittle fracture characteristics of steel and the rivetted hulls of these ships were seen as safer than the all welded hulls of US built ships. While a crack can start in a rivetted plate it will almost certainly stop at a rivetted joint, while in a welded ship a crack could travel right round the hull.

CONVERTING THE QUEENS

Consideration was given to converting the liners *Queen Mary* and *Queen Elizabeth* into aircraft carriers and in 1942 a design was provided by John Brown in conjunction with the DNC. Particulars included a flying-off deck of 500ft × 66ft; a landing deck of 416ft × 125ft; two hangars of 670ft × 45ft each (one port, one starboard) an armament of four twin 4in and five four-barrel pom-poms and 72 aircraft. This scheme was abandoned in June 1942.

The British escort carriers were generally successful as ships but there were a few problems. The increased windage of the hangar structure meant that heavier anchors and cables were needed on conversion. The existing windlasses were retained and these were often overloaded resulting in frequent breakdowns.

The original fit of four arrester wires, one safety wire and a single crash barrier proved inadequate and was increased where possible. Ventilation to living spaces near the hangar had to be improved by fitting forced exhaust.

Comparision with US built escort carriers is not easy since the USN design was a more expensive ship, intended to support opposed landings as well as for trade protection. *Activity* cost £850,000, and *Campania* £1,520,000 much less than the $11 million of the *Commencement Bay* class. In consequence the US ships were bigger and faster with more aircraft and much better aviation equipment.

The MAC ship *Empire Macandrew*, as completed in 1943.

MoD

Empire Maccoll in November 1943.

MoD

The *Amastia* was converted into a MAC ship from a merchant tanker.

Shell

VULNERABILITY

There were major differences in the approach to vulnerability. An enquiry into the loss of the US built HMS *Avenger,* which blew up when torpedoed, showed that bombs and depth charges were stowed against the ship's side and had been detonated by splinters from the torpedo hit. In all RN operated ships and some American vessels, longitudinal bulkheads were then built 15ft in from the side and weapon stowage confined to the spaces between the bulkheads. Stability of the first four US built ships to be transferred to the RN was inadequate to survive the flooding of two compartments and 1000 tons of ballast was added together with empty oil drums in the wing tanks.

1 The Royal Navy's *Tracker* class were US built lend-lease vessels, this is HMS *Battler* as completed.

IWM

2 The US built carrier HMS *Pursuer* in an arctic swell on 31 March 1944, during Home Fleet operations covering the Russian convoys JW58/RA58. In the background is the carrier *Furious*.

MoD

HMS *Dasher* was lost due to an accidental petrol explosion, blamed by the RN on lack of safety precautions in the design and by the USN on British lack of experience. Extensive modifications were made to the petrol stowage in the RN ships leaving them with a capacity for 36,000–52,000 gallons instead of the design figure of 151,000 gallons.

The later group of ships – *Ameer* class – were all buil at the Seattle-Tacoma yard and then proceeded to Van couver for a 6-week modification programme. The afte end of the flight deck was extended and given a 'round down' to improve air flow. The US ships were built ver quickly, using prefabrication to a large extent togethe with a standardised range of fittings, often made by firm not accustomed to ships. In consequence there were a number of teething troubles to put right. Together with a 5- and 6-week work up it took 20–27 weeks from com pletion to the first operation. This led to complaints from the USN but, in practice, their own record with th *Bogue* class was little better.

REFERENCES
[1]D K Brown 'The Development of the Aircraft Carrier prior t WWII', *Interdisciplinary Defence Review 1983*
[2]K Poolman *Escort Carrier 1941–1945* (Ian Allan 1972)

The M Class Submarine Monitors

By Thomas A Adams

HM submarine *M1* as built.
/SPL Collection, via author

he *M* class 'monitor submarine' appears to have been
rst discussed in September 1915, at the initial meeting
f the Submarine Development Committee. This
ommittee, which sat under the Chairmanship of the
Controller, Admiral Tudor, was charged with consider-
g questions of British submarine designs. Of the six
ems listed on their agenda, one was recorded as the
monitor submarine'. Interestingly, the minutes show
at the term 'monitor submarine' was actually used for
ant of a better term. What actually generated the ini-
al idea to include the subject on the agenda has been
ifficult to define, but there is some evidence to suggest
at one reason was the fact that the torpedo was
ntrustworthy as a weapon and this caused more
mphasis to be placed upon gun power.

The question of designing a boat to actually take a
2in gun was considered and as a result of discussion,
onsideration was also given to a 7.5in gun with a range
f 8000yds, with an aircraft for spotting. The Commit-
e decided that the Director of Naval Construction
ONC) should actually prepare plans for two sub-
arines:

i a boat with a low velocity gun having a large capacity
shell; and
ii another with a high velocity gun firing a projectile of
around 200lbs. Two guns of around 7.5in calibre to be
carried if possible and with armour protection provided.

By the date of the Committee's second meeting, on 2
October, representatives of the DNC had produced one
design for a vessel to carry a 12in/23 calibre gun and
not the 7.5in as had been decided previously. There
was initially no agreement on the purpose and role of
this 'monitor submarine'. Finally it fell to Commo-
dore(S), a Commander S Hall, who was in favour of the
large low velocity gun, to submit his views and arguments. The Director of Naval Ordnance (DNO) was
also asked to produce estimated ballistics of the proposed 12in gun, and the DNC to report approximately
the displacement, dimensions etc, on a submarine to
carry:

a a modern 12in gun; and
b to carry two 12in guns – one forward and one aft.

Commander Hall's arguments were based on a
number of factors:
a Submarines found it increasingly difficult in bringing
off successful torpedo attacks due to (i) the high speed
and zig-zagging course of the enemy, and (ii) the comparatively low speed of torpedoes and resulting errors

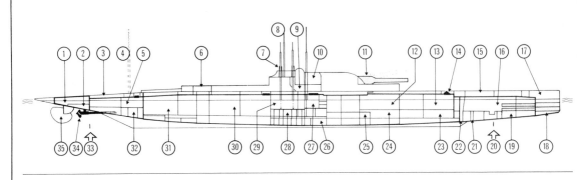

M Class Submarine 1916

ADAMS NAUTICAL RESEARCH SERVICE
VISUAL PRODUCTION ©

KEY: 1 Steering gear compartment, **2** Aft trimming tank, **3** Aft free flooding spaces (controlled), **4** Radio mast (alternative positon), **5** Crew quarters, **6** 12pdr HA gun housing, **7** Periscope(s), **8** Radio mast(s), **9** 12in magazine, **10** Loading and director tower, **11** 12in BL gun (depress 5°, elevate 20°, train 15°), **12** Officers' quarters, **13** Auxiliary machinery compartment, **14** Torpedo loading hatch, **15** Forward free flooding spaces (controlled), **16** Torpedo room, **17** Free flooding space (controlled), **18** 4 torpedo tubes (18in on *M1/M2*) (21in on *M3/M4*), **19** Forward trimming tank, **20** Position of fore hydroplanes, **21** Forbes log tank, **22** Chain locker, **23** No 1 Battery tank, **24** No 2 Battery tank, **25** Distilled water tank, **26** Hydraulic tank, **27** Hydraulic machinery room, **28** No 3 Battery tank, **29** Control room, **30** Engine room, **31** Main motors and after machinery compartment, **32** 12pdr magazine, **33** Position of aft hydroplanes, **34** Twin screws, **35** Rudder.

Viewed from astern, the *M3* after her conversion to a minelayer in 1927. The mines were stowed inside the casing and laid through its after end – the opening being closed by a door which opened radially, hence the odd shape at the after end of the casing.

WSPL Collection, via author

due to wrong estimation of the enemy's speed and course.

• If a submerged submarine observed a ship, came to the surface, fired a large shell, then there was no time for the enemy ship to evade.

• A submarine could only carry a small number of torpedoes, whereas a large number of gun shells could be carried.

The Committee's reasons for finally deciding upon the building of the 'monitor submarine' are recorded as:

i that a boat with a 12in gun would find its own opportunities for action in the North Sea, if the enemy became active (which in 1915 was considered very likely).

ii if the gun failed, there still remained a good fighting boat.

iii the boat should effect surprise when it came into action.

iv The Admiralty should be abreast of any enemy developments in that direction.

Submarines *K18–K21* had been ordered in February 1916, but before building commenced, The Admiralty decided to substitute them with four *M* class boats. Consequently, an order was placed with Vickers to build the first *M* class boats – *M1* taking the place of *K18*. *M2* (ex-*K19*) was ordered from Vickers in May 1916. In August 1916, Armstrong Whitworth received orders to build two more – *M3* (ex-*K20*) and *M4* (ex-*K21*).

The building and construction of *M1* was accelerated after some early delays and she came into service in June 1918, just a short time before the end of the war. Immediately, questions arose as to her future and it was actually suggested that *M2–M4* should be completed without the 12in gun and be refitted for overseas patrols. The First Sea Lord, however, turned this down and ordered that they be completed as originally designed.

But what of this original design? It was obviously governed by the 12in gun, its mounting and auxiliary spaces, but also by the fact that the main engines, motors and batteries used were to be the same as was then being fitted in the *L* class submarines.

CONSTRUCTION

The *M* class were partial double hull boats with the double hull extending for about 65 per cent of the length. Built to withstand a diving depth of 200ft, 12.8lb frames were used, spaced 21in and 18in apart. The pressure hull was built from 25lb and 22lb plating and the outer hull from a variety of 30, 25, 20, 18, 15 and 10lb plating – a strange mixture. However, most of the lower outer hull was actually built to pressure standards with the main ballast tanks reportedly tested to 50lb/sq in and designed to withstand diving depth. There were 11 watertight bulkheads making 12 internal main compartments all tested to 35lb/sq in.

MAIN TANKS

The class was designed with 20 external main ballast tanks (numbered 1 to 10, port and starboard) with a total capacity of some 375 tons. To improve the submerged stability two tanks were converted into buoyancy tanks before completion and therefore they actually only had 18 main ballast tanks with a total capacity of 337 tons.

To achieve quick diving – reportedly 90 seconds – scoop valves were fitted to the ballast tanks, just below the water line and also additional Kingston valves were fitted. All the venting valves were worked by telemotor and together with the scoop valves could be operated from the central control room.

The outer hull as it continued forward to the bows, created three controlled free flooding spaces with a total capacity of 27.5 tons. A similar tank aft had a 15-ton capacity.

Additionally the *M* class boats had 9 compensation tanks with a capacity of 46 tons and 12 auxiliary ballast tanks with a capacity 105 tons.

MAIN MACHINERY

This comprised two Vickers single-acting, 4-stroke, 12-cylinder diesels with bore 14.5in, stroke 15in – developing 1200bhp at 380-400rpm. One engine was coupled to each shaft, driving a 3-bladed, 5ft10in diameter propeller, each of which weighed 14.96cwt and had a flat surface area of approximately 12.15sq ft.

MAIN MOTORS

Two single armature type motors were coupled together on each shaft, giving 800bhp per shaft for a total of 1600bhp at 300rpm (220 volts at a rating of 1½ hours). Additionally an auxiliary propelling motor of 20hp was fitted to operate on the starboard shaft only.

FUEL TANKS

Fifteen external tanks were designed to carry 76.36 tons of oil fuel. HM Submarine *M2* differed slightly in that her No 9 (p & s) main ballast tanks were fitted for oil fuel, giving her a total bunkerage of 110 tons.

BATTERIES

The battery outfit comprised a total of 336 Exide lead acid cells weighing 137.42 tons. They developed 220 volts with a full speed duration of 1½ hours.

HYDROPLANES AND STEERING GEAR

The fore and aft sets of hydroplanes were 'drowned' as in the *E* type boats, and were activated by a 3hp motor. Total plane area was 41sq ft (forward) and 60sq ft (aft). The steering gear was on a telemotor control system incorporating hand gear. The rudder area was some 67sq ft.

TORPEDO ARMAMENT

The *M1* and *M2* were fitted with four 18in bow tubes with a total load of 8 torpedoes. *M3* and *M4* had a similar fit but used 21in torpedoes, these boats being some 10ft longer to provide for the larger torpedoes.

GUN ARMAMENT

The main feature of the *M* class submarine was its 12in BL gun of 40 calibres. The gun, the loading chamber and director tower was forward and incorporated in the bridge superstructure; the 12in magazine, shell room and hydraulic machinery room occupied about 30ft of the length of the pressure hull, directly below the gun. Forty rounds of 12in ammunition and shell were carried.

The gun was designed to train through 15°, elevate to 20° and depress to 5°. The loading operation was carried out on the surface and both loading and firing was carried out from inside the loading chamber. The muzzle of the gun was fitted with a watertight tampion electrically controlled from the loading chamber.

The 12in guns are understood to have been Mk IX and came from a *Majestic* class battleship. The gun and mounting weighted 120 tons and the 40 rounds of ammunition some 29 tons.

It must not be overlooked that these boats were fitted aft with a 12pdr (3in) HA gun, this being on a 'disappearing' mounting which when not in use folded with the gun into the after casing. This gun had a separate magazine for 72 rounds of ammunition.

The *M3* entering harbour. The 12pdr gun aft was on a disappearing mounting which could be lowered into the casing.

WSPL Collection, via author

HM SUBMARINE M1

The *M* class prototype, reported to have handled well when submerged. The gun and mounting were classed as satisfactory and no damage was reported during gun trials. Surface speed trials were conducted on the Stokes Bay measured mile, where she reached only 14.7kts

TABLE 1: PARTICULARS OF M CLASS

Length oa	295ft 9in (303ft for *M3/M4*)
Length bp	280ft (290ft for the *M3/M4*)
Length wl	290ft
Breadth	24ft 8in
Breadth, inner hull	20ft
Depth	18ft 6in
Depth, inner hull	16ft 6in
Draught	15ft 9in
Displacement	1601 tons (surface), 1950 tons (submerged)
Surface speed[4]	16kts at 2400 bhp
Submerged speed[4]	10kts at 1600 bhp
Surface endurance[4]	2500nm at 16kts[1]
	4000nm at 10kts
Submerged endurance[4]	10nm at 10kts
	80nm at 2kts
Diving Depth	200ft[2]
Periscopes	2 × 30ft[3]
Complement	65 officers and ratings

[1]. *M2*'s endurance was increased by 45 per cent due to larger fuel capacity.
[2]. In practice it was unlikely that 100ft would have been passed.
[3]. One was fitted as a rangefinder and one used for gun control.
[4]. Design figures.

TABLE 2: PARTICULARS OF TANK NUMBERS/CAPACITIES

	No	Capacity
Main ballast tanks (internal)	2	14.89
Main ballast tanks (external)	18	337.2
Controlled free flooding spaces	3	42.5
Trimming	2	9.23
Auxiliary ballast tanks	12	105.3
Compensating fuel tanks	9	42.61
Oil fuel (external only)	15	76.36
Lubricating oil tanks	2	10.00
Fresh water	3	17.30
Distilled water	1	2.00
Store room	2	7.8
Hydraulic tanks	1	13.93
Magazines (including shell room)	3	94.2

TABLE 3: COMPARISION OF BUILDING WEIGHTS WITH L CLASS (TONS)

	M1/M2	L1-8
Hull	662	354
Main machinery, motors and batteries	248	248
Auxiliary machinery	33	33
Equipment and services	119	87
Spares and sundries	12	12
Ballast keel	140	44
Torpedo armament	23	29
Gun armament	146	6
	1483	813
Oil fuel and Lubricants	87	56
Fresh water	17	9
Auxiliary ballast weight	114	42
	1601 tons	920 tons

However, the water was considered shallow for such a large boat and she reportedly achieved 15.4kts on another occasion. New propellers were ordered, however, in an attempt to obtain her designed speed of 16kts. On 12 November 1925 she was lost after a collision with SS *Vidal*, off Start Point.

HM SUBMARINE M2

The submarine *M2* was actually converted in 1928 to a submersible seaplane carrier. The 12in gun was removed and a large hangar fitted in lieu, with a large handling crane on its roof. A catapult was fitted on the wide horizontal forward casing to operate a Parnell Peto seaplane. This conversion, undertaken at Chatham Dockyard, was a great success. *M2* retained her original good underwater handling and quick diving ability. Records show that she could surface from periscope depth, open hangar, catapult aircraft, secure hangar and dive in a total of 5 minutes. She was lost on 26 January 1932, when conducting flying operations off Portland Bill.

TABLE 5: M2 POST-CONVERSION PERFORMANCE

Speed	14.1kts (surface), 6.4kts (submerged)
Endurance (surface)	2350nm at 14kts
	3700nm at 10kts
Endurance (submerged)	1.7 hours at 6kts
	6.0 hours at 4kts
	12.00 hrs at 1.9kts
Fuel capacity	97.5 tons

HM SUBMARINE M3

Converted in 1927 to an experimental minelayer. The submarine *M3* had her 12in gun removed and twin mine rails were laid on top of her hull. The rails, running for some two-thirds of the boat's length, were enclosed in the free-flooding casing. She could carry 100 mines and was considered to have been a great success. Work with her led to the design and building of the *Porpoise* class minelaying submarines. *M3* was scrapped in 1933.

HM SUBMARINE M4

M4 was laid down in 1917 but work was suspended in 1918. On 30 November 1921 her hull was sold to her builders.

SOURCES

DNC Records of Warship Construction 1914–1918
Technical History Vol II (TH21)
Ship Histories (Naval Library)

TABLE 4: BUILDING DATES – M Class Submarines

	M1	M2	M3	M4
Building yard	Vickers	Vickers	Armstrong	Armstrong
Ordered	2.1916	5.1916	8.1916	8.1916
Laid down	7.1916	13.7.1916	4.12.1916	1917
Launched	9.7.1917	15.4.1919	14.10.1918	Cancelled
Completed	17.4.1918	14.2.1920	9.7.1920	

This and the other photographs accompanying this article are
of a remarkable 1200 scale model of the battleship *Yamato*
built by Michael Wünschmann.

Jürgen Peters

The Japanese Super Battleship Strategy Part 1

By Hans Lengerer

On 22 April 1930 the London Treaty for the limitation
and reduction of naval armaments was concluded. The
Japanese naval leadership did not agree with the terms
of the treaty, informed the nation that they considered
it a threat to national security, and opposed it with
great energy. The basic reason for this position was
that, in addition to the primary battle vessels (battleships and battlecruisers), even the 'quasi-primary battle
vessels' – the heavy cruisers equipped with 8in
(20.32cm) guns – were restricted in numbers to below
70 per cent of the American tonnage. The battleships
and battlecruisers had been limited to a ratio of 5
(USA) : 5 (England) : 3 (Japan) in the Washington
Treaty of 6 February 1922. Within the Navy Ministry,
the Admiralty staff and the Fleet, officers of all ranks

complained that, with her forces reduced to this level
Japan would not be in a position to fight successfull
against the USA.

It was only after protracted internal argument, whic
led amongst other things to the resignation of the chie
of the Admiralty staff, that the Japanese governmen
succeeded in convincing the naval chiefs that the quar
titative restriction did not necessarily mean a qualita
tive limitation. The Navy accepted this, and the treat
was signed, while at the same time, the naval budge
was expanded to facilitate the modernisation of existin
warships and the construction of new vessels c
improved power – the latter to include a new battleshi
design which ultimately became the *Yamato* class.

THE DESIGNER

Amongst the Japanese naval architects of this time, the individual who carried the responsibility for the design of new warships was Captain (of shipbuilding) Kikuo Fujimoto. He was the senior designer of the well-known 'special-type destroyers' (*Tokkai Kuchikukan*) of the *Fubuki* class, and he demonstrated his new theory of warship design by the use of a novel clean

TABLE 1: Planning Programme for 18in Gun Battleships

Building Programme	3rd	4th	5th	6th
Number of ships	2	2	3	4
Design Year	1936	1937	1941	1941
Project commencement of construction	1937	1939	1942	New plan

silhouette for the destroyers. Fujimoto was a man of great foresight – amiable, prepared to compromise but an extravagant drinker. He prepared the way to his position as designer of Japan's last generation battleships by his success with the *Fubuki* design, which departed from orthodox theories of shipbuilding, the new hull form with its higher centre of gravity, proving excellent. When he designed the four cruisers of the *Mogami* class, which featured five 15.5cm triple turrets, he applied the same principles. Incidentally, it is interesting to note that the dimensions of the *Yamato* were proportionally similar to those of the *Mogami*, and this

fact brought the following comment from a British specialist in shipbuilding: 'I am surprised that the Japanese shipbuilders know any theory!' – in fact stability was excellent.

He also decided to adopt 20cm twin turrets for the secondary armament in the new battleship, which was to be built as a replacement for a ship to be taken out of service, in accordance with the Washington Treaty. Moreover, he decreed that the substructure for the 15cm and 20cm turrets was to be of such a design that they could be mounted in the same barbettes. Thus the smaller guns could easily be replaced by the larger, should the disarmament treaties end and war break out. This provided a rapid means of increasing the number of 8in gun cruisers, of which the Japanese Navy did not have sufficient number.

Fujimoto proposed a further surprising plan. He wanted to design the new battleships in such a way that the 18in triple turrets could be replaced by 20in twin turrets, as it seemed that this calibre was likely to appear in due course as a result of the fierce competition in the acquisition of larger battleships. At the time of the London Treaty's signing the government and Navy agreed that Japan had no alternative but to aim for qualitative advantage if they were to stay on level terms, should the treaties terminate, or Japan withdraw from the Treaty.

CONSTRUCTION PLANS

Preparations for the building of the new battleships had been in progress since 1930, although the real preparatory work did not begin until 1934, 14 years after the 8-8 Fleet, and in 1937 the ship was laid down. The

TABLE 2: PLANNED ORGANISATION FOR BATTLESHIPS OF THE COMBINED FLEET

Fleet	Division	Ships
		Position October 1938 — planned for 1944
1st	1st	4 super battleships (2 from 3rd and 2 from 4th building programmes)
1st	2nd	*Nagato, Mutsu*
2nd	3rd	*Fuso, Yamashiro, Ise, Hyuga*
2nd	4th	*Kongo, Hiei, Haruna, Kirishima*
		Position in October 1938 — planned for 1950
1st	1st	4 super battleships (2 from 5th and 2 from 6th building programmes)
1st	2nd	4 super battleships (2 from 3rd and 2 from 4th building programmes)
1st	3rd	*Nagato, Mutsu*
2nd	4th	*Fuso, Yamashiro, Ise, Hyuga*
2nd	5th	*Hiei, Kirishima*
3rd	14th	*Kongo, Haruna*
		Position on 17 January 1941 — planned for 1950
1st	1st[1]	4 super battleships (4th building programme)
1st	2nd[2]	3 super battleships (5th building programme)
2nd	3rd[1]	4 super battleships (2 from 3rd and 2 from 4th building programmes)
2nd	4th	*Nagato, Mutsu*
2nd	5th	*Fuso, Yamashiro, Ise, Hyuga*
2nd	6th	Two *Kongo* class battleships

Notes: 1 Division to include eight B class (*Akizuki* Type) AA destroyers
2 Division to include four B class AA destroyers

TABLE 3: JAPANESE PLANS FOR BATTLESHIP SUPERIORITY

	1936	1941	1946	1951

JAPAN

Yamato x 7
18in x9

gun replacement

Yamato x 7
20in x6

Super-Yamato x 4
20in x 8

New BB 16in

USA

18in

20in

Japanese supremacy in gun
power for 10 years

Remarks: _ _ _ _ under construction

_____ in service

A close up of the quarter deck showing the after 18in gun
mounting and the comprehensive aircraft arrangements.

Jürgen Peters

The model of *Yamato* from the starboard bow.

Jürgen Peters

new shipbuilding policy had decided that the super-battleships were to be armed with 18in guns, a calibre which had not been adopted by any other Navy to that time (except for the British in the 'large light cruiser' *Furious* with its 18in gun, but this gun had a barrel length of only 35 calibres, and had nothing like the performance of the guns intended for the *Yamato* class). This policy was to be kept a closely-guarded secret.

The policy of secrecy held out well: before 1944 the Americans had no plans for battleships with 18in guns. If the war had not broken out in the Pacific, the Japanase Navy would eventually have had 4 battleships with 18in weapons in service, and a further 7 under construction. In theory she would have had at her disposal 11 battleships with 18in guns compared with the 17 new battleships of the US Navy, (from BB55 *North Carolina* to BB71 *Louisiana*), all of which had 16in guns.

The decision to build four new battleships in expectation of the 'foreseeable' re-expansion in naval armament' had been made as early as 1924. The specific plan followed in 1936: namely two battleships in the Third Naval Armament Supplementary Programme of 1937 (abbreviated as 3rd Programme – *Maru San*

Keikatu) and a further two in the Fourth Naval Armament Supplementary Programme *(Maru Yon Keikatu)*. Two ships of the *Kongo* class were to be scrapped, so that a total of 12 battleships would be available. In the meantime the USA passed the 20 Per Cent Fleet Expansion Act in May 1938. The Admiralty staff reacted by expanding its plans to include a further 2 battleships but in 1941 it became clear that Japan would still not be able to counter the expansion of the US Fleet with their current plans when the American 11 Per Cent Fleet Expansion Act and the Two-Ocean Fleet building programme (70 per cent expansion) of 1940 were passed. Consequently the Navy included one further battleship in the Fifth Naval Armament Supplementary Programme of 1942 *(Maru Go Keikaku)* and two more in the Sixth Naval Armament Supplementary Programme *(Maru Roku Keikaku)*, although the latter programme did not progress beyond initial studies. The planning for the battleships with 18in guns ran as shown in table 1.

FUTURE PLANS

Although neither Japan's industrial capacity nor her financial position would have allowed it, a 'dream fleet' was drawn up for the year 1950, which included 19

TABLE 4: CONSTRUCTION PLANS FOR 18in GUNS (February 1934)

	Period	Years
Design:	1934 – end 1936	3
Manufacture of fittings:[1]	1934 – mid 1937	3½
Test construction of barrels and barbettes:	Spring 1934 – end 1937	3¾
Proof firing and range tables:	1938	1
Test construction and turret mounting:	Mid 1935 – Spring 1938	2¾
Building turrets for first ship:	1937 – autumn 1939	2¾
Fitting turrets in first ship:	Autumn 1939 – Spring 1940	½
Building turrets for second ship:	1938 – autumn 1940	2¾
Fitting turrets in second ship:	Autumn 1940 – Spring 1941	½

Note: 1 For twin turret, quad turret would have taken 6 months longer (4 years). Development of fittings would have run parallel with main programme, experimental work being completed 6 months sooner (end 1936).

TABLE 5: CALCULATED WEIGHTS OF GUN BARRELS

Calibre (ins)	Length (cals)	Weight (tonnes)
14	45	85
16	45	102
16	52.5	123
18	50	170
19.3	47	150
20	50	240

battleships, 20 aircraft carriers, 43 cruisers (including 6 super-cruisers) and 131 other warships (including submarines). Part of this plan was that the battleships of the United Fleet (*Rengo Kantai* = 4 battleships) should be integrated into the First Fleet (*Dai ichi Kantai* = 7 new battleships, 6 old battleships) and the second Fleet (*Dai ni Kantai* = 2 old fast battleships). The planned organisation of the battleships is shown in table 2.

The four new battleships in the 6th Programme were intended to be 100,000-ton ships with 8–20in guns. The three battleships in the 5th Programme were to be fitted with 6–20in guns. Twin turrets were to be fitted exclusively. This was Fujimoto's idea, which had so strongly influenced the Admiralty staff.

This strategic concept took absolutely no account of the considerable development in aircraft technology. As a result the belief prevailed that the side whose ships possessed the largest guns would win the battle. For this

reason the Japanese Navy was convinced that it could maintain its dominance in the Western Pacific, and that a war would not break out between the USA and Japan before an American battleship with 18in guns could be brought into service. The real reason for fitting 18in guns on the mammoth battleships of the *Yamato* class, contrary to the worldwide trend towards disarmament, was that Japan hoped that this measure would tend to suppress any possible Pacific war. This was Japan's

TABLE 6: COMPARISON OF HEAVY GUN TURRET MOUNTINGS

Type	Revolving Weight (tonnes)	Total Weight of Guns (tonnes)	Notes
14in/45 twin	700	187	*Hyuga* type
16in/45 twin	1060	268	*Nagato* type
16in/52.5 triple	1730	442	
18in/50 twin	1850	437	
18in/50 triple	2570	623	Projected
18in/50 quadruple	3350	824	designs
20in/50 twin	2750	661	
20in/50 triple	3790	940	
20in/50 quadruple	4900	1246	

national strategy, the basic reasons for which lay not least in that country's difficult economic position.

Fujimoto estimated that battleships with 18in guns could serve as 'Peace Goddesses of the Pacific' for a

A close-up of the superstructure, viewed from the starboard side.

Jürgen Peters

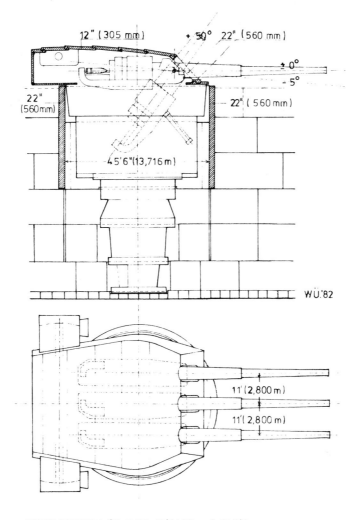

DEVELOPMENT OF THE 18'(460mm) GUNS
(94 SHIKI (TYPE) 16" (406 mm) TRIPLE GUN TURRET) WÜ.82

The Type 94 Shiki 16in (40.6cm) triple turret. *Drawn by Michael Wunschmann from material supplied by the author.*

period of around five years. In any case the Admiralty staff used this period as the basis for deciding between 16in and 18in guns, after which the USA would also possess the larger calibre. For this reason he decided to install 20in guns from the start in the four ships which were to be laid down from 1941 onwards, and completed in 1946.

His overall plan was based on the replacement of all the 18in triple turrets by 20in twin turrets as soon as the US Navy began to construct battleships with 18in guns and also on his assumption that there would be a period of a further five years of peace which the Americans would require in order to build battleships with 20in guns. He probably estimated that the outbreak of a latent war could be delayed by a total of 10 years by

this shipbuilding policy. Whether Fujimoto explained this carefully worked-out strategy to anybody – a strategy which admittedly presumed that the USA would behave as predicted – is not clear. Table 3 shows graphically this strategy.

GUN REPLACEMENT

Replacing the guns in large warships is a difficult task, but is not impossible. The limit, up to that time, was the replacement of the 6in guns in cruisers by 8in guns. In the case of the 18in and 20in it was possible, provided that careful attention had been paid in the initial design stages, but there remain two major problems. The first concerns gun blast. Even in the case of the 18in guns of the *Yamato* the high gun blast affected the entire ship

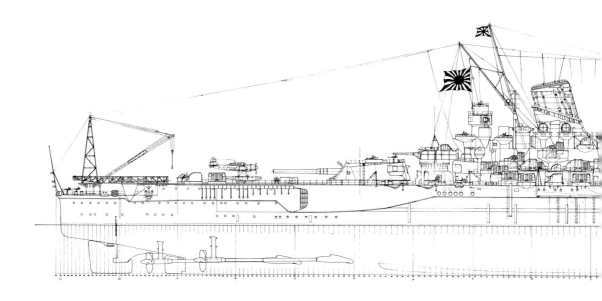

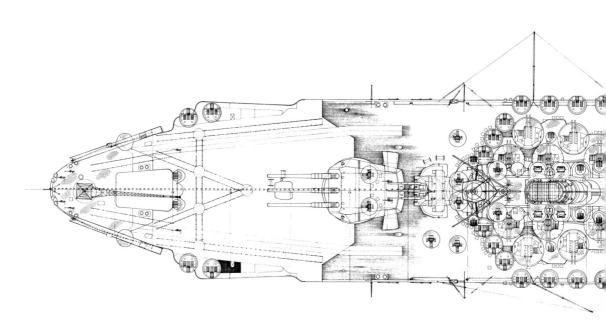

Yamato. Drawn by the author.

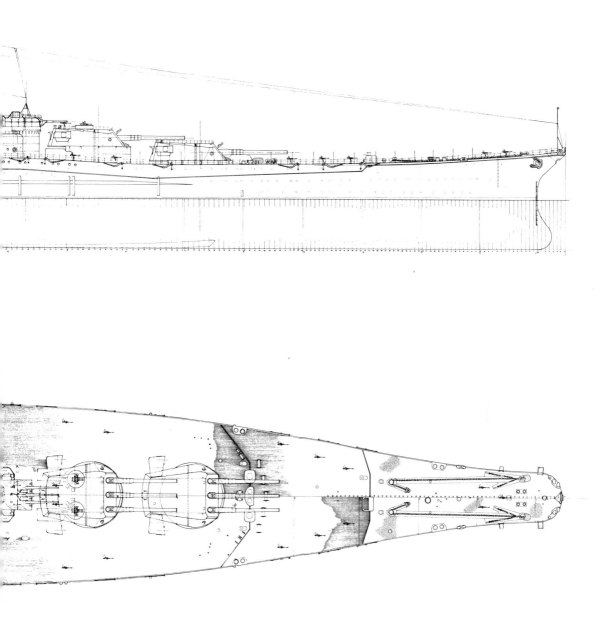

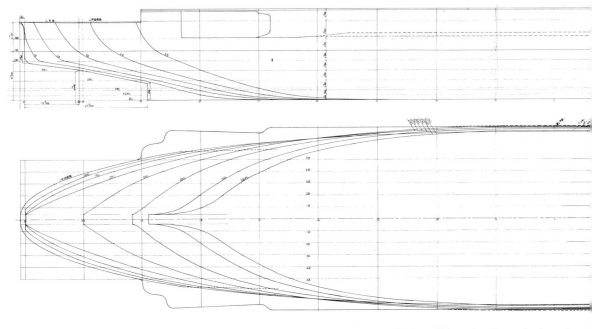

Yamato Body and Lines plan. *Drawn by the author.*

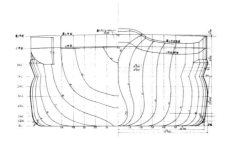

when a salvo was fired, causing some of the machine guns to stop working, and other operational difficulties with the range finders, the radar systems, observation points and so on. The blast would have destroyed the aircraft and auxiliary boats if they had been subjected to its effects on deck. The measures aimed at reducing the effects were very difficult and called for considerable design change over other battleships. As much greater difficulties were to be expected with the 20in

TABLE 7: STUDIES FOR 18in GUNS (10 April 1934)

Study:	A	B	C	D
Gun type:	Relatively light	Heavy	Heavy	Lighter than C
Length (calibres):	50	50	45	45
Maximum elevation (degrees):	50	45	45	45
Barrel weight (tonnes):	180.5	200	183	183
Turret weight (tonnes):	2654.5	2819.6	2580.6	2502
Weight of turrets (tonnes):	7964	8459	7742	7506
Weight of shell and charges (130rpg):[1]	2260	2260	2210	2210
Total weight for ship	10,224	10,719	9952	9716

Note: 1 Weight includes charge cases

TABLE 8: BALLISTIC DATA FOR 18in GUN DESIGNS

Length (calibres):	45	50
Muzzle velocity (m/s):	780	820
Range at 35° elevation (m):	37,200	40,200
Range at 40° elevation (m):	39,000	42,500
Range at 50° elevation (m):	40,200	43,900
Performance at range of (m):	20,000/30,000	20,000/30,000
Angle of elevation:	12°43′/23°16′	11°23′/20°28′
Angle of fall:	16°39′/32°23′	14°52′/28°50′
Time of flight (sec):	32.52/56.32	30.66/52.48
Striking velocity (m/s):	521/474	549/490
Penetrating power (vertical) (in):	22.2/–	23.6/–
Penetrating power (horizontal) (in):	–/10.2	–/9.8
Dispersion (m):	110/71	120/76
Hit probability:	0.707/0.332	0.759/0.373

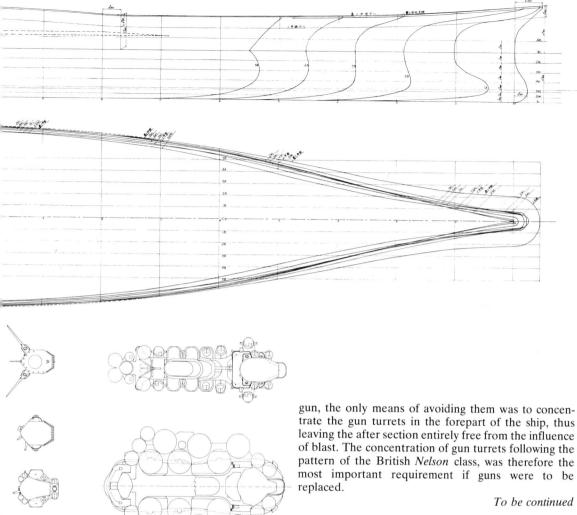

gun, the only means of avoiding them was to concentrate the gun turrets in the forepart of the ship, thus leaving the after section entirely free from the influence of blast. The concentration of gun turrets following the pattern of the British *Nelson* class, was therefore the most important requirement if guns were to be replaced.

To be continued

Plans of *Yamato*'s superstructure decks. *Drawn by the author.*

This overhead view of the model gives an excellent impression of *Yamato*'s general layout

Jürgen Peters

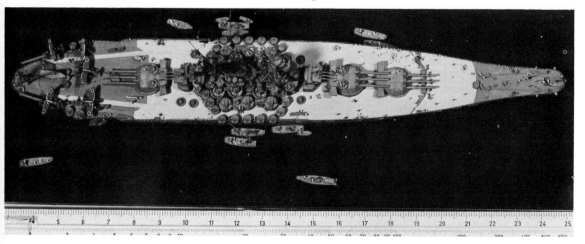

British Naval Guns 1880~1945 No 8

By NJM Campbell

The cruiser *Norfolk* in 1937. She carried eight 8in Mk VIII guns in twin MkII mountings, which were also fitted in her sister, *Dorsetshire*, and in *York*. Early County class cruisers employed the MkI (*Kent* class) or MkI* (*London* class) mountings, while the cruiser *Exeter* carried the final version of the 8in twin mounting, the MkII*.

MoD

8in Mk I It was originally intended to make 8 of these 25.5 calibre guns of which 2 each were to be mounted in *Agincourt, Minotaur* and *Northumberland*, but in the event only 2 were built and they were used as powder proof guns. They were examples of the first, and worst, Woolwich all-steel construction with the hoops made from hammer-welded steel coils. The forged trunnion piece was screwed to the breech coil and originally at least they were not chase hooped.

8in Mk II This only differed from Mk I in being 29.5 calibres. It was intended to make 8 of which 2 were for *Neptune* and it is believed 2 for *Sultan* and 1 for *Bellerophon*, but only 2 were built and joined the Mk I as powder proof guns. They were later lined to 6in and chambered as 6in Mk VII.

8in Mk III Of improved construction compared with the above, with the hoops machined from steel forgings. It was 25.6 calibres and originally without chase hooping. The construction comprised 'A' tube/breech piece, 'B' hoop, 'B' tube (not to muzzle), with 'B' hoop linked to the breech piece by a key ring in halves/5 hoops including trunnion hoop, over key ring and breech piece, and small hoop over the muzzle. The breech block screwed into the breech piece and there was a bronze sheath over the breech end as hood and counterweight. The elevating band was shrunk on.

On chase hooping the trunnion hoop, key ring and hoop over it, part of the 'B' hoop and the small muzzle hoop were removed. Over the breech piece and part of 'B' hoop were shrunk a 'D' hoop and trunnion hoop interlocking with breech piece and 'B' hoop, and in front of the trunnions were shrunk '3B' and '2C' hoops. The bronze counterweight was removed, reducing oa length by 3.8in and the trunnions were now 5.2in nearer the muzzle.

It was originally intended to mount 10 guns in *Bellerophon* with 2 each in *Triumph, Sultan, Northumberland, Agincourt, Achilles, Shah, Raleigh* and *Inconstant*, but only *Bellerophon* ever mounted them. Her original outfit was not chase hooped, and the VB Mk I mountings allowed elevations of +10° to −4½°. Chase hooped guns (one each) were in the gunnery school gunboats *Bustard*, on VB Mk I mounting, *Bonetta, Pike* and *Snap*, on VCP Mk I mountings which allowed elevations of +15° to −5°.

Altogether 24 guns were made, 14 by RGF Woolwich and 10 by EOC as Pattern 'E'.

8in Mk IV Similar to Mk III but 29.6 calibres. It was originally not chase hooped with construction as Mk III except that there were six instead of five hoops. After chase hooping it again resembled Mk III, but there were '5B' and '1C' hoops and the trunnions were moved 9.4ins.

Originally 8, reduced to 2, were to be mounted in *Triumph*, 4 in *Swiftsure*, 2 each in *Sultan* and *Neptune* and 1 in *Bellerophon* but in the event they were limited to 2 each in *Mersey*, *Severn*, *Forth* and *Thames* on VCP Mk I mountings allowing elevations of +15° to −5°. 13 guns were made, 2 by RGF and 11 by EOC as Pattern 'F'.

8in Mk V A 25.6 calibre design which was never made. It was not chase hooped to the muzzle and differed from Mk III in having fewer external components and an alpha tube and liner inside the 'A' tube.

8in Mk VI Originally intended as a 29.6 calibre version of Mk V, the construction was altered as follows: 'A' tube/breech piece, taking breech block, '1B' tube, '2B' tube to muzzle/'C' tube over part of '1B' and '2B'/jacket interlocking with breech piece, trunning ring interlocking with 'C' tube and breech piece, 'D' hoop. The guns were used to rearm the Indian monitors *Magdala* and *Abyssinia* replacing their former 10in RMLs. The twin turrets were converted by Elswick to hydraulic training and the guns were in Vavasseur mountings but the elevation, originally 13° with the 10in RMLs, has not been found. The gun design was by RGF but all 9 were made by EOC though there does not appear to have been a Pattern letter.

8in Mk VII An old design of 26 calibre gun of mixed steel and wrought iron construction of which 5 were purchased from Elswick, 4 of these being mounted at Singapore in old type long recoil barbette mountings. Some were chase hooped before issue with a reduction of 25.5 calibres, and one of those that were not, blew its muzzle off in 1891. They were replaced by Mk VIIA of 26 calibres which was similar in construction to Mk VI.

The original Mk VII was Elswick Pattern 'H', and guns of the same general type were mounted in vessels of the Australian states and in Australian and New Zealand coast defences. Thus Pattern 'D' was in *Albert* and *Protector*, 'D' in *Victoria*, 'G' in *Gayundah* and *Paluma* while 'I' was in Australian and 'L' in New Zealand coast defences.

The performance of all these early 8in BL guns did not differ very much and the shells of 180lb to 210lb could be handled by two men. A proposal was made in 1898 to introduce a new 8in gun with a 250lb shell and MV of 2700fs, but this shell was too heavy for two men, and the 7.5in with 200lb shell was developed instead. A new 8in gun was not introduced until the construction

The cruiser *York* c1932–33.
MoD

of the Washington Treaty cruisers which had complete power loading.

8in Mk VIII This 50 calibre gun was mounted in twin turrets in all the Washington Treaty cruisers, the *Kent* class with *Australia* and *Canberra* having Mk I mountings, the *London* class Mk I*, the *Norfolk* class and *York* the improved Mk II and *Exeter* Mk II*. Elevation limits were +70° to −3° except in Mk II* with +50° to −3°.

In all, 168 guns were made including 2 prototypes, and these and the last 26 were built without wire winding. The remainder were intended to begin life as Mk VIII* with 'A' tube, wire, 'B' tube, overlapping jacket, breech ring and breech bush, and on lining with tapered inner 'A' tubes became Mk VIII. Owing to troubles with 'A' tube forgings half the wire wound guns had inner 'A' tubes initially.

The last 26 guns with no wire were known as Mk VIII**, and were built with tapered inner 'A', 'A' tube, jacket to 170in from muzzle, breech ring and breech bush. All guns had Welin screw breech blocks with hydraulic or hand Asbury mechanism, and all were fully interchangeable.

During the Second World War 6 Mk VIII** were mounted on single 70° mountings in the Dover – Folkestone area.

The turrets were complicated and gave considerable trouble initially, but the guns seem to have performed well, though the originally specified 2900fs MV was reduced for better life and accuracy.

8in Mk IX and X These guns were intended for triple turrets in projected cruisers which because of various wartime pressures never got beyond sketch design. Mark IX* was to have 'A' tube, jacket, breech ring and breech bush with a slightly modified Mk VIII Breech mechanism. On lining with a tapered inner 'A' tube, it would become Mk IX. One gun was ordered from Vickers Armstrongs in April 1941 but on introduction of new design rules based on Vickers Armstrong's practice of stressing at 24/27 instead of 20/27 of the yield point, it was abandoned in favour of the much lighter Mk X* which would become Mk X on lining. Apart from weight, construction was to be as in Mk IX* but a new design of breech mechanism was to be used. The order was cancelled in October 1942.

PARTICULARS OF 8in GUNS

	8in Mk III	8in Mk IV, VI	8in Mk VIII	8in Mk IX, X
Weight (tons)	13.4 (not c hooped) 14.4 (c hooped)	14.3 (not c hooped) 15.0 (c hooped) 13.9 (Mk VI)	17.2	17.0 (Mk IX) 12.5 (Mk X)
Length oa (in)	226.3 (not c hooped) 222.5 (c hooped)	258.3 (not c hooped) 254.5 (c hooped, Mk VI)	413.1	413.2
Length bore (cal)	25.6	29.6	50.0	50.0
Chamber (cu in)	3050 3350 (later)	3050 3350 (later, Mk VI)	3646	4300
Chamber length (in)	34.5 38 (later)	34.5 38 (later, Mk VI)	50.1	58.3
Projectile (lb)	210	210	256	290
Charge (lb)/type	100/Pr' Bl 104/Pr'Br 28.7/Cord 20	118/Pr' Br 32.6/Cord 20	66/SC205	72.2/SC205
Muzzle Velocity (fs)	1987 (Cord) 1953 (Sighted)	2200 (Pr' Br) 2145 (Cord) 2150 (Sighted)	2805	2670
Range (yds/elevation)	7200/10° at 1953fs	c10700/15° at 2150fs	30650/45°	31300/45°

A Majestic Revolution Part 1

By Karl Lautenschläger

The *Majestic* class pre dreadnought HMS *Illustrious* fires her 12in guns during gunnery practice.

Tom Molland

In 1895, the Royal Navy put the first of nine *Majestic* class battleships into service. In doing so, Britain precipitated a naval revolution as significant as the one that followed the commissioning of HMS *Dreadnought* in 1906. Today, this transition is hardly recognized, let alone understood. Yet with the perspective of nearly a century, the transformation of battle fleets that began in the late 1890s can be seen as one of the dramatic changes in combat capability at sea. This review is intended to illuminate little known but important details of that transformation. It also provides a case study in the way technology has been adopted to produce substantive change in warfighting capability.

Four sets of technology were brought together for the first time in the *Majestics*. Combining these particular technologies enabled battle fleets to fight effectively at three times the maximum range that had been possible before. Furthermore, the *Majestics* were the first war-

ships whose armament and protection were consistently effective on the open ocean, particularly in rough seas.

The *Majestics* were the first predreadnoughts in a strict sense of the term. As distinct from the ironclads and armourclads which preceded them and the dreadnoughts which followed, predreadnought battleships represented a specific type for important technical reasons. If the dreadnought type is considered to be revolutionary, then the predreadnought too was a revolutionary development and not merely an evolutionary extension of the armourclad. Both the predreadnought and the dreadnought types took time to develop fully. In the first case, four years elapsed after the first ship of the type entered service before all of the necessary equipment had been installed to realise its full potential and make its fighting capabilities significantly better than its predecessors. In the case of the dreadnought, it took even longer. Once fully equipped, however, the new ships made all earlier designs immediately obsolete. Updating older ships with new technology was not possible, because the new types were fundamentally different.

The four technologies that combined to make predreadnoughts fundamentally different from armour-clads were: 1) high velocity, heavy ordnance; 2) quick-firing, medium calibre guns; 3) face-hardened, alloy steel armour; and 4) telescopic gunsights. Other technologies were being introduced in warships throughout the 1890s, but these four were basic to the reformation of the battleship.

HIGH VELOCITY GUNS

High velocity guns were a significant advance over earlier naval artillery, because they gave projectiles the momentum required to have high striking velocity and small dispersion at long range. By way of comparison, most rifled guns in the major navies before 1895 had muzzle velocities of 1300fs to 2000fs. High velocity guns had muzzle velocities of about 2400fs to 3000fs.

The key to improved performance was propellant. Black powder, used in all naval guns until the 1880s, gave a sudden hammer-like impulse to the projectile, and then its propelling energy dropped off sharply. A bigger charge could impart more energy to the projectile, but the sharp explosive characteristic of black powder put extensive strain on the gun. The rapid dissipation of the explosive pulse, and the danger of bursting the gun, kept muzzle velocities for guns using granulated black powder below 1600fs.

What was needed was slow burning powder that would maintain relatively high pressure on the projectile, accelerating it down the entire length of the barrel.

The early broadside ironclad *Agincourt*.
P A Vicary

From 1860, there were several attempts to inhibit the burning rate of black powder. One approach was to press the powder into a block and then break it into pebbles. Another was development of brown powder by changing the proportions of potassium nitrate (saltpetre) and sulphur, adding a small amount of sugar, but underburning the charcoal. Some progress was made, but since black powder and its derivatives are mechanical mixtures, it was difficult to regulate its burning rate and improve its efficiency. With brown powder and longer guns, muzzle velocities could reach 2200fs. But without a technological breakthrough, heavy guns had reached the limit of their performance.

SLOW BURNING PROPELLANTS

Development of chemical compound explosives for use as propellants brought the improvements that were necessary. Chemical explosives based on nitrate compounds burned more slowly than black or brown powders, putting a sustained propelling force on the projectile. This permitted the projectile to accelerate smoothly down the barrel. Chemical propellants were also more efficient. Almost the entire explosive turned into expanding gas and thus propelling energy, whereas 50 to 60 per cent of black or brown powders remained after detonation as partially burned particles. Since there was no solid residue and much less smoke produced by the new propellants, they were called smokeless powders. Even with more energy per unit weight, a charge of chemical propellant did not strain the gun tube as severely as the old powders did, because peak pressure was lower and it was applied over a longer time.

Smokeless propellants were made from nitrocellulose

The battleship *Trafalgar* as completed in 1890 with short funnels. With her sister ship *Nile* she was (excluding the hybrid *Hood* of 1891) the last of the British low freeboard, turret armourclads. Her protection consisted of compound armour, of 14in to 20in thickness and she was the first British capital ship to carry a secondary armament of QF guns.

P A Vicary

or from nitrocellulose and nitroglycerin. The first successful smokeless propellant was a nitrocellulose type invented by Paul Vieille in 1886 and immediately adopted by the French navy as 'Poudre B'. Alfred Nobel developed the first of the so-called double base propellants in 1887 and named it 'ballistite'. It was improved by Frederick Abel and J Dewar and adopted by the Royal Navy in 1890 as 'cordite'. Other navies followed the French or British lead.

The change from mechanically mixed propellants to chemically produced propellants opened considerable potential for improving gun performance, but the first battleships to benefit were not in service for several more years. In order to take advantage of the sustained explosive pressure of smokeless propellants, guns had to be built with longer barrels. This allowed projectiles to be accelerated to much higher velocities before leaving the muzzle. Longer guns, in turn, demanded redesigned mountings. Thus, it was not until the end of 1895 that the first battleships with high velocity heavy guns entered service.

Some of the last battleships commissioned with low velocity guns and the first with high velocity guns are listed in Table 1. In several cases, the first battleship commissioned with high velocity guns was not the first having all of the basic characteristics of a true predreadnought. The transitional guns are a sampling of guns with intermediate muzzle velocities or high velocities but very light projectiles. Neither proved effective against battleship armour at the new fighting ranges.

QF GUNS

The second technology that contributed to the transformation of battle fleets was the quick-firing gun. The impetus for the development and adoption of this type of weapon for naval use was the search for an antidote for surface torpedo attacks. Mounted on battleships, cruisers and torpedo boat destroyers, the quick-firing gun decided the issue of battle fleet supremacy in the face of the torpedo boat threat. Less widely recognized is the fact that the same weapon became a major factor in battleship-versus-battleship tactics, and it remained so for well over a decade.

The essence of predreadnought battleship armament was a mixed calibre main battery. The idea of designers was to obtain a balance between hitting power and rate of fire. While the heavy 12in guns pounded away slowly, eventually penetrating the adversary's armour, medium calibre quick-firing guns would deliver a hail of explosive projectiles, wrecking unprotected upperworks, inflicting casualties, and undermining morale. This approach led to the inclusion of at least two and often three calibres of guns in a predreadnought battleship's main battery.

Since torpedo defence batteries on later dreadnought type battleships were 6in calibre, we today tend to think of that size of gun in a secondary battery. However, in battleships that prevailed between about 1899 and 1911, guns of 5in to 8in calibre were an essential part of the *main* battery. The torpedo defence battery in these ships was usually made up of much lighter guns.

The inventions necessary to make quick-firing guns an important part of battleship armament came together gradually. They included fast-operating breech mechanisms, cartridge ammunition of cannon calibre, and pedestal mountings. Fast-operating breech mechanisms were invented and perfected in France by 1866 and in Germany by 1868. Either the De Bange interrupted screw or the Krupp sliding wedge became the model for fast-loading breeches adopted by all of the major navies.

ABLE 1: INTRODUCTION OF HIGH VELOCITY HEAVY GUNS

				AP proj (lbs)	MV (ft/sec)	Ship Class	Last Unit Commissioned
ow Velocity Guns							
3.4in	28 cal	1884	Fr	926	1969	Marceau	14 Mar 1891
3.4in	28 cal	1881	Fr	926	1969	Neptune	Feb 1893
3.5in	30 cal	Mk II	GB	1250	2016	Royal Sovereign	12 Jun 1894
3.5in	30 cal	Armstrg	It	1250	2014	Re Umberto	4 May 1895
2in	35 cal	Oboutov	Ru	714	2090	Navarin	1896
2in	35 cal	Mk II	US	870	2100	Iowa	16 Jun 1897
ransitional Guns							
0in	40 cal	Armstrg	It	452	2398	E. Filiberto	6 Sep 1901
3in	35 cal	Mk II	US	1130	2200	Illinois	16 Sep 1901
4in	40 cal	Krupp	Ge	309	2739	Wittelsbach	13 Apr 1904
4in	40 cal	Skoda	AH	505	2312	Ferdinand Max	31 Dec 1907
igh Velocity Guns							**First Unit Commissioned**
2in	35 cal	Mk VIII	GB	850	2400	Majestic	12 Dec 1895
3.4in	42 cal	1887	Fr	926	2600	Brennus	1896
2in	40 cal	Armstrg	Ja	850		Fuji	17 Aug 1897
2in	40 cal	Oboukov	Ru		2602	Tri Sviatitelia	1897
2in	40 cal	Mk IX	GB	850	2612	Formidable	10 Sep 1901
2in	40 cal	Mk III	US	870	2600	Maine	29 Dec 1901
2in	40 cal	Armstrg	It	850	2526	R. Margherita	14 Apr 1904
1in	40 cal	Krupp	Ge	529	2690	Braunschweig	15 Oct 1904
2in	45 cal	Skoda	AH	992	2625	Franz Ferdinand	15 Jun 1910

METAL CARTRIDGE CASES

Machine guns, using rifle calibre cartridge ammunition, were also developed in the 1860s, the most notable by Richard Gatling and Benjamin Hotchkiss. Putting the propellant in metal cartridges instead of cloth bags sol-

The after twin 12in turret of a Majestic class battleship.
Courtesy J A Roberts

ved the problem of having a breech that could be opened quickly but still be gas-tight when it was closed for firing. Either attached to the projectile, or as a separate piece in larger guns, the metal cartridge served as the obturator in quick-firing guns. Since a single cartridge replaced two or more bags of propellant, loading time was shortened further.

The Nordenfelt 1in quick-firing gun was introduced for use against torpedo boats in 1877 but not until the

TABLE 2: REPRESENTATIVE MEDIUM CALIBRE QF BATTERIES

	Guns in Broadside				Common Proj (lbs)	Nominal Service rds/min	Broadside lbs/min
Armorclads							
Trafalgar	3	4.7in	40 cal	I	45	10	1350
Royal Sovereign	4	6in	40 cal	I	100	8	3200
Marceau	8	5.5in	45 cal	1891	66	8	4224
Jaureguiberry	4	5.5in	45 cal	1891	66	8	2112
Kearsarge	7	5in	40 cal	III	50	5	1750
Friedrich III	9	5.9in	40 cal		99	7	6237
Predreadnoughts							
Majestic	6	6in	40 cal	II	100	8	4800
Formidable	6	6in	45 cal	VII	100	8	4800
King Edward VII	2	9.2in	45 cal	X	380	2	5520
	5	6in	45 cal	VII	100	8	
Shikishima	7	6in	40 cal	Arm	100	7	4900
Czarevitch	6	6in	45 cal		89	7	3738
Maine	8	6in	50 cal	VIII	105	7	5880
Virginia	4	8in	45 cal	VI	260	2	
	6	6in	50 cal	VIII	105	7	6490
Connecticut	4	8in	45 cal	VI	260	2	5050
	6	7in	45 cal	II	165	3	
Republique	9	6.5in	45 cal	1893	115	6	6210
Liberte	5	7.6in	50 cal	1902	253	3	3795
Braunschweig	7	6.7in	40 cal		119	5	4165

advent of smokeless propellants could cartridges be made light enough for rapid manual loading of guns of 5in or larger calibre. For example, an early British 6in quick-firing gun used a 55lb charge of brown prismatic powder. When cordite was introduced, the propellant charge for this gun could be reduced to 13lbs. The prob-lem of smoke dissipation between firings was also solve with the adoption of smokeless propellants.

The other necessary element was a gun mount tha was easily trained and pointed. Obviously, a centra pivoting pedestal mount was the answer, but this becam practical only with the development of effective hyc raulic recoil dampeners. J Vavasseur designed the firs pivot mount with hydraulic recoil brakes in 1881.

The forward turret of the battleship *Majestic* trained on the starboard beam.
Courtesy J A Roberts

Military personnel practising with 6pdr Hotchiss QF guns, one of the most successful of the early anti-torpedo boat guns adopted by the Royal Navy.

Courtesy J A Roberts

INTRODUCTION OF THE SECONDARY BATTERY

The British Admiralty adopted the 4.7in 40pdr QF gun in November 1887 and the 6in 100pdr in October 1890. The French navy adopted a series of quick-firing guns from 3.9in to 6.5in in 1891 and undertook a programme to convert hundreds of old breech-loaders to quick-firing guns. The German navy officially adopted a series of quick-firing guns in April of the next year. Thereafter, all German naval guns with metal propellant-cases, including 9.4in and 11in guns, were designated *Schnellade Kanone*. All of the major navies were soon including quick-firing armament in their designs for new battleships and replacing old-style breech-loaders with quick-firing guns on existing units.

The quick-firing portion of the main battery adopted as standard in the Royal Navy was six 6in guns mounted along each side of the ship. At a sustained rate of fire in service, a six-gun battery could deliver 48 100lb projectiles per minute. This amounted to 4800lbs of high explosive and shrapnel on a target every minute. Other navies adopted mixes of projectile weight and gun numbers that enabled a broadside battery to deliver at least 3000lbs of projectiles per minute. Toward the end of the predreadnought period, a second calibre of heavy guns was added, and in a few ships, quick-firing guns were eliminated except as a torpedo defence battery of 4.7in or smaller. The Japanese *Kawachi* and *Settsu* had heavy guns of uniform calibre but mixed bore length and muzzle velocities in their main batteries. It was probably beyond the technology of that day to calibrate two different types of guns to the same central fire control system. If so, these ships were technically predreadnoughts and not dreadnoughts as is so often claimed.

IMPROVED PROTECTION

The third important technology gave battleships significantly better protection. The advent of cemented, alloy steel not only provided a much better armour material than had been available before. It also permitted a much improved distribution of protection.

One problem with armour was mating two material properties which seemed to nullify one another. To be effective, armour needed both a hard penetration-resistant face and a tough body which was not prone to shatter. It was like trying to combine the properties of glass and clay in the same material. Wrought iron was tough in that its relative softness localised the shock of impact, but that softness meant lower resistance to penetration. Simple steel could be made very hard by tempering. It could resist penetration and denting because large portions of the plate were called into play in absorbing the energy of impact. However, this meant that it was also brittle and more prone to crack than wrought iron.

The other problem with armour was one of effectiveness versus weight. Improved resistance was gained by casting a steel face on a thick wrought iron plate in what was called compound armour. Later, nickel was added to all-steel armour to increase its toughness and reduce its tendency to shatter. Both compound and nickel steel armour were effective against the latest projectiles when they were first introduced. However, even then, if either of these types of armour was thick enough to resist perforation by heavy projectiles, it was too heavy to protect a vessel's high sides and its main armament.

A very thick compound or simple steel armour belt could extend only a few feet above the waterline, or protect a relatively small portion of a ship's length. More expensive protection would have an adverse effect on stability and consume an excessive amount of the ship's displacement. Therefore, armourclad battleships were designed either on the British model, with low freeboard, or on the French model, with high unpro-

A 6in QF gun on a late Victorian cruiser, such weapons helped to revolutionise the nature of the battleship in the 1890s.

Courtesy J A Roberts

tected sides. Low freeboard presented a smaller target of which more could be protected, but it meant that the guns could be aimed and operated only in calm seas. High freeboard allowed guns to be worked in rough seas, but unprotected sides produced the likelihood of flooding above the armour belt and the danger of capsizing.

FACE HARDENING

The solution to both the material and weight problems came with the advent of face-hardened, alloy steel armour. Face-hardening, or cementing, was the application of carbon at very high temperatures for a long time. The carbon, which increased hardness but also brittleness, was confined to the face of the armour plate. Alloys of nickel, chromium, and later molybdenum made the steel body tough and aided the cementing process.

Low impurity steel could be produced in the 1860s, but three decades passed before armour technology went through its most important transformation. The Schneider Company of Creusot, France, introduced nickel steel in 1889. The next year, H A Harvey, working at the Washington Navy Yard, introduced his face-hardening process. The firm of Friedrich Krupp soon

took the last steps to complete this major advance by adding chromium to the nickel steel alloy in 1893 and developing decremental gas carburizing in 1895.

Krupp cemented, chromium nickel steel was adopted quickly by the navies of the world, and it became the standard for rating armour effectiveness. Krupp cemented armour was about $1\frac{1}{2}$ times as effective as compound armour and over twice as effective as wrought iron armour. The whole range of armour types can be compared in general terms. The same calibre and type of projectile that was stopped just short of complete penetration by 15in of wrought iron, could also be stopped by 12in of compound armour, 12in of oil tempered steel, 11.5in of nickel steel, 7.5in of Harvey cemented steel, or just 6in of Krupp cemented armour. Refinements of the Krupp process and of steel alloys brought variations from country to country, so that this comparative index is only nominal.

What the comparison shows is the dramatic improvement in the effectiveness of armour plate. This meant that much less weight was required to provide a given amount of protection. The savings in weight could be used to increase extent of protection on battleships, particularly to increase the height of protective side armour.

To be continued

he LS 30R naval Rarden gun on show at the Royal Navy
ngineering exhibition in 1981.
nna Hogg/Defence

The Naval Rarden Gun

By Antony Preston

n 19 March 1981 the new naval version of the British
rmy's 30mm Rarden gun was demonstrated publicly
•r the first time at the Royal Navy's Fraser Gunnery
ange at Eastney.

The Rarden gun had already proved very successful as
high-velocity weapon for use against armoured cars
nd similar lightly armoured targets. The Royal Navy,
though running out of 20mm Oerlikon Mk 7 and
0mm Bofors L/60 guns and needing a new light auto-
iatic gun for what is commonly known as 'junk-
ashing', had not expressed any desire for a replace-
ient. The initiative came from the Defence Sales
•rganisation, which was aware of an export require-
ient for such a gun; DSO accordingly approached the
.oyal Ordnance Factories and Laurence Scott Elec-
omotors of Norwich to discuss the possibility of
iavalising' the Rarden.

THE DESIGN

In 1977 Laurence Scott and Electromotors decided to
go ahead with a private venture adaptation of their
already highly successful Optical Fire Director (OFD) to
provide a power-driven, line-of-sight stabilised gun-
mounting. This programme reached fruition in the
autumn of 1980 when the LS 30R Naval Rarden was
shipped aboard the frigate *Londonderry*, the Admiralty
Surface Weapons Establishment (ASWE) trials ship.
These firing trials proved that the mounting met its
design specifications, and in 1981 the same mounting,
now on a rolling platform at the Fraser Gunnery Range,
underwent further tests by the Royal Navy. The demonstration in March was preceded by a firing of 15 spaced
single shots from the standard 20mm Mk 7, giving a very
vivid demonstration of the widely differing ballistics of
the two weapons. Whereas the Oerlikon's tracer rounds

The Rarden mounting undergoing shock and environmental testing.

Plessey, courtesy of Defence

floated lazily through the air the Rarden's rounds appeared to travel quickly over a noticeably flatter trajectory. The target was a barely discernible iron boiler lying on a shingle bank at 1100m distance, and the gun made good shooting in two 15-round bursts, using both APDS and HE ammunition. What was equally impressive was the quick reaction to a couple of jams caused by defective ammunition; the Rarden gun can be dismantled by one man and the 6-round magazine can be cleared instantly.

During the sea trials 80 per cent hits were made on a 2m square target in Sea State 5. The dispersion was less than three milliradians, proving that the new mounting has done nothing to diminish the Rarden's reputation for accuracy – 'the world's largest sniper's rifle' as described by an eminent small arms expert. The characteristics of the gun make it ideal for the peacetime duties of warships, giving them the ability to immobilise merchant vessels by accurate shooting at ranges below 4000yds. The APDS round is used in this role to penetrate not only the shell-plating of a ship but the engine block as well. No specific anti-aircraft role is envisaged

but the 70° elevation of the mounting permits it to fire a a helicopter or the superstructure of a large merchant man, for example.

THE MOUNTING

The mounting is stabilised on the line-of-sight by tw rate-integrating gyros and tracking is done with binocular sight. Aim-off and range are estimated by th operator, using the calibrated graticule in the binocula and it is possible to fit an image-intensifier for low-ligh conditions. The Mk 1 version demonstrated how it i controlled locally by the operator, using a joystick t control the training and elevating servos, with both ve ocity and rate-aided modes of control available. Tw more versions are being developed, Mk 2 and Mk 3, th former capable of being controlled and fired remotel they will be fitted with coarse/fine synchros for transmi ting bearing and elevation to a second system. This wi enable the gun to function as an optical director, a usefu adjunct when the Naval Rarden is mounted on a larg ship. Although the magazine is easily replenished b 3-round clips the Mk 3 will have a clip-on magazin carrying 21 rounds' meeting requirements from pro pective customers for sustained fire. In addition to th improvements of the Mk 2 the Mk 3 will have an o mount digital predictor. Using pre-set data, range an racking rates, an aiming point can then be predicted and injected into the binocular, giving the operator a form of head-up display.

PARTICULARS OF THE LS 30R GUN MOUNTING

Weight of gun Mounting Complete	800 Kg
Height Overall (Gun Horizontal)	2m
Swept Radius (Gun Horizontal)	2.2m
Elevation Arc	+70° to −20°
Training Arc	±160° standard
Training Velocity	30°/sec
Elevation Velocity	30°/sec
Elevation Acceleration	120°/sec²
Training Acceleration	120°/sec²
Electrical Power	2kVA
	50VA
Maximum Rate of Fire	90 rounds/minute
Maximum Continuous Burst	6 rounds (21 rounds with extra magazine)
Barrel length	2.44m
Calibre	30mm

CONCLUSION

The demonstration showed that the LS 30R mounting has lived up to expectations. It requires no penetration of the deck other than a small-diameter channel for the power cable, and because of the design of the gun, imposes only a low deck-loading. As the mounting is based on a proven piece of naval equipment it is designed for the sea-environment, and the only improvement needed to the gun was an extra coating of weatherproofing. The barrel-life is 10,000 rounds but the ROF recommend that barrels are withdrawn at 3750 rounds to provide a big safety margin.

Clearly the mounting is an ideal replacement for the 20mm and 40mm guns currently used by the Royal Navy and other navies. The original 20mm is now quite out-classed and the supply of 40mm Mk 3, Mk 5 and Mk 7 guns is now quite exhausted. In any case the 40mm was designed as an anti-aircraft gun and does not have the right ammunition to match the 30mm's APDS against ship-targets. The current need is for what might be called 'middle-level' sophistication for the offshore role: ease of maintenance, accuracy but not massive overkill, and a high rate of fire. At a time when an automatic 76mm automatic mounting costs £1 million and even a twin 30mm automatic will leave no change out of £350,000 the estimated cost of the Naval Rarden at £150,000 must make it an attractive proposition.

The prototype Mk1 LS 30R stabilised mounting for the 30mm Rarden gun on its rolling platform, designed to simulate ship motion at the RN's Fraser Gunnery Range.

Laurence, Scott and Electromotors Ltd, courtesy Defence

The US Monitors Part 1

By Francis J Allen

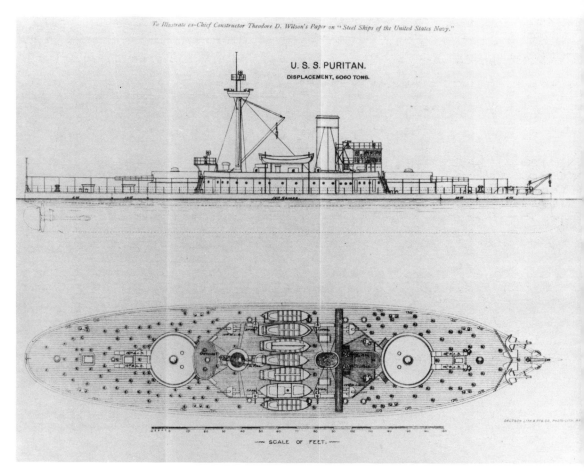

To Illustrate ex-Chief Constructor Theodore D. Wilson's Paper on "Steel Ships of the United States Navy."

U. S. S. PURITAN.
DISPLACEMENT, 6060 TONS.

— SCALE OF FEET. —

Official plan of USS *Puritan* (BM-1), 1893.

US Naval Museum

It is my intention in this article to deal with the subject of the six monitors which were built between the 1870s and the early 1900s. They preceded the *Arkansas* class of monitors both in concept and construction, as they were under 'repair' for many years.

In order to gain some perspective on this idea of 'repair', it will be helpful to briefly review the post Civil War naval history of the United States Navy. Immediately after this war, there was a surplus of monitors in the Navy, the budgets were shrinking and doing so faster than the fleet could. 'The shortage of funds for new construction, or even the maintenance of good vessels

was not due only to departmental bickering, but even more to a public and Congress little short of hostile. I must be remembered that it was normally considered very un-American to have anything vaguely resembling an effective fighting force. This, coupled with congressional indifference to technological change could have only boded ill for the Navy.'[1]

With the acute shortage of money, the Navy found a deception that enabled them to start new construction. The US Navy simply 'repaired' existing warships, building new vessels, bearing the same names as older monitors from the period of the Civil War. Under this system, construction could only '. . . proceed at a snail's pace during the years of naval stagnation, although considerable sums of money were dribbled on them under some cloudy contractual dealings.[2]

USS *Puritan* at the Norfolk Navy Yard, Norfolk, Va, in May 1902.

National Archives

USS *Miantonomoh* (BM-5), close up photo of the 10in guns and turret, with laundry!

US Naval Museum

If it could be maintained that the monitors authorised by Congress in 1898, the *Arkansas* class, were antiquated before they were commissioned in 1902–1903, how much more so were the monitors built for the US Navy that had preceeded them. As it was, the American Navy by the beginning of the twentieth century had acquired ten '. . . of these wallowing curiosities . . .'[3] with the intention of using them for harbour and coast defence. The appropriateness of such a policy as harbour and coastal defence for a navy on the brink of world responsibility and power is a topic for discussion at a later time.

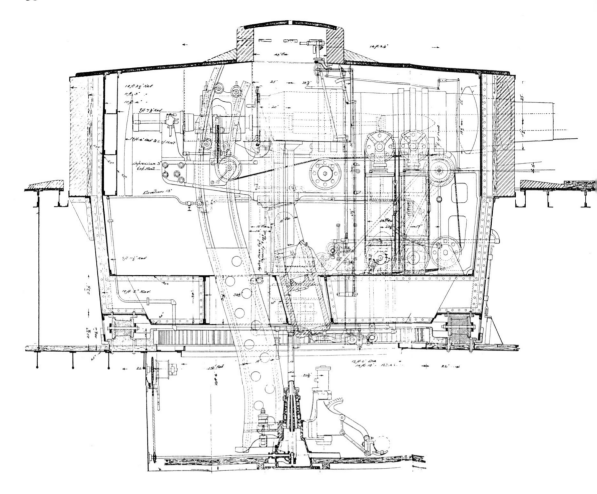

The pneumatic powered gun turret of the USS *Amphitrite*.

These ships were built for that purpose and it is within that framework that they must be viewed.

'Like the Civil War ironclads from which they had descended, these ships were characterised by low speed; heavy armour protection; broad, flat hull design; shallow draught and extremely low freeboard, which made them terribly wet at sea but also inconspicuous targets.'[4]

Those monitors which came before the *Arkansas* class, being laid down in 1874, can be divided into three groups: **1** USS *Puritan*, the oldest and the heftiest; **2** the *Amphitrite* class of four ships, most noteworthy for their unbearable heat and the pneumatic system of the *Terror*; and **3** the USS *Monterey*, the newest and most modern.

USS PURITAN

The original USS *Puritan* was launched in July 1864 but remained unfinished at the war's end and when finally scrapped brought only $43,000.

The new *Puritan* was 'repaired' to plans drawn up in the 1860s. The ship was the largest of the six pre-*Arkansas* class monitors, topping the scales at a dainty 6060 tons. Started in 1874, the construction of the *Puritan* took over twenty years, including a ten-year lapse of interest '. . . until Congress voted money for her completion as one of the steps in the creation of a new navy.'[5] In time the *Puritan* was completed at the New York Navy Yard with a hull of iron and mounting four 12in rifles in modern barbette turrets.[6] In fact so much time had passed between the laying down of the *Puritan* and her commissioning that Frank M Bennett, a former Assistant Engineer, US Navy, wrote 'The machinery presents one of the earliest example of compound practice in this country, and is interesting chiefly as an object for antiquarian investigation.'[7]

The *Puritan*'s one moment of glory was her duty of shore bombardment and blockade performed in the Caribbean during the Spanish-American War.

THE AMPHITRITE CLASS

As a class of warships the ships of the *Amphitrite* class were designed as smaller and lighter versions of the *Puritan*, at about 3990 tons.

The same system of 'repair' was originally applied to these monitors, the *Monadnock* being 'repaired' by the

Phineas Burgess Yard at Vallejo, California; the *Terror* by the Granys Co of Philadelphia, Pa; *Amphitrite* by Harlan and Hollingsworth of Wilmington, Delaware; and the *Miantonomoh* by John Roach of Chester, Pa. All of these monitors were eventually taken over and completed at navy yards.[9]

The *Amphitrite* class as a group could well have been voted the hottest things afloat but not for reasons of success. With battle hatches and superstructure doors closed to keep the sea out, and with the outside temperature varying between 50° and 72° Fahrenheit the *Amphitrite*'s engine room ranged from 120° to 160°. These temperatures were thought of as being somewhat severe![10] At Hampton Roads, shortly after the above temperatures had been recorded, the *Amphitrite* underwent full power steam trials. At that time the Board of Inspection and Survey recorded that the engine room thermometer ranged from 138° to 158° Fahrenheit and that in the fire room registered between 157° and 170°.[11] These extremely high temperatures made the *Amphitrite* and her sister ships very inefficient warships. Excessively high temperatures were reported for the *Puritan*, the *Miantonomoh* and the *Terror*. The cause of this was the '. . . lack of provision in the engine and boiler spaces [for proper ventilation]. These regions became so hot that little useful work could be done in them, and the lack of air was such as to actually ruin the furnace

USS *Monadnock* (BM-3) in commission at Mare Island, California, 20 February 1896.

US Naval Museum

doors.[12] At one time a Board of Officers reported that the air that was trapped between the boilers and the iron, main deck reached 202° Fahrenheit.[13]

To correct these conditions the Navy Department authorised the following:

> Four large ventilators with revolving cowls were put through the protective deck into the fire room, one in each forward corner and the other over the two after boilers. The ash hoist tube formerly screened by the boats and smoke pipe was built several feet higher and fitted with two branches, one on each side of the smoke pipe. The latter was boxed in where it passed through the ward room. Two ventilators were also let into the top of the engine room a previously existing uptake pipe with a close-fitting mushroom cap being utilized as the trunk of one of these.
>
> The immediate effect of these additions was remarkable. By admitting outside air to the oven like spaces over the boilers, the fire room temperature was reduced to a living figure, and the ward room deck above it ceased to resemble the top of a stove. The same improvements resulted in the engine room.[14] With these improvements the *Amphitrite* was able to obtain 10.72kts in speed trials.[15]

THE PNEUMATIC GUN MOUNTING

In 1896, the date of the commissioning of the USS *Terror*, the pneumatic system with which she was fitted was both innovative and unique to her. The system was invented by Mr H A Spiller of the Pneumatic Gun and Power Co and this system was installed in the *Terror* under the supervision of Mr E D Eldridge. The original contract called for the completion of the work in 1889 but this was not met owing to design changes by the Government and the contractors. The air compressors

USS *Monadnock* (BM-3) under construction at Vallejo, California. The Mare Island Navy Yard is seen in the background.
US Naval Museum

USS *Monterey* (BM-6) off Portland Oregon, August 1893
US Naval Museum

Stern view of the USS *Monterey*, (BM-6).
National Archives

were of a special compact design from the Norwalk Iron Works; one was located by each of the turrets. The turrets were turned by means of two engines in each turret which were fed by the compressors. These engines in turn worked the turrets by means of worm gears in contact with a large internal cast steel gear.[16] The maximum turning arc of the turret was 270°. 'Elevation of the gun was controlled by a ram . . . bearing on the lower side of the rear transom of the gun carriage.'[17] Compressed air in the recoil cylinders was used to absorb the shock of the gun firing. There were two recoil cylinders per gun and they were attached to the saddle of the gun. The piston inside the cylinders remained stationary while the cylinders recoiled with the gun.

The central column in each turret carried '. . . sleeves which received air from the supply pipes and distributed it to the various motors above. The centre of the column carried a shaft for operating the steering mechanism. Each turret also contained a lever and rheostat for electric steering; the wires being led down the central column.'[18]

Within the confines to the turret not only was it necessary to accommodate the guns crews, the guns, hoists, etc, but due to the lack of a conning tower, the captain also had to find some room. The conning of the ship was then done from the platform of the forward turret. The rudder was handled by pneumatic steering gear which comprised:

> Two athwartship cylinders, whose pistons are attached to the same heavy piston rod, firmly secured to castings built into the ship . . . At midlength the piston rod carries a slotted head, the brasses of which permit the sliding of the tiller as its angularity changes . . . The Distribution of air [for the cylinders of the steering system] is effected by a simple slide valve receiving its motion from a float lever, one end of which is controlled by an arm projecting from the rudder head. The float lever receives its initial motion from a threaded spindle working a nut on the lever . . . So long as there is a supply of air the principle of the float lever insures motion of the tiller in obedience to the screw spindle.[19]

Steering wheels were provided with a geared index which acted as an indicator of the rudder's motion, or more precisely the motion the rudder should have had as a result of the action given to the screw spindle of the float lever, the indicator not being directly connected to the rudder. In each turret in addition to the above mentioned indicator, in the floor above the central column there was a circular index composed of two concentric circles, one showed the rotation of the turret while the other indicated the angle of the helm.

To cap this system, a muffler of sorts was built up from vessels, or pipes, containing pebbles into which the exhaust pipes of the pneumatic cylinders discharged.

The pneumatic system on board the *Terror* and the hydraulic system on the *Amphitrite* can only be compared in one respect – that of coal consumption. During a period of sixteen days while both ships were at Charleston Harbour, in the winter, burning coal from the same stock, *Amphitrite* burned 84.35 tons while the *Terror* burned 129.25 tons. As neither ship was under way during this sixteen-day statistical period and as both vessels ' . . . are the same in size, with boilers exactly the same and have the same demands upon their auxiliary machinery it must be that this difference in coal consumption is due to the great (demands of the) air compressors of the *Terror* . . .'[20] This was according to Mr Bennett.

Reputed to be the best of her class, the USS *Monadnock* had been fitted with modern machinery, in particular the high pressure boilers which were able to give a constant supply of all necessary power for her turrets and machinery.[21]

To be continued

FOOTNOTES
1 *Warship International:* 'Controversial Cruisers', Gene T Zimmerman, No 4, 1974, p334.
2-4, 8 *American Steel Navy,* John D Allen
5-7, 9-15, 20-21 *Journal of the American Society of Naval Engineers:* 'Reconstructed American Monitors', Frank M Bennett, Vol IX, 1897.
16 *Journal of the American Society of Naval Engineers:* 'The USS *Terror* and the Pneumatic System' T W Kinkaid, Vol IX, 1897.

The *Jaguar* at some time during 1933–35.
Drüppel

GERMAN TORPEDO BOATS AT WAR
The Möwe & Wolf Classes

By Pierre Hervieux

This study deals with the German type 1923 and 1924 torpedo boats, of which twelve were launched between 1926 and 1928. In the German Navy the first six were known as the *Raubvogelklass* (Bird of Prey class) and the remainder as the *Raubtiesklasse* (Wild Beast class). On the outbreak of war in September 1939 only eleven remained in service, as one vessel, the *Tiger* (Kapitanleutnant Neuss) of the 5th Torpedo Boat Flotilla, had sunk on 25 August 1939, east of Bornholm Island in the Baltic, in collision with the destroyer *Max Schultz* (Z3). It was an inauspicious start but subsequently the two classes were successfully engaged in some very active front line service which lasted until mid 1944. In consequence, they received the nickname *Kanalarbeiter* (Channel worker) as they were mainly employed in the English Channel.

Between 3 and 20 September 1939 the 5th Torpedo Boat Flotilla (Korvettenkapitan Heyke) with *Greif, Möwe, Albatros, Kondor* and *Falke*, and the 6th Torpedo Boat Flotilla (Korvettenkapitän Wave) with *Leopard, Seeadler, Iltis, Wolf, Luchs* and *Jaguar*, were engaged in several operations with light cruisers, destroyers and minelayers, and helped to lay the 'Westwall' mine barrages in the North Sea.

In November 1939 the 6th Flotilla consisting of *Leopard, Seeadler, Iltis* and *Wolf*, together with the light cruisers *Königsberg* and *Nürnberg* were employed in escorting destroyers returning from minelaying operations off the English coast. On the 13th and 18th they covered four and three destroyers, respectively, returning from minelaying off the Thames Estuary (*Wolf* was not included in the second operation) and on the 19th, with the addition of the light cruiser *Leipzig*, they met three destroyers returning from the Humber Estuary.

THE SKAGERRAK AND NORWAY
At the end of November the flotilla began operating against merchant ships in the Skagerrak, the first such raid on the night of 21/22nd involved the armoured ship *Deutschland* and the light cruisers *Köln* and *Leipzig* escorted by the *Leopard, Seeadler* and *Iltis*. A second raid was made three days later employing the same

ships, reinforced by *Wolf*. Similar operations followed in December and between the 14th and 16th *Jaguar* and *Seeadler* captured six merchant vessels. On the 1 February 1940 the *Iltis* was in collision with the submarine *U15* in the North Sea and the U-boat was lost. On 20 February 1940 the *Luchs* and *Seeadler*, together with four destroyers, carried out another shipping raid in the Skagerrak.

Eight of the torpedo boats were involved in the invasion of Norway: the *Leopard* and *Wolf* being in Group 3 (the invasion force for Bergen); the *Greif, Luchs* and *Seeadler* to Group 4 (Kristiansand South and Arandal); and the *Albatros, Kondor* and *Möwe* to Group 5 (Oslo). The latter group became involved in heavy fighting with Norwegian forces in Oslofjord on 9 April 1940; the *Albatros* (Kapitänleutnant Strelow) was fired on by the patrol boat *Pol III* (214 tons, 1926) but the fight was rather unequal and, consequently, a short one, the Norwegian vessel being sunk by the torpedo boats 4.1in guns. Fourteen survivors were rescued by German forces. On the following day *Albatros* was damaged by coastal artillery while supporting the occupation of Bolarne and was herself lost after being beached. On the same day, off Kristiansand, the *Grief* had the unpleasant duty of sinking the *Karlsruhe* with a torpedo after the cruiser had been seriously damaged by torpedoes from HM Submarine *Truant* (Lt Commander Hutchinson).

The class itself was also to suffer further; the *Leopard* (Kapitänleutnant Trummer) was rammed and sunk by the minelayer *Preussen* during a mining operation in the Skagerrak on 30 April and the *Möwe* was torpedoed and badly damaged by HM submarine *Taku* (Lt Commander Byl) off the Norwegian coast on 9 May. *Möwe* was not

The *Wolf* as completed in black paint scheme, without AA guns and the recognition letters WO (later changes to WL) on her bow.

Drüppel

recommissioned until April 1942 when she joined a *Torpedo-Schulfotille* prior to rejoining the 5th Torpedo Boat Flotilla.

In mid 1940 the class provided escorts for the damaged battlecruisers *Scharnhorst* and *Gneisenau* which sailed home separately, from Trondheim to Kiel, on 21 June and 25 July respectively. In the initial operation the escort was provided by the *Greif, Kondor, Falke, Jaguar* and four destroyers. Off Utsire, the force was attacked by six Swordfish aircraft without success, two of the enemy planes being shot down. The *Scharnhorst* arrived safely in Kiel on 23 June. *Gneisenau* was covered initially by the cruiser *Nürnberg* and four destroyers, which were joined later by the *Iltis, Jaguar, Wolf, Seeadler* and *Luchs* (Kapitänleutnant Kassbaum). On 26 July the *Luchs* was torpedoed, probably by HM submarine *Thames*, off the Norwegian coast. The torpedo boat broke in two and quickly sank while the submarine survived a counter attack with depth charges and escaped.

MINELAYING OPERATIONS
Before being transferred to Western France the torpedo boats were involved in several minelaying operations in the south west North Sea. On the night of 7/8 August 1940, the *Falke, Kondor* and *Jaguar*, together with three smaller torpedo boats, escorted the minelayers *Roland, Cobra* and *Brummer* when they laid the offensive mine barrage SW1. The same vessels, plus *Iltis* and two small torpedo boats, covered a similar operation a week later, on the night of 14/15th, by the minelayers *Tannenberg, Roland* and *Cobra* (barrage SW2). On 31 August, north west of Texel, the British 20th Destroyer Flotilla ran into these minefields and the destroyers *Esk* and *Ivanhoe* were lost (the latter finally sunk by HMS *Kelvin* on the following day). A third destroyer, *Express*, was severely damaged and put out of action for 13 months.

1

2

Mine barrage SW3 was laid by the *Roland, Tannenberg* and *Cobra* between 31 August and 2 September, the escort being provided by *Falke, Iltis, Jaguar* and *Greif* of the 5th Flotilla, four smaller torpedo boats and three destroyers. On the night of 6/7 September another minefield (SW0) was laid in the English Channel, the escort once again being provided by the 5th Flotilla (this time including *Kondor*), together with three T1 class torpedo boats. Finally during 30 September/1 October 1940 offensive mining operation Werner was carried out off Dover, covered by the 5th Flotilla (KorvettenKapitän Henne, with *Greif, Kondor, Falke* and *Seeadler*).

ACTION IN THE CHANNEL

On the night of 8/9 October 1940 the 5th flotilla (*Greif, Kondor, Falke, Seeadler, Wolf* and *Jaguar*) reconnoitred an area off the Isle of Wight. Two days later, at 1930 (German time – British time 1 hour earlier) on 11 October, the same vessels, less *Jaguar*, sailed from Cherbourg to operate against merchant shipping in the same area. Proceeding north east at 21kts they reached a position at approximately 50°25N/01°05W at 23.20 when two vessels were sighted at a distance of 2-3 miles bearing port 345°. Identified by the German ships as coasters, these were in fact the armed trawlers *Listrac* and *Warwick Deeping* which were patrolling in line ahead on a westerly course at 5kts with *Listrac* leading. The German ships immediately altered course west toward the enemy and at 23.37, opened fire at range of 3600m on the *Warwick Deeping*. *Listrac* switched on her identification lights, and was also fired on, receiving a hit in the boiler room, which caused an explosion. The sinking *Listrac* was then hit by a torpedo fired by *Greif* and blew up. The surviving crew abandoned ship and were picked up on the following day. Meanwhile, the *Warwick Deeping*, hit two or three times and enveloped in smoke, was attempting to escape northwards toward the coast, with *Kondor* and *Falke* in pursuit. *Kondor* fired three torpedoes, which missed, and the trawler finally succumbed to the combined gunfire of the two torpedo boats at 23.58; there were a few survivors.

The Flotilla returned to its westerly course and at 00.07 sighted the French submarine chasers *CH6* and *CH7* (now under the Polish Flag) off the port bow. Closing the range to about 1000m the torpedo boats opened fire at 01.11 and soon reduced the enemy vessels to drifting wrecks. However the 'chasseurs' proved difficult to sink and a great deal of ammunition was expended before they finally succumbed. About 40 survivors were rescued by *Greif* among whom were French

sailors who at first refused to be picked up – knowing that they could be transferred to the Vichy authorities and sentenced to death (Vichy France having made peace with Germany her citizens were breaking the law in continuing to fight).

The flotilla reformed at 01.50 and steered east at 23kts until 02.20 when they turned to a south easterly course. At 03.25, in position 51°10N/01°25W *Greif* reported four (actually five) enemy destroyers bearing 140° at a range of 5000m and on a westerly course. In the face of a superior force and with their ammunition running low the torpedo boats had little choice but to avoid action and immediately turned to the west, increased speed to 28kts and began to lay a smoke screen. The British vessels were in a position which could force the torpedo boats away to the north or west but, behind their smoke screen, the 5th flotilla gradually turned southward onto a course toward the French coast. Fortunately the British reaction was slow and it was not until they were almost in the wake of the German vessels that action commenced. After illuminating the area with starshell the destroyers opened fire at about 03.25, the first salvo falling between *Greif, Seeadler* and *Kondor* without causing damage. Some of the HE shells passed very close over *Kondor* to explode 100m to 200m beyond the starboard bow. The smoke screen proved very effective against the starshell illumination and, in order to locate their target, the British used their searchlights but with little success.

To avoid revealing their position, the torpedo boats did not fire their guns but, using the enemy gun flashes as a point of aim, the *Wolf* and *Falke* each fired three torpedoes – the results of which were not observed. *Kondor*, with a destroyer close in her wake, dropped three depth charges to deceive the enemy into believing that mines were exploding – the ships were by this time in an area mined by the British. The fall of shot from the destroyers gradually became more and more erratic and finally, at about 04.00 contact was lost. The flotilla altered course for Brest at about 05.50 and headed south with Cap de la Hague on their beam. However, forty minutes later they were ordered by Naval Group Command West to proceed to Cherbourg where they all arrived safely, and undamaged at 10.25. The 'unknown' British destroyers with which they were engaged were *Jackal, Jaguar, Jupiter, Kelvin* and *Kipling*.

On the night of 17/18 October 1940 the 5th Flotilla consisting of *Greif, Kondor, Seeadler, Falke, Wolf* and *Jaguar* covered a sortie toward the western entrance of the Bristol Channel by four destroyers.

RETURN TO MINELAYING

At the end of the month the class returned to providing escorts for minelaying operations, the first taking place on the night of 29/30 October when *Iltis* and *Jaguar* were employed in offensive minelaying operation 'Alfred' off Dover. The same ships covered a similar operation ('Oskar') off Dover on the night of 2/3 December, while on the following night operation 'Marianne', also off Dover, was covered by *Greif, Kondor, Falke* and *Seeadler*.

Luchs in about 1938.
Drüppel

Möwe in 1942.
Drüppel

1

2

By the end of the year only one German destroyer *(Richard Beitzen)* was still operational so the torpedo boats bore almost the entire responsibility for covering minelaying operations. For example on the night of 22/23 December *Greif, Falke* and *Seeadler* went to the west side of the North Sea to cover operation 'SWa' and on the night of 7/8 January 1941 *Kondor* and *Wolf* covered operation 'Renate' off Dover. On her return from the latter operation *Wolf* was lost on a mine off Dunkirk, losses among her crew including the commander, Oberleutnant zur see Peters.

On the night of 23/24 January the *Iltis, Seeadler* and *Richard Beitzen* covered the offensive minelaying operation 'Weber' off the south coast of England. This minefield was probably responsible for the loss of two cargo vessels – *Ben Rein* (156 tons) off Falmouth on 17 February and the *Shoal Fisher* (689 tons), in position 50°10N/04°50W, on 23 February. It is also worth mentioning that the following vessels were lost off Dover in mine barrages 'Werner', 'Alfred' and 'Renate': the British cargo ship *Adaptity* (372 tons) in position 51°44N/01°17E on 5 October 1940. The Norwegian cargo ship *Hundvaag* (690 tons) near the South Goodwins on 1 November 1940. The British cargo ship *Baltrader* (1699 tons) in position 51°41N/01°18E on 9 November 1940. The British motor barge *Ability* (293 tons) in position 51°45N/01°11E on 18 November 1940. The British Cargo ship *Ryal* (367 tons) in position 51°32N/01°04E on 24 November 1940. The Trinity House tender *Strathearn* (683 tons) in position 51°45N/01°10E on 8 January 1941.

After operation 'SWa' (21/22 December) *Greif* and *Seeadler* sailed to Cuxhaven whence they sailed at 16.20 on 16 January 1940 in company with the blockade runner *Alstertor,* arriving three days later, at 22.00 on the 19th, at Dunkirk.

On 23 January 1941, the *Falke* was at Christiansand in Norway where she received orders to join three T1 class torpedo boats to escort *Scharnhorst* and *Gneisenau* through the Skagerrak in the initial stages of Operation 'Berlin' (break-out into the Atlantic). At 12.08 on 26 January she was back in Bergan having successfully completed her small part in this operation. On the night of 3/4 February together with four smaller torpedo boats she escorted the minelayers *Tannenberg, Königin Luise* and *Brummer,* in Operation 'Rugen' off the Norwegian coast. After which she went to Stavanger.

The *Falke* off St Malo in 1942 or 1943

Author's collection

Greif and *Kondor* in 1943.

Drüppel

OPERATION AUGSBERG

In February 1941 *Seeadler, Greif, Kondor* and *Falke* were sent to Rotterdam for refit and repair leaving the flotilla with only two boats – *Jaguar* and *Iltis*. This latter pair were employed in minelaying operations, themselves laying mines near Eastbourne on the nights of 25/26 February and 5/6 March in operations 'Augsberg A' and 'Augsberg B'. In the former the two torpedo boats sailed from Cherbourg at about midday on 25th and sailed toward Boulogne at 25kts in order to deceive any enemy observers into thinking that they were attempting to break through the Dover Straits. However, off Boulogne they altered course west toward the English coast and at 00.42 the first mine was dropped. Each vessel laid 40 mines, the last at 01.39, and returned safely to Cherbourg at 09.57 on 26th. For 'Augsberg B' they sailed from Cherbourg at 20.22 on 5 March, began laying their mines at 04.43 the following morning and finished an hour later at 05.42. They passed Cap d'Antifer, north of Le Havre, at 08.10 and were back in Cherbourg at 12.28.

The 'Augsberg' minefields caused the loss of five British vessels: HM armed trawlers *Keryado*, off Newhaven on 6 March, and *Gullfoss*, off Dungeness on 9 March; and the cargo ships *Corina* (870 tons), *Sparta* (708 tons) and *Waterland* (1107 tons) all in position 50°55N/00°35E on 10 March.

KAPITÄNLEUTNANT HARTENSTEIN

Between October 1939 and March 1941 the *Jaguar* was commanded by Kapitänleutnant Hartenstein, who was later to command the submarine *U156*, becoming famous for his humanity in rescuing the survivors of the *Laconia* after he had sunk that ship. However, before he left *Jaguar* he was to take her on two final operations. On 9 March 1941, with the *Iltis* in company, he covered the *Hipper* during the cruisers speed trials which took place off the Ronde, in the sheltered roadstead of Brest, for a period of 24hrs. Finally on 21 March, again in company with *Iltis*, he sailed from Brest to meet and escort the *Gneisenau* and *Scharnhorst* on their return from Operation Berlin. The battlecruisers were met in the north of the Bay of Biscay and the whole force arrived safely in Brest on the morning of the 22nd in company with the mine destructor ships *Sperrbrecher 8* and *Sperrbrecher 9*.

By this time *Jaguar* and *Iltis* were seriously in need of refit and repair and were ordered to return to Germany. Consequently at 23.00 on 23 March 1941 they sailed from Cherbourg, passing Calais at 08.30 the following morning. In the North Sea the two torpedo boats were attacked by British aircraft (one of which was shot down by the *Jaguar*) without loss to the German vessels and both anchored safely in the roadstead of Heligoland at 10 minutes past midnight on 25 March 1941. Subsequently *Iltis* sailed for Schiedam in Holland, where she arrived on 9 April for refit and repair by the Wilton Shipyard. *Jaguar* was transferred to Rotterdam for the same purpose, the work being carried out by the Smith Shipyard.

To be continued

WARSHIP PICTORIAL
Surcouf under refit

By Francis J Allen

Surcouf, launched at Cherbourg on 18 October 1929, was the French version of the large 'cruiser' type submarines which were produced by most of the major naval powers, after the First World War. Like those vessels she was inspired by the large German U-boats of the 1914–18 period, proved expensive and impracticable and was not repeated. She was designed for long range operations against trade and her smaller torpedoes (she was fitted with four 400mm torpedo tubes as well as eight 550mm torpedo tubes) and two 8in guns were largely intended for use against merchantmen – the latter helping to ensure that she would not have to foreshorten an operation due to lack of torpedoes (she carried 14 550mm and 8 400mm). She also carried two

37mm AA guns. The vessel displaced 3205 tons (surface)/4304 tons (submerged), was capable of speeds of 18.5kts (surface)/10kts (submerged) and had a range of 10,000nm at 10kts.

After the fall of France in June 1940 *Surcouf* escaped from Brest and sailed for Britain where she was taken over. She was subsequently transferred to the FNFL and was mainly employed on patrol work in the Atlantic until lost in collision with the US merchantman *Thomson Lykes* in the Gulf of Mexico on 18 February 1942. The accompanying photographs were taken in late 1941 while *Surcouf* was under refit at Portsmouth Navy Yard, New Hampshire, USA.

Surcouf's port quarter on 1 September 1941. Note the size of the rudder, the port aft hydroplane and the staggered arrangement of the twin screws.

USN

Viewed from forward, the *Surcouf* in No 2 dry dock, Portsmouth Navy Yard on 1 September 1941.

USN

Surcouf's starboard quarter, 1 September 1941.
USN

A midships view from abaft the conning tower on 1 September 1941. Note the two 37mm AA guns mounted abaft the bridge – the structure below these guns was a watertight hangar for a small Besson MB411 seaplane – one of the items of equipment intended to enhance her qualities as a commerce raider.

USN

A close up of *Surcouf*'s twin 8in gun mounting, which, as can be seen, was streamlined into the forward end of the conning tower. The 8in/50 cal guns had a range of 30,000yds at 30° elevation and were of the same 1924 model as fitted in the heavy cruisers of the *Duquesne* and *Suffren* classes and the *Algerie*.

USN

The *Surcouf* on completion of her refit, 9 November 1941.
Note the two-colour camouflage.
USN

The conning tower of *Surcouf*, 9 November 1941.
USN

FORTHCOMING NAVAL TITLES FROM CONWAY

US NAVAL WEAPONS

Every gun, missile, mine and torpedo used by the US Navy from 1883 to the present day

Norman Friedman

A truly encyclopaedic work, Norman Friedman's latest book gives detailed specifications for each weapon and backs each entry with an authoritative discussion of why the weapon was developed and how it functioned in service. To complete the picture, full descriptions of the essential electronics – fire control systems, radars, sonars and other sensors – are included, together with analyses of US Navy thinking on strategy and tactics as it affected weapons development and procurement.

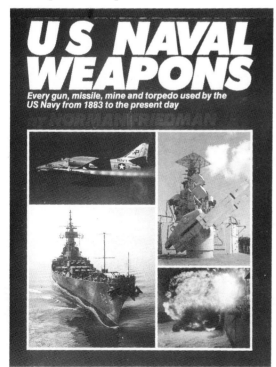

310 × 216mm (12¼" × 8½"), 288 pages, 200 photographs, 150 line drawings. ISBN 0 85177 240 4. **£18.00** *(plus £1.80 postage and packing when ordering direct). March*

A CENTURY OF NAVAL CONSTRUCTION

The History of the Royal Corps of Naval Constructors

D L Brown RCNC

Published to mark the centenary of the Royal Corps, this book offers a completely new insight into the factors governing British warship construction as well as the wider issues of Royal Navy Policy. The ancestry of the Corps can be traced back to the eighteenth century, but the story is carried right up to the present; vessels designed by the Corps are the only warships to have seen action against modern weaponry, and the book concludes with an analysis of the lessons of the Falklands conflict.

241 × 156mm (9½" × 6"), 384 pages, 92 photographs, 20 line drawings. ISBN 0 85177 282 X. **£20.00** *(plus £2.00 postage and packing when ordering direct). March*

CONWAY'S ALL THE WORLD'S FIGHTING SHIPS 1947-1982

Part I: The Western Powers

The fourth volume of Conway's four-volume history of iron and steel warships provides a clear but comprehensive review of postwar naval affairs, from the largest issue to the minute technicalities of warship design. It has been necessary to divide this volume into two parts in order to include the details of every significant warship built (and many that were only projected). The first covers the NATO navies, its associates like France, and other Western-orientated powers such as Japan, Australia and New Zealand. Part II contains the navies of the Warsaw Pact, non-aligned countries and minor navies and will be published in the Autumn.

310 × 216mm (12¼" × 8¼"), 256 pages, 250 photographs, 240 line drawings. ISBN 0 85177 255 0. **£25.00** *(plus £2.00 postage and packing when ordering direct). April*

From your local bookshop or
Conway Maritime Press Ltd
24 Bride Lane, Fleet Street, London EC4Y 8DR

72

BALTIC EPISODE

A CLASSIC OF SECRET SERVICE IN RUSSIAN WATERS

BALTIC EPISODE

Captain Augustus Agar V.C.

Captain Augustus Agar VC

Early in 1919 a flotilla of the Royal Navy's Coastal Motor Boats was sent to Finland to organise the rescue of an important British agent in Leningrad. Captain Agar led the flotilla and *Baltic Episode* is his own account of the daring exploits accomplished by his tiny torpedo boats, culminating in the sinking of the cruiser *Oleg*, for which Agar won the Victoria Cross. A tale of bravery, fantastic ingenuity and perseverance – but also a fascinating glimpse of the Baltic at a crucial stage in its history.

203 × 134mm (8" × 5¼"), 264 pages, 15 photographs, 3 maps. ISBN 0 85177 276 5. **£6.95** *(plus £1.00 postage and packing when ordering direct). January*

From your local bookshop or
Conway Maritime Press Ltd
24 Bride Lane, Fleet Street, London EC4Y 8DR

Conway Maritime Press

COMPLETE CATALOGUE OF BOOKS 1983

Conway Maritime Press

Our 1982/1983 catalogue, containing details of all our new titles and a complete back list of our titles already published, is now available.

For a free copy, ring 01-583 2412 or write to:
Conway Maritime Press Ltd, 24 Bride Lane, Fleet Street, London EC4

NEW CATALOGUE NOW AVAILABL

EDITORIAL John Roberts

This year marks the centenary of the Royal Corps of Naval Constructors, an event which should receive much more attention than it will, no doubt, actually receive. Very few people outside those professionally concerned and those with an interest in naval matters would know of its existence and very few understand the very great contribution it has made to the development of warships in the last 100 years. Hopefully, the events of this year may help to enlighten many people.

The year is to be marked by a 'Centenary Exhibition' at the National Maritime Museum, which will open on 3 May and run until September when it is expected to go on tour, visiting principally the Royal Dockyard cities and, naturally, the city of Bath where the RN's principal design facility has been based since 1939. A television documentary has also been produced, but there is some doubt as to whether it will actually appear, while the GPO are to issue a commemorative cover and postmark on Centenary Day, 21 August 1983. Furthermore, the publishers of *Warship* have produced the centenary history (*A Century of Naval Construction* by D K Brown, £20).

The First School of Naval Architecture was formed in 1811 and although this initiated a system which subsequently produced a number of notable naval architects, including William White and Phillip Watts, it did not give the Navy the truly professional body of naval architects required by the rapidly developing technology of the ironclad era. The solution was provided by William White who laid down the principles for the formation of the RCNC in 1880. The system he proposed for the training and career structure of the Admiralty's design team was approved by the Brassey Committee in 1882 and officially established in the following year. Since then, the RCNC has left its mark not only on British warships but on worldwide warship design.

In the case of the aircraft carrier for example, much is made of how far ahead of the British, the Americans and Japanese were in the Second World War. However, this relates largely to carrier employment and naval aircraft development, not to ship design. Until the 1920s the RN was the only navy with an aircraft carrier, and set the pattern of carrier design and equipment. The USA, Japan and France obtained substantial assistance from the RCNC in developing their own carriers, France being given the plans of *Eagle* and Japan the plans of *Argus*. Subsequently the RCNC led aircraft carrier design in such things as the introduction of the escort carrier and the angled flight deck.

This ability to lead the field can be seen in all aspects of warship design and construction both conventional and innovative. William White's predreadnought fleet was, for all the criticisms levelled at it, one of the most powerful groups of ships for its time ever built; the RCNC initiated the development of the escorts and landing craft of the Second World War; and, more recently, designed the world's first gas turbine warship and the first major ships to be constructed of glass reinforced plastic.

On a more detailed level the RCNC has combined with their scientific colleagues to improve submarine strength and control, introduce noise reduced propellers ten years in advance of any other navy (this will be the subject of a forthcoming technical article in *Warship*) and provided much of the expertise to convert the ideas of others into practical propositions. In all this they have been supported by the Royal Dockyards (in more recent years with reorganised management and improved equipment). What can be achieved by the RCNC and the Dockyards when given the full support of the Admiralty is well illustrated by the rapidity with which two ships were designed and constructed – the battleship *Dreadnought* of 1906 and the nuclear submarine *Dreadnought* of 1963. These and many other events mark a century of achievement which included not only the development of warships but the design of the world's first tank and the early development of airships: few, if any, similar organisations could match the achievements of the RCNC.

WARSHIP PICTORIAL

Owing to space limitations the Warship Pictorial on Naval Guns, planned for this issues has been held over to *Warship* 27.

GERMAN TORPEDO BOATS AT WAR
The Möwe & Wolf Classes

By Pierre Hervieux

Part 2

The *Möwe* with the 5th Torpedo Boat Flotilla off Le Havre on
9 July 1943. Ahead of her is an *Elbing* class torpedo boat,
either *T22* or *T23*.

Drüppel

On 13 May 1941, repairs in Rotterdam being over, *Greif*,
Kondor and *Seeadler* left the harbour for Kiel. They then
went to the Central Baltic for individual exercises; *Falke*
and *Jaguar* following soon after. On 16 June all five ships
sailed north where they were employed on a large
number of escort missions until the end of August. These
missions were between Frederikshaven, Horten, Skagen
and Christiansand, escorting in particular the light cruisers *Emden*, *Leipzig* and *Nürnberg*.

The 5th Torpedo Boat Flotilla was present for the
Channel Dash, five of its six boats (*Seeadler*, *Falke*,

Kondor, Iltis and *Jaguar*) under the command of Fregat-
tenkapitan Moritz Schmidt, setting out from Dunkirk
and at 13.26 on 12 February 1942 to join the German
Naval Force in the narrowest part of the English Channel off Cape Gris Nez. During the air attack *Jaguar* was
near missed and damaged by a bomb.

A month later, on the evening of 13 March 1942 the
5th Torpedo Boat Flotilla left Vlissingen (Holland) with
the same 5 boats to escort the auxiliary cruiser 'Schiff 28'
Michel which was sailing for the Atlantic. There were
also 9 'M' type minesweepers. They passed the Dover
Straits once again, this time in the opposite direction,
and at about 04.00 on the morning of 14 March the first
British MTBs attacked, without result. Three hours later
the German force was off Le Touquet. Soon afterwards

enemy MTBs and four destroyers hove in sight but the German vessels opened rapid fire and the British withdrew. Later a third attack took place; six MTBs from Dover, escorted by three MGBs and supported by the destroyers *Walpole, Windsor, Blencathra, Fernie* and *Calpe*, were involved in a fierce engagement which included the German shore batteries as well as 'Schiff 28' herself. The *Fernie* and *Walpole* were damaged without German loss except that 'Schiff 28' was hit once. Le Havre was reached a few hours later, St Malo on 15 March and, still escorted by the 5th Torpedo Boat Flotilla, 'Schiff 28' *Michel* reached La Pallice on 17 March from where she set out for the Atlantic on 20 March 1942.

ST NAZAIRE
On the morning of 27 March 1942, about 120 miles south-south-east of Ushant, around 06.30, the submarine *U593* (Kapitanleutnant Kelbling) was attacked by the destroyer escort HMS *Tynedale* and was claimed as sunk by the British ship. In fact the U-boat escaped and sent a radio message signalling the presence of three destroyers and ten motor launches. This was part of the British force en route for the raid on St Nazaire (it will be noted that, by a strange coincidence, on 12 December 1943, in the Mediterranean, the same *U593*, with the same Captain, met the *Tynedale* once more, torpedoing and sinking her together with her near sister *Holcombe*! This tough customer was herself sunk on the following day by a US and a British destroyer, after a 32-hour search, Captain Kelbing becoming a prisoner). After having received *U593*'s message the German Admiralty ordered the five torpedo boats of the 5th Flotilla to sail that afternoon. On the following morning, being about 100 miles off the coast they were advised of the attack on St Nazaire and at once turned back and increased speed to 26kts. At 06.43 a motor launch was sighted by *Jaguar* (Kapitanleutnant Paul) who opened fire with her light AA guns. This was *ML306* (75 tons, 1941) which returned the fire very courageously. At 06.51 the *Jaguar* stopped firing, leaving the ML stopped and out of action. On board there were 16 crew members and 14 commandos, of which 9 seriously injured and 7 killed during the action. *Jaguar* sent a boarding party to *ML306* and the 23 survivors were taken prisoner, including the ML's captain who, unhappily, later died of his wounds. On the *Jaguar*, 3 men were wounded, one of them seriously. The *Falke* (Kapitanleutnant Hoffman) also reported to have sunk an MTB which was set on fire and sunk by three shells (4.1in). This was probably *MTB74* (39 tons, 1941) which had stopped to pick up two survivors from the water and was lost after leaving St Nazaire. A brief action also took place between the five German torpedo boats and the British destroyer escorts *Atherstone* and *Tynedale*, without result. After being captured *ML306* was repaired by the Germans and renumbered *RA9*. She was sunk on 14 June 1944 (not 16 August) during an air raid on Le Havre.

THROUGH THE DOVER STRAITS
Another Channel Dash occurred for four of the torpedo boats (*Kondor, Falke, Iltis* and *Seeadler*) when they received the order to sail from Brest for the Hook Van Holland! On 8 May 1942 they left Brittany and after a stop at Cherbourg, which they left at 20.30 on the 10th headed for Boulogne at 23kts. At 02.00 on 11 May they were off Fecamp; Boulogne was reached slightly past 07.00, where they stopped until 19.30, when the sailed again, passing Cape Gris Nez at 23kts at 20.30. Off Gravelines speed was reduced to 12kts. At 23.30 off Dunkirk the Flotilla was attacked by British MTBs which continued until 23.50. Off Ostend speed was increased to 21kts. The torpedo boats were off the Hook Van Holland around 04.05 but a thick fog obliged them to wait and they only came into harbour at 10.20. This

Falke in 1943
Drüppel

Iltis as she appeared prewar; this view was taken at some time during 1933–35.

Drüppel

dangerous mission had been undertaken so the boats could once more escort an anxiliary cruiser, the 'Schiff 23' *Stier*, through the Dover Straits. *Stier* was in Rotterdam, with orders to sail for the Atlantic under the false identity of *Sperrbrecher 171!* With sixteen motor minesweepers she left Hook Van Holland at 16.30 on 12 May 1942, the four torpedo boats sailing half an hour later. For the passing of the Dover Straits in the opposite direction it suffices to say that in the early hours of 13 May, after enduring shelling from British coastal batteries, there was an attack by three British MTBs (*MTB219, MTB220* and *MTB221*). *Iltis* was torpedoed at 04.00 and *Seeadler* at 04.09, both sinking quickly, north of Boulogne. *MTB220* (35 tons, 1941) was sunk, with her entire crew of 10, by gunfire from the *Seeadler*. It is not clear which MTBs sank the *Iltis* and *Seeadler*, as only *MTB221* claimed a hit on a torpedo boat. *MTB220* having already been sunk could not have been responsible, so either *MTB221* sank both or *MTB219* sank one of them. The German losses were *Seeadler* 84 men, *Iltis* 34 men, her captain, Kapitanleutnant Jacobsen, being among them. The auxiliary cruiser continued her journey during the following nights by small stages; Le Havre, Cherbourg, La Pallice and finally Royan where she arrived on 19 May 1942 without further incident, still accompanied by *Falke* and *Kondor*. From the Gironde Estuary the ship broke out into the Atlantic undetected on 20/21 May being escorted, for a while, by

Falke, a *Sperrbrecher* and several patrol boats. *Kondor*, having trouble with a salted-up condenser, could not join them; she was sent back to Germany for essential refit and repairs, leaving *Falke* alone in Western France. On 5 November 1942 this torpedo boat, in company with two *T13* class units, left La Pallice at 18.00 to meet the transport *Templin*, which was in sight at 20.45. On the following morning they were joined by three 3 'M' class minesweepers. From about midday several air attacks began, the last one taking place at 18.16, then darkness came and all the ships safely reached La Pallice.

On 12 November, repairs being over, *Kondor* left Kiel in company of the brand new torpedo boat *T23*, for La Pallice. Off Texel they were involved in a skirmish with two British MTBs. They stopped in Hook Van Holland, sailing again for Brest and La Pallice where they arrived on 21 November 1942.

BLOCKADE RUNNERS

On 29 November 1942 the Italian blockade runner *Cortellazzo* set out from Bordeaux en route to Japan, escorted by *Kondor*, *Falke* and two *T22* class torpedo boats. After the escort turned back, a Sunderland flying boat found her on 30 November and, being located by the destroyers *Quickmatch* and *Redoubt*, the latter ship sank her with a torpedo on 1 December.

On 28 March 1943 the Italian blockade runner *Himalaya* set out for Japan from the Gironde, escorted by *Falke* and four other torpedo boats, but after the departure of the escort in the area of Cape Finisterre she had to return when located by British air reconnaissance. Met by *Kondor* and three other torpedo boats, the *Himalaya* returned to Bordeaux on 30 March. On 9 April another attempt to break out was unsuccessful, in spite of a strong escort of three destroyers, *Kondor* and four other torpedo boats. The ship was forced to return after enduring heavy air attacks.

MINELAYING

Between 4 and 6 June 1943 the 5th Torpedo Boat Flotilla (Korvettenkapitan Koppenhagen) accomplished two mining operations in the English Channel with *Möwe* (at work again, after a long absence), *Falke*, *Greif*, *Kondor* and *T22*. Between June and August 1943 German U-boat tankers and damaged submarines were escorted several times by *Falke*, *Greif*, *Möwe*, *Jaguar* and *Kondor*. On 3 and 5 September 1943, *Möwe*, *Kondor* and three other torpedo boats carried out the mining operations 'Taube' and 'Rebhuhn' in the English Channel. On 29/30 September 1943, *Kondor*, *Greif* and three other torpedo boats carried out the mining operation 'Talsohle' in the Channel. On 22 March 1944, north of Fécamp, *Möwe*, *Kondor*, *Greif* and *Jaguar* laid a barrage of 180 mines and on the night of 27/28 March 1944 the boats of the 5th Torpedo boat Flotilla (since 11 November 1943 under the command of Korvettenkapitan Hoffmann) laid a five-row protective float barrage to defend the barrages already laid. The boats then moved to Brest, via Cherbourg, on 29/30 March. From 17 to 19

Seeadler wearing the new flag of the Third Riech – the prewar appearance and the swastika flag date the photograph between November 1935 and 1939.

Drüppel

April the same Torpedo Boat Flotilla, comprising *Kondor*, *Möwe*, *Greif* and two other units, was transferred from Brest to Cherbourg as distant cover for a convoy. On the night of 21/22 April *Kondor*, *Möwe* and *Greif* laid a protective float barrage, consisting of 145 floats, from Cherbourg and on the following night they were deployed again from Cherbourg, against British MTBs. They were attacked near Cape Barfleur, but the British failed to gain any success and *MTB671* was sunk by gunfire on 24 April. On the night of 26/27 April *Kondor*, *Greif* and *Möwe* laid a barrage of 108 mines north of Cherbourg and on the following night laid another defensive barrage of 108 mines off Cherbourg. When avoiding a British fighter bomber attack, the force ran into a British minefield and *Kondor* was damaged. On 30 April *Möwe* and *Greif* carried out two, and on 1 May, one defensive mining operation when barrages 'Blitz' '28', '38A' and '39' were laid with 260 mines.

The torpedo boat *Jaguar* sailed from Brest for Cherbourg where she arrived on 23 May and on the following night proceeded with *Kondor*, *Greif*, *Falke* and *Möwe* to Le Havre. On the way *Greif* was hit during fighter bomber attacks, collided with *Falke* and sank on 24 May. *Kondor* was again badly damaged by a mine but survived.

D DAY

On 6 June 1944 the Allied Operation 'Neptune', the amphibious phase of Operation 'Overlord', the greatest combined operation of all time, the landings in Normandy, took place. The invasion fleet comprised 7 battleships, 2 monitors, 23 heavy and light cruisers, 3

gunboats, 105 destroyers, 1073 sloops, corvettes, frigates minesweepers, armed trawlers, MTBs, MGBs, MLs etc ... plus over 4000 landing craft and transports. To oppose this formidable fleet, the German Navy in the Channel area had 5 torpedo boats and 39 MTBs and of the latter, 5 were non-operational. Only three torpedo boats were available: *Jaguar*, *Möwe* and *T28* (Flotilla leader); *Falke* was not operational following her collison with *Greif* on 24 May and *Kondor*, severely damaged by a mine on the same day, was not ready in time to take part in any attack against the invasion fleet. Around 03.00 on 6 June the headquarters, established ashore, warned Korvettenkapitan Henrich Hoffman (leader of the 5th torpedo Boat Flotilla) that the enemy was approaching, big ships having been detected in Seine Bay, sailing south. The warning was probably issued from a radar station in Cherbourg which had not been destroyed by bombing and was able to work in spite of jamming. Hoffman's Flotilla commanders were called to a meeting. The three available boats passed Le Havre harbour's jetties at 04.42 and at 05.05 the first Allied planes were sighted. Six minutes later the Flotilla leader signalled, '6 large shadows ahead', just as she emerged from a smoke screen, and at 05.18 air attacks began against the small German force. All the flak guns of the three torpedo boats opened a fierce fire. At 05.31 other fighter bombers attacked but the only result was 2 torpedo tubes damaged and unserviceable aboard the *T28*. At the very same time battleships and cruisers were clearly seen off Ouistreham. This was the British 'Force S' which comprised the battleships *Warspite* and *Ramillies*, monitor *Roberts*, headquarters ship *Largs*, cruisers *Mauritius*, *Arethusa*, *Scylla*, *Danae*, *Dragon* and *Frobisher*, escorted by 13 destroyers! AT 05.35 steaming in line ahead at a speed of 28kts, the three torpedo boats launched 16 torpedoes (*Jaguar* and *Möwe*, 6 each and *T28* 4) at a range of 6500m. Shortly afterwards, shells fell around the torpedo boats, which returned fire with their 4.1in guns prior to escaping into the smoke screen and disappearing without damage. On their way back to Le Havre at 05.45 they were again attacked by fighter bombers but safely reached the harbour around 06.15. Two of the torpedoes they fired passed between the battleships *Warspite* and *Ramillies*, a third went straight toward the Headquarters ship *Largs* (ex-French *Charles Plumier*) which only escaped by going astern at full power. The destroyer *Virago* signalled that another one had narrowly missed her. A fifth hit the Norwegian destroyer *Svenner* amidships, and she, broken in two, sank very quickly with the loss of 34 men (32 Norwegians and 2 British liaison personnel). The *Svenner* (Lieutenant-Commander Tore Holthe) ex-British *Shark*, was a brand new destroyer, commissioned on 18 March 1944 and had never fired her guns in anger. Nobody will deny that the spirit that led to this attack and the way it was accomplished would be an honour to any navy. In the night of 6/7 June 1944, *Jaguar*, with the Flotilla Leader on board (*T28* being in dock) and *Möwe* unsuccessfully attacked two Allied destroyers off Le Havre. In the night of 8/9 June *Jaguar*, *Möwe* and *T28* became involved in an engagement with the British 55th

Chasseur 13, sister to *Chasseurs 6* and *7*, at Brest on 21 July 1945.

Author's collection

MTB Flotilla, off Cap de le Héve. The Germans also reported that there was a destroyer group in support comprising about six units. On the following night *Jaguar*, *Möwe* and *T28* sailed from Le Havre to attack an Allied destroyer patrol consisting of the *Glaisdale* (Norwegian), *Ursa* (British) and *Krakowiak* (Polish) but was outmanoeuvred by the latter. *Falke* was now repaired so in the next operation, on the night of 12/13 June, she joined *Möwe*, *Jaguar* and *T28*. Scarcely one hour after sailing two fighter bomber attacks were repulsed and at 02.37, off Le Havre, two Allied destroyers were encountered, *Stord* (Norwegian) and *Scorpion* (British); *Möwe* and *T28* attacked them unsuccessfully with torpedoes. Afterwards on their way back to harbour, the four torpedo boats were again subjected to air attacks without result except for minor splinter damage.

For a week, these small torpedo boats and the E-boats harassed the Allied patrols and since the Allied naval forces were not getting the better of them it was decided to ask RAF Bomber Command to mount a massive 'carpet' bombing of their base. Thus on the night of 14/15 June 325 four-engined Lancaster heavy bombers raided the harbour of Le Havre. *Falke* received 5 heavy hits and *Jaguar* 4, both capsizing. *Möwe* was hit by a stick of explosive and incendiary bombs. At 00.45 a second wave of bombers dropped bombs for 15 minutes. At 05.00 *Möwe* turned onto her beam-ends, starboard side and sank. Losses were slight among the crews, for as soon as the bombers approached all the men took cover in the E-boat bunker, only the light AA artillery gunners staying on board.

However there was still one *Möwe* class torpedo boat afloat, the *Kondor*, which escaped destruction during the air raid although badly damaged by it. Consequently the very last unit of these very active and aggressive torpedo boats was not sunk by the Allies, for the Germans scuttled *Kondor* themselves on 28 June 1944. There was still one intact torpedo boat in the harbour of Le Havre, the miraculously undamaged *T28*. What happened to her is another story that will be covered in a future article concerning the *T22* class torpedo boats.

Northern Patrol Part 2

By Donald L Kindell

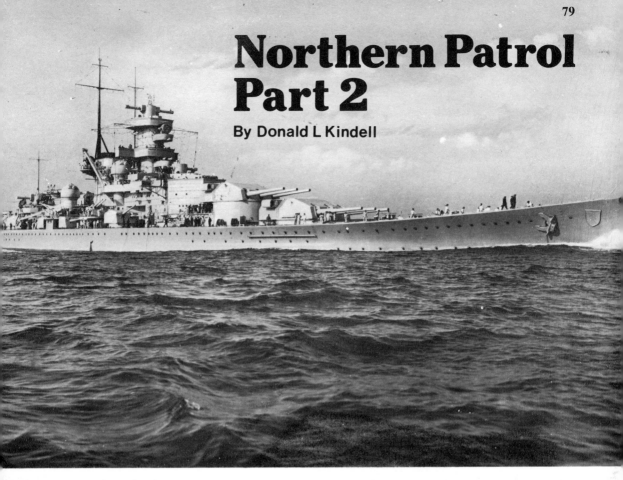

The German battlecruiser *Scharnhorst*, pre-war.
CMP

The German battlecruisers *Gneisenau*(flagship of Vice Admiral Wilhelm Merschall) and *Scharnhorst* had sortied from Wilhelmshaven on 21 November to raid in the Atlantic. They were accompanied by the light cruisers *Köln* and *Leipzig* and the destroyers *Giese, Arnim* and *Galster* until late on the 21st when the escort was detached for operations in the Skagerrak. South of Iceland, the battlecruisers were to put pressure on British shipping in the North Atlantic to draw attention away from the *Graf Spee* in the South Atlantic where allied hunting groups were concentrating.

During the afternoon of 23 November, the Northern Patrol was disposed as follows: in the Denmark Strait were the cruisers *Norfolk* and *Suffolk* and the AMCs *California, Chitral* and *Transylvania*; in the Iceland-Faroes Channel were the cruisers *Newcastle, Delhi, Ceres* and *Calypso* and the AMC *Rawalpindi* (*Delhi* was actively engaged in chasing a German merchant ship); finally, the cruisers *Caledon, Cardiff* and *Colombo* were operating to the south of the Faroes.

THE LOSS OF RAWALPINDI

At 15.07 on the 23rd, *Scharnhorst* came upon *Rawalpindi* southeast of Iceland. The AMC attempted to outrun the German ship, and at 15.51, radioed that she had sighted an enemy battlecruiser, adding a few minutes later that this warship was the *Deutschland* which the British believed was still at sea. Finally, at 16.03, *Scharnhorst* came within range and opened fire, followed by *Gneisenau* at 16.11. *Rawalpindi* was soon wrecked and set afire, but *Scharnhorst* was hit in return by one of *Rawalpindi*'s 6in shells, which hit the quarter deck and caused some splinter casualties among the crew.

Scharnhorst picked up six survivors from *Rawalpindi* and *Gneisenau* picked up 210. The burnt-out hull rolled over and sank shortly before 20.00. The following day, *Chitral* picked up an additional eleven survivors from a life-boat; some 271 crew members were lost.

The *Newcastle,* on station next to *Rawalpindi*, received her SOS and steamed towards her location. At 18.16, she actually sighted *Gneisenau* and a minute later *Scharnhorst*, but both disappeared in a rain squall and *Newcastle* lost touch at 18.24. Subsequently she was joined by *Delhi*, which had abandoned her pursuit of the German merchant ship, and both vessels searched to the northwest and northeast until the dawn of the next day but never regained contact.

1

1 The ill fated AMC *Rawalpindi*.
CMP

2 *Chitral* as an AMC.
CMP

Admiral Forbes, in response to *Rawalpindi*'s sighting report, sailed from the Clyde at 19.30 with *Nelson* and *Rodney*, the cruiser *Devonshire*, and the destroyers *Faulknor*, *Forester*, *Fortune*, *Firedrake* and *Fury* and headed for a position off the Norwegian coast in order to intercept the enemy ships as they returned to Germany.

joined by *Diomede* and *Dunedin*, which came out from Loch Ewe and took station off North Rona to patrol the western approaches to Fair Island Channel. The *Dragon*, at Loch Ewe, was the only Northern Patrol cruiser not involved in this operation. The *Sheffield* departed Loch Ewe and proceeded towards the reported position of the German ships, joining *Newcastle* and *Delhi*, while the destroyers *Tartar*, *Kandahar* and *Kashmir* departed Scapa Flow with orders to locate and shadow the German forces. In the Denmark Strait, *Norfolk* and *Suffolk* were ordered to proceed towards Bill Baily's Bank, while the three AMCs on patrol with them were ordered to withdraw from patrol and return to port at once (it was while returning to port that *Chitral* rescued the *Rawalpindi* survivors). The *Glasgow* with the destroyers *Maori* and *Zulu*, at sea since the 20th looking for the German liner *Bremen*, were to the northeast of the Shetlands.

The allied convoy CN3, just leaving the Firth of Forth at this time, was recalled and its escorts, the destroyers *Inglefield*, *Imperial* and *Isis*, joined the Glasgow group. Additionally, the destroyers *Imogen*, *Impulsive*, *Kingston and Bedouin* at Rosyth put to sea to join the *Southampton* group (en route one of these destroyers was detached to patrol the Pentland Firth). The destroyers *Somali*, *Mashona*, *Ashanti* and *Punjabi*, recently departed Belfast escorting the dummy battleships *Waimana* and *Pakeha*, were ordered to join Forbes at sea after sending their charges back into port.

The battleship *Warspite* which had departed Halifax with convoy HX9 on 18 November, was ordered to leave the convoy and take station in the Denmark Strait. The battlecruiser *Repulse* with the carrier *Furious* also sailed from Halifax with orders to steer east protecting the convoy routes and sweeping for the German ships. However, when *Repulse* was damaged by heavy weather, both ships returned to Halifax and, to replace them, the *Hood*, with the destroyers *Exmouth*, *Echo* and *Eclipse*, sailed from Plymouth on 25 November. They rendezvoused with the French battlecruiser *Dunkerque* and the destroyers *Mogador* and *Volta* which had departed Brest on 25 November. These ships proceeded to position 60°N, 20°W, whence they made a sweep which lasted through to the end of the month.

British submarines already on patrol were the *Thistle*

At sea, off the Clyde, the destroyers *Fame* and *Foresight* joined Forbes. Other large scale dispositions were also made: the cruisers *Southampton*, *Edinburgh* and *Aurora* with the destroyers *Afridi* and *Gurkha* sailed from Rosyth for the Fair Island Channel. The *Caledon*, *Cardiff* and *Colombo*, patrolling south of the Faroes, were off the Skaw, *Triad* off the Lindesnes, *Sturgeon* off Horn Reef and *L23* southwest of the Lister Light. Additionally, submarines of the 2nd and 6th Flotilla left Rosyth on the Firth of Forth and Blyth on the Tyne, respectively, to patrol southwest of Lister Light.

At 16.00 on 24 November, Forbes redisposed his fleet off Norway to intercept the German ships. Forbes placed *Norfolk* and *Suffolk* of the 1st Squadron; *Glasgow, Southampton* and *Edinburgh* of the 2nd Squadron; *Caledon* and *Diomede* of the 7th Squadron; *Colombo, Cardiff* and *Dunedin* of the 11th Squadron; and *Newcastle* and *Sheffield* of the 18th Squadron in a patrol line, keeping his battle squadron deployed to the northwest of this line and the *Aurora* and seven destroyers as a strike force south of the line, off Utsire. The line was moved north at 07.00 on the 25th but despite all these efforts, *Scharnhorst* and *Gneisenau* arrived back at Wilhelmshaven on the 27th with only storm damage.

DECEMBER OPERATIONS

The Northern Patrol sighted 56 ships and sent 23 into Kirkwall for inspection from 24 November to 7 December and in the following period, 8 December 1939 to 4 January 1940, 164 ships were sighted and 59 sent into Kirkwall.

In view of *Nelson's* damage by magnetic mine on 4 December, Forbes decided (on 9 December) that, as his heavy ships could not now leave harbour to support the Patrol, it would have to be reduced and the AMCs were consequently ordered to return to port. However, he ordered them out again on 17 December to counter possible attempts by a number of German merchant ships to run the blockade and return to Germany. Forbes sailed with *Warspite, Barham, Hood* and *Repulse* to cover the Northern Patrol, and the movement of convoy ON5 which departed Methil on 16 December. The *Warspite* and *Hood* arrived back at Greenock on 26 December, but *Barham* and *Repulse* were still at sea covering the Patrol until 28 December. Off the Clyde Estuary on the 28th, *Barham, Repulse* and the destroyers *Isis* and *Nubian* were contacted by the German submarine *U30* which was able to torpedo *Barham* and escape. *Repulse* left the group and proceeded, unaccompanied, at high speed into the Clyde while *Faulknor* and *Mashona*, and later *Foxhound*, departed Loch Ewe to assist *Barham*. The battleship was able to get into the Clyde but was under repair and refit until 16 July 1940.

Vice Admiral Max K Horten turned over command of the Northern Patrol to Vice Admiral R H T Raikes on 20 December to assume the post of Vice Admiral Submarines, Home Fleet.

The old 'C' and 'D' class cruisers began to be withdrawn from the Patrol and restationed in less trying stations at the end of the year and by the spring of 1940 *Caledon, Calypso, Ceres, Delhi* and *Dragon* had been transferred to the Mediterranean; *Dunedin* and *Diomede* to the West Indies; *Colombo* to the East Indies; and finally *Cardiff* was assigned as Training Ship for the Gunnery School. Their place was filled by additional AMCs and the cruisers of the Home Fleet squadrons. The new AMCs joining the patrol were *Andania, Ausonia, Canton, Corfu, Derbyshire, Forfar* and *Wor-*cestershire in November and *Carinthia, Laconia, Patroclus* and *Wolfe* in January 1940.

1940

A total of 342 ships were sighted by the Northern Patrol from 5 January to 14 February and 79 were sent into Kirkwall. While the Patrol did not make any German interceptions, there was one loss indirectly attributed to them. The German merchant ship *Bahia Blanca* (8558 tons) attempting to evade the Patrol by hugging the ice line, ran onto the ice and sank in the Denmark Strait, northwest of Iceland, on 10 January.

From 15 January to 29 February, 92 ships were sighted and 24 sent into Kirkwall and on 21st the Northern Patrol had its first success since *Konsul Hendrik Fisser* was captured on 23 November, when the *Manchester* and *Kimberley* captured the German merchant ship *Wahehe* (4709 tons) which had departed Vigo on 10 February. It was the first sign of the substantial improvement for, as the winter subsided, interceptions for the Northern Patrol picked up again in March. From 1st to 14th, 98 ships were sighted and 12 sent into Kirkwall. Four German merchant ships were encountered and all four scuttled themselves upon being ordered to stop: on 2 March, *Wolfsburg* (6201 tons) scuttled herself when intercepted by the cruiser *Berwick; Arucas* (3359 tons) which had departed Vigo on 10 February, scuttled herself when stopped by the cruiser *York* on 3 March; *Uruguay* (5846 tons) scuttled herself when intercepted by *Berwick* on 6 March; and, on 13 March *Coruna* (7359 tons) scuttled herself when stopped by *Maloja*.

From 15 March to 31 March, 138 ships were sighted and 13 sent into Kirkwall for inspection while one, the German merchant ship *Mimi Horn* (4007 tons) which had departed Curacao on 5/6 March, scuttled herself when intercepted by *Transylvania* in the Denmark Strait on 28 March.

Fifty-four ships were sighted and twelve sent into Kirkwall from 1 to 9 April but on this last day the Norwegian campaign began, followed a month later by the invasion of the Low Countries. Although, despite these events, the Northern Patrol was to continue, heavy demands for ships elsewhere left the patrol very thin and it achieved few interceptions thereafter; the accomplishments of the 'Phony War' period were never to be repeated.

SELECTED BIBLIOGRAPHY

Primary sources

ADM 53/various – Ships logs
ADM 187/various – Pink List
ADM 199/24 – Convoy Reports
ADM 199/362 – Rosyth War Diary
ADM 199/399 – Home Fleet War Diary
ADM 199/2195–2197 – Home Fleet War Diary (Northern Patrol)

Published

Lloyds Register of Ships, London 1940
The War at Sea, Volume 1, 1940, by S W Roskill HMSO, London 1954
Chronology of the War at Sea 1939–1945, J Rohwer Arco Publishing, New York 1972

Askold as built.
CMP

Askold Part 2

By Andrzej M Jaskuła
Translated by Adam Śmigielski

HULL AND ARMOUR

The hull was divided into 13 watertight compartments by 12 transverse bulkheads and was so designed that she would not sink even when two adjoining compartments flooded. She had a double bottom over 60% of her length, extending to the side as far as the armoured deck in the region of the engine room. The ship had a very low forecastle and consequently she was wet forward. The hull was strengthened (especially the upper deck) as a result of trials in August 1901 when unpleasant vibrations were caused, mainly by the outer screws, when the rpm was higher than 110. At the same time the bearings were working too hard and the use of main armament caused cracks in the hull structure. The hull was too lightly built and needed strengthening in the region of

the gun foundations, while the weak superstructure restricted the arcs of fire of the main armament. In all 83 tonnes of steel were added to the hull and after additional work the hull weighed 3058 tonnes against the designed figure of 2972 tonnes. Main engines and boilers weighed 140 tonnes less than specified (1130 tonnes instead of 1270) but armament and ammunition were 50 tonnes heavier than the anticipated 495 tonnes. As a result of all these additions the normal displacement rose to 6135 tonnes and with 1065 tonnes of coal on board to 6273 tonnes. The metacentric height at full load was 0.88m. Despite these modifications there was still some vibration when steaming at high speed, which affected the ship's compasses.

Askold had an armoured deck over her full length, 0.35m above the waterline on the flat but sloped to end underwater at the sides. Horizontal armour had a thickness of 50mm and consisted of 40mm nickel steel plates on 10mm deck plating. The sloped part of the deck was 75mm thick, of which 60mm was formed by nickel steel plates and ended 1.4m below the waterline. It was sloped at an angle of 40°.

Over the engine room a domed armoured glacis 100mm thick protected the engine cylinders; the glacis had armoured hatches and ventilation gratings in it. The steering engine compartment was similarly armoured.

All the openings over the boiler rooms were protected by 38mm plates standing vertically between armoured deck and battery deck. Other openings in the horizontal part of the deck had armoured hatches. All ammunition routes above the armoured deck, were protected by

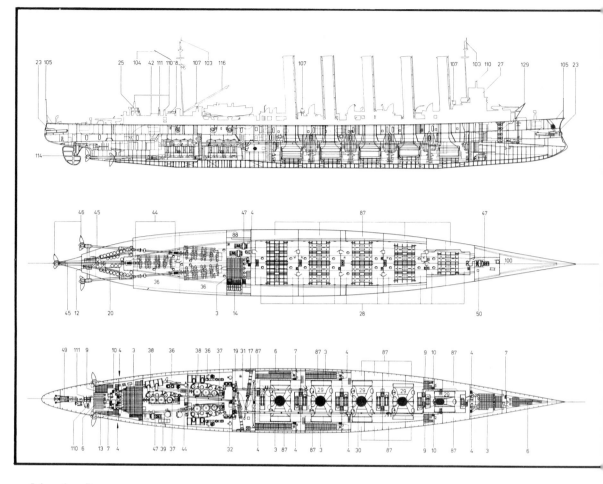

Inboard profile

Double bottom (boiler foundations shown in the larger boiler room are schematic)

Hold and magazines

Armament 1 152mm QF gun; **2** foundation of 152mm gun; **3** 152mm magazine; **4** 152mm hoist **5** 75mm QF gun; **6** 75mm magazine; **7** 75mm hoist; **8** 47mm QF gun; **9** 47mm magazine; **10** 47mm hoist; **11** foundation of the 37mm gun, **12** ammunition room; **13** ammunition room; **14** torpedo warhead magazine; **15** bow torpedo tube; **16** stern torpedo tube; **17** submerged torpedo tube; **18** above water torpedo tube; **19** torpedoes; **20** magazine for mines.

Armour and Command posts 21 armoured deck (slope line); **22** CT tube, **23** armoured cover of torpedo tube; **24** conning tower; **25** after command post; **26** chartroom; **27** pilot house.

Machinery 28 boiler room; **29** boiler; **30** forward boiler group steam pipe; **31** after boiler group steam pipe; **32** main steam pipe; **33** boiler room blower (steam driven); **34** ventilating trunk/gangway; **35** funnel uptake; **36** engine room; **37** engine; **38** main condenser; **39** auxiliary condenser; **40** engine room blower (electric driven); **41** engine room casing; **42** engine room hatch; **43** gangway; **44** thrust bearing; **45** port shaft; **46** port screw.

Other machinery 47 main 70.4kW dynamo; **48** 35.2kW dynamo; **49** steering gear; **50** compressor.

Accommodation 51 captain's day cabin; **52** captain's bedroom; **53** captain's cabinet; **54** executive officer's bedroom; **55** executive officer's office; **56** officer's cabin; **57** officer's wardroom; **58** chief of staff; **59** bedroom; **60** steward; **61** petty officer's cabin; **62** petty officer's mess; **63** crew's quarters; **64** chapel.

Domestic rooms and others 65 engineer's office; **66** ship's office; **67** pantry; **68** bakery; **69** officer's galley; **70** petty officer's galley; **71** galley; **72** crew's galley; **73** stoker's laundry; **74** drying room; **75** workshop; **76** sick bay; **77** sick bay stores.

Toilets, baths etc 78 captain's bathroom and WC; **79** executive officer's WC; **80** officer's bathroom; **81** officer's WC; **82** petty officer's toilets; **83** machinist's bath; **84** crew's bath; **85** crew's toilets; **86** sick bay bathroom and WC.

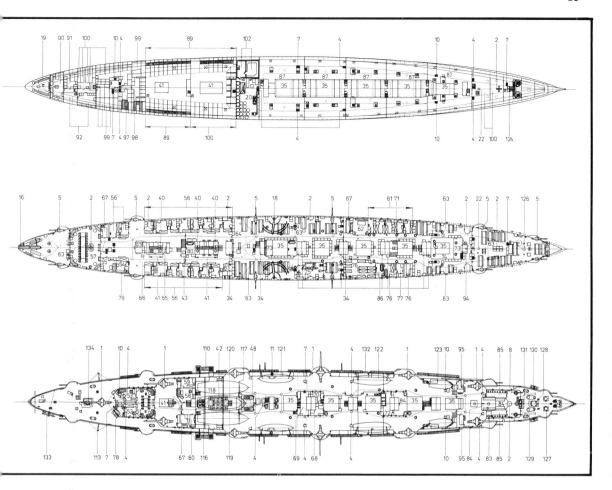

Armoured deck

Battery deck

Upper deck

Stores, etc 87 coal bunker; **88** oil tank; **89** engineering stores; **90** ordnance stores; **91** spare parts for torpedoes; **92** boatswain's store room; **93** store; **94** locker; **95** store; **96** medical store; **97** captain's stores; **98** wardroom stores; **99** sea biscuit store; **100** provisions; **101** food in barrels; **102** refrigerator room.

Rigging, hull and deck arrangement 103 topmast; **104** gaff; **105** jackstaff; **106** ensign staff; **107** searchlight; **108** hammocks; **109** accommodation ladder; **110** compass; **111** steering wheel; **112** ship's bell; **113** propeller guard; **114** rudder.

Boats 115 steam driven boat winch; **116** boat derrick; **117** boat skids; **118** steam launch; **119** longboat; **120** pinnace; **121** gig; **122** cutter; **123** jolly boat.

Anchors and associated machinery 124 anchor capstan donkey engine; **125** chain locker; **126** chain reduction gear (transmission); **127** anchor capstan; **128** mooring capstan; **129** anchor davit; **130** forward anchor; **131** spare anchor; **132** midship anchor; **133** stern anchor; **134** capstan.

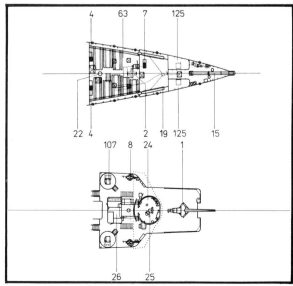

Bow TT platform

Forward superstructure deck

Drawings by Andrzej M Jaskula

TABLE 1: DISPLACEMENT, DIMENSIONS AND OTHER DATA

Legend displacement:	6000 tonnes with 720 tonnes of coal on board (some sources give 5900 tons)
Length:	132.1m oa, 130.0m wl
Breadth on frames:	15.0m
Depth:	10.2m
Draught (legend):	6.2m
Coal:	legend load 720 tons, maximum 1050–1100 tons.
Range:	6500nm with 1100 tons of coal at 10kts as designed (according to Soviet data the range was 3140–3300nm at an unspecified speed).
Complement:	573–580 officers and men (according to Soviet sources there were 20 officers and 514 petty officers and men).

38mm tubes leading to the upper deck. The armoured conning tower, situated on the forward superstructure, had 150mm sides, 40mm roof and 30mm floor and was connected to the protective deck communication by an 80mm thick tube, which had an internal diameter of 400mm and housed electrical wiring, voice pipes and other communication equipment.

Bow and stern torpedo tubes were protected with armoured plates of 40mm thick (above) and 60mm (side). The ship's sides were completely unprotected but there were coal bunkers which afforded some protection against small shells. The main armament had only small splinter shields which proved of little use in actual combat.

MACHINERY

Askold's machinery spaces were very long – 7.15m due to the necessity to locate three sets of powerful engines, a large number of boilers and extensive coal bunkers in a long and very narrow hull. There were also problems in the placing of the auxiliary machinery to allow for ease of maintenance.

The ship had 9 double-ended Thornycroft-Schulz watertube boilers placed in 5 watertight compartments, the first compartment containing only one boiler and the remainder two each. All main boilers were designed for a working pressure of 17kg/cm² and were tested for 22kg/cm². Total heating surface was 5020m² and grate area 104m². Thornycroft-Schulz small-tube boilers were chosen because of their high size power ratio and their simple construction. The ship needed less time to raise steam from cold than was the case with nearly all other cruisers of the period, and the boilers were so designed that their construction prevented flames from going into the funnels.

Each of the two groups of boilers had its own steam pipe which was in turn connected to the ship's main steam supply at the engine room bulkhead. The steam pipes were approved by the MTK only after lengthy discussions, the Russians hinting that these pipes were of poor quality.

Askold was powered by three four cylinder vertical triple expansion engines. The cylinders had diameters of 930mm (1), 1440mm (2), and 1630mm (3 and 4) and a stroke of 950mm. Each of the engines had its own surface condenser.

The engines driving the outer screws were situated side-by-side in the forward engine room and there was no longitudinal dividing bulkhead because of the narrowness of the hull. The centre screw was connected to the third engine placed in the after engine room. The designed power of all three engines combined was 19,000ihp for a maximum speed of 23kts. The boilers could be forced easily to give 23,000–24,000ihp.

The propeller shafts were divided into three sections, and the three-bladed bronze propellers had a diameter of 4.5m and pitch of 6.86m (outer) and 4.3m and 6.83m (centre).

SEA TRIALS

The first shipyard trial was conducted on 1 August 1901 in the Eckernförde Gulf. *Askold*, displacing 6070 tonnes, developed 22,900ihp which gave a speed of 22.9kts in the shallow (25m deep) water. Results for each engine were as follows:

starboard engine	7770ihp	130rpm
centre engine	7560ihp	128rpm
port engine	7570ihp	130rpm

During the trial all 9 double ended boilers were used at a steam pressure of 17kg/cm². The trial was conducted in fair weather on a smooth sea.

Official speed trials took place on the Nowa Karczma (Neukrug) measure mile near Gdansk. The ship was run on the mile four times sometime during August or September 1901. The following results were recorded at a displacement of 5950 tonnes, and a mean draught of 6.17m:

1	23.30kts	20,160ihp
2	23.45kts	19,940ihp
3	23.61kts	20,060ihp
4	23.08kts	18,470ihp
mean	23.36kts	19,650ihp

The final trials took place on 28 and 30 September 1901 at the measure mile near Bornholm and lasted for 6 hours each:

Date	28 Sept	30 Sept
Power (ihp)	20,390	20,420
rmp	125.2	126.4
speed (kts)	23.4	23.8
coal consumption (kg/ihp/hr)	0.85	0.83

These last trials were conducted on a displacement of 6100 tonnes and all 9 boilers were in use. Maximum power achieved on trials was 23,600ihp which corresponds to a speed of 24.4–24.5kts in deep water.

On all trial runs *Askold* was run by Russian naval personnel, it being considered by the Russians as a good training opportunity. Trials also confirmed the high economy of the Thornycroft-Schulz boilers. The ship was a fast steamer and she could also raise steam for

Askold, probably taken at Shanghai.
CMP

23kts from cold in less than two hours. Coal consumption was less than anticipated at 0.87kg/ihp/hr for both full speed and cruising.

Askold had good manoeuvrability thanks to the powerful steering engine and a large rudder area. The turning circle was only two ship's lengths (good for a ship so long and narrow). In the case of main steering failure there was a hand steering position. In all, four steering positions were provided in the ship: pilot house, conning tower, aft command post and in the steering engine compartment (local steering).

OPINIONS ON THE MACHINERY
Detailed observations of the behaviour of the machinery were conducted during the entire voyage to Port Arthur, China. The triple screw arrangement had many advantages over other designs; the ship could for example cruise with only one engine operating and the two outer screws turning free. As one engine produced only 6600 to 6800ihp it gave good fuel economy at cruising speeds. Under natural draught the ship had a range of 4100nm at 10kts with 1117 tonnes of coal (c65 tonnes of coal a day). When steaming at 13.5kts the range shrank to 3250nm and at 23kts to 1550nm (c400 tonnes a day).

It is interesting to compare *Askold*'s and the US built *Varyag*'s performance. The first ship used 7400 tonnes of coal for 18,500nm when on *Varyag* the consumption was twice as high and reached 8500 tonnes for 8000nm.

ELECTRIC PLANT
The ship was fitted with six dynamos driven by small donkey steam engines. Four were of 70.5kW and located under the armoured deck, and two others of 35.2kW each were placed on the upper deck. The voltage was 105. There were 46 electric motors throughout the ship (14 for the ammunition hoists, 24 for blowers, 7 for impeller bilge pumps and 1 in the workshop), 750 electric lamps and 6 searchlights.

ARMAMENT
The main armament consisted of 12 single 152mm L/45 QF guns fitted with small splinter shields. Two of these guns were fitted on the centreline fore and aft, and had an arc of fire of 270°. The other guns were mounted in the ship's sides (six of them in sponsons) on the upper deck. This arrangement of guns was proposed by the shipyard, because it offered the advantage of allowing 5 guns to fire fore and aft.

The secondary armament consisted of 12 single 75mm L/50 QF guns on the battery deck. Eight of them (four forward and four aft) were placed in so called *Schwalbennester* and so it was possible to fire them along the ship's course.

The light armament consisted of 8 47mm QF guns and two 37mm guns fitted on the upper deck and in the superstructure. In addition there were two 7mm machine guns and two Baranovsky 64mm guns for a landing party.

The ship was fitted with 14 ammunition hoists: 8 for the 152mm guns, three for the 75mm guns and three for the 47mm guns. The electric motors driving them were mostly installed on the battery deck. It was also possible to operate the hoists by hand. All hoists were connected by an elaborate rail system, so all guns could be well supplied with ammunition from more than one hoist as required. There was an extensive ventilation system to prevent the temperature in the magazines from rising higher than 35°C. Magazines could be flooded in 15 minutes.

There were six 380mm torpedo tubes, one each in the bow and stern, and four side tubes (two of them submerged and mounted on special platforms) located between the boiler rooms and engines. The ship also carried some anchor mines and mortar mines. It is worth noting that the ship's steam launches could be armed with one of the ship's 47mm guns or a torpedo tube and machine gun or eventually one of the Baronovsky 64mm landing guns.

During the First World War *Askold* had a slightly different armament(two bow 75mm QF guns were removed together with all 47mm and 37mm guns, and two additional 47mm AA guns were fitted; the ship was also fitted to act as a minelayer. Definite information on this period is lacking but it seems that *Askold* had her torpedo tubes changed to 3–4 tubes for 457mm torpedoes.

The Japanese Super Battleship Strategy Part 2

By Hans Lengerer

THE PROBLEM OF DISPERSION

The second problem was the reduction in the number of guns. Nine guns would be reduced to six. A high hit probability could only be maintained if the angle of dispersion of the fall of shot was also reduced. In fact the Japanese Navy did have difficulties with the dispersion arc of their guns.

The *Myoko* class of cruisers, the design of which was completed in 1923 by the famous architect Dr Yuzuru Hiraga, and which Fujimoto altered in part after the ship was laid down, were famed for their high speed, their powerful armament and armour, and were recognized by experts as excellent cruisers. In fact they did have one fatal weakness: a very low hit percentage/probability.

In 1932 the cruisers *Nachi* and *Myoko* carried out a gunnery firing practice on the cancelled minelayer *Aso* (ex-Russian armoured cruiser *Bayan*) at ranges between 15,800m and 22,300m. Although the salvoes were on target, not one single strike was recorded because of the

Port profile of Michael Wünschmann's 1/1200 scale model of Yamato *as in April 1945.*

Jürgen Peters

enormous dispersion (approx 350m). *Aso* was finally sunk on 8 August 1932 by the new (model 91) armour-piercing shell, fired from the *Myoko*. This result came as a severe shock to the Naval authorities. The fact of the matter was that the *Myoko* class always caused some trouble whenever artillery practice was carried out during manoeuvres. The experts came to the conclusion that the cause lay in the combination of the massive steel structures of the forward and aft gun turrets and the flexible structure of the hull.

The *Takao* class was intended as successor to the *Myoko* class; in this design the later Vice Admiral (shipbuilding) Iwakichi Ezaki was made responsible for reducing dispersion, in order to improve the hit probability. The distance between the gun turrets in 'A' and 'Y' positions was reduced by one gun turret's length. This brought the bridge over the efflux of the forward funnel, giving it its massive appearance. Nevertheless, the problem of inadequate hit probability was not wholly solved in this class.

In the *Mogami* class, as part of the third modification, the third gun turret was arranged higher than the second, and turrets No 3 and 4 ('C' and 'X') were integrated with

the superstructure deck. This arrangement subjected the barbettes to powerful internal stresses, which at times caused the turrets to jam. For example, during the official gun trials of *Mogami*, turrets 'C' and 'X' could not be trained. It eventually proved possible to solve this problem simply by improving the method of fixing the barbette to the ship's hull.

In the *Tone* class, as part of the fourth revision (these ships were again designed by Ezaki under the leadership of Fujimoto) the fifth gun turret was dispensed with, and all four turrets were concentrated forward. These cruisers were very popular in the Japanese Navy. With the introduction of the type 98 discharge delay unit, which allowed shells to be ripple fired at intervals of 3/100 of a second, the problem of excessive dispersion was finally solved. The concentration of the turrets forward was an experiment with a dual purpose: on the one hand it was an attempt to reduce dispersion, but it was also an experimental version of the turret arrangement planned for the *Yamato*. The latter investigation was planned for 1934.

DESIGN PROBLEMS

Fujimoto was very eager to adopt new technologies, especially in the case of new battleship design. The study of indirect protection by the use of a greater number of watertight compartments, the introduction of electric welding and the careful observation of diesel drive development were all initiated by Fujimoto. But there were many problems.

The Japanese Navy faced some problems when the design of the new battleships was discussed shortly before the London disarmament conference. A High Level Technical Conference was held in 1929, with the aim of laying down general policy for the replacement of the *Kongo* class. The conference members were dismayed when Vice Admiral Dr Hiraga, the predecessor

of Fujimoto as head of the planning office of the fourth Shipbuilding division of the Navy design office *(Kaigun Kansei Honbu)*, made his proposals. Hiraga had lost his post in 1925 as a result of a tendency to adhere too strongly to his own ideas. He worked in the research division of the Navy *(Kaigun Gijutsu Honbu)* and in this capacity attended the High Level Technical Conference. Hiraga presented his own privately drawn-up design, which reflected his personal views. He was an excellent designer who believed stoutly in the principle of direct protection. In his design everything was squeezed together to protect the short vital region of the citadel. However, the arrangement of part of the medium artillery in casemates was very old-fashioned.

His plan was opposed by that of Fujimoto, whose design criterion was designated a 'Kampon plan'; a ship of far more modern concept, in which emphasis was placed on indirect protection.

Although Hiraga's proposal had a whole series of weak points (*eg* no indirect protection, medium artillery in casemates), and also tended to be the result of a study of shipbuilding theory which disregarded strategic aspects – an area in which Fujimoto's design excelled – the Conference tended towards acceptance of the Hiraga plan. In the end a follow-up conference was never called, as the London Conference began, and with the signing of the treaty the moratorium on battleship construction was extended further. Incidentally, 16in guns were planned for both ships. A short description is contained in Appendix I.

HIRAGA'S DESIGNS

Hiraga and Fujimoto had been classmates at the Imperial University of Tokyo, but were very different personalities. Hiraga was a typically conservative technical student and a serious technician, who collected data assiduously, and analysed his information day by day.

Hiraga's *Kongo* replacement (1928) – external profile

All drawings by Michael Wünschmann

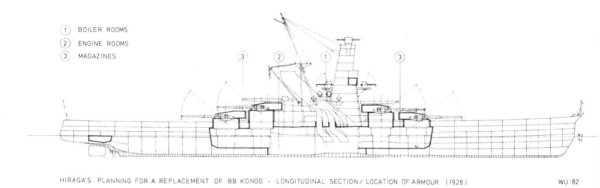

① BOILER ROOMS
② ENGINE ROOMS
③ MAGAZINES

Hiraga's design for the replacement of the battleship *Kongo* – longitudinal section and armour layout (1928).

But he was never quite able to take more than one step at a time. For example, he was confronted with a problem with the battleship *Nagato* namely that smoke from the forward funnel collected in the bridge. Fujimoto immediately suggested an alteration to the shape of the funnel. Hiraga rejected this suggestion with the words: 'The shape of a battleship should be upright!' Later he altered the funnel, without consulting Fujimoto, and even took the shape to a more extreme form in his design work of 1928 and, as we shall see later, even in 1929.

The light cruiser *Yubari*, on the design of which his reputation was based, was a very modern ship in shape and in the use of the armour as an integral part of the ship's structure, but the strategic concept hardly differed from that of the *Tenryu* class. The vessel had a lower speed than those ships, and its poor seakeeping ability made it less than a true cruiser, with the result that it could only be used off the Chinese coast and in the South Pacific. The IJN wanted large cruisers with great range, but Hiraga took no account of this strategic viewpoint. Even the *Furutaka* class, which was an enlarged version of the *Yubari*, was a product of his dogmatic convictions. On these cruisers the supply of shells and cartridges to

the guns could not keep pace with the rate of fire of the guns because of the manual transfer system installed. Fujimoto was given the task of improving on this feature and in response he designed *Aoba* and *Kinugasa*.

Hiraga, who had designed the battleships *Kaga* and *Amagi* as well as the cruisers mentioned above, was in fact an outstanding propounder of theory, against whom hardly anyone was able to argue.

The characterictic features of his designs were: a slender hull, lightweight machinery installation, high speed, heavy gun armament, and weight saving measures wherever possible. One result of these features was the wide dispersion characteristic of the guns, for which two reasons can be brought to light here: (a) the distortion of the hull; (b) vibration of the bridge, with all the consequent problems concerning rangefinder, fire control units etc.

Hiraga also preferred the direct method of protection, and defended the vital region with thick armour, being prepared to accept lower speed as a result. In contrast to this Fujimoto preferred the indirect method of protection, as the explosives experiments with the battleship *Tosa* in 1924 had shown that the only systems which

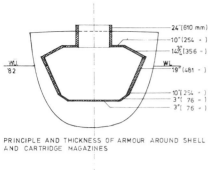

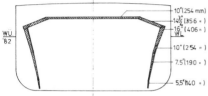

PRINCIPLE AND THICKNESS OF ARMOUR AROUND SHELL
AND CARTRIDGE MAGAZINES

PRINCIPLE AND THICKNESS OF ARMOUR OF BOILER AND
ENGINE COMPARTMENTS

Close up of the forward turrets and superstructure on the
Yamato model.

Jürgen Peters

could withstand damage to any real extent were hull
subdivision into a large number of watertight compartments, and a multi-layer torpedo protection system at a
lower level. It would not be an exaggeration to say that
the *Yamato* sank because its buoyancy was insufficient
to withstand severe damage. In theory the armoured
citadel would have been capable of keeping the ship
afloat if it had remained watertight.

A further design by Hiraga for a fast battleship exists,
the drawings for which are dated 7 September 1929, and
was presumably intended to counter the British *Nelson*
design. As it has not been documented before now,
Appendix 2 carries some details of this design. This ship
was probably the origin of the *Yamato* design, although
we cannot exclude the possible influence of the 1928
design for the *Kongo* replacement in respect of the
superstructure, which was concentrated in the midship
region.

RESEARCH PROGRAMME
The second phase of the battleship design, subsequent to
the Washington Treaty, began in 1932. Fujimoto and
Ezaki worked together, but design work was interrupted
from 1929 to 1934. Research work for the new battleship continued however, for Fujimoto was, as already
mentioned, very interested in the introduction of new
technologies, the areas of research being as follows:

a Research on diesel engines. On the submarines support ship *Taigei* in 1933, in which electric welding was also used extensively in place of the standard rivetting, in order to gain experience in the new technique.
b The concentration of turrets foreward, in the *Tone* class in 1934, as already mentioned, with the aim of keeping the afterdeck free from the destructive effects of gun blast, and also to test triple turrets.
c Research on bow forms on the training battleship *Hiei* in 1935.

During this period Fujimoto arranged for his protégé Ezaki to take a post on the Admiralty staff, in addition to his post in the Navy's design office. This was an unusual move initiated personally by Fujimoto to help him to achieve his secret strategy. At the same time he tried to ensure that Hiraga should be kept in the dark about his designs, for Hiraga's position made it possible for him to learn the details of the designs of his former subordinate. It would have been better if he had expressed his opinions during the earlier design period, or at the High

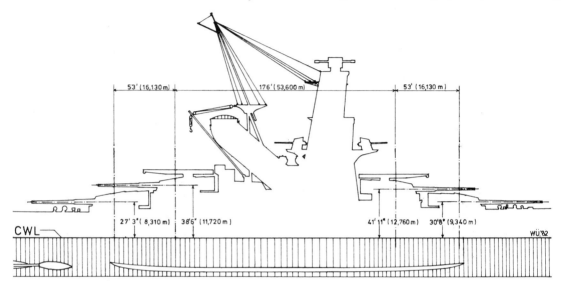

Hiraga's *Kongo* replacement (1928) – arrangement of main gun turrets.

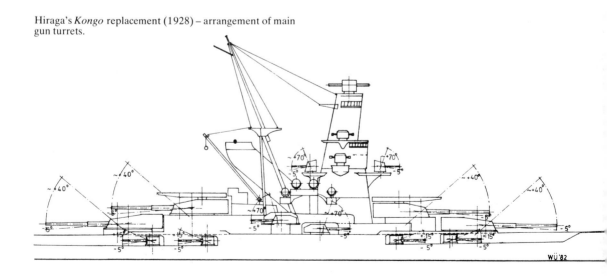

Hiraga's *Kongo* replacement (1928) – gun elevation profile.

The *Yamato* model viewed from ahead.
Jürgen Peters

Level Technical Conference. However, he did not because he had preferred to present his own private design, which had nothing to do with the Naval design office. To avoid a repetition of this situation he ordered Ezaki to cooperate with the Admiralty staff.

Fujimoto developed the ideas of concentrating the new battleships triple turrets forward, and of powering the ships with diesel engines, and used Ezaki to convince the Admiralty staff of his views.

In 1934 he began preparations for the design of the new battleship, at the same time starting development work on the 18in and 20in super guns, which were to use a common cartridge and shell transport system, and also have the same dimensions to facilitate exchange. Tables 4 to 8 show the initial plans and studies (see *Warship* 25).

FUJIMOTO'S DESIGN

On 31 August 1934 a preparatory conference was held to lay down the principles for the construction of battleships after the end of the treaty period. After the chairman of each committee had presented his paper (study of past and future of Naval armaments races; study of gun manufacture; the political situation in the USA and Britain; preview of the annual Navy budget up to 1943; standards for the calculation of shipbuilding costs and the maintenance of the Navy), Fujimoto presented the design of a battleship with 20in guns (Table 9).

TABLE 9: FUJIMOTO's SUGGESTED DESIGN FOR A BB WITH 20IN GUNS (1934)

Displacement (tons):	50,000 standard
	60,000 trials
Length:	290m
Beam:	38m
Draught:	9.8m (trials)
Armament:	12–20in (4×3), 16–15.5cm, 8 to 10–12.7cm AA, some MG, no torpedo tubes
Aircraft:	12
Catapults:	3
Armour:	11in deck, 16in side
Engines:	Mixed turbine/diesel drive, 140,000bhp = 30kts
Range:	12,000nm/16kts
Fuel:	*c* 6,000 tons

This shipbuilding philosophy was an enlargement of that of the *Mogami*: longer and broader in the beam than the actual *Yamato*, but smaller in draught. More heavily armed, but more lightly armoured and with a higher speed, it was closer to the design of a battlecruiser than that of a battleship.

It was Fujimoto's misfortune that the well-known accident to the torpedo boat *Tomozuru* had occurred just before the conference. Her capsize in a storm was a great shock. For about a year the Navy studied the stability of all its ships, making improvements where required.

Fujimoto was responsible for the design of the *Tomozuru*. His authority as head of the design office was therefore informally restricted for a period, until the actual cause of the capsize was made clear. The final decision was that the accident had been an inevitable result of the development of new building techniques, and that of the Admiralty staff shared the responsibility. as it had demanded too much from the designers. Fujimoto, who had been relieved of his post, was called back to the Navy's design office. Unfortunately he died on the day after his recall to his former office on 9 January 1935, without revealing his revolutionary strategy.

Rear Admiral (shipbuilding) Keiji Fukuda took over his post. He was a typically devoted engineer, loyal to the last. As a trusted, faithful pupil of Hiraga he developed his own designs in accordance with the demands of the Admiralty staff, which were laid down in October 1934, and had been classified as a Military Secret *(Gunki)*. They are included in Table 10. A few preliminary studies had been made before this time, all of which contrasted with Fujimoto's strategy. Examples are shown in Tables 11 and 12.

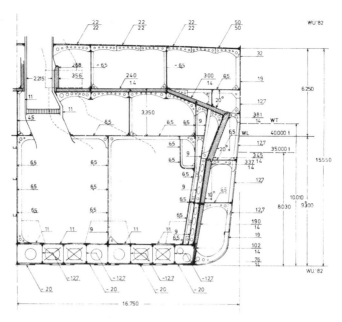

ALL DIMENSIONS IN MILLIMETERS

1928:
HIRAGA'S PLANNING FOR THE REPLACEMENT OF BB KONGO

Hiraga's *Kongo* replacement (1928) – midships section (all dimensions in mm).

TABLE 10: ADMIRALTY STAFF REQUIREMENTS FOR BATTLESHIPS, OCTOBER 1934

Main Armament:	8–46cm guns
Secondary Armament:	12–15.5cm (4×3) or 20cm (4×2) guns
Speed:	30kts
Range:	8000nm/18kts
Immunity zone:	20,000–35,000m against heavy shells

Notes: (a) It was forbidden to quote the calibre of the 46cm guns. (b) Hiraga's proposal to mount both twin and triple turrets was formally rejected at this time. (c) The last official statement of the primary characteristics of the *Yamato* was issued in 1942 and was well removed from reality. These figures were as follows (with actual figures in parentheses): waterline length 235m (256m); max beam 31.5m (38.9m); draught 9.15m (10.4m); standard displacement 42,000 tons (65,000 tons); speed 25kts (27kts); boats 14; armament 9–40cm (45.6cm), 12–15.5cm, 12–12.7cm; searchlights 8; machinery 4 sets turbines, 16 Kampon boilers, 90,000shp (150,000shp).

ABLE 12: COMPARISON OF PRELIMINARY BATTLESHIP STUDIES WITH MUTSU, AUGUST 1934

	28,000-ton type	35,000-ton type	55,000-ton type	Mutsu
standard displacement (tonnes):	28,000	35,000	55,000	38,318
rial displacement (tonnes):	30,000	39,000	58,000	42,700
ength (m):	212	232	259	220.8
eam (m):	29.6	32.5	36	35.05
raught (m):	8.75	9	9.76	9.3
ngines:	Diesel	Diesel	Diesel	Turbines
ower (bhp):	57,000	72,000	100,000	80,000
peed (kts):	25	25.6	26	24.4
ange (nm/kts):	10,000/18	10,000/18	10,000/18	7000/16
ain armament:	9–35.6cm (3×3)	9–40.6cm (3×3)	9–45.6cm (3×3)	8–40.6cm (4×2)
econdary armament:	12–15.5cm (6×2)	12–15.5cm (6×2)	8–15.5cm (4×2)	20–14cm (20×1)
A armament:	8–12.7cm (4×2)	8–12.7cm (4×2)	8–12.7cm (4×2)	8–12.7cm (4×2)
atapults:	2	2	2	1
ircraft:	4	4	4	3
ide armour (in):	12.3	15	19/18	–
eck armour (in):	7.7	8.5	12/10	–
mmunity zone against 35.6cm shells (m):	20,000–30,000	17,000–28,000	20,000–35,000	
mmunity zone against 40.6cm shells (m):	22,000–26,000	–	25,000–30,000	–

ABLE 11: EZAKI's DESIGN FOR A BATTLESHIP WITH 5.6CM GUNS (Preliminary study of 5 July 1934)

DESIGN STUDY

rmament:	9–45.6cm (3×3)	9–45.6cm (3×3)
	12–15.5cm (4×3)	12–15.5cm (4×3)
	8–12.7cm AA (4×2)	8–12.7cm AA (4×2)
achinery:	6 shaft diesel	4 shaft diesel motors
HP:	140,000	140,000
peed:	31–33kts	28kts
ange:	10,000nm/18kts	–
ength:	990ft	950ft
eam:	126ft	125ft
raught:	34ft	32ft
isplacement:	67,000 tons standard	50,000 tons standard
	70,000 tons trials	70,000 tons trials
mmunity zone	20,000–35,000m (magazines)	20,000–30,000m, (magazines)
	26,000–30,000m (machinery)	25,000–30,000m (machinery)

Note: Immunity zones are for 45.6cm shells

APPENDIX 1: HIRAGA'S DESIGN FOR KONGO REPLACEMENT 1928

Standard displacement:	35,000 tons
Trial displacement:	39,200 tons
Operational displacement:	44,000 tons
Tons per inch immersion:	129.6
Length (oa):	768ft
Length (wl):	760ft
Beam (max):	110ft
Draught:	30ft 6in
Freeboard:	27ft 6in (forward)
	30ft 6in (amidships)
	23ft 6in (aft)
Armour:	15in belt at waterline, reducing to 13.8in at lower edge; 13.2in upper belt; 7.2in lower belt; torpedo bulkhead 4in at top, 3.5in at bottom; 9.4in middle deck on flat, 11.75in middle deck on slope (inclined at 20°); 19in turrets above roller path, 17in below roller path; 10.6in upper funnel protection, 14–17in lower funnel protection; 3in (roof) and 5in (sides) steering compartment; 19in conning tower.
Immunity zone:	17,000–28,000m
Length of citadel:	321ft
Width of citadel:	50ft 3in
Height of side armour:	5ft 9in
Height of deck armour:	13ft (forward), 11ft (midships), 13ft (aft)
Main armament:	10–16in (2×2, 2×3)
Secondary armament:	16–6in (8×1, 4×2)
AA armament:	8–4.7in (4×2)
Torpedo tubes:	2–24in
Main machinery:	4 shaft geared turbines; 4 boilers of 12,500hp each and 4 boilers of 7500hp each; 80,000shp = 26.3kts
Auxiliary machinery:	4–500kW turbo generators, 2–250kW diesel dynamos

his detail view of the starboard side of the superstructure
nows well the concentration of the AA armament amidships
 keep it as clear as possible of the blast effects of the
amato's 18in guns.

irgen Peters

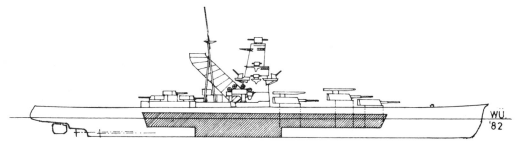

Hiraga's design for a fast battleship, dated 7 September 1929.

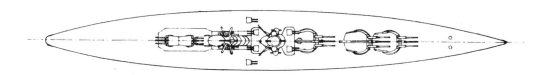

APPENDIX 2: HIRAGA'S PROJECTED DESIGN FOR A FAST BATTLESHIP WITH 18in GUNS

Standard displacement:	62,000
Trial displacement:	65,000 tons
Length (wl):	289.5m
Beam (wl):	37.1m
Draught:	10.23m
Armament:	9–45cm (3×3), 9–20cm (3×3), 12–12.7cm AA (6×2)
Immunity zone:	Magazines, turrets and CT 20,000–30,000m, machinery 25,000–30,000m against 45cm shells
Machinery:	Combined diesel/turbine engines, 200,000bhp = 32kts (engine room area 61m × 30m)
Range:	10,000nm/18kts
Fuel capacity:	5500 tons

Weights (tons):

Hull	17,350
Armour	22,589
Fittings	2,170
Machinery	4,650
Armament (guns)	11,935
Armament (torpedo)	50
Aircraft	100
Others	11

Armament weights (tons):

45cm turrets	2,630 × 3 =	7890
45cm shell (150/mount)	653 × 3 =	1959
45cm charges	135 × 3 =	405
45cm cartridge cases	73 × 3 =	219
		10,473 tons
20cm turrets	224 × 3 =	672
20cm shells (150/mount)	80 × 3 =	240
		912 tons
AA mountings (6)		140
AA shells (200/mount)		88.5
AA shell cases		34.5
		263
Machine guns		287
Grand Total		**11,935 tons**

As naval aviation evolved out of the experiments o First World War and the years immediately follow the specialist requirements of carrier-borne ai rapidly became apparent and, by and large, t characteristics have ensured that the developme land-based and ship-based machines has proce down separate, if parallel, avenues. Early shipb operations by wheeled aircraft were, perforce, ducted by landplanes, then adapted landplanes, an only comparatively recently that some considerable scious efforts have been made to produce mach effective in either environment, chiefly in hope reducing costs. Nevertheless, expediency (some ma desperation) has determined that the avenues merged at several points in the meantime, and now has this been more apparent than in the procurer programmes for the Fleet Air Arm in the late 1930 early 1940s.

The Norwegian campaign in the spring of 1940, Royal Navy carriers were deployed in support of B forces ashore, showed up in sharp focus the major s coming in the Fleet Air Arm inventory: the absence fleet air-defence fighter of sufficient speed to

Warship Wings No 5 HAWKER S

By Roger Chesneau

Sea Hurricane Mk IA being hoisted on to a land-based catapult during experimental firings. The aircraft still bears RAF code letters – indeed, CAM-operated aircraft were generally flown by RAF pilots. Note the six 3in rocket tubes which will be attached to the catapult trolley as a propulsion unit. For launch, the aircraft's undercarriage will be retracted.

enemy strike aircraft. Martlets were on order from the United States, but the only short-term solution seemed to be the adoption of standard RAF fighters, a move encouraged by the apparent ease with which such aircraft were flown off and landed aboard *Glorious*, off Norway, without any form of mechanical shipboard aid.

URRICANE

The German bombing campaign over the British mainland during the summer of 1940 delayed the transfer of Hurricanes to the Fleet but by the end of the year a batch of aircraft had been earmarked: with modifications no more complex than the installation of radio equipment compatible with Navy requirements, catapult attachment lugs and a simple V-form arrester bolted on to a locally strengthened fuselage frame, they were available within weeks and had entered service on board *Furious* by July 1941 (Sea Hurricane Mk IB). A parallel programme witnessed an even more limited conversion, simply the attachment of catapult lugs, to enable one-shot take-offs to be made from CAM (Catapult Armed Merchant) Ships and fighter catapult ships to provide some sort of response to anti-convoy missions by German long-range attack aircraft based in France.

Although the ex-RAF Hurricanes provided Royal Navy carriers with their first single-seat monoplane fighter aircraft and one with a performance to match its

Ranged for take-off, six Sea Hurricane IBs aboard *Indomitable,* 1942. Note tie-downs below wing tips.

HAWKER SEA HURRICANE MK IB – SPECIFICATION

Overall length:	32ft
Span:	40ft
Max height:	8ft 9in
Wing area:	257.5ft²
Engine:	1 × Rolls-Royce Merlin II piston engine, 1030hp
Max speed:	315mph at 12,000ft; climb from sea level 2300ft/min
Combat radius:	200nm
Weight:	4900lb empty; 6900lb normal loaded
Weapons:	8 × 0.303 Browning machine guns

adversaries, and although the aircraft was used to great effect, particularly in the Mediterranean in the spring and summer of 1942, its unsuitability for carrier operation was clear. Primarily, it possessed no wing-folding capability and although its extreme dimensions were small enough for it to be struck below on board the older fleet carriers (though not on *Ark Royal* or her armoured successors), the ships' capacity was seriously compromised with the aircraft embarked. Moreover, the latter had insufficient range to be a really effective all-round naval interceptor, other than in the point defence role; this shortcoming had already been appreciated before the aircraft's entry into Royal Navy service, and attempts to improve endurance ranged from the fitting of auxiliary external fuel tanks to a bizarre scheme which resulted in one Hurricane being experimentally fitted with a jettisonable full-span second wing. Deck landing and take-off problems were aggravated by the aircraft's

A substandard photo that does, however, give a good indication of the V-form arrester gear fitted to carrier based Sea Hurricanes. This is another Mk IB; other variants included the IC and IIC, both fitted with four 20mm cannon.

All photos: Fleet Air Arm Museum

relatively high stalling speed (about 75kts) and poor forward visibility with the tail on deck. Conversely, the wide-track undercarriage and the overall sturdiness of the airframe at least enabled landings to be more positive than with some other adapted landplanes.

The Sea Hurricane remained in front-line carrier service for about a year only, until superseded by specialist machines with more appropriate naval characteristics or higher speed. The aircraft served aboard the fleet carriers *Furious, Eagle, Victorious, Formidable* and *Indomitable*, the escort carriers *Avenger, Biter, Chaser, Dasher, Striker, Vindex, Nairana* and *Pegasus*, and also aboard *Argus* and *Unicorn* when they were pressed into service as front-line units in 1942–43. In convoy defence duties it also embarked on board CAM-ships and MAC-ships.

HMS CAMPANIA 1914~1918

By John M Maber

RMS *Campania* entering No 7 Dry Dock, Birkenhead, on 31 October 1914 prior to modifications for naval service by Cammell Laird.

MoD

Campania as first modified for service as an aircraft carrier. Note the flying off ramp over the forecastle.

IWM

On the 14 November 1910 Eugene B Ely piloting a Curtiss pusher biplane was launched successfully from an 83ft long ramp erected above the forecastle of USS *Birmingham*, a 3750-ton scout cruiser then preparing to get under way in Hampton Roads, Virginia. This first flight from the deck of a ship nearly ended in disaster, since the aircraft actually touched the water before gaining sufficient air speed to climb away and make for the shore near Norfolk some $2\frac{1}{2}$ miles distant, but the episode did mark the first tentative step towards the eventual realisation of the concept of an aircraft carrier.

The US Navy was not alone, however, in seeking to assess the potential of the aeroplane in a naval environment and on 10 January 1912[1] Lieutenant C R Samson, piloting a Short S.27 biplane, made a successful flight from a railed launch track rigged forward on the battleship *Africa*, then moored off Sheerness. On the 9 May following, in Weymouth Bay, Samson flew the Short S.27 from the battleship *Hibernia*, steaming at $10\frac{1}{2}$kts into the wind, and following further trials from this vessel the series was completed with the launch of probably the same aircraft, piloted on this occasion by Lieutenant C J Malone, from the battleship *London* on 4 July 1912.

At this stage the Royal Navy was somewhat ahead of the US Navy in terms of both technique and expertise in the operation of aircraft from a warship at sea and, with this accumulated experience to hand, the Admiralty next sought to explore the potential of ship-borne aircraft for working with the fleet.

HERMES

On 7 May 1913 the thirteen year old protected cruiser *Hermes* recommissioned under the command of Captain G W Vivian as parent ship for the fledgling Naval Air Service. In addition she was equipped to operate with the fleet as a seaplane carrier. A canvas hangar housing a seaplane on a wheeled trolley topped a launching ramp forward, whilst aft another canvas shelter accommodated a second aircraft which could be handled over the ship's side by derrick to take off from the water. In addition provision was made for the necessary aircraft support stores and some 2000 gallons of aviation fuel. Thus equipped it was intended that the *Hermes* should take part in the 1913 fleet manoeuvres and on 18 July at Sheerness she embarked her two aircraft, a Short S.64 'Folder' seaplane and a French Borel seaplane. In the event the latter suffered damage in a gale and was replaced by another French aircraft, a Caudron G.III amphibian.

The fleet exercises started in earnest on the 24 July and both aircraft were flown during the next few days although it was not until the 29th that the forecastle launching platform was brought into use to put the Caudron aloft with the vessel steaming at 10kts before a light breeze. Unfortunately, the weather in general was poor with gales interrupted by spells of fog and the trials proved anything but conclusive. However, the programme continued throughout that summer, some thirty flights being made in all although the launching platform was used only twice!

ARK ROYAL

HMS *Hermes* paid off into reserve at Chatham in December 1913 but in the meantime it had been decided that an incomplete mercantile hull should be purchased for fitting out as a purpose designed seaplane carrier with a flying-off deck some 130ft long and steam cranes to handle the aircraft both in and out of the below-deck hangar and over the ship's side. The hangar, 150ft long by 45ft broad, was to accommodate ten seaplanes. Negotiations with the Blyth Shipbuilding Co resulted in the acquisition in May 1914 of a suitable hull which, in the wake of the necessary modifications, was launched in the following September as *Ark Royal*. The new vessel first commissioned in December of that year and in January 1915 was despatched to the eastern Mediterranean where her primitive seaplanes were employed on reconnaissance and gunnery spotting, without any con-

Campania in her final guise, with split forward funnel, on 5 April 1916.

spicuous success, in the early months of the Dardenelles campaign.

With a maximum speed of only 10½kts the *Ark Royal* was obviously unsuitable for fleet work and following the outbreak of war in August 1914, three 21kt cross channel steamers[2] were taken up for fitting out as seaplane carriers. These three vessels were employed in the abortive attack staged against Cuxhaven on Christmas Day 1914.

CAMPANIA

For work with the Grand Fleet, however, a larger ocean going vessel was required and in November 1914 the Admiralty purchased from the shipbreakers, T W Ward & Co, the former Cunard liner *Campania*, a North Atlantic veteran dating from 1893. She was in a poor state but little had been done towards her demolition, other than stripping out some of the cabin fittings, and the price was low.

Built by the Fairfield Shipbuilding & Engineering Co at Govan, the 12,950-ton (gross) *Campania* was completed for the Liverpool to New York express service of the Cunard Steamship Co in 1893. A twin-screw vessel engined with 5-cylinder triple expansion machinery, she could maintain 21kts in service and soon brought the Atlantic Blue Riband back to her owners' houseflag. Change was rapid on the North Atlantic throughout the years preceding the First World War however, and the *Campania* and her sister *Lucania* were soon left behind in the battle for the travelling public's affection. Completion of the 45,647-ton *Aquitania* in May 1914 brought about her withdrawal from service although she did undertake two further voyages on the Anchor Line berth from Glasgow before being laid up pending sale. The outbreak of war in August 1914 resulted in the return of the *Campania* to the North Atlantic trade but she was virtually worn out and in the course of her final

voyage, arriving back in Liverpool on the 15 October, could manage only 17½kts. Her sale to T W Ward followed.

CONVERSION AND TRIALS

In the event, the *Campania* spent little time idle for on 31 October she was brought round to Birkenhead and docked in Cammell Laird's No 7 Dock for survey prior to purchase by the Admiralty. Although found to be in poor condition she was acquired outright for £32,500 on the 27 November 1914, arrangements having been made in the meantime for her overhaul by Cammell Laird & Co. The contracted work involved also fitting out as an armed merchant cruiser with eight 4.7in QF guns and the necessary communications facilities for fleet work in line with plans prepared to meet the requirements of her former status as a reserve merchant cruiser. To equip the vessel for her proposed role as a fleet seaplane carrier, however, a light flying-off deck some 120ft long was to be provided, extending the length of the forecastle and necessitating the suppression of the two forward 4.7in mountings, removal of the foremast and the installation of the necessary seaplane handling and recovery derricks immediately forward of the bridge and between the funnels. In this guise HMS *Campania* commissioned on the 17 April 1915 under the command of Wing Captain Oliver Schwann, RNAS and on the 6 August Flight Lieutenant W L Welsh, piloting a Sopwith Schneider seaplane was launched successfully from the deck with the ship steaming into the wind at 17kts. The aircraft was mounted on a wheeled trolley but there were no guide rails and difficulty was experienced in maintaining the alignment of the machine within the limited confines of a flying-off deck inclined at 0° 15′ towards the bow. Lift off was achieved on this occasion in about 80ft.

In the light of the difficulty experienced it was realised that either the aircraft must be given more power, by means of some externally applied acceleration (*ie* a catapult), or the flying-off deck itself must be sharply inclined down towards the bow. Although apparently the simpler solution this latter alternative, in fact, posed constructional problems in the case of the *Campania* which, without further radical alterations to the configuration of the vessel, would seriously impede the working of aircraft between the hangar in the former forward hold, the flight deck and the flying-off deck. In fact little was done at the time to improve the capability of the *Campania* as an aircraft launch platform and she continued to work with the fleet in the more limited role of a conventional seaplane carrier, hoisting her aircraft out over the ship's side to operate from the water when required.

FURTHER MODIFICATION
A lengthy report by Captain Schwann dated the 8 October 1915 outlined the *Campania*'s shortcomings whilst stressing that it would be a great mistake to pay her off since '. . . no other method of carrying out aerial scouting work for the fleet is as promising as that of employing *Campania* for the purpose.'[3] This plea was supported by Admiral Sir John Jellicoe, the Commander-in-Chief Grand Fleet, and in November 1915 she was taken in hand by Cammell Laird & Co for extensive alterations. The work involved the splitting of the fore funnel to permit the erection of a much more steeply sloped (about 3°) flying-off deck 200ft long thus facilitating the launch of heavy seaplanes from wheeled trollies. Under the after end a two part hangar, each section with its own trunked hatch, housed the ten Sopwith Schneider and Short 184 floatplanes which were worked out betweeen hangar and flight deck by derrick. Suppression of the original bridge and the erection in lieu of a small navigating bridge above and clear of the deck enabled the aircraft to be manhandled forwarded with their wings folded to the launch position ready to be prepared for flying off.

Aft, the mainmast and structure were cleared away to enable the vessel to operate an observation kite balloon, for the working and stowage of which a protective canvas tent could be rigged on deck above the balloon hold when required. Auxiliaries included a hydrogen producing plant (Silicol Plant) and the necessary hauling down winches for the balloon. The ship's armament now comprised six aged 4.7in low angle guns and one 3in anti-aircraft gun.

HMS *Campania* recommissioned, still under the command of Captain Schwann, in April 1916 and it is interesting to note that photographs of her taken in the Mersey on the 5th of that month still show clearly her name, merchant ship style, on the starboard bow (and presumably likewise on the port bow). In her new guise she proved successful, considering the contemporary state of the art of shipborne aircraft operation, and the Commander-in-Chief of the Grand Fleet with which she continued to work requested that further vessels of this type be made available for fleet duty. Despite the fact that she could not now manage more than 18kts at best she took part in a number of Grand Fleet sweeps of the North Sea but missed Jutland through not receiving her sailing signal in time to leave Scapa Flow with the remainder of the fleet!

Obviously the material state of the *Campania* left much to be desired and at a conference on board the fleet flagship *Iron Duke* on the 12 October 1916 the '. . . Third Sea Lord was asked to make special arrangements for the rapid repairs of the defects now existing in *Campania* . . . He was informed that if the strengthening necessary entails giving up the balloon equipment, the Commander-in-Chief is prepared to do this . . .'[4]

AIRCRAFT REPLACEMENT
Eventually the *Campania* rejoined the fleet and in February 1917 is was proposed that the Sopwith Baby seaplanes, which had replaced the earlier Sopwith Schneider aircraft, should be replaced in turn by Sopwith Pup aeroplanes (*ie* wheeled) since it was considered that they would be far more effective in an anti-Zeppelin role. These machines, embarked later in that year, had necessarily to alight on the water to await picking up and were fitted with flotation bags in order keep afloat. This change apart, however, the ship continued to be beset by the problems of old age, her machinery in particular being prone to frequent breakdowns. Thus in August 1917 Admiral Sir David Beatty, who had taken over as Commander-in-Chief Grand Fleet towards the end of November 1916, told Rear Admiral Lionel Halsey (Third Sea Lord) '. . . we are still dependent on the *Campania*, a vessel brought into the Fleet two years ago and which was now utterly unreliable for ordinary sea work.'[5] In the wake of this complaint it was proposed that, following the planned entry into service of the aircraft carriers *Argus* and *Cavendish* (later *Vindictive*), the *Campania* should be converted for training with the addition of an 'alighting deck' aft and possibly a catapult. Pending the delivery of these new vessels, however, Admiral Beatty proposed that the *Furious* and *Campania* '. . . be fitted with flying-on decks and hangars aft, with means of transporting all machines to the flying-off deck . . . In considering this question [*ie* the numbers of reconnaissance and torpedo aircraft to be embarked] it must be remembered that the future life of *Campania* cannot be expected to be long.'[6]

In the event nothing further was done to enhance the operational capability of the *Campania* apart from the embarkation in 1917–18 of Fairey Campania float planes as replacements for the Short 184 type. This aircraft, which took its name of course from the ship, is of particular interest since it was the first designed specifically for carrier-borne operation. Eventually five were embarked together with eight Sopwith '1½ Strutters', two-seat aeroplanes employed for reconnaissance and anti-submarine patrols, which could be struck down in the hangars with their wings detached. Like other carrier-borne wheeled aircraft the '1½ Strutters' were fitted with inflatable flotation bags.

THE LOSS OF CAMPANIA
In April 1918 the Fleet, and with it the *Campania*, moved its base from Scapa Flow to the Firth of Forth and it was while lying at anchor off Burnt Island on the 5 November 1918[7] that she met her end. In the midst of a

This sequence of photographs shows the *Campania* sinking in the Firth of Forth on 5 November 1918 after being damaged in collision with the *Glorious* and *Royal Oak*.

CPL

8.00am

8.20am

8.30am

8.40am

ale in the early hours of the morning she dragged her anchors and fouled first the ram bow of the battleship *Royal Oak* before dragging on across the bow of the cruiser *Glorious*. Badly holed the *Campania* drifted on with a steadily increasing list to port until 08.50 when she settled on the bottom with her masts and funnel tops clear of the water. There was no loss of life. The regulation court martial followed on 18/19 December when the officer of the watch on deck at the time was sentenced to be dismissed the ship for failing to keep a proper lookout. Captain Lindsay was cleared of blame.

Although practically worn out at the time of her purchase much had been achieved and considerable experience accumulated in the course of HMS *Campania*'s three and a half years operational service with the fleet. The *Campania* herself was never fitted with a 'flying-on' deck but this next logical step in the development of the aircraft carrier concept featured in the re-design of the converted cruisers *Furious* and *Vindictive* (ex-*Cavendish*) together with provision also for the movement of aircraft from the 'flying-on' deck aft to the 'flying-off' deck forward. The penultimate stage in this process of development involving the complete suppression of the funnels and conventional bridge structure was achieved in the design of HMS *Argus*[8] which commissioned for service in September 1918 as the first 'true' aircraft carrier with a large box hangar and a full length flight deck served by electric lifts. In October successful flying trials were carried out from the Argus with a 'dummy' island rigged on the starboard side of the flight deck to simulate the proposed arrangements for the aircraft carriers *Eagle* and *Hermes*. Thus, with the proving of this design feature, the evolution of the prototype fleet carrier was all but complete.

As for the *Campania*, her wreck lies, nearly three quarters of a century after the event, where she foundered on the 5 November 1918 still with the remains inside the hangar of her seaplanes and, apparently, a Rolls Royce armoured car![9]

NOTES

1 Statements that the first flight by Lieutenant Samson took place in December 1911 have since been discounted. (See *To Ascend from a Floating Base* by R D Layman. Associated University Presses, Inc, Cranbury, New Jersey, USA 1979.)

2 The *Empress, Engadine* and *Riviera* of the South Eastern & Chatham Railway. Each was fitted with a canvas hangar aft to house three seaplanes which were handled over the ship's side by derrick.

3 Letter dated 8 October 1915 from Captain O Schwann to the Vice Admiral Commanding Second Battle Squadron. (*Documents Relating to the Naval Air Service*, Vol 1, Navy Records Society, 1969. Hereafter referred to as *Documents**)

4 Extracts from Minutes of Conference held on board HMS *Iron Duke* on 12 October 1916 between Admiral Sir John Jellicoe, C-in-C Grand Fleet and Rear Admiral F C T Tudor, 3rd Sea Lord (*Documents**)

5 Minutes of a Conference between Admiral Sir David Beatty, C-in-C Grand Fleet and Rear Admiral Lionel Halsey, 3rd Sea Lord in August 1917. (*Documents**)

6 Letter dated 24 September 1917 from Admiral Sir David Beatty to the Admiralty entitled *Aircraft Requirements of the Grand Fleet*. (*Documents**)

7 Captain J C H Lindsay, RN had been appointed in command 16 August 1918.

8 Laid down by Wm Beardmore & Co in June 1914 as the passenger liner *Conte Rosso* for the Italian flag Lloyd Sabaudo S A. Purchased on the stocks and renamed August 1916.

9 Information supplied by Mr David Lyon.

*Transcripts of Crown copyright records in the Public Record Office appear by permission of the Controller of H M Stationery Office.

WARSHIP DETAILS No3
Type VII U boat

Developed from the Type VIIA and VIIB, the Type VIIC was the most prolific of the German U-Boat types that served in the Second World War, over 570 having been commissioned by the end of hostilities. The drawing shows the Type VIIC in its original configuration, although early boats did vary slightly in detail, in particular in conning tower design. Later in the war considerable modifications were made to the type, new vessels being built to the improved standard and old boats refit-

ted. These alterations included suppression of the main gun and the net cutter, the extension of the conning tower – largely to accommodate an increased AA armament, the addition of radar, a snorkel and improved underwater detection and defence equipment.

(Drawing from the next in the 'Anatomy of the Ship' series *The Type VII U-Boat*, originally to have been published in May but postponed until autumn 1983 owing to the illness of the author.)

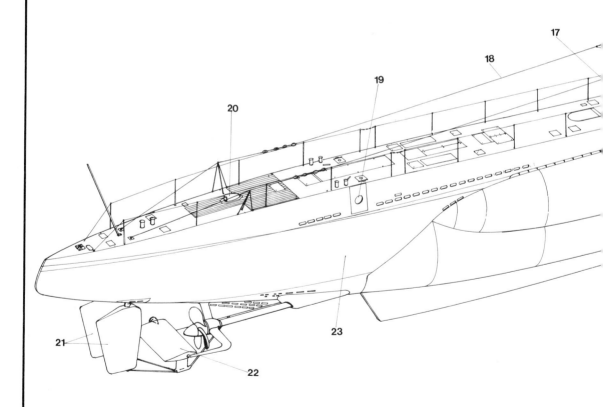

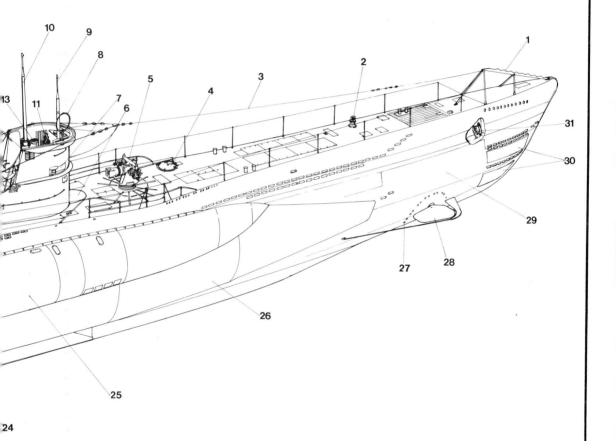

1 Net cutter; 2 Winch; 3 Jumping wires and W/T aerial; 4
Water tight ready-use locker; 5 88mm C35 gun; 6 Compass
casing; 7 Navigation light; 8 DF loop aerial; 9 Air-search
periscope; 10 Attack periscope; 11 Torpedo aimer; 12
Ventilators; 13 Compass; 14 20mm C/30 AA gun; 15 Ensign
staff; 16 Bell; 17 Water tight ready-use locker; 18 Jumping
wire and W/T aerial; 19 Diesel engine exhaust; 20 Stern light;
21 Twin rudders; 22 After hydroplane; 23 After casing; 24
Keel; 25 Saddle tank; 26 Pressure hull; 27 Holes for sound
detector; 28 Forward hydroplane; 29 Forward casing; 30
Torpedo-tube doors; 31 Anchor (starboard only).

A Majestic Revolution Part 2

By Karl Lautenschläger

High armoured sides were one of the predreadnought's most important features. They made high freeboard an advantage instead of a liability by giving protection to buoyancy, stability and vital areas in rough seas. No armour could defeat all existing guns, but the high walls of Krupp cemented armour on predreadnoughts were proof against all but the very latest high velocity guns at the new extended battle ranges.

Much has been made of the important new trend in battleship design supposedly introduced by the high freeboard *Royal Sovereign* class. Actually, these ships were hardly better protected than contemporary French battleships, whose basic design dated from a decade earlier. It was the *Majestic* and her sisters that were revolutionary in their scheme of protection. Naval architects consider 10 degrees to be a moderate angle of

A fine portrait of HMS *Illustrious* in Victorian livery. She and *Hannibal* were the last pair of *Majestics* to enter service. Four 12pdr torpedo defence guns are visible amidships on the upper deck. Not apparent in any external photo are the telescopic sights so essential to the predreadnought gunnery system.

USN

pective when one realises that before 1900, only one major naval action was fought out of the sight of land.

FIRE CONTROL

The fourth critical element in the transformation of battleships was a significant advance in fire control technology. Current works on battleship gunnery invariably concentrate on gun power, while ignoring fire control. Yet the state of fire control technology is a fundamental determinant of combat effectiveness in any naval weapon system.

The change from open sights to telescopic fire control gave predreadnought battleships the capability to shoot accurately out to about 7000yds. This was more than three times the maximum fighting range using open sights. The reason was more than a matter of mere magnification. Using an open sight, the gunner had to line up a rear sight, front sight and the target. Since the human eye cannot focus on objects at different distances at one time, a compromise had to be made by focusing more or less on the front sight and attempting to keep the target and rear sight in line. This meant that a target the size of a ship had to be inside 2000yds if it was to be hit consistently.

Developments in gun mounts, such as hydraulic recoil dampers and refined train and elevation mechanisms, increased the potential for accurate shooting at longer ranges. But the lack of adequate fire control equipment continued to be a crucial limitation. The battle between the American and Spanish fleets off Santiago demonstrated just how crucial. In spite of an overwhelming American superiority in gun power, over 98 per cent of the American ammunition fired went into the sea.

Telescopic sights enabled the gunner to focus on the target. Deficiencies in a gunner's eyesight could also be corrected with adjustments in the telescope's optics. These features, and fine cross hairs, allowed accurate aiming and thus consistent hitting out to 7000yds. High-velocity heavy and quick-firing guns gave battleships armaments that were effective as well as accurate at that range.

A dramatic indicator of the effect of the change from old open sights to telescopic fire control is the contrast between the battle in the Yellow Sea on 10 August 1904 and the engagement in the Tsushima Straits on 27 May 1905. Both actions were between Japanese and Russian battle fleets. Traditional accounts of the first battle stress that both sides opened fire at the extreme range for that time of 14,000yds. In fact, the major part of both actions was fought at between 4000 and 7000yds. The Japanese had technical advantage and superior training in each battle. Yet the first was inconclusive and the second was decisive.

heel. The side armour of armourclad battleships, even at designed and not full load displacement, submerged at 2 to 4 degrees angle of heel. At normal draught, the *Majestic*'s side armour did not submerge until the ship reached 14 degrees heel.

Metallurgy thus made it possible for battle fleets to fight effectively on the high seas. The significance of the advent of high seas combat capability is placed in pers-

The quarterdeck of HMS *Hannibal* of the *Majestic* class. The 12in guns rotated in a sloping armoured box atop a stationary armoured barbette. Today, we call this a turret, but in the 1890s, it was called a hooded barbette. Its perforated roof provided ventilation for the gun crew and confirms that the *Majestics*, like all predreadnoughts, were not expected to fight at ranges where plunging fire would be a hazard.

USN

The critical difference between the two battles was the type of fire control available to the Japanese. An oft quoted report to the British Admiralty submitted by an observer of the August 1904 battle notes that the Japanese had neither telescopic sights nor mechanical telegraphs. They relied on ranges taken from a single range finder and passed by speaking trumpet and blackboard. As the system broke down in the din of battle and the range decreased, shooting in the Japanese battle fleet increased in accuracy. In the months following the first battle, the Japanese navy, with the aid of the Royal Navy, changed its fire control methods and adopted new equipment. With telescopic sights on each individual gun, the outcome of the next major battle was much different.

The telescopic sight was developed gradually for shipboard use. It has been introduced in the British army as early as 1857, but aboard ship the shock of gun recoil at least threw the sight out of alignment if it did not damage it with each firing. A practical telescopic sight needed a sturdy mounting that moved with the gun carriage but was isolated from the gun's recoil. It also needed a linkage to the gun carriage in the form of a parallel motion device, because in turrets, sights were mounted some distance from the gun in a hood on the turret roof or up behind the turret front face. Lastly, a telescopic sight needed adjustments in elevation and azimuth, and optical correction for the gunner.

The first steps toward a practical telescopic gun sight were taken in the US Navy in 1892. The efforts of Bradley Fiske and H C Mustin in the US Navy and Percy Scott in the Royal Navy were largely responsible for the fact that both of these services had practical telescopic turret sights by 1899. These were improved further, and as the new sights gained acceptance in the Anglo-American fleets, other navies followed their lead. Since the new sights could be fitted easily, the final step in the transformation was taken quickly, once the technology was developed and available.

The lack of flare at the bow of HMS *Magnificent* is apparent in this view. Her high freeboard is accentuated by the four sailors leaning on the lifelines at the bow. Freeboard of the *Majestics* was 25ft at the bow and 17ft 3in amidships at load draught.

USN

THE PREDREADNOUGHT ERA

The predreadnought era may be dated from 1899 to 1911. Introduction of the new type began in 1895, and the Royal Navy clearly led in this transformation, as it would in the next. HMS *Majestic* and her sister, *Magnificent*, both commissioned for service in the Channel Fleet on 12 December 1895. Eighteen months later, the Channel battle squadron had been brought to its desired strength of six *Majestic* class predreadnoughts and two *Royal Sovereign* class armorclads. By 1899, when the telescopic sight had been refined sufficiently for combat use, there were also three predreadnoughts in the British Mediterranean Fleet and many more building for it.

The next country to commission a true predreadnought was Japan, with her British-built *Shikishima*, delivered in 1900. Russia and then the United States followed in 1902. Thus, it is logical to date the transition from 1895 when the first unit was commissioned, and the beginning of predreadnought predominance from 1899 when the first force with fighting capability was deployed and fully equipped.

When did the dreadnought eclipse the predreadnought battleship? The oft repeated statement that the launching of HMS *Dreadnought* in February 1906 made all existing battleships obsolete does not stand up to critical analysis. Launching a ship does not make her operational, and one ship does not transform a navy.

The *Dreadnought* herself underwent extended trials, adjustments, and alterations. She was attached to the Nore Division, Home Fleet during this period, but she did not join the active battle fleet until March 1909. The world's second dreadnought battleship, HMS *Bellerophon*, did not become operational until April of that year. The second country to have a dreadnought in service was Germany, with HMS *Nassau*, which completed her trials in May 1910. A year later, the Royal Navy added its eighth dreadnought to the Home Fleet for the world's first complete dreadnought battle squadron.

The all big gun main battery of the dreadnought type allowed it to fight effectively at 12,000 to 14,000yds, out of the effective range of medium calibre guns on predreadnoughts, but this could happen only after a suitable fire control system had been developed. In simple terms, it was the mating of centralised fire control with all big gun armament that doubled fighting ranges and rendered the predreadnought hopelessly inferior in firepower. Centralised fire control required a director, an elevated spotting position, a gun battery calibrated according to a common reference in train and elevation, and reliable communication between the elements of the system. The first battleship to have a uniform calibre main battery and all of the necessary elements of an effective central fire control system was HMS *Neptune*. She was commissioned for service in the First Battle Squadron, Home Fleet on 11 May 1911, with the Royal Navy's first director fire control system already fitted. Thus, director control was introduced in the same year that the first dreadnought squadron was available. Introduction of the dreadnought type certainly started with the commissioning of HMS *Dreadnought* in

The *Bouvet* was one of sixteen high-freeboard French battleships usually placed in the predreadnought category. However, their very low armour belts causes them to be considered armourclads here. At normal displacement, the *Bouvet*'s belt rose only 19in above the waterline, submerging at 2.68 degrees angle of heel.

USN

The *Royal Sovereign* class was important in British Naval expansion under the Naval Defence Act of 1889, but these ships represented little that was technically innovative. Their 13.5in guns used the old mechanical mixture propellant for a muzzle velocity of only 2016fps. Of ten heralded as the first high freeboard battleships, they followed similar French designs by several years and had the same deficiencies in their scheme of protection.

USN

December 1906. However, it seems unreasonable to date the supersession of the predreadnought before 1911.

THE DEFINITIVE TYPE

The *Majestic* ushered in a new type of battleship that predominated in the fleets of the world for more than a decade. The new type was significantly better than its predecessors. The combat capabilities that came with the technology of the predreadnought era thus represented a new minimum standard in battle fleet performance.

The technology and the standard can be summarised briefly. Battleship main armament, controlled by on-mount telescopic sights, was accurate to about 7000yds. High velocity heavy guns in the main battery could perforate at least 6ins of vertical Krupp cemented steel at that range. A second type of gun in the main battery

American predreadnoughts, such as the *Minnesota* shown here, usually carried three calibres of ordnance in their main batteries. The thirteen battleships of the *Virginia*, *Connecticut* and *Mississippi* classes carried four 12in, eight 8in and eight to twelve 6in or 7in guns in obvious adherence to the spectrum-of-fire concept.

USN

could fire at least 3000lbs of high explosive projectiles per minute at a single target. Floatation, stability and vital compartments were protected by the equivalent of at least 6ins of vertical Krupp cemented armour, up to a height allowing a 10-degree list before belt submersion. The predreadnought was able to fight effectively in rough seas, because of her freeboard (at least 16ft for a length of 375ft or more), the height of her guns above water, and the vertical extent of her protection.

The transformation of battleships did not take place in isolation. Other technical developments such as wireless telegraphy, capped projectiles and shipboard electricity gave the battle fleet important new capabilities. The torpedo-boat destroyer finally joined the battle fleet as an effective oceangoing weapon after 1907, and development of the battleship continued gradually until

the dreadnought revolution. However, the important point is that the technical developments that produced the first true predreadnought represent a fundamental change: a discontinuity in the evolution of battleship design.

TABLE 3: PREDREADNOUGHT BATTLESHIPS

All warships that met the five main criteria of the predreadnought battleship type are listed by class in order of completion. The date of keel laying provides an indication of when design work had advanced enough so that construction could begin, as well as an indication of building rates.

In simplified terms, the criteria are:

a on-carriage fire control, efficient to 7000yds.

b heavy guns can perforate 6in or more of vertical Krupp cemented type armour at 7000yds.

c medium guns can deliver 3000lbs or more of explosive projectiles at a single target.

d at least 6ins of Krupp cemented armour or equivalent, over 60 per cent of the ship's length, to a height allowing a 10-degree list at LWL before side armour will submerge.

e at least 16ft freeboard forward.

	Laid down	Commissioned for service
GREAT BRITAIN		
Majestic	4 Feb 1894	12 Dec 1895
Magnificent	18 Dec 1893	12 Dec 1895
Prince George	10 Sep 1894	26 Nov 1896
Jupiter	26 Apr 1894	8 Jun 1897
Victorious	28 May 1894	8 Jun 1897
Mars	2 Jun 1894	8 Jun 1897
Caesar	25 Mar 1895	13 Jan 1898
Hannibal	1 May 1894	10 May 1898
Illustrious	11 Mar 1895	10 May 1898
Canopus	4 Jan 1897	5 Dec 1899
Ocean	15 Feb 1897	20 Feb 1900
Goliath	4 Jan 1897	27 Mar 1900
Glory	1 Dec 1896	1 Nov 1900
Albion	3 Dec 1896	25 Jun 1901
Vengeance	23 Aug 1898	8 Apr 1902
Implacable	13 Jul 1898	10 Sep 1901
Formidable	21 Mar 1898	10 Oct 1901
Irresistible	11 Apr 1898	4 Feb 1902
Bulwark	20 Mar 1899	18 Mar 1902
London	8 Dec 1898	7 Jun 1902
Venerable	2 Jan 1899	12 Nov 1902
Queen	12 Mar 1901	7 Apr 1904
Prince of Wales	20 Mar 1901	18 Mar 1904
Russell	11 Mar 1899	19 Feb 1903
Exmouth	11 Aug 1899	Jun 1903
Duncan	10 Jul 1899	8 Oct 1903
Montagu	23 Nov 1899	Oct 1903
Albemarle	8 Jan 1900	12 Nov 1903
Cornwallis	19 Jul 1899	9 Feb 1904
Swiftsure	for Chile	21 Jun 1904
Triumph	for Chile	21 Jun 1904
King Edward VII	8 Mar 1902	7 Feb 1905
Commonwealth	17 Jun 1902	9 Apr 1905
New Zealand	9 Feb 1903	11 Jul 1905
Dominion	23 May 1902	5 Aug 1905
Hindustan	25 Oct 1902	22 Aug 1905
Britannia	4 Feb 1904	2 Oct 1906
Africa	27 Jan 1904	6 Nov 1906
Hibernia	6 Jan 1904	2 Jan 1907
Agamemnon	15 May 1905	Apr 1909
Lord Nelson	18 May 1905	Apr 1909

JAPAN	Laid down	Completed
Shikishima	29 Mar 1897	26 Jan 1900
Hatsuse	10 Jan 1898	18 Jan 1901
Asahi	18 Aug 1897	31 Jul 1900
Mikasa	24 Jan 1899	1 Mar 1902
Katori	27 Apr 1904	20 May 1906
Kashima	29 Feb 1904	23 May 1906
Iwami	for Russia	Jun 1907
Hizen	for Russia	23 Nov 1908
Satsuma	15 May 1905	23 Mar 1910
Aki	15 Mar 1906	11 Mar 1911*
Kawachi	1 Apr 1909	31 Mar 1912*
Settsu	18 Jan 1909	1 Jul 1912*

RUSSIA	Laid down	Completed
Retvizan	5 Nov 1898	25 Mar 1902
Czesarevitch	24 May 1898	Aug 1903
Kniaz Potemkin	10 Sep 1898	1903
Imperator Aleksandr III	10 May 1900	24 Oct 1903
Borodino	24 May 1900	1904
Orel	3 Jun 1900	Sep 1904
Kniaz Souvoroff	8 Sep 1901	1904
Slava	1 Nov 1902	1905
Sviatoi Evstafi	11 Nov 1904	5 Aug 1910
Ioann Zlatoust	27 Nov 1903	11 Aug 1910
Andrei Pervosvanni	11 May 1905	27 Jul 1910
Imperator Pavel I	11 May 1905	7 Sep 1910

UNITED STATES	Laid down	Commissioned
Maine	15 Feb 1899	29 Dec 1902
Missouri	7 Feb 1900	1 Dec 1903
Ohio	22 Apr 1899	4 Oct 1904
Rhode Island	1 May 1902	19 Feb 1906
Virginia	21 May 1902	7 May 1906
New Jersey	2 Apr 1902	12 May 1906
Georgia	31 Aug 1901	24 Sep 1906
Nebraska	4 Jul 1902	1 Jul 1907
Louisiana	21 Mar 1903	2 Jun 1906
Connecticut	10 Mar 1903	29 Sep 1906
Vermont	21 May 1904	4 Mar 1907
Minnesota	27 Oct 1903	9 Mar 1907
Kansas	10 Feb 1904	18 Apr 1907
New Hampshire	1 May 1905	19 Mar 1908
Mississipi	12 May 1904	1 Feb 1908
Idaho	12 May 1904	1 Apr 1908

GERMANY	Laid down	Joined the fleet
Braunschweig	24 Oct 1901	Dec 1904
Elsass	28 Sep 1902	May 1905
Preussen	14 Jun 1902	1 Oct 1905
Hessen	15 Apr 1902	4 Mar 1906
Lothringen	1 Dec 1902	1 Jul 1906
Deutschland	20 Jul 1903	26 Sep 1906
Pommern	22 Mar 1904	11 Nov 1907
Hannover	7 Nov 1904	13 Feb 1908
Schlesien	19 Nov 1904	21 Sep 1908
Schleswig-Holstein	18 Aug 1905	22 Sep 1908

ITALY	Laid down	Delivered
Regina Margherita	20 Nov 1898	14 Apr 1904
Benedetto Brin	30 Jan 1899	1 Sep 1905
Regina Elena	27 Mar 1901	11 Sep 1907
Vittorio Emanuele	18 Sep 1901	1 Aug 1908
Napoli	21 Oct 1903	1 Sep 1908
Roma	20 Sep 1903	17 Dec 1908
Pisa	20 Feb 1905	1 Sep 1909
Amalfi	24 Jul 1905	1 Sep 1909
San Giorgio	4 Jul 1905	1 Jul 1910
San Marco	2 Jan 1907	7 Feb 1911*

FRANCE	Laid down	Commissioned for service
Republique	2 Dec 1901	Dec 1906
Patrie	1 Apr 1902	1 Jul 1907
Democratie	1 May 1903	Jan 1908
Liberte	Nov 1902	Mar 1908
Justice	Apr 1903	15 Apr 1908
Verite	1 May 1903	Jun 1908
Danton	Feb 1908	1 Jun 1911*
Condorcet	23 Aug 1907	25 Jul 1911*
Voltaire	20 Jul 1907	1 Aug 1911*
Diderot	20 Oct 1907	1 Aug 1911*
Mirabeau	4 May 1908	1 Aug 1911*
Vergniaud	Jul 1908	18 Dec 1911*

AUSTRIA-HUNGARY		
Erz Franz Ferdinand	12 Sep 1907	15 Jun 1910
Radetzky	26 Nov 1907	15 Jan 1911*
Zyriniyi	20 Jan 1909	15 Sep 1911*

CHILE		
Constitution	26 Feb 1902	in Royal Navy
Libertad	26 Feb 1902	in Royal Navy

GREECE		
Averoff	1907	1911*

*Obsolete upon commissioning.

EVOLUTION

Naval historians have concentrated on the policy changes that led to naval expansion in the 1890s. British writers say it was the Naval Defence Act of 1889 that ushered in the modern era. Americans cite the Bill of 1883 that authorised construction of the steel warships known as the ABCD ships. For German historians, Admiral Tirpitz's Naval Bill of 1898 signalled the Reich's construction of a modern battle fleet. But this perspective can be misleading if it is used to explain the important developments in naval technology. Technical improvements in warships came about quite independently of political decisions to expand navies.

For a number of reasons, the nature of the transformation in material has not been adequately explained. It is hoped that this brief essay represents a step toward correcting that deficiency. The approach taken here has been to examine how technology improved the combat capabilities of battleships in the most important and fundamental ways. The emphasis here is on the combat potential of a ship as an integrated set of ordnance, fire control, protection and platform components. The new standards of performance that came with the predread-

The USS *Ohio*, painted in white and buff. A sister was the second *Maine* and the first true predreadnought commissioned in the US Navy. Eleven earlier steel battleships, including the first *Maine*, were technically armourclads.
USN

The *Czesarevitch* was the second true predreadnought to join the Imperial Russian Fleet. This French-built ship was designed with the high sides and exaggerated tumblehome typical of French battleships, but she carried an 8in upper belt 7ft above her design waterline, allowing a 10.5-degree heel before the belt submerged.
USN

The *Deutschland* exhibited the German tendency to mount lighter guns in an attempt to gain a high rate of fire. However, the 28cm 'fast-loading' gun fired its 529lbs projectile at about the same rate as foreign 12in (30.5cm) guns having 850lb projectiles. Seven 17cm guns in each broadside battery made up the rest of the *Deutschland*'s main armament.

USN

Japan's *Mikasa* (shown here) and the Greek *Averoff* are the only predreadnought battleships still in existence. Neither was built in her country of service. The *Mikasa* is a fine example of British predreadnought design and the *Averoff* is an Italian-built sister to the *Pisa* and *Amalfi*.

USN

nought were a product of something more complex than obvious physical features. The usual measures of gun calibre and maximum armour thickness tell us little about the predreadnought transition. Guns actually got somewhat smaller in calibre but at the same time they became more powerful. It was the type and extent of protection, not its maximum thickness, that was important. Advances in fire control were an essential element of the change. Yet they are not an obvious feature in a photograph and are seldom mentioned in most current writings on battleships. Obviously, combat performance also depends on crew training and proper functioning of equipment, but by clarifying the technical limits of combat potential, we gain a more realistic basis for measuring fleet proficiency in a given period.

As a case study, the transition from armourclads to predreadnoughts points to several conclusions. First, basic technology existed long before it was refined sufficiently for practical application. Second, invention and development of various technologies took place in different countries, and inventions from several people and countries were often integrated to provide solutions to technical problems. Third, not all of the countries that had the technology were to adopt it for naval use in a timely manner. France, for example, led in developing some of the most important technical components of predreadnoughts, but the French navy was the last to deploy a squadron of these ships before the dreadnought era. Lastly, the technical features of a warship must be evaluated as an integrated whole if the capabilities of the weapon system are to be fully understood.

British Naval Guns 1880-1945 No9

By NJM Campbell

7.5in Mk I A 45 calibre gun of Vickers design with inner 'A' tube, 'A' tube, wire winding nearly to the muzzle, 'B' tube and jacket. There was a shrunk collar at the rear end of the 'A' tube and this and a screwed ring at the rear, secured the 'B' tube and jacket longitudinally. The breech bush for the Welin type block, screwed into the 'A' tube and the link type breech mechanism was attached to a lug band seated on the jacket. Mk I* differed in having a breech ring to which the breech mechanism was attached, shrunk over the rear end of the 'A' tube and screwed to the jacket, and Mk I**differed from Mk I* in having a thicker rear end to the 'A' tube and a larger diameter breech ring. There was apparently no shrunk collar.

Altogether 33 guns were made including 3 prototypes as the army originally showed some interest. Of the total 13 are known to have been Mk I* and 4 either Mk I* or I**. Steel choke was not unusual and some guns had cannelured rings. They were carried by the *Hampshire* class armoured cruisers in 4 single, turret type, Mk I mountings which allowed 15° elevation, and also as replacements by the monitor *M26* in an adapted Mk III mounting.

7.5 in Mks II and V Mk II which was of similar construction to Mk I** with 'pure-couple' breech mechanism, and Mk II* which only differed in the 'A' tube being thickened over the breech bush, were 50 calibre Vickers designs intended for the coast defence of India against Russian cruisers. Originally 22 were to be made of which 6 were to be mounted at Bombay, 5 at Karachi, 4 at Madras, 3 at Aden and 2 at Rangoon. As a result of the Russian disasters in the Russo-Japanese war, this programme was drastically reduced to 19 guns of which 5 were transferred to the navy but never used, and the most ever mounted were 6 at Bombay and 2 at Karachi.

Of the naval guns apart from the 5 above, 16 were Mk II** and 40 were Mk V. Mk II** was not homogenous, 2 guns being to Woolwich design, 8 to slightly differing Elswick designs and 6 to Vickers design. All the Mk Vs were to a Vickers design. In brief Mk II** differed from II** in a generally thicker 'A' tube with correspondingly less wire, a thicker inner 'A' in some and the rear end of the jacket reinforced by a screwed or shrunk 'C' hoop immediately in front of the breech ring. Mk V was like II** but there was no 'C' hoop, the jacket being thickened instead. Steel choke was again a problem and many guns had cannelured rings.

The guns were carried by the *Achilles* and *Minotaur* class armoured cruisers in 4 and 10 single, turret type Mk II mountings allowing 15° elevation. The former class had Mk II** except *Warrior* with 3 Mk V, while the latter class had Mk V with one Mk II** in *Shannon* and two in *Defence*.

In late June 1918 6 guns were offered to the army for lining to high velocity AA weapons but were declined, and 25 guns were in existence as a reserve during the second World War but without mountings. Two guns made for Canada prior to the First World War were known as Vickers Mk C and only differed in rifling details.

7.5 in Mk III This was the 50 calibre Elswick Pattern 'A' introduced with the battleship *Swiftsure*. The gun was built with an 'A' tube, breech piece and 1 'B' and 2 'B' tubes, wire for 63% of length, 'C' tube and jacket. The breech bush which took a cylindrical screw block with Elswick breech mechanism, screwed into the breech piece and the breech ring and 'ring connecting hydraulic buffer' were secured to the jacket. There were 14 guns to this construction and 2 spares to Mk III* which had an inner 'A' tube, 'A' tube, wire for 63% length, 'B' tube and jacket with breech bush screwing into the 'A' tube, breech ring and 'ring connecting hydraulic buffer'.

The *Swiftsure* had 14 guns in Mk III casemate type mountings allowing 15° elevation (possibly 14° for main deck guns) and they were later fitted in the monitors *M21, M23* and *M26*. When the *Swiftsure* was disarmed in mid 1917, one gun was mounted for coast defence at Yarmouth and one at Lowestoft, while 10 guns and 8 mountings went to the Belgian coast for counter-battery work. These shore mountings were on Arrol platforms and could be wedged up to give 8° more elevation.

7.5 in Mk IV The Vickers 50 calibre Mk 'B' introduced with the battleship *Triumph*, sister to *Swiftsure*. The construction comprised an 'A' tube, full length 'B' tube into which the breech bush for the Welin block screwed, wire for 49% of length, jacket and screwed collar at rear. There was a 'ring connecting hydraulic buffer' but no breech ring. The 14 guns of this type were lost in the *Triumph* and the 2 spares were Mk IV* with inner 'A' tube, 'A' tube, full wire, 'B' tube and jacket, the breech bush screwing into the 'A' tube and the rest as in Mk IV. These two were later in *M24* and *M25*.

The Mk IV casemate type mountings are believed to

The cruiser *Frobisher* in 1944-45. She and her sisters carried the 7.5in Mk VI gun, the last weapon of this calibre to see service in the RN.

CMP

have allowed 15° elevation and the 'as fitted' drawings of *Triumph* show clearance for this, though 14° is quoted on them.

7.5 in Mk VI A 45 calibre gun ballistically as Mk I, but of improved construction with tapered inner 'A' tube, 'A' tube, full wire and full length jacket with breech ring, shrunk collar and breech bush for the Welin block, screwed into the 'A' tube. Asbury breech mechanism was fitted. In all 44 guns were made and were carried by the *Hawkins* class cruisers and the aircraft carrier *Vindictive*.

The mountings were CPV with power elevation and training. Max. elevation was 30°. There were a good

many spares by the time of the Second World War and a 3 gun battery was installed at South Shields from July 1941 to August 1943. In additon 7 went to the Dutch West Indies in 1939, 3 to Canada in 1940 and 4 to Mozambique in 1943. Of these last 2 were lost en route and replaced in 1944 by 2 guns from South Shields.

7in/10 ton Mk I Originally intended to be mounted in sponsons in the cruisers *Mersey* and *Severn*, 3 guns and 1 mounting were included in the 1884–5 estimates but cancelled. An experimental gun was made on army account and delivered in 1887–8. It was built with an 'A' tube, breech piece taking the screw block and hoops to the muzzle. The outer layer comprised a long hoop, trunnion hoop and another hoop. The bore was 36 cals, chamber 37 × 9.5in and with 160lb shell and 100lb pebble charge, MV was 2250fs. It was later lined to a long experimental 4.7in QF.

PARTICULARS OF 7.5IN GUNS, MKS I to VI

	7.5in Mk I**	7.5in Mks II**, V	7.5in Mks III, IV	7.5in MK VI
Weight, incl BM (tons)	13.76	15.06	15.75 (III) 16.06 (IV)	13.79
Length oa (in)	349.2	386.7	388.2 (III) 386.7 (IV)	349.2
Length bore (cals)	45	50	50	45
Chamber (cu in)	4500	4500	3720 (III) 3725 (IV)	4500
Chamber length (in)	55.062	55.062	46.337 (III) 45.525 (IV)	54.66
Projectile (lb)	200	200	200	200
Charge (lb)/type	61/MD26	61/MD26	54.25/MD26	61.875/SC150
Muzzle Velocity (fs)	2765	2827	2781	2770
Range (yds) – 2 crh	14008/15°	14328/15°	14088/15°	–
– 4 crh	15215/15°	15571/15°	15309/15°	21114/30°

Notes: 4crh shells were limited to the Mk VI gun, the *Minotaur* class and monitors. The 4crh figures are taken from accurate range/MV data, but those for 2crh shells are probably about 200 yards too high.

HM Submarine Torpedo Boat No 1

by Commander Richard Compton-Hall

John Philip Holland. The original caption in the New York newspaper of 1899 read 'What me? Afraid?'

On 5 November 1913 the *Naval and Military Record* carried a brief report headlined, 'OBSOLETE SUBMARINE SUNK – ACCIDENT OFF THE EDDYSTONE'.

About a mile and a half off the Eddystone Lighthouse there was lost on Thursday submarine *H-1* [meaning *Holland I*] but happily the accident was not attended by loss of life. The vessel was one of the first three [actually five] of the Holland type built for the British Navy twelve years ago, but in the meantime the progress in the design and construction of submarines has been so rapid that the type has in all essential details become obsolete ...

The report went on to say that *Holland I* (as she has generally become known, being the first of the class) had

been offered for sale by auction at Portsmouth in October 1913 and the whole of her equipment had been sold with her with no obligation on the part of the purchasers to break anything up except that the torpedo tube had to be 'mutilated'. The Royal Navy's first submarine was bought by T W Ward Limited for £410 and she left Portsmouth almost immediately under tow from the tug *Enfield* bound for the shipbreaker's yard on the Welsh coast. While passing the Eddystone Light the tugmaster noticed that his tow was settling rapidly and he prudently slipped the tow, leaving the little submarine to sink slowly to the bottom 35 fathoms below.

RAISING HOLLAND I

That might have been the end of the story if somebody had not turned up the newspaper cutting in the Plymouth Library and sent it to the Royal Navy Submarine Museum at Gosport. If the wreck was still there it was obviously of the greatest interest and importance.

Late in the evening of Tuesday 14 April 1981 the minehunter HMS *Bossington*, searching on behalf of the Museum, made contact by sonar with a substantial object on the seabed at a depth of 63m. By midnight the diving vessel *Seaforth Clansman* had moored accurately over the position and lowered a diving bell, with a naval deep-diving team and an underwater television camera, down to the reported contact. At 2.15 on the morning of 15 April the diving officer was able to signal that the wreck was 'confirmed as a small submarine of correct dimensions for Holland class'. At noon a further signal was made: 'Submarine in reasonably sound condition. Hull is heavily encrusted but easily identifiable and sits with keel approximately two feet into the seabed with a slight list. Nets and fishing tackle abound.'

HM Submarine *No 1* had been found, and a salvage operation was initiated straight away by the Museum. Naval divers and salvage experts agreed to undertake the task as their major annual training exercise; and although bad weather delayed operations considerably, broad wire strops were successfully passed around the hull in August 1982 and the submarine was made ready for lifting by the salvage vessel *Pintail* from the considerable depth of more than 200ft.

RMAS *Pintail* now commenced a series of lifts, moving into shallower water each time to overhaul the tackles for the next lift. Navigation had to be exact in order to avoid shallow patches and other wrecks. In all, six lifts were necessary before the submarine was brought safely into Plymouth Sound and laid gently on the harbour bottom just off Drake's Island on 5 September 1982. The salvage divers then removed about half of the 60 battery cells to lighten the submarine with a view to lifting her entire by crane; but, in the event, it was

HM Submarine No 1 (*Holland I*) in Portsmouth Harbour
*c*1904.

decided to dock her and this was successfully accomplished in No 12 Dock, Devonport Dockyard on 30 November – a historic day. It was important not to let the submarine break surface until the last moment because contact with air would immediately cause severe corrosion; so the docking was, for the first time ever, made blind and fully submerged with the submarine hanging from *Pintail*'s horns. In fact, the Naval Constructors at Devonport were less than two inches out in their calculations and the tailor-made cradle fitted the hull almost precisely. Sheer professionalism had ensured that the entire salvage operation, from start to finish, went without a hitch and with absolutely no fuss.

PRESERVATION

When the dock was pumped out it was immediately apparent that *Holland I* was in exceptionally good condition after 69 years submerged. The first operation, carried out by Waterblast Limited of Hornchurch, was to blast the hull clean with dual water-jet guns at around 8000lbs per sq in. These guns deliver 16 gallons per minute with a velocity approaching 800mph (compared with about 40mph from an ordinary garden hose). Within a couple of hours, the hull was gleaming and, apart from three small holes where fishing nets had rested against it, there was virtually no corrosion inside or out. The torpedo loading hatch had already been opened, without any trouble by the divers; and the conning tower hatch simply swung back on its one remaining hinge when the Museum Director first boarded the submarine in dock.

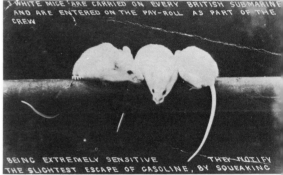

Postcard *c*1905

An extremely effective new rust converter and inhibitor, Fertan, was now applied inside and out by Fertan Limited of Hounslow and, apart from some external casing plates and the hydroplanes (which had been recovered earlier) HM Submarine *No 1* looked, in a very short space of time, practically immaculate. Fertan had already been used, for trial purposes, on the hydroplanes and other parts that had been brought up and sent to the Museum earlier and had proved all that the company claimed of it. Without any doubt, the Waterblast and Fertan operations could advantageously be applied to ships and submarines in general to say nothing of steel bridges and the like. The speed with which water at high pressure cleans off surfaces down to bare metal and removes salts is remarkable – and a great deal quieter than old-fashioned windy hammers. Fertan leaves a black, durable surface on sound metal while converting any rusty areas to a very solid material as hard as steel itself.

RMAS *Pintail* with *Holland I* hanging from her horns.

One of the two wire purchases on board the salvage vessel *Pintail*. The weight of the submarine was more than 100 tons.

It was decided to cut the submarine into three sections so that, when she arrived at the Museum, visitors could see inside; and this had the great advantage of making removal (on Army tank transporters thanks to the Royal Corps of Transport) much easier. *Holland I* now stands proudly outside the Royal Navy Submarine Museum at Gosport in Hampshire close by the submarine base where she first saw service during the reign of King Edward VII at the beginning of the century. She had already attracted world-wide interest because she is the only surviving example, apart from a considerably later version in Sweden, of the brilliant Irish-American John Philip Holland's invention which was adopted by the United States, British, Russian, Japanese, Scandinavian, Dutch and Chilean navies; and, furthermore, her shape is remarkably like that of a modern nuclear submarine – short, fat, stubby and ideal for underwater speed and control. J P Holland had it right from the beginning!

HISTORICAL BACKGROUND

What may have been forgotten is the extreme reluctance of the British Admiralty to have submarines at all when they were first conceived. Clearly, if they were successful they would threaten the magnificent Victorian surface fleets which had won the Empire. Underwater boats were far from popular. In fact, the Controller of the Navy in 1900 denounced them and advocated that submariners in wartime should be hanged as pirates. The Royal Navy only contracted to build five Holland boats under licence from the Holland Torpedo Boat Company in America, at the shipbuilding yard of Vickers Sons & Maxim, Barrow-in-Furness, as an experiment to see just how dangerous and effective they might be. Most senior officers sincerely hoped they would fail and only a few visionaries like the redoubtable Admiral Jackie Fisher supported the idea with any real enthusiasm. 'In all seriousness,' wrote Jackie with his customary capitals, 'I don't think it is EVEN FAINTLY realised – THE IMMENSE IMPENDING REVOLUTION WHICH THE SUBMARINES WILL EFFECT AS OFFENSIVE WEAPONS OF WAR . . .' How right he was; and

Holland I was the start of it all.

The fact is that these tiny boats, each 63ft 10in long or 'a yard shorter than a cricket pitch' as the Edwardian press typically described them, were extremely successful within their capabilities which were certainly, by modern standards, limited. Displacing 113 tons on the surface and 122 tons dived, *Holland I* had a surface speed of 7kts with her 8-cylinder Otto petrol engine and her batteries drove her at 5kts submerged. Her maximum diving depth was 100ft although the greatest depth which any of the class is known to have reached was 87ft. Tactically, she was a match for surface vessels of the period with one 18in torpedo tube and two reload torpedoes and practice attacks were demonstrably successful. She enjoyed one great advantage over the similar *Adder* class submarines in the United States Navy: she had a fixed periscope, rigged like a mast, and she did not have to 'porpoise' up and down to glimpse a target through the thick glass scuttles set into the short, heavy brass conning tower. American submarines were, incidentally, called pig-boats after the mariners' name for porpoises – 'sea-pigs' – and not because of living conditions on board!

Holland I was launched on 2 October 1901 amidst considerable secrecy and without the usual fanfare – 'with every privacy' as the press put it. She had, nominally, a crew of 2 officers and 6 ratings but she usually took more men than this to sea (each man carrying on board his own camp-stool) because training was a do-it-yourself business and there were no training facilities ashore. But, in addition, like most other petrol-driven submarines in the years to come, she carried three white mice suspended in a cage close to the engine to give warning of petrol fumes and carbon monoxide which were then the most significant hazards underwater. One commanding officer was actually commended by the Commander-in-Chief for continuing a practice attack 'despite the fact that the mice had already died'. Less foolhardy officers immediately surfaced their boats and ventilated thoroughly as soon as the mice became uneasy!

The *Holland* boats were sometimes scornfully referred to as mere toys; but there is clear evidence that they were far more than that, for three of them were once sailed for war against the Russian fleet following the notorious Dogger Bank incident. In October 1904 a

Holland I breaks surface for the first time after 69 years submerged.

highly disorganised Russian Squadron under Admiral Rozhdestvensky, with morale and maintenance in hopeless disarray, sailed from Libau in the Baltic bound for Japanese waters. The fleet was ultimately to meet defeat at the battle of Tsushima, but one night, during the voyage south through the North Sea, some of the lookouts thought that they had sighted Japanese gunboats coming in to attack. How the Japanese could have arrived in the North Sea was not clear, but the sailors panicked and fire was opened on what turned out to be a group of British fishing trawlers. A great deal of damage was done at point-blank range and several fishermen were killed. Three *Holland* boats and three more submarines of the new 'A' class were immediately prepared for war and sent to sea ready for action. Admiral Jackie Fisher, the First Sea Lord, happened to be ill but, roused from his sickbed, he decided that the incident was not worth war; so the boats were reluctantly recalled. But there is no doubt that they were prepared for battle.

In No 12 dock, HM Dockyard Devonport before waterblasting the hull clean of marine growth and scale. Only the 'horizontal rudders' (hydroplanes) and vertical rudders are missing; sections of these were recovered earlier and they will be repaired and replaced. The lifting strops are still in place.

ITTINGS

olland I served faithfully for a dozen years, mainly perating from Fort Blockhouse on the Gosport side of 'ortsmouth Harbour where she has now returned. Doubtless she was indeed obsolete by 1913 but, very ortunately, the instructions to 'mangle the torpedo tube' vere not obeyed and her batteries, although clearly repared for lifting out, were not removed. The magnifient porcelain 'heads' (WC – Doulton No 612) was also eft intact, tucked away on the starboard side forward by ie torpedo tube. It was equally fortunate, however, that ost of the instrumentation and pipe lines amidships ere stripped out before she sailed for the breaker's ard because if they had been left in they would almost ertainly have set up electrolytic corrosion with the hull. s it is, the hull is virtually unpitted. But some intriguing quipment was left on board and one piece in particular, very complex muffler tank on the exhaust system, is ystifying. It could conceivably have resulted from Hol-

land's much earlier experiments with running a petrol-driven submersible fully submerged well below the surface, using air for the engine from compressed air bottles and discharging the exhaust through a system of non-return valves. There is certainly no record of *Holland I* using her engine while dived but she did have to shut down, relying only on a tall air-inlet mast, when running on the surface in bad weather.

Another surprising feature is the row of circular glass scuttles overhead in the hull to supplement the scuttles in the 2ft conning tower. A glance at a Second World War X-Craft (which is comparable in size to *Holland I* although less beamy) will show where midget submarine X-Craft designers took their ideas from. Indeed, sub-

Waterblasting starts. Its effect can clearly be seen where bright shining metal is starting to appear.

marines in every navy today owe their development to the Irish-American inventor's first successful warlike design – a design which, ironically, he embarked on originally in the 1870s as a means of destroying the British fleet and thus, in some unexplained way, gaining independence for his native Ireland.

The arrival of *Holland I*, alongside her comparatively huge descendant HMS *Alliance* which was opened to the public eighteen months ago, must surely make the Royal Navy Submarine Museum the foremost of its kind in the world. The Museum is dedicated to the memory of submariners lost in peace and war; but it has now also become a fitting memorial to the father of all submariners everywhere – John Philip Holland.

NOTE

A book by Commander Richard Compton-Hall telling the story of the early submariners and their extraordinary boats is being published by Conway Maritime Press in May 1983. It is entitled *Submarine Boats: The Beginnings of Underwater Warfare* (£10.50 net).

The mysterious exhaust box aft by the Jack (which the divers inadvertently mounted at the wrong end).

The Story of HMCS Protector

By Ross Gillett

Protector as built
R Gillett

In July 1882, motions were brought forward in both houses of the South Australian Parliament for a cruiser-type warship, capable of defending the local coastline. At the suggestion of Sir Wm Jervois, Sir Wm Armstrong & Co of Newcastle-upon-Tyne were chosen to build the vessel, named *Protector*, for approximately £40,000 to £50,000. The builder's estimate was £63,000. The contract authorising construction was signed on 16 November 1882, the time alloted being fourteen months.

A considerable number of alterations were incorporated during the vessel's time on the builder's ship, delaying completion until May 1884. On 19 June, *Protector* was ready for sea. She was officially commissioned and during the day undertook her initial speed trial run over a four-hour period, the average speed attained being 14kts. The guns were then tested in the open sea.

Sir Wm Jervois recommended *Protector* would be most suitable for Marine Board duties, but the Board denied this, claiming she would only be of service to them so far as 'an eagle might be used for catching flies'. Despite the Marine Board's rather poor opinion of *Protector*, she was, nevertheless, the perfect ship for her role. An armament comprising one 8in and five 6in guns ranked her amongst the most powerful gunboat-type vessels yet constructed. The South Australian authorities rightly classed her as a cruiser and as a cruiser she was referred to up until her transfer to Commonwealth and RAN control. It was estimated that maintenance costs would amount to £10,000 per annum.

Protector sailed from Newcastle on 27 June 1884, and arrived in Gibraltar on 5 July. Sailing via Malta and Port Said, she anchored at Suez on 25 July. Rigged as a topsail schooner the 'cruiser' sailed on to Colombo, leaving there on 25 August. During her voyage to Adelaide *Protector* flew the blue ensign. She left King George's sound on 24 September, and on 30 September, arrived at Port Adelaide.

Protector's first commanding officer was Commander J C P Walcott, RN, who brought her out from England

and served as C-in-C of the South Australian Naval Forces until August 1893, when he was succeeded by Captain Creswell.

ARMAMENT

Protector's largest weapon, the 8in Woolwich-Armstrong breech-loading rifle, was mounted at the bow. The gun weighed 12 tons and could fire a 180lb shell 7500yds using a charge of 60lbs of black powder. The gun measured 18ft in length, and was mounted on an 11½-ton Elswick carriage.

The smaller 6in BL variants were mounted, two on each beam and one at the stern. Like the larger weapon the 6in guns were of Woolwich-Armstrong design, and could shoot a projectile over 7200yds. Each 6in gun weighed 4 tons, was 14.4ft long and was protected by 1in thick steel shields. An 80lb shot was fired using a 34lb charge.

Four 3pdr Hotchkiss QF guns were mounted on the hurricane deck and amidships near the funnel. Each weighed ¼-ton and was 6.72ft long. Five Gatling machine guns capable of firing 1200 rounds per minute were also carried. Originally 32 Martini-Henri rifles, 12 revolvers, 30 swords and a quantity of boarding pikes and axes

Protector at Port Adelaide with her sailing rig removed.
South Australian State Library

were carried onboard. Later in her career the number of small arms increased to 200 – 0.45in rifles, 100 breech-loading revolvers, 100 cutlasses and 30 boarding pikes.

During the First World War *Protector* lost most of her original guns and was rearmed with 2–4in, 2–12pdr and 4–3pdr weapons.

APPEARANCE

Upon her arrival in Adelaide *The Advertiser* reported:

Protector's outward appearance is that of a low decked vessel built up several feet from the bow to right aft. She is divided into watertight compartments by 4 transverse bulkheads. The main deck is laid with teak planks 2½in thick. On the main deck are the galleys, officers' quarters and principal steering gear. The Captain's cabin is on the lower deck, there being an entrance to it, aft, just in front of the stern gun. It is upholstered in Morocco, the woodwork being of mahogany.

Crew's quarters are on the lower deck forward. Magazines are on the main deck, one fore and one aft. They are built of steel plates lined with lead so as to be perfectly watertight.

Above the main deck, extending from about midships to the low forward deck, is a square hurricane deck, on which is fixed a conning tower formed of inch steel plates. It contains duplicate steering wheels, with speaking tubes to various parts of the vessel, as well as chart tables and boxes.

During her career, *Protector* carried several paint schemes, the last being naval grey. In 1914 her 8in gun was removed and the bow built-up. Years later she was sold out of service and again altered when converted into a lighter.

In 1918 *Protector* lost her funnel overboard, but managed to make port.

R Gillett

With her rig reduced and armament removed, *Protector* was employed at Flinders Naval Depot as a stores ship.

RAN

THE CAREER OF PROTECTOR

Protector led an uninteresting life up to the turn of the century, being based solely in South Australian waters. Her only acitivites comprised regular deployments on station in Largs Bay. Usually she was placed on the slipway for refitting and then proceeded to the bay. The cruiser's periods on station after 1893 were from March 1894 to August 1894; October 1894 to May 1895; August 1896 to 1897; and October 1899 to March 1900. On 22 March 1900, she was taken in tow by the SS *Edith* to Fletchers slip where her hull was cleaned and maintenance carried out.

She remained at Port Adelaide until August when the South Australian warship was offered to, and accepted by, the Imperial Government for service in China as part of the Colonial Naval Force. The ship was provisioned and fuelled and sailed for China on 6 August. After visiting Sydney, from 10 to 12 August, *Protector* made for Brisbane, where Captain Creswell assumed command of the ship at 2.30pm on 14 August. Creswell commended, 'I was glad indeed to see the sturdy little ship steam into a berth in the Brisbane River. It was indeed a stroke of luck that brought me back into my old force, every soul of whom I knew so well.' Creswell had previously served as Commandant of the South Australian Naval Forces until April 1900, when he took up the position of commander of the Queensland Marine Defence Force.

One day in port proved sufficient to recoal and replenish stores, and on 15 August, *Protector* proceeded down the Brisbane River. The cruiser steamed to Thursday Island via the Barrier Reef in charge of a pilot. At Thursday Island *Protector* again replenished her small water tanks from the large reservoir at the fort. On 23 August, the vessel got underway and, employing sails when possible, arrived at Manila at the end of the month. Hong Kong was reached on 9 September, a Sunday afternoon. To the surprise of a dockyard official, who

enquired about the ship's defects, he was told that there were none.

The British Commodore received Creswell and immediately asked when would *Protector* be ready for action. Creswell replied, 'At once.' The Commodore, surprised as he was, put the dockyard at the disposal of the Australian warship. *Protector*, in the meanwhile was being coaled cleaned and her sides painted.

At 1410 hours on 19 September, *Protector* steamed for Woosung, arriving there four days later. Another quiet passage found her at Shanghai on 26 September. The Tartar city Shan Hai Kuan was *Protector*'s last port and the site of the Boxer uprising. She arrived there on 11 October, to find preparations in full-swing for an attack on the Boxer-controlled forts. However, fate decided otherwise and the Boxer army retreated, the forts capitulating. *Protector* had steamed thousands of miles and saw no action, her work, as Creswell described it, 'consisting of odd jobs and services here, there and everywhere.'

The gunboat left for Shan Hai Kuan on 19 October, and returned to Hong Kong harbour on 12 November. *Protector* left for Amboina twelve days later and, sailing via Thursday Island, reached Brisbane on 14 December. After two days Captain Creswell gave up charge of the

Sold out of service and with her upper works removed, *Protector* was renamed *Sidney* and used as a lighter.

RAN

ship to Captain Clare and she sailed for Sydney, and finally Adelaide. When leaving Sydney, on 2 January 1901, the ship was cheered by the fleet as she passed down the harbour. Finally on 6 January, she arrived in Adelaide, 153 days out.

In the years up to the creation of the Australian Fleet, *Protector* was active around the southern and eastern seaboards. As well as maintaining her patrols from Largs Bay, the gunboat steamed to Sydney, Newcastle, Hobart, Port Arthur and Melbourne in 1905. After these duties she sailed once more to Tasmania, calling into Launceston, Devonport and Hobart. During her stopover in Hobart *Protector* collected the Tasmanian Torpedo Boat *TB No 1* and towed the vessel back to Adelaide, arriving there in early May. The following year she again sailed interstate, visiting Melbourne, Sydney and Hobart.

In 1911, she was re-boilered and integrated into the Royal Australian Navy. From September 1913, she served as a tender to *Cerberus*. When war broke out in 1914, *Protector* began service as a depot ship to the submarines *AE 1* and *AE 2*, and in this role was ordered to German New Guinea on 28 August. After the surrender of these colonies on 17 September, she remained based at Rabaul as a port guard ship until she proceeded to Sydney on 4 October.

Up to October 1915, when she sailed to the Cocos Island in the Indian Ocean, *Protector* was based in Melbourne. Two months were spent in the Indian Ocean,

reporting on the wreck of the German cruiser *Emden*, before the ship returned to resume duties as tender to *Cerberus*. Before the end of the War *Protector* saw some sea-going duty and for a period acted as a minesweeper in Victorian coastal waters.

In May 1920, *Protector* transported the advance party to Flinders Naval Depot at Western Port Bay in preparation for the official opening on 1 September. On 1 April, 1921, she was renamed *Cerberus*, becoming a tender to the new Naval Depot. In turn the old monitor *Cerberus* was renamed *Platypus II*.

Protector today, 98 years after first commissioning.

R Gillett

In 1943 *Sidney* is run ashore on Heron Island off the Queensland coast.

R Wright Collection

DISPOSAL

Finally in June 1924 *Protector*'s forty-year naval career came to a close when she was paid off for disposal. Sold to Mr J Hill of Melbourne for £677.50, *Protector* was dismantled. Her armement, turrets and engines, and all moveable parts were sold at auction. Conversion work to a lighter was completed in November 1929, her old ammunition magazines now serving as a tank for approximately 300 tons of oil fuel.

In 1931, she was renamed *Sidney* and sold to the Victorian Lighterage Co for use as a wool lighter. During July 1943, she was requisitioned for war service by the US Army. En route to New Guinea and off Gladstone, she was damaged in a collision with a tug and abandoned. Her hulk was taken to Heron Island (now a resort island) and later sunk for use as a breakwater. Her rusting remains are still visible to this day. No attempt has been made to recover the old cruiser due to her poor condition and it appears likely that she will remain a feature of the island well past her 100th year.

PARTICULARS OF PROTECTOR	
Type:	Steel Cruiser (later Gunboat)
Displacement:	920 tons (555 gross)
Length:	185ft oa, 180ft 6in pp
Beam:	30ft
Draught:	12ft 6in
Machinery:	Two compound surface condensing engines
Horsepower:	1500 (750hp each engine)
Speed:	14kts (maximum)
Bunkers:	150 tons of coal
Armament:	1–8in, 5–6in, 4–3pdr, 5–10 barrelled Gatling guns, various small arms (see armament notes)
Complement:	90 officers and ratings
Cost:	£65,000

The US Monitors Part 2

By Francis J Allen

While the ships of the *Amphitrite* Class '. . . were still under construction monitor enthusiasts added a sixth one, the 4084-ton *Monterey* for defence on the West Coast.'[22] Although authorised in 1887 she was building at the Union Iron Works of San Francisco, California between 1890–93 at a contract price of $1,628,950. For this price, the US Navy received a ship that was ordinary for her type, reactionary in battle array and only slightly innovative in her machinery.

As built, the armour and armament were consistent with earlier practice. The armoured belt extended the

Official plans of the USS *Monterey* (BM-6)
US Naval Museum

full length of the ship, providing for the protection of the vessel from 2.5ft above the water line to 2ft below the water line. The belt had a thick central section which tapered from 13in at the top to 5in at the armour shelf with some 9in at the water line. This extended for 118ft of the ship's length. Forward and aft of the central citadel, the armour first tapered from 8in or 9in above the water line to 4in at the shelf. This in turn was followed by a final section forward and aft, where the armoured belt was 6in thick decreasing to 4in at the shelf. The armour protection for the turrets was as follows: forward barbette 13in, aft turret 8in; aft barbette $11\frac{1}{2}$in, aft turret $7\frac{1}{2}$in thick. The deck protection consisted of two layers whose total thickness, running from

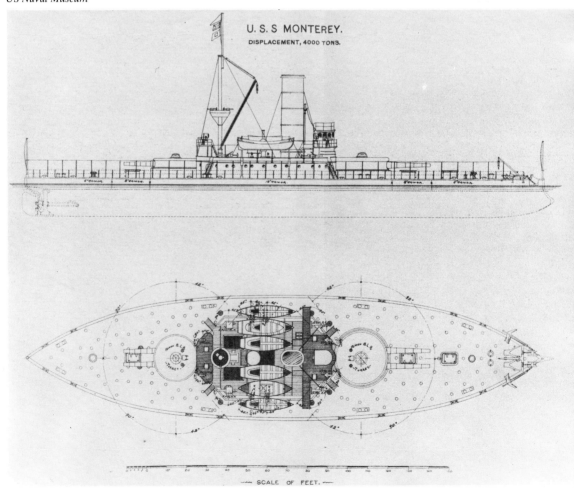

U. S. S MONTEREY.
DISPLACEMENT, 4000 TONS.

~~ SCALE OF FEET. ~~

USS *Monterey* (BM-6) seen in drydock at San Francisco
US Naval Museum

the stem to the aft side of the aft barbette, was 3in and aft of that, 2in.[23]

The armament of the *Monterey* consisted of two 12in guns forward, weighting 46 tons each, and two 10in guns aft, weighing 27 tons each; both pairs were mounted on barbette turrets. There was provision for six 6pdr guns on the superstructure deck, two 1pdr on the bridge and two 1pdr in the military tops.

HULL STRUCTURE

The structure of the hull was standard for its day. The ship's double bottom, extending from frame 5 to frame 77, accounted for 107 of the *Monterey*'s 223 water-tight compartments, these being divided by water-tight transverse frames into nineteen groups. Mounted abreast each other in their own water-tight compartments, were the ship's two vertical direct-acting, triple-expansion engines; a water-tight door being provided in the central longitudinal dividing bulkhead for communication at working platform level. Coal bunkers were located fore and aft of the engine and boiler rooms, three on each side of the ship and two athwartships at the forward end of the boiler rooms, divided by longitudinal bulkhead.[24] These coal bunkers did not extend to the sides of the ship. The total capacity was 195.2 tons of coal.

MACHINERY

The working of the turrets and guns, as well as the steering of the ship and the operation of the battle hatches, was by means of hydraulic pressure. Hydraulic machinery was also used for checking the recoil of the

USS *Monterey* in drydock at San Francisco, California, during the latter stages of her construction, about 1892.
US Naval Museum

guns, running the guns out, hoisting the ammunition and the steering gear. The operating pressure for the turrets and steering gear was 600psi and the machinery for these operations was built by the Dow Pump Works of San Francisco, California.[25] Steering of the ship could be handled from the pilot house, conning tower or the steering-gear room.

For driving the *Monterey* through the water, her designers selected two adjustable pitch, three-bladed, screw propellers of 10ft 2in diameter. They had both axially and radially expanding pitches. The hubs were spherical and had a diameter of 3ft. 'The port propeller is left handed and the starboard right handed . . .'[26] To these were attached propeller shafts of 33ft 9in in length. As was the case with all of the shafting, the propeller shafts were made of forged steel.

The ship's electrical plant comprised three Edison marine dynamos of 200 amperes and 80 volts at 400 revolutions. There were 348 incandescent lamps for a total 6144 candle power on twelve circuits. Four additional circuits were provided for as many Mangin projectors.[27]

The *Monterey* had, among its many features, one which harkened back to the days of the American Civil War. This ship could 'submerge'. The submerging was accomplished by '. . . admitting water into the double bottom. Nine flushing Kingstons were provided for this purpose, located at the side of the ship on the berth deck and in passageways . . . The water is admitted . . . by sluice gates.'[28] The monitor could be lowered in the water until just a few inches of her freeboard was left above the water line. She was then at her fighting trim.

Of all the characteristics of the USS *Monterey*, the one which particularly set her apart from her contemporaries was her boiler arrangement. As the demand for increased armour and armament became more pressing, reductions in weight had to be achieved elsewhere and the Bureau of Steam Engineering proposed the use of four coil boilers in conjunction with two single-ended Scotch boilers. These six boilers were divided equally between two water-tight compartments, separated by a midship longitudinal bulkhead. Each boiler room contained one cylindrical and two Ward boilers. For the cylindrical boilers, the plates, furnace, tubes, rivets and braces were of steel while the grate bars were of wrought iron.

TABLE 1: PARTICULARS OF USS MONTEREY'S SCOTCH BOILERS

Length:	10ft 7in
Outside diameter:	11ft 2in
No of furnaces (corrugated):	2
Outside diameter of furnace:	3ft 10in
Inside diameter of furnace:	3ft 6in
Length of grate:	6ft 3¾in
Outside diameter of tubes (steel):	2¼in
Length of tubes between tube sheets:	7ft 4⅞in
Tube heating surface:	1252.72sq ft
Plate heating surface:	199.82sq ft
Total heating surface:	1452.54sq ft
Grate surface:	44sq ft
Volume of furnaces and combustion chambers above grate:	182cu ft
Load on safety valves:	160psi
Test pressure:	250psi

'In the Ward boilers, the coils and vertical, central drum (were) of wrought steel, the manifolds and heads of the central drum of cast steel, the grate bars of cast iron and the boiler casing of light sheet iron, lined with fire brick and tiles; the top of the casing also, is of light iron.'[29]

TABLE 2: PARTICULARS OF USS MONTEREY'S WARD BOILERS

Outside diameter – annular grate:	10ft 2in
Inner diameter – annular grate:	3ft ¾in
Outside diameter-casing at furnace:	11ft 1in
Outside diameter-casing above furnace:	10ft 8in
Height of casing-floor to cover:	8ft 3in
Height of central drum from floor:	11ft 6in
Length of central drum-outside:	10ft 9in
Test pressure:	300psi
Heating surface-total:	2970sq ft
Volume of steam space:	18cu ft
Voume of water space:	86cu ft

During the *Monterey*'s trials, which were run between Hunter's Point and Red Rock in San Francisco Bay, favourable results were obtained from her combination of cylindrical boilers and Ward boilers. A selected list of figures from the *Monterey*'s totals are given in Table 3.

TABLE 3: USS MONTEREY – TRIAL RESULTS

Displacement at mean draught on trial:	4000 tons
Area of wetted surface:	19,203sq ft
Average speed:	13.6kts
Slip (mean) of both screws:	18.73%
Revolutions (mean) of both engines:	161.51rpm
Temperature – Engine rooms:	109.3 port
	109.4 starboard
Temperature – Fire rooms:	145.5 port
	131.1 starboard
Collective IHP both main engines:	4986.87
IPH per ton of propelling machinery, boilers and water:	12.95

SERVICE

It was during the Spanish-American War that these warships were given their only chance to fire their guns in anger. The *Amphitrite, Miantonomoh, Puritan* and *Terror* were acceptable for service with Rear Admiral Sampson's fleet because of the increase, on paper at least, that was obtained in fire power. The Admiral was not greatly pleased with the general performance of the monitors '. . . they caused him endless trouble and delay, especially since the monitors' limited coal capacity required that they frequently be taken under tow by the larger warships.'[30] In this condition they resembled '. . . at the end of hawsers . . . reluctant truants being dragged to school.'[31] For all their shortcomings, they were given bombardment and blockade duties in the Caribbean area.

At about the same time that Sampson's monitors were in the Caribbean, the USS *Monadnock* and the USS *Monterey* were crossing the Pacific Ocean to augment Commodore George Dewey's forces in the Philippines. When the *Monterey* steamed past Corrigidor on 4

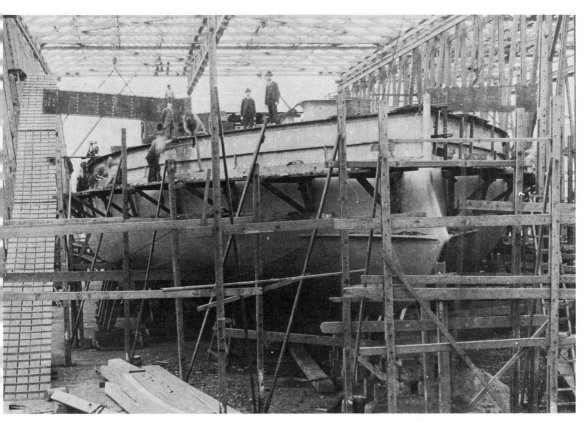

USS *Monterey* on the stocks at the Union Iron Works, San Francisco, California, about 1890–91.

US Naval Museum

August Dewey had the edge he felt he needed to handle the Spanish forts at Manila.

It was perhaps inevitable that the assessment of these warships in service would not be favourable, for the heat of the tropics plus their own internally produced heat, added to the impossibility of keeping the ships dry while at sea, produced conditions of poor habitability. The monitors' gunnery also suffered from their low freeboard and their tendency to roll heavily.[32]

A few words should be said about basic concept of monitors in the late nineteenth century as weapons of war for what was even then a two-ocean navy, though admittedly on a small scale.

Many of the men in responsible positions believed in the monitor as a practical means of harbour defence, and did so following the Navy's experience with monitors during the American Civil War. Their experience with monitors led them to view the warships of this category as an inexpensive way to protect the ports of the nation, not only because they were small vessels but because the necessary '. . . crews (were) small at the most and (could) be considerably reduced by some changes in organisation . . .'[33] Though underlying these reasons there was a reluctance to give up something which had been proved by trial and error, there were those who felt that the monitor, as ships which were immediately avail-

able for completion, should only be finished and commissioned as a means of expanding the navy. In 1881 the then Secretary of the Navy, William H Hunt, although denouncing the monitor as a type, advocated their completion 'solely as a choice of evils.'[34] In the end, however, it is fair to state that the technical concept of a low freeboard, heavily armed warship (*ie* a monitor) was not so much at fault, since the Army was at the same time, in a frenzy of building and modernising coastal fortifications. The problem was centred more in the abstract idea of the best harbour defence being based at the harbour itself. This made little sense for a growing navy that was beginning to see beyond the boundaries of its own coast line. By 1904 the Secretary of Navy, Charles J Bonaparte was able to state, as opposed to views held just a few years before, that '. . . it was thought that vessels of a special type were needed for coast defence . . . this idea is now outgrown . . . old horsey in our naval policy.'[35]

SHIP HISTORIES
(From *American Steel Navy*)

USS Amphitrite: Partially constructed by Harlan & Hollinsworth, Wilmington, Del; laid down *c*1874; launched 7 June 1883; completed at Norfolk Navy Yard; commissioned 23 April 1895; served as a Naval Militia training ship 1910–1917; sold 3 January 1920; converted into a 75 room floating hotel for use at Beaufort, SC, and Fort Lauderdale, Fla; scrapped in 1951.

USS *Monterey* showing the installation of 'Big Betsy', a 12in rifle, in her forward turret, at the Union Iron Works, San Francisco, California, on 23 January 1892.

US Naval Museum

USS *Monterey*'s after turret, taken prior to the installation of the guns and the armour. Taken at the Union Iron Works, San Francisco, California, about 1891.

US Naval Museum

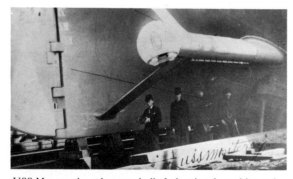

USS *Monterey*'s underwater hull aft showing the rudder and starboard shaft. Taken just prior to her launch, in April 1891.

US Naval Museum

USS *Puritan*, 1897.

National Archives

USS Miantonomoh: Partially constructed by John Roach & Sons, Chester, Pa; laid down *c*1874; launched 5 December 1876; completed at New York Navy Yard; commissioned 27 October 1891; stricken 3 December 1915 and employed as a gunnery target; hulk sold 26 January 1922.

USS Monadnock: Partially constructed by Continental Iron Works, Vallejo, Cal; laid down *c*1874; launched 19 September 1883; completed at Mare Island Navy Yard; commissioned 20 February 1896; stricken 2 February 1923.

USS Terror: Partially constructed by Wm Cramp & Sons, Phila, Pa; laid down *c*1874; launched 24 March 1883; completed at New York Navy Yard; commissioned 15 April 1896; stricken 15 December 1915 and employed as a gunnery target; hulk sold 10 March 1921.

USS Puritan: Partially constructed by John Roach & Sons, Chester, Pa; laid down *c*1874; launched 6 December 1882; completed at New York Navy Yard; commissioned 10 December 1896; stricken 27 February 1913 and employed as a gunnery target; hulk sold 26 January 1922.

USS Monterey: Built by Union Iron Works, San Francisco, Cal; authorised 3 March 1887; commissioned 13 February 1893; sold 25 February 1922.

SHIP'S DATA

PURITAN

Length on Load Water line:	289ft 6in
Extreme Breadth:	60ft 1½in
Mean Draught:	18ft
Normal Displacement:	6060 tons
Armament:	4–12in, 35 cal breech-loading rifles; 6–4in, 40 cal rapid-fire guns; 6–6pdr; 2–1pdr; 2–37mm.
Maximum Armour Thickness:	14in (sides); 8in (turrets)
Engines:	Twin-screw, horizontal compound
Performance:	12.4kts; 3700 ihp
Complement:	22 officers; 208 men

MONTEREY

Length on Load Water line:	256ft
Extreme Breadth:	59ft
Mean Draught:	13ft 10in
Normal Displacement:	4084 tons
Armament:	2–12in, 35 cal breech-loading rifles; 2–10in, 30 cal breech-loading rifles; 6–6pdr; 4–1pdr; 2 Gatlings
Maximum Armour Thickness:	13in (sides); 8in (turrets)
Engines:	Twin-screw, vertical triple-expansion
Performance:	13.6kts; 5244 ihp
Complement:	19 officers, 172 men

USS *Monterey* on 15 July 1924.
National Archives

AMPHITRITE CLASS

Length on Load Water line:	259ft 6in
Extreme Breadth:	55ft 10in
Mean Draught:	14ft 6in
Normal Displacement:	3990 tons
Armament*:	4–10in, 30 cal breech-loading rifles; 2–4in, 40 cal rapid-fire guns; 2-6pdr; 2-3pdr; 2-1pdr; 2-37mm.
Maximum Armour Thickness*:	9in (sides); 7½in (turrets)
Engines**:	Twin screw, inclined compound
Performance (Amphitrite):	10.5kts; 1600 ihp
Complement:	26 officers, 145 men

*Miantonomoh had 2–10in, 30 cal and 2–10in, 35 cal breech-loading rifles. *Miantonomoh* and *Terror* had 7in armour on sides, 11½in armour on turrets, no barbettes, and no 4in guns.
**Monadnock had twin-screw, horizontal triple-expansion engines, providing 12kts at 3000ihp.

FOOTNOTES

22, 30, 31, 33, 34 *American Steel Navy* by John D Allen
23–29 *Journal of the American Society of Naval Engineers* 'The Contract trials of the USS *Monterey*' by Howard Gage and Emil Theiss, Vol V.
32 *Journal of the American Society of Naval Engineers* 'Reconstructed American Monitors' by Frank M Bennett, Vol IX, 1897.

USS *Monadnock* off the Mare Island Naval Yard in 1898, just prior to her voyage to the Far East. USS *Camanche* can be seen in the background.

US Naval Museum

USS *Terror* at New York, 23 April 1897.

National Archives

USS *Monadnock* taken in China 27 January 1901 – 28 November 1904.

National Archives

NTONY PRESTON'S ARTICLE ON THE RN'S 1960 RUISER DESIGNS from Michael Vlahos

here is something very wrong about this article. The esign portfolio presented is authentic, and is undoubdly entitled something like 'Cruiser Sketches: 1960'. nfortunately, the designs date from a decade before. hese are cruisers from the design minds of the late 940s, and certainly no later than 1950.

Of four cruiser types, only one has a guided missile /stem, and obviously as an afterthought-modification f design one, an all-gun ship. Mr Preston himself admits at the staff requirement for Seaslug dates from as early s 1946. The 'Counties' were designed in the mid-1950s ith Seaslug as their main system, but by the end of the 950s a new area-defence system was in development, e Sea Dart. Why would Admiralty designers envisage n antiquated area-defence system for their warships of e future, especially when the first-generation system, easlug, by 1960 had proven to be a complete and irefully concealed failure?

These are gun-cruiser designs. The main gun system, a avalized version of the Army Green Archer progimme, was scrapped for naval use when Green Archer self was cancelled, around the time of the Sandys port. A navalized Green Archer, *a concept of the late* 940s, was long dead by 1960.

Now take Mr Preston's comment about the close-in A system, the 'DACR'. He calls it 'an updated version f the 40mm Bofors Mk 6'. Why, again, would designers ttempt, in 1960, to introduce an updated version of a /orld War II gun-AA system, to *replace* the newly itroduced Seacat, which had been introduced, among ther ship types, in the 'County' class DLGs, which Mr reston insists *preceded* the '1960 Cruisers'?

Finally, I cannot ignore the presence of torpedo tubes three of these designs. By 1960, tubes were being emoved from the Type 12 *(Whitby)* frigates which, hen originally designed in the late 1940s, were given 2 torpedo tubes. It must be remembered as well that ven then, torpedo doctrine had almost completed its ansformation in the Royal Navy from anti-ship to nti-submarine employment. One looks in awe at such esigns as the 'Small Cruiser of 1960' with as many tubes s the *Emerald* of 1926, and must surely wonder, in the perational context of 1960, why?

Unfortunately, in all other aspects of the designs – hull orm, boat-handling equipment, gun directors, radars, rmour thickness and disposition – the '1960 Cruisers' eek of the late 1940s. No self-respecting warship esigner of 1960 would put a Type 984 radar on a ship at could not hope to see operational service until *1970* the earliest*, when the eagerly awaited Anglo-Dutch -D radar, then in active development, would be ready or service by 1965. The boat-handling, armour scheme, nd hull form would be archaic for 1960. Why were ese ships ever called '1960 Cruisers'?

One can discern an answer in the very nature of the planning process. A military institution must always look ahead, not only in its contingency plans, but in its expectational order of battle as well. An overall assessment of potential enemy capabilities – as they can be expected to evolve in the future – must be made, before specific force-planning projections can be hazarded for one's own service. A recent published example of this was the Anthony Cave-Brown edition of 'Dropshop', which he called 'America's Plan for War with the Soviet Union in 1956'. Of course, the war-planning documents he reproduces originated in the world of 1948. The JCS of that moment was prudently, and typically, attempting to describe a conflict scenario set some eight years into the future, given current projections of the growth of Soviet capabilities. They were attempting to show what American and Allied military forces would be necessary to win their war forecast for 1956.

In the 1947–50 period, Admiralty designers were given a similar task: 'Given what we know about current trends in the development of the Soviet Navy, what cruiser-types should we think about developing to meet this threat, given systems and design practices either available now or projected for the next decade?' To the world of 1948, '1960' was a resonant benchmark-date to capture the future.

In 1948, a medium-calibre dual-purpose gun system seemed to offer good prospects both for area-defense AA and possible surface action against the newly emergent *Sverdlov* cruiser. Remembering the kind of surface action sustained by the Royal Navy in the Norwegian and Barents Seas in the last war, a heavy torpedo armament – to counter a convoy attack by big Soviet cruisers – might have appeared highly appropriate.

Antony Preston replies:
I am most grateful to Professor Vlahos for his comments, which underline the problem of researching British official records under the 30-year Rule. It is also a classic example of the risk in getting only a small part of a design-history, without supporting documents.

I must confess that I was puzzled when I was shown these four sketch designs labelled '1960 Cruisers', but as nothing else could be found at the time I could only try to give an explanation for them. Even though in theory all documents up to 1953 are available, it is never quite so easy as the Public Record Office officials give priority to political papers rather than ship-design files.

Information which I have looked at since that short note appeared in *Warship* indicates that the four sketch designs were prepared to illustrate a paper at the end of 1948 for a conference the following year. The Director of Naval Construction was replying to Naval Staff papers trying to define the essential functions of cruisers, and the DNC put forward what he saw as essential features. To act offensively a cruiser should have:
1. surface guns
2. long- and short-range AA armament
3. speed, endurance and seakeeping
4. protection against splinters at least, over all vital parts
5. torpedo armament
6. ability to attack aircraft and submarines
7. ability to direct aircraft
8. ship-to-air guided missiles
9. accommodation for HQ staff and good communications

Ideas on the future were constrained by the earliest dates at which new weapons would become available. The 6in Mk 26 twin and the 3in/70 Mk 6 twin would be available in 1953, but the 5in and the new close-range weapons would not be ready until 1957, and Seaslug was a year behind them. The fire-control systems were subject to similar time-scales.

Although there had been talk of the desirability of nuclear propulsion (even gas turbines had been discussed) there was no likelihood of such luxuries being available in time, and so a steam plant of the *Minotaur* or improved *Daring* type was chosen. The four turbines and boilers would have been in four combined boiler/engine rooms. Special attention was to be paid to the positioning of weapons, to avoid interference and physical fouling at any angle of training. This was because the guns concerned were to be automatic weapons with high training speeds.

If a single funnel was adopted there would be the need for very long horizontal uptakes. If a complement of only 650 was achieved accommodation with cafeteria messing could be worked in below the upper deck, but if as DNC expected, it rose to 950 a superstructure deck would have had to be provided. This would have meant a ship of not less than 17,500 tons deep.

The final comment is that if the design studies were criticised as entirely conventional (in 1948 terms) it was only fair to emphasise that they used only equipment likely to be available by 1958.

ICEBREAKER from Charles D Maginley, Deputy Director, Canadian Coast Guard College, Sydney, NS

The icebreaker in the background of the photo of the newly completed launches at a Canadian port is the *J D Hazen* (compare the photo of the same ship in drydock on page 178 of *Usque Ad Mare* by Thomas E Appleton, DOT Ottawa, 1968). Some subsequent photos show her with lengthened funnels.

The *J D Hazen* was completed by Canadian Vickers in 1916 and sold to the Russian government who renamed her *Mikula Seleaninovitch*. She was captured by French forces during the intervention of 1919 and brought to France as a prize of war. In 1923 she was bought back by the Canadian government and served on regular ice breaking duties under the name *Mikula* until scrapped in 1937.

The name has been preserved by the present CCG *Mikula*, an ex-lightship which serves as a training vessel for the Canadian Coast Guard College.

From Arthur B Harriss, Commander RCNR, Troy Michigan

In As&As of *Warship* 23 you show a photo of motor launches, thought to have been taken in Montreal in 1915 or 1916. You asked if anyone could identify the icebreaker visible in the background.

In the 1959 *Transactions of The Society of Naval Architects and Marine Engineers* there appeared an article by J Gorden German titled *Design and Construction of Icebreakers*. Mr German started by giving a short history of icebreaking in the St Lawrence River, and he described the ships which have been built for that service.

In 1916 Canadian Vickers Ltd built an icebreaker named *J D Hazen*, 292ft oa, 57ft 6in beam, 4960 tons displacement, 8000hp on two shafts, reciprocating steam engine of course. The profile drawing matches the photo – twin funnels and masts, forecastle, and especially the backward rake of the stem.

The article shows under *service* 'Archangel – White Sea', and a name change to *Mikula Selianinovitch*, so it seems likely that she was sold to the Imperial Russian Government when new or fairly new. I hope this is of some assistance.

The accompanying table is based on the information sent by Commander Harris.

PARTICULARS OF J D HAZEN

Built:	1916
Built at:	Montreal
Length:	292ft (oa), 275ft (pp)
Beam:	57ft 6in (moulded)
Load draught:	19ft 3in
Load displacement:	4950 tons
Complement:	90
Trial speed:	15.5kts
HP:	8000ihp
rpm:	130

Note: from the above it seems fairly certain that the photograph which appeared in *Warship* 23 shows the *Hazen* as just completed or in the final stages of fitting out at Montreal in 1916; a fuller completion date would allow a more accurate dating of the photograph.

FORTHCOMING NAVAL TITLES FROM CONWAY

US NAVAL WEAPONS

Every gun, missile, mine and torpedo used by the US Navy from 1883 to the present day

Norman Friedman

A truly encyclopaedic work, Norman Friedman's latest book gives detailed specifications for each weapon and backs each entry with an authoritative discussion of why the weapon was developed and how it functioned in service. To complete the picture, full descriptions of the essential electronics – fire control systems, radars, sonars and other sensors – are included, together with analyses of US Navy thinking on strategy and tactics as it affected weapons development and procurement.

310 × 216mm (12¼″ × 8½″), 288 pages, 200 photographs, 150 line drawings. ISBN 0 85177 240 4. **£18.00** *(plus £1.80 postage and packing when ordering direct). March*

A CENTURY OF NAVAL CONSTRUCTION

The History of the Royal Corps of Naval Constructors

D L Brown RCNC

Published to mark the centenary of the Royal Corps, this book offers a completely new insight into the factors governing British warship construction as well as the wider issues of Royal Navy Policy. The ancestry of the Corps can be traced back to the eighteenth century, but the story is carried right up to the present; vessels designed by the Corps are the only warships to have seen action against modern weaponry, and the book concludes with an analysis of the lessons of the Falklands conflict.

241 × 156mm (9½″ × 6″), 384 pages, 92 photographs, 20 line drawings. ISBN 0 85177 282 X. **£20.00** *(plus £2.00 postage and packing when ordering direct). March*

CONWAY'S ALL THE WORLD'S FIGHTING SHIPS 1947-1982

Part I: The Western Powers

The fourth volume of Conway's four-volume history of iron and steel warships provides a clear but comprehensive review of postwar naval affairs, from the largest issue to the minute technicalities of warship design. It has been necessary to divide this volume into two parts in order to include the details of every significant warship built (and many that were only projected). The first covers the NATO navies, its associates like France, and other Western-orientated powers such as Japan, Australia and New Zealand. Part II contains the navies of the Warsaw Pact, non-aligned countries and minor navies and will be published in the Autumn.

310 × 216mm (12¼″ × 8¼″), 256 pages, 250 photographs, 240 line drawings. ISBN 0 85177 255 0. **£25.00** *(plus £2.00 postage and packing when ordering direct). April*

From your local bookshop or
Conway Maritime Press Ltd
24 Bride Lane, Fleet Street, London EC4Y 8DR

SUBMARINE BOATS

The Beginnings of Underwater Warfare

by Richard Compton-Hall

In May 1983, *Holland I*, the only surviving example of the world's first practical submarine design, will go on display to the public as the focal point of a new gallery in the Submarine Museum at Gosport. The author, the director of the museum, was the inspiration behind the search for and ultimate raising of *Holland I* and he has planned his book to celebrate this event. *Submarine Boats* is a witty and perceptive account of the early years of submarine development, including the more weird and wonderful inventions but concentrating on the brilliant designer John Philip Holland, and it is illustrated with a spectacular collection of early photographs, which were collected from the huge archives of the Submarine Museum.

240 x 184mm (9½" x 7¼"), 192pp, 150 black and white photographs, 50 line drawings. ISBN 0 85177 288 9. May 1983. £10.50 (plus £1.60 post and packing when ordering direct).

From your local bookseller or by post from
Conway Maritime Press Ltd.
24 Bride Lane, London EC4Y 8DR.

EDITORIAL John Roberts

Debating why various warships have become popular provides an interesting sidelight on the study of naval history. There are some obvious conclusions to be drawn big ships, particularly battleships and battlecruisers, are always popular and, of course, any with an exciting service career draw the interest of writers, from those who originally reported the events concerned to the historians who subsequently outline the battles of the past.

Among British capital ships, being sunk seems to increase popularity considerably although a closer examination tends to cloud this simple statement to some extent. *Hood* was well known and popular throughout her career, and the dramatic circumstances of her loss have served mainly to increase the interest in her rather than create it. On the other hand *Ark Royal* became famous for her exploits in the earlier part of the war, in particular because her activities were reported extensively as part of the propaganda war, and how much her loss which was less than spectacular, affected her subsequent popularity is difficult to say. Certainly none of the other major British carriers lost (*Courageous, Glorious, Hermes* and *Eagle*) can claim similar popularity.

One event which seems to emphasise the loss of a vessel as a major contributing factor to its popularity is the loss of *Prince of Wales* and *Repulse*. The former is distinctly more popular than her four sister ships, which removes appearance as a factor, and both *King George V* and *Duke of York* have equal claims to fame due to their war records. Similar comments apply to *Repulse*, which draws more attention than her sister *Renown* and also to the *Royal Oak* (although her four sisters were not extensively involved in the major events of the war). An exception is the *Queen Elizabeth* class, of which *Warspite* is easily the most popular vessel, due to her spectacular war record, while the only ship of the class lost, *Barham*, has received little attention.

With cruisers and smaller vessels the same criteria do not seem to apply, for although many of the most famous, such as *Exeter, Kelly* and *Cossack*, were lost their fame was created before they sank. It seems likely that the loss of non-capital vessels is accepted because such ships cannot, and are not, expected to be invulnerable whereas the sinking of a major ship is cause for a detailed analysis because such ships, if still not invulnerable, are at least expected to survive very serious damage. This applies particularly to the loss of *Prince of Wales* and *Hood*, both of which were the subject, and still are, of considerable debate, but not to such vessels as *Royal Oak* and *Barham* which were old, virtually obsolete vessels whose loss, if no less shocking, was less surprising.

It seems that popularity owes a good deal to wartime propaganda for many of the ships which received substantial attention in the media during the early years of the war have continued to be the 'well known' ships of the period. I emphasise the early years of the war because once the Allies began to land on the European mainland, the naval side of the war was reported much less, as the developing situation ashore drew more and more attention. The early years were of course much more critical as well, and later naval battles, although no less exciting in many cases, did not necessarily have a major effect on the course of the war. Thus the battle between *King George V* and *Bismarck* receives more attention than that between *Duke of York* and *Scharnhorst*.

TORPEDO WARFARE:

A Successful Prediction by D J Lyon

The torpedo cruiser *Serpent*, of the *Archer* class, which was completed in 1888. She carried one fixed torpedo tube in the bow and two torpedo launching carriages on the upper deck, one forward and one aft. The latter could be traversed across the deck for firing on either side; the embrasures for these can be seen in the photograph at bow and quarter.

CPL

This article is modified from three separate and differing papers given on the development of torpedo vessels in the Royal Navy at the 1979 Maritime Science Symposium at Greenwich, the 1979 Naval History Conference at the US Naval Academy, and the 1980 meeting of the International Committee on Military History at Bucharest.

In the eighteenth century warships fought broadside to broadside with the aim of pounding the enemy into submission, killing the crew, smashing the masts and spars and, if necessary, delivering the *coup de grâce* by boarding. Capture was the main intention, and it was extremely rare for a ship to sink during battle. Twentieth century naval battles, however, have resulted in sinkings, not captures, the taking of prizes having become as rare as foundering in action had been before.

Perhaps the most important of the several reasons for this reversal was the introduction of underwater explosive weapons, the submarine mine and the locomotive torpedo, which became regular items in naval arsenals during the second half of the nineteenth century. The torpedo was the more important and more effective of the two weapons, not least because it produced another revolution in naval warfare in that it made possible the sinking of the largest vessels by much smaller craft without the certainty of destruction of the smaller craft in suicidal attack, as had been the case with that self destructive weapon, the fireship.

THE WHITEHEAD TORPEDO

The 1860s were the decisive decade in the introduction of such underwater weapons, as it was during the American Civil War that the spar torpedo and submarine mine were first used successfully in action to sink ships. Also by the end of the decade the brilliant emigré English engineer, Robert Whitehead, had developed a workable, if primitive and not particularly reliable piece of equipment, the 'fish' torpedo, the world's first guided weapon.

From its first trials, Whitehead's torpedo was clearly of great potential, and during the remaining years of the nineteenth century it attracted a great deal of enthusiasm. It posed a definite threat to the survivability of the large, expensive and hitherto unchallenged battleship, and therefore attracted the support of politicians anxious to obtain cuts in defence spending, just as much as it appealed to young naval officers avid for early independent command and for a means of challenging the thinking of elderly and conservative admirals. The 'David and Goliath' appeal of small, fast torpedo boats attacking massive battleships won many adherents for the torpedo amongst journalists and the public at large. Small navies found in the torpedo boat a possible answer to their coastal defence problems at a price they could

HM 1st Class Torpedo Boat *029* in South African waters shortly before the First World War. She was a 125ft Thornycroft boat built in 1885.

afford. Other, larger navies, in particular that of the French, saw torpedo warfare as a way of countering the Royal Navy's superiority in numbers of large ships, and of attacking Britain's vital overseas trade.

Naturally there was a great deal of theorising on the strategic and tactical potential and use of the new weapon, not to mention the possible defences against it, and a good deal of thought was put into the problem of how best to carry the torpedo in action. It is on this issue – what would now be called the 'weapon system' aspect – that I intend to concentrate. More especially, I shall be tracing the way in which one particular set of predictions, those made by the small group of naval and Royal Engineer officers who formed the Torpedo Committee of 1873, were developed in practice.

THE COMMITTEE REPORT
The Royal Navy had been aware of Whitehead's exper-

The gun/torpedo vessel *Curlew* of 1885 which, at 950 tons, was about half the size of the contemporary *Archer* class torpedo cruisers but carried the same torpedo armament with one fixed tube and two traversing carriages.
CPL

iments from 1868, and after trials in 1870 had decided to manufacture the new weapon. The Committee was set up to report on all aspects of the use of the new weapon and to make recommendations about both this and possible defences. The resulting printed report was clear, comprehensive and sensible. It included the following four proposals for ways in which torpedoes could be taken to sea.

The first was that the new weapon should be added to the armament of existing types of warship – battleships, cruisers and sloops – and, as a result, by the end of the 1870s most major war vessels in the Royal Navy carried torpedoes. One British cruiser, the large unarmoured frigate *Shah*, became the first ship to fire a torpedo in anger, during an unsuccessful engagement with the Peruvian ironclad *Huascar* in 1877, but although battleships and cruisers continued to be fitted with torpedo tubes up to the time of the Second World War, they made comparatively little use of them in action.

Second, torpedoes could be carried by ships' boats, and again this proposal was adopted with great enthusiasm. In the last quarter of the nineteenth century nearly all types of of boat large enough to carry a torpedo were so fitted, and this included pulling and sailing boats as well as steam-powered craft. It was natural that this should be so, as the Royal Navy had a long tradition

HMS *Sandfly*, launched in 1887, was one of the first of the Navy's torpedo gunboats. Note the 14in torpedo tube in the bow, and the recess for the side 14in tube amidships. A fourth tube was arranged in the stern.

Photomatic

carried six second-class boats. However it was not until torpedo aircraft went to sea in aircraft carriers that a modified form of this concept really proved itself. In 1940 as HMS *Illustrious'* strike of Swordfish torpedo bombers raided Taranto the trumpets sounded with no uncertain voice.* And in the long run, in another element, this part of the 1873 Committee's suggestion saw its final justification.

Launched in 1894, *Hazard* belonged to the last class of torpedo gunboats to be built for the RN. She carried a fixed 18in tube in the bow and twin revolving tubes on each side amidships.

Tom Molland

of using ships' boats to attack enemy vessels in their own harbours, into which they had been driven by British blockade. Indeed special torpedo boats, known as 'second class torpedo boats' were developed for carrying aboard larger warships. They were very popular for a short while, large numbers being built during the late 1870s and early 1880s for the Royal Navy, but they proved to be too fragile and unseaworthy for prolonged use and were eventually supplanted by the more solid, but slower, steam picket boats, which were conventional general-purpose ships' boats capable of carrying torpedoes. They were also built of wood, as opposed to the single-purpose second-class boats which were of steel construction. In the early 1880s ships intended to act as both torpedo boat carriers and depot ships appeared: in the Royal Navy there was the converted merchantman *Hecla* and the purpose-built, cruiser-like *Vulcan*, which

The last two proposals of that Committee, however, were the most immediately important ones for the development of torpedo vessels. They were, respectively, the construction of purpose-built sea-going torpedo vessels for use with the fleet, and the adapting of small, fast steam launches of the type recently developed for river use by firms such as Thornycroft and Yarrow, for carrying torpedoes for harbour and coastal defence. The first of these two proposals led to a series of false starts, the second to the development of the torpedo boat, which was eventually to evolve into the successful sea-going torpedo vessel, the destroyer.

*'Vox Non Incerta' was *Illustrious'* motto.

VESUVIUS AND POLYPHEMUS

Even before the 1873 Committee was convened the Royal Navy was considering designs for torpedo vessels. The first to be built, a small and slow vessel called *Vesuvius*, was hardly spectacular; usually, if noticed at all, she is dismissed as an experimental vessel of little importance or interest. It is true that she spent her life in the dull but vital tasks of training, and of experimental tender to the torpedo school, but it would appear that she was originally intended to be capable of operational use. Unfortunately, I have been unable to locate any discussion of her design, anything that would approximate to the modern 'Staff Requirements', but it would seem that she was intended for attack by stealth, probably under the cover of night. She had a very low freeboard, engines which were intended to be as nearly noiseless as possible, and vents at deck level for the smoke (though a funnel was added whilst she was completing). In practice she might have proved a better choice for an attack on a hostile harbour than the fragile and unreliable early torpedo boats, but her maximum speed of 9kts was enough to condemn her in contemporary eyes, and what might have been a worthwhile alternative to the high-speed torpedo boat was never developed any further.

She did, however, have a much larger and more spectacular successor. This was the torpedo-ram *Polyphemus* of 1881. She combined high speed (17kts), armour protection (a 3in thick layer over the top of a cigar-shaped hull), a very low silhouette and a powerful submerged torpedo tube armament (five tubes plus reloads). She also incorporated another fashionable weapon of the later nineteenth century in the form of a strong steel ram. This however was not, as has so often been said, the chief weapon of the ship; she was intended primarily as a torpedo ship, the ram serving as a secondary weapon (and also as a standby in case the submerged torpedo tubes, for which she was the experimental vessel, did not work). They were in fact successful, and the *Polyphemus* would have proved a formidable antagonist to her battleship contemporaries, with their few, slow firing, short-ranged and, above all, slow-traversing guns. However, the almost simultaneous advent of the quick-firing gun somewhat altered the situation in the battleship's favour. This combined with the fact that there was never the chance to try her concept in action, and that she was a ship for which there was little or no use in peacetime, ensured that she had no successors.

UNREALISTIC SPEEDS
A few 'torpedo cruisers' were built in the early 1880s, in a somewhat half-hearted attempt to produce sea-going torpedo ships, but they were unsatisfactory both as

Naval cadets undergoing torpedo instruction, with an 18in torpedo, aboard the 1st class cruiser *Theseus* in 1896.

The Hawthorn Leslie '30-knotter' torpedo-boat destroyer
Roebuck of 1901.

Tom Molland

cruisers and as torpedo vessels.

Meanwhile vast numbers of torpedo boats were being built. These, as has already been mentioned, were derived from the slender, steel-hulled river launches which were the fastest water craft of their day. Speed was their chief feature and remained so – speed obtained at the expense of most other desirable features such as seaworthiness and habitability, and speed moreover which could only be obtained on unrealistic trials, with the vessels 'tuned up' to their maximum efficiency and run by specialised crews in the finest possible weather. Trials speeds bore little resemblance to the effective service speed of an ageing vessel with an average crew, which might be as much as one-third less. The demand for speed for speed's sake, which was long a major factor in warship design (and is not dead yet), is perhaps the most outstanding example of the tendency, particularly in late Victorian times, for technological possibilities, rather than operational requirements, to be the chief influences on design. The development of the torpedo boat, and the first destroyers, was dominated by the demand for more and more speed. It was not until the 'River' class destroyers of the early 1900s that a class appeared intended to make a reasonable speed in a seaway rather than in a flat calm, a change which demanded a sturdier and bigger hull, instead of the light hull almost completely filled with yet more boilers and more powerful engines than before which had previous

been the pattern of development.

Of course, other factors than the demand for speed influenced the development of the torpedo boat. Torpedoes increased in speed and power, and machine guns and then quick-firers were fitted for self-defence and for brushing aside enemy boats. There were increases in size to cope with demands for better habitability and more seaworthiness as well as those for more powerful machinery, the former demands being the result of practical experience throwing some doubt on the optimistic predictions of torpedo boat builders and enthusiasts. A factor which operated against the steady increase in size was a persistent demand for torpedo vessels to be inconspicuous, low in the water and small. However the chief impression one gains from studying the development of the torpedo boat in detail is that there was little real effort made to analyse the basic factors in design, no serious attempt to work out whether speed or stealth were more important. For example, though there was a great deal of talk about tactical details, such as the minutiae of flotilla formations and the like, with the hindsight given by a knowledge of the methods of operations research and the combat experience of two world wars this theorising looks extremely superficial. We now know, for example, that during the Second World War the most successful motor torpedo boat attacks were made at low speed using stealth and surprise. High speed was only used for a quick getaway after detection. Wartime experience has also emphasised the importance of an adequate and reliable sea speed, as against very high speed in calm weather.

DESTROYER DEVELOPMENT

As the torpedo boat grew in size, seaworthiness and numbers, so the need to find a counter to it became more urgent. Each time a larger type of torpedo boat was ordered one of its tasks was always stated to be that of screening the fleet against the attacks of other smaller torpedo boats. At least one class, the 125-footers, were briefly referred to as 'torpedo boat destroyers'. The main reason for placing small guns on torpedo craft was to enable them to fulfil this function.

Another approach to the problem was to revert to the idea of building specialised sea-going torpedo ships, smaller versions of contemporary cruisers with a good torpedo armament, powerful machinery and light guns. These were the 'torpedo gunboats' or 'catchers'. They were accounted failures because they had insufficient speed to catch contemporary torpedo boats, a shortcoming due as much to difficulties with their boilers as to any failing in the design. Again, one can criticise the Navy of the late nineteenth century for sloppy thinking. The main aim of the type was to prevent torpedo boats attacking the fleet; although one way of doing this was to chase and destroy torpedo boats, close escort was at least as likely to achieve the object, and for that high speed, though definitely desirable, was not essential. As escorts the torpedo gunboats would have been useful vessels.

The scaling down of a larger type having been accounted a failure, the alternative of scaling up the

Originally classed as a destroyer, the flotilla leader *Swift*, seen here in 1911, was reclassified due to her exceptionally large size.

NMM

torpedo boat itself was adopted instead, with considerable success. The first 'torpedo boat destroyers' or, as they were later to be known, 'destroyers' were the result of a collaboration between the specialist torpedo boat builders, Thornycroft and Yarrow, and the Controller of the Navy, the celebrated 'Jackie' Fisher. It is worth noting that the relative importance of purely technological factors in the conception of these ships is underlined by the fact that it was only with torpedo vessels that the Admiralty allowed design leadership to pass out of its own hands into those of a commercial shipbuilder. *Daring* and *Decoy, Havock* and *Hornet*, the first destroyers, were still very much in the torpedo boat tradition, with trial speed being the dominant element in design. These '26-knotters' were succeeded by '27', '30' and finally '32-knotters', all in the same line of development, and the last of total failure. Finally, the aforementioned 'River' class redressed the necessary balance in design between speed and seaworthiness, with their raised forecastles and stronger hulls. With them the wheel had revolved until the torpedo launch type recommended by the 1873 Committee had evolved into a true sea-going torpedo vessel.

THE CMB

By growing to this size, and in the process not only proving an effective counter to the torpedo boat but also replacing it in its role of torpedo attack, the destroyer inevitably created a gap at the bottom of the scale, a need for a small, fast coastal torpedo boat, which was shortly to be filled thanks to the development of a lightweight and compact power source in the internal combustion engine. The demands of the First World War,

One of the *Swift*'s two 18in torpedo tubes

HMS *Viceroy*, a Thornycroft 'special' of the classic 'V' and 'W' classes which formed the basis for the majority of British destroyer construction between the wars.

MTV4, one of a pair of CMBs built by Thornycroft for the Finnish Navy in 1928; she was later renamed *Syöksy*. She is seen here on trials.

combined with Thornycroft's experience in building fast hydroplane racing boats, produced the coastal motor boat (CMB), the first successful motor torpedo boat (MTB). They were intended, interestingly, to be lowered from the davits of major warships (though this was rarely done in practice) like the old second-class torpedo boats. Inevitably, demands for greater seaworthiness, range and weapon load led to the MTB, in turn, steadily growing in size. The original 40ft CMBs were followed by 55ft and then 70ft boats, and subsequent developments have made the modern MTB, usually known as the Fast Patrol Boat (FPB), of very much the same size as the first destroyers.

To revert to the development of the main sea-going torpedo vessel, which is what the destroyer had become, the destroyers of the period up to 1916 showed a steady but unspectacular programme of detail improvement and slow growth in size since the 'River' class, if we except the somewhat unsuccessful anomalies of the 'Tribal' class and the huge *Swift*, which were the result of Fisher's addiction to superlatives and simple-minded slogans as a substitute for constructive thought in ship design. The development in size and armament was, however, inadequate for the exigencies of war in the hard conditions of the North Sea. More torpedoes were needed if adequate salvoes were to be fired to ensure a hit at long range, for war experience showed that the old idea of the torpedo as a precision sniper's weapon could not apply at the long ranges at which battles were fought; instead, a 'shotgun blast' of several torpedoes had to be fired. A new form of torpedo boat, the submarine, had already demonstrated its deadliness, and destroyers had to be fitted to carry weapons to deal with this new

menace, just as they had to carry guns capable of shooting at high angles to deal with the danger of aircraft attack. To meet this set of requirements a new class was designed, the 'V & Ws', perhaps the most successful destroyers ever built, primarily for dealing with surface targets. With their four superimposed gun mounts, multiple torpedoes and sturdy hulls, they established the basic concept for British (and much foreign) destroyer design until the requirements of anti-aircraft fire and anti-submarine operations eclipsed all other factors during the course of the Second World War.

We can thus see how the predictions of the 1873 Committee were fulfilled in the half-century or so afterwards, sometimes in rather tortuous and unexpected ways. Of course new inventions like the submarine and the aircraft modified the pattern considerably, though it is only fair to add that much of the most successful work of submarines, particularly American and German, was done on the surface rather than submerged, with the submarines acting as sea-going torpedo boats whose ability to disappear below the waves was merely as additional benefit, comparatively rarely used during night attacks. For a group of men attempting to predict the future of a brand-new weapon at a time usually known as 'the dark ages of the Victorian Navy', the 1873 Committee did not do badly.

MAIN SOURCES
Ship plans, specifications and Ships Covers (ADM 138 series) in the NMM, Admiralty Collection (for torpedo boats and craft, and destroyers).
1873 Torpedo Committee Report (copy in the NMM Phipps Hornby Collection).
Ship plans, specifications and correspondence in the NMM Thornycroft Collection.
HMS *Vernon* (Naval Torpedo School): Annual Torpedo Reports (set in the Library of the NMM).

THE STEAM SUBMARINE SWORDFISH by John M Maber

At the end of 1910 the Royal Navy had in service no fewer than 67 submarines comprising the five single hulled craft of the 'Holland' class and successive developments of this design forming the 'A', 'B' and 'C' classes. The 'Hollands' had been built by Vickers, Sons & Maxim Ltd at Barrow in the wake of an agreement between the Admiralty and the Holland Torpedo Boat Co.[1], but a subsequent agreement between the former and Vickers severed the Holland connection and gave Vickers the virtually exclusive right to build in Great Britain submarines developed on behalf of the Admiralty. An exception was made in the case of vessels built in the Royal Dockyards. In the event, of this group all

but six were built at Barrow the remainder, all of the 'C' class, being laid down in pairs at Chatham between 1907 and 1909.

In the meantime, in November 1910, Captain Roger Keyes RN had been appointed as Inspecting Captain of Submarines with a directive to bring about the integration of the Submarine Service in respect of all operational matters with the remainder of the Fleet. He was to advise also on future development and to this end Commander A P Addison, a submarine experienced torpedo specialist, was co-opted by Keyes as his technical advisor. this move led in turn to the formation of a Submarine Advisory Committee[2] which amongst its early decisions recommended the building of two types of submarine, a small 'coastal' class for local defence and a larger, better armed, 'overseas' class for offensive operations.

Launch of the Scott-Laurenti submarine
S2 at Greenock, 14 April 1915.
MoD

Termination of the agreement giving Vickers a near monopoly in the construction of submarines for the Royal Navy was subject to two years notice and an impasse was reached early in 1911 when the Admiralty sought assurance in the matter of meeting the future requirements of the Fleet. In the first place, however, a consortium known as the Submarine Torpedo Boat Co came into being in an attempt on the part of the shipbuilding industry to break the Vickers' monopoly, but the fact remained that no other private shipbuilder had experience in the design and construction of submarines and as a result the infant was still born. However, formal notice of the Admiralty's intention to end the agreement with Vickers was given on the 31 March 1911 although for a further two years, of course, construction of the new 'E' class was restricted to the facilities available at Barrow and Chatham. As an interim measure, a proposal was made that suitable shipyards might be licensed to undertake the construction of submarines to existing foreign designs. This move provoked much criticism and in fact the British 'E' class proved operationally superior. On the other hand, Submarine Service opinion welcomed the opportunity to assess foreign developments in the field of submarine design and in particular the potential of the double hull mode of construction favoured in both France and Italy.

DOUBLE-HULL DESIGNS
In 1909, Scotts' Shipbuilding & Eng Co of Greenock had been granted a licence by Fiat San Giorgio of Spezia to build submarines of Laurenti partial double hull design for service under the British flag. Such craft were already in commision with the Italian Navy and in August 1911 Admiralty representatives visited Spezia to inspect the *Medusa* and *Velalla* of this type then under construction by Fiat San Giorgio. Apparently the team was impressed with what they saw and this, coupled with the increased stability and improved seakeeping qualities possible with a double hull design, led to the placing of an order with Scotts' in December 1911 for a submarine (*S1*) of the Laurenti type engined (2 shafts) with Scott-Fiat diesel machinery. Orders for *S2* and *S3* followed in June 1913.

In the wake of visits to Italian and other shipyards and the accompanying discussion on the merits, or otherwise, of a double hulled concept the Admiralty called together the Submarine Committee to make further recommendations on future submarine designs, taking into account the needs of the fleet. Amongst other proposals in February 1912 the committee advocated the building of an 'overseas' submarine of double hull design capable of 20kts on the surface and of a brief burst at high speed while submerged. With a surface displacement of about 1000 the proposed vessel was to be considerably larger than 'overseas' submarines of the 'E' class then under construction while a ship shaped hull would contribute to the sea keeping qualities necessary for extended passage on the surface. The weapon fit was to include two bow, two beam and two astern torpedo tubes.

Vickers were invited to submit their proposals for an 'overseas' submarine aligning to this specification but it soon became apparent that they would be unable to meet the demand for 20kts surface speed. Despite this limitation, the sketch design for a partial double hulled submarine of 1270 tons surface displacement was accepted and in March 1913 the keel of the vessel, to be named *Nautilus*, was laid at Barrow. Machinery design aligned with contemporary practice and for surface propulsion the twin screws were driven by Vickers single acting 12-cylinder diesel engines each of 1850bhp, enlarged versions of the heavy oil engines fitted in the 'D' and 'E' class submarines. Already, however, doubts had been expressed concerning the reliability of untried engines of this size and output with the result that the Admiralty decided to look once again at the possibility of some alternative design to meet the requirements laid down by the Submarine Committee. Thus, while Vickers were developing *Nautilus* design, an approach had been made, through the agency of Scotts', to Fiat San Giorgio in order to establish what Signor Laurenti might be able to offer in answer to the staff requirement.

DESIGN OF SWORDFISH
In view of the high power called for the Fiat company was reluctant to recommend the employment of diesel engines and as an alternative Laurenti produced the sketch design for an 856-ton partial double hulled submarine of similar configuration to the twin screw Scott-Laurenti 'S' class but propelled on the surface by geared turbine steam machinery developing 4000shp for an estimated 18kts.

The order for the Royal Navy's first steam submarine, to be named *Swordfish*, was placed with Scotts' Shipbuilding Co on 8 August 1913, only five months after that for *Nautilus* had been placed with Vickers. The eventual designed developed by Scotts worked out somewhat heavier, at 932 tons surface displacement, than that conceived by Signor Laurenti but the leading dimensions remained unchanged, the overall length being 231ft 3in and the beam 22ft 11in. The propulsion machinery for surface drive comprised a Parsons geared impulse-reaction turbine set of 2000shp coupled to each shaft and taking superheated steam at 250psi from the single Yarrow boiler. As a result of the increased displacement, however, the estimated endurance for the parent Fiat-Laurenti design of 3500nm at 10kts on one engine only was stated by her builders to have been reduced to 3000miles at 8.5kts; on the other hand no reference has been seen to other than the designed surface speed of 18kts although, in the absence of any trials results, this figure cannot be confirmed and in all probability was never achieved. Astern turbines on each shaft were built into the low pressure turbine casings.

Diving was centrally controlled via a telemotor system plus an electric drive for housing the funnel and closing the valve to seal the boiler uptake. Shutting down the boiler and preparations for diving occupied about 1¼ minutes including the change over to electric

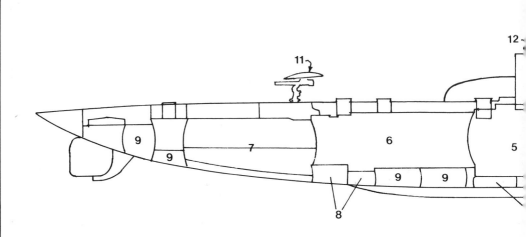

General arrangement of *Swordfish* as built:
1 Forward torpedo room, **2** Forward battery, **3** Broadside
torpedo room, **4** Control room, **5** Boiler room, **6** Engine room,
7 After battery, **8** Oil fuel, **9** Ballast tanks, **10** Conning tower,
11 Disappearing gun mounting, **12** Funnel.

*Based on Admiralty draughts (NMM) dated 1917, drawn by
John Roberts*

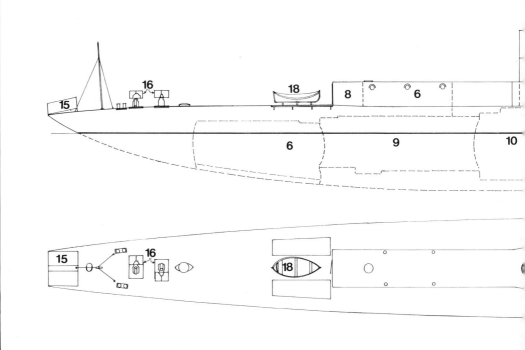

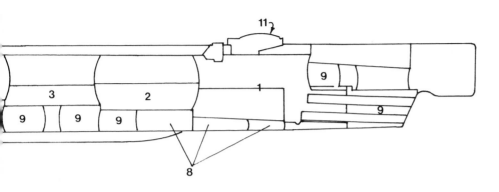

Swordfish as converted to a surface patrol boat.
1 20in searchlight, **2** Galley, **3** 4in gun, **4** Funnel, **5** Galley, **6** Crew accommodation, **7** Officers' smoking room, **8** Engine room hatch/vent, **9** Engine room, **10** Boiler room, **11** Control room, **12** Wardroom, **13** CO's cabin, **14** Officers' bathroom, **15** Depth-charge chutes, (3 Type D depth charges in each), **16** Depth-charge thrower, **17** 20ft collapsible boat, **18** 10ft collapsible boat.

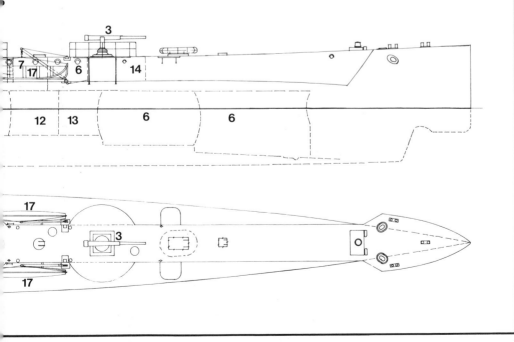

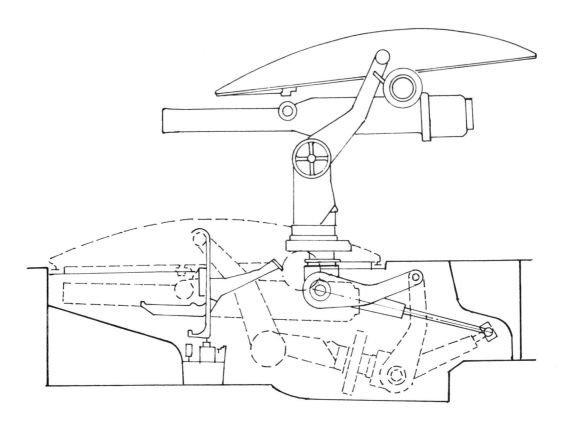

Disappearing 3in gun mounting as fitted in *Swordfish*
Drawn by John Roberts

drive. Submerged the two main motors together developed a total of 1400bhp to give a maximum speed of about 10kts, the endurance in service being some 60nm at 6kts. There were two battery sections each of 64 cells.

The *Swordfish* design, based on Laurenti principles, incorporated a double hull for about 75% of the total length and provided for a ship-shaped upper structure with a broad weatherdeck. This configuration needs to be compared with the single hulled saddle tank design of the 'E' classes which were given only a narrow free flooding casing by way of superstructure. The early 'E' class (*E1* to *E8*) had been the first British submarines with internal watertight bulkheads of which there were two. Later vessels of the class had three but in the Laurenti designed 'S' class and *Swordfish* there were no fewer than ten and seven bulkheads respectively, thus stressing the importance ascribed to subdivision and watertight integrity in Italian submarine design.

The torpedo outfit comprised two 21in torpedo tubes forward, stepped one above the other and set well back from the stem in a cut-up from the keel to preserve the fine lines of the bow, and four 18in tubes amidships, two mounted on each beam. Reload torpedoes were carried for each tube. Two 3in guns on disappearing mountings housed beneath watertight hoods to maintain the streamlined form completed the weapon fit. These were brought to the firing position when required by the action of hydraulic rams.

CONSTRUCTION AND TRIALS

Swordfish was not laid down until the last day of February 1914, a little more than five months before the nation went to war against Germany. Thereafter construction work lagged while resources were diverted to matters of more immediate importance, as also was the case at Barrow where the diesel engined *Nautilus* suffered an even more protracted period of gestation. Eventually *Swordfish* was put afloat on 18 March 1916, the process of fitting out being presumably well advance since this stage was completed some four months later in July of that same year. In view of the lack of any operational experience in the working of a steam submarine, comprehensive basin trials were carried out before the vessel left Greenock involving, initially, closing down for diving while remaining surfaced to permit monitoring of engine and boiler room ambient temperatures and atmospheric conditions. Once these factors had been established with safety of personnel in mind, basin diving trials followed and thereafter trials were undertaken at sea proving that

HM Submarine *S1* (ex-*Swordfish*) during trials in the Gareloch. The hood for the forward 3in gun is clearly visible.

Author's Collection

conditions in general differed little from those in contemporary diesel engined submarines.

SAFETY MEASURES

An interesting aspect of the design of this craft and the other Scott-Laurenti submarines was the attention paid to emergency arrangements, a feature which appears to have received scant consideration in the design of contemporary British, ie Vickers, submarines. Indicator buoys and a telephone buoy, capable of being released from within the submarine in the event of an accident, were provided together with external air connections and a charged high-pressure air line which could be used to refresh the air in any manned compartment or the living spaces. In addition the main ballast tanks could be blown from not only a valve in the control room but also via valves in the forward and after ends.

DESIGN PROBLEMS

In the meantime *Swordfish* had been commission on 28 April 1916 under the command of Commander Geoffrey Layton RN, being at the same time renamed *S1*[3] although no doubt her ship's company and others continued to use her former title. Acceptance followed on 21 July 1916 but in fact, although nominally a unit of 2nd Submarine Flotilla[4] based on HMS *Dolphin* at Gosport, trials continued in an attempt to rectify various defects and design problems. In particular, surfacing was accompanied by a marked loss of stability, presumably due to inability to clear rapidly the controlled free flood spaces forming the upper part of the double hull structure. Despite the strenuous efforts made by design staff and the ship's company to bring *S1* to an operational state, stability problems continued to beset post-acceptance trials, but these material matters apart, there remained also the question of how should she be employed! Too slow to work with the Fleet should any such requirement arise, her potential value as a warship was in practice no better than that of contemporary 'E' and 'G' class diesel engined 'overseas' submarines, in addition to which the complexity of her diving arrangements compared unfavourably with the simple drill practised in the former classes. Actual diving times are not known but certainly preparations for diving in

S1 took, as stated above, about 1¼ minutes.

Five months of post-acceptance trials failed to resolve outstanding problems and eventually *S1* was laid up at Gosport pending a decision as to her future.

CONVERSION TO PATROL CRAFT

Early in 1917, with the German submarine assault becoming increasingly dangerous in so far as Britain's shipping interests were concerned, there was a desperate need for anti-submarine vessels and presumably this prompted the seemingly unlikely conversion of *S1* for a surface patrol role. Structural alterations included the addition of a raised forecastle together with a bridge and wheelhouse, and the provision of a taller fixed funnel. To what extent the submarine features were stripped out is not known but presumably the battery was replaced by ballast and such equipment as the hydroplane gear deleted. Likewise the 'disappearing' gun mountings and the torpedo tubes together with their associated fittings were removed, the hull openings being blanked, and a weapon fit appropriate to her new role installed. This outfit comprised depth charges and a pair of 3in, 12pdr, guns on high angle (HA) mountings. Her steam plant remained unchanged.

In July 1917, *S1* reverted to her former name as HMS *Swordfish* and on 10 August she recommissioned at Portsmouth as a patrol vessel. Acceptance followed on completion of trials in October 1917 but it was 24 January 1918 before she joined 1st Destroyer Flotilla, based at Portsmouth, to become operational for the first time, albeit her metamorphosis complete in the guise of an anti-submarine patrol vessel. Her appearance failed to belie her former role, however, for despite the built up structure her hull retained the marked tumble-home begat by her well rounded lines.

DISPOSAL

Little is known of her subsequent wartime career, although presumably it involved no contact with the enemy. *Swordfish* remained a lone oddity[5], taken up for her new role when there was a pressing need for anti-submarine craft of any kind, once hostilities ceased the requirement faded and she found no place in the post-war Fleet. Taken out of service on 30 October 1918, a few days before the Armistice, *Swordfish* had disappeared from the Navy List by January 1919 although in fact she lay at Portsmouth until July 1922 when eventually she was acquired, presumably for breaking up, by

The patrol vessel HMS *Swordfish*
(ex-HMS Submarine *S1*, ex-*Swordfish*)
awaiting breaking-up together with the
submarine *G14*.

IWM

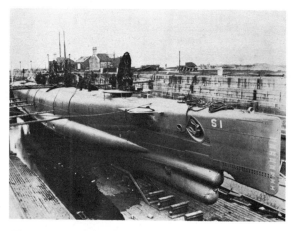

The submarine *S1* (ex-*Swordfish*) in dry
dock showing the forward 3in gun,
partially housed, and the forward 21in
torpedo tubes set back from the stem in
the cut-up from the keel.

MoD

H G Pounds of Portsmouth. However, this was not to
be and in the following year Pounds resold the hulk to
Hayes of Porthcawl.

Swordfish had seen little service but on the other
hand much had been learned and in particular the
arrangements for closing the boiler uptake and housing
the funnel formed the basis for the system employed in
the 24kt (surface) 'fleet' submarines of the 'K' class.
She represented an early attempt to achieve a high surface speed utilising the limited resources of the day but,
as was again to be demonstrated in the design of the 'K'
class, the fossil fuelled steam submarine with its complexity was not the answer. Such craft took too long to
dive and also to restore boiler pressure on surfacing.
Too large, too vulnerable and lacking any clearly
defined role, *S1* (ex-*Swordfish*) and her successors represent, at most, an interesting exercise in submarine
design, for there was little they might do which could
not be undertaken at less expense and with greater efficiency by other means.

1 Acquired with Holland's patents by the Electric Boat Co of
New York in 1897.
2 Cdr A Addison, Cdr C Little, Lt-Cdr H Lawrence, Lt-Cdr M
Nasmith, Lt-Cdr C Craven (of Vickers) and Engineer Cdr R
Skelton.
3 The Scott-Laurenti design diesel submarine *S1* had been
transferred to the Italian Government in July 1915, followed
by *S2* and *S3* in September of that same year.
4 Subsequently transferred to 6th Submarine Flotilla.
5 The aged petrol engined submarines *B6, 7, 8, 9* and *11* of
1906 were converted to surface patrol boats in Malta for
service in the Adriatic in 1917 being renumbered *S6* to *S11*
respectively.

The Japanese Super Battleship Strategy Part 3

By Hans Lengerer

Michael Wünschmann's 1:1200 scale model of *Yamato* in 1945.
Jürgen Peters

STABILITY AND STRENGTH

Fukuda used plans A 140 from A to D and further as his reference. The idea of protecting the magazine more strongly than the engine and boiler rooms, which Ezaki had introduced in the design of the *Takao* class, disappeared again in the development of these designs, as it was at variance with Hiraga's ideas. In October 1935 the Fourth Fleet was caught in a typhoon during the autumn manoeuvres, and many of the warships were damaged;

this incident showed up the inadequate strength of the hulls designed by Fujimoto. Incidentally, Fujimoto's devoted pupil Ezaki was then dismissed from his post, and was about to be moved to the Naval dockyard at Kure. It was only the opposition of the Admiralty staff that reversed the decision. We can only presume that the Admiralty staff wished to have a successor to continue Fujimoto's work. Nevertheless, Ezaki was 'put on ice', as he was given the task of working on the examination of hull strengths, and he was never again to produce a design for a new warship.

Fujimoto always strove to embrace new theories of shipbuilding, and he designed warships whose safety

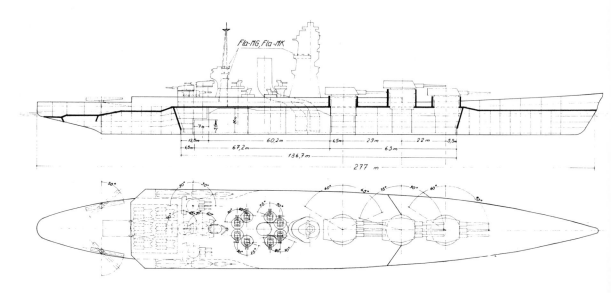

Sketch design A140/A.

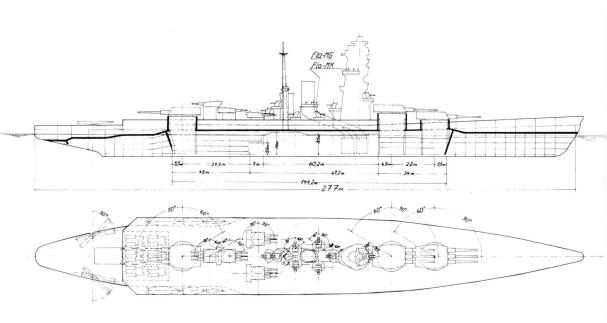

Sketch design A140/A1.

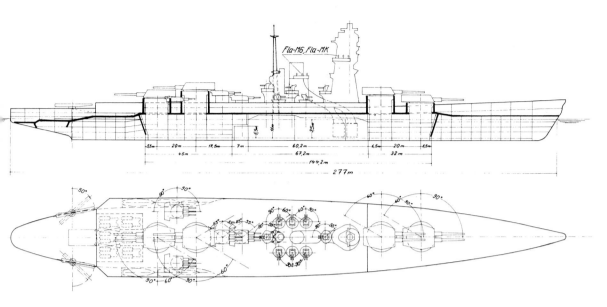

Sketch design A140/A2.

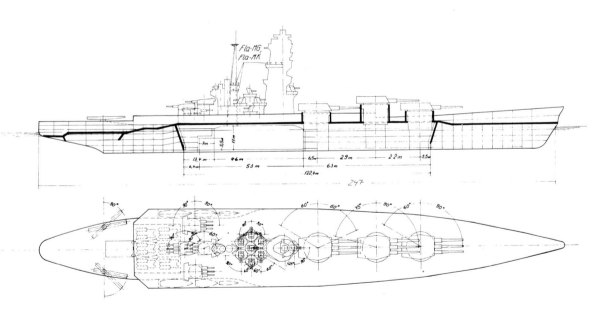

Sketch design A140/B.

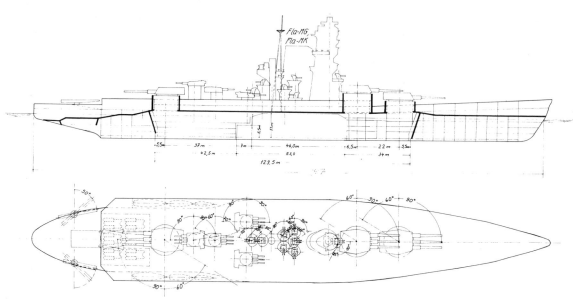

Sketch design A140/B1.

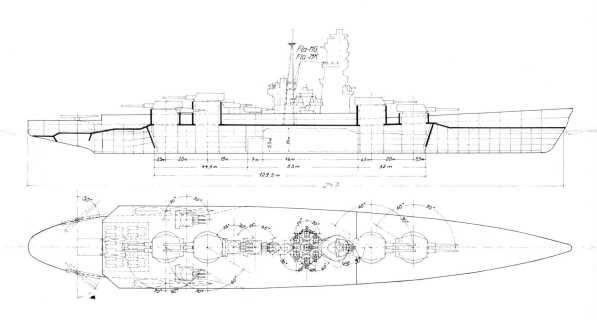

Sketch design A140/B2.

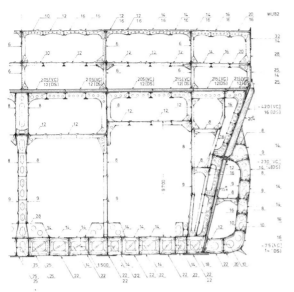

Midships section of *Yamato* design (9 March 1936) showing thickness' of plating in mm

Drawings by Michael Wünschmann from material supplied by the author

margin was reduced to the absolute minimum, with the aim of obtaining ships with superior battle power to those of foreign opponents. Unfortunately for him the reserves of safety were not up to the loads placed on the vessels in terms of stability and hull strength.

It is possible that he foresaw the occurrence of the shipbuilding catastrophes already mentioned (in fact it was the Admiralty staff which forced the technical experts into a corner with its ever more extreme demands, and had dismissed Hiraga, when he refused to fulfill these demands), and was therefore very eager to cooperate with the Admiralty staff in introducing new technologies. But the Naval chiefs were suspicious of this cooperation, and forbade consultation on design details between the Naval design office and the Admiralty staff; a system which Fujimoto had practised so skilfully with Ezaki. Hence it became impossible for the engineers in the design office to exchange their views frankly with those of the Admiralty staff.

Hiraga, who at this time was a reserve officer and was called up as temporary advisor, ordered Fukuda to remove Fujimoto's ideas one after another from the design of the new battleship. Hiraga was a friend of the Navy Minister and the chief of the Admiralty staff, and pressed them hard to adopt his ideas, exploiting the mistrust of the shipbuilding officers that they harboured at that time.

FUKUDA'S DESIGNS
Designs A, A1, A2, B, B1 and B2, and also C and D, were Fukuda's, and are shown in Table 13. They show the superiority of his plans in respect of the separation of the gun turrets according to orthodox theory. This was in contrast to the Admiralty staffs, view which insisted on their concentration forward as in the British *Nelson* class. This arrangement followed Fujimoto's philosophy, a solution which he considered to be the only possible means of facilitating conversion to 20in guns.

On 10 March 1935, plan A 140 was fixed, the characteristics of which make clear the influence of Hiraga as adviser and the connection with his plan for the *Kongo* replacement ship and his design of 1929: superstructure massed together in the centre, direct system of protection, full-length armour deck, inclined side armour, integration of the armour material into the hull shell, and the aircraft and hangar arrangement. Eight plans, namely those shown in Table 13, were completed in time for the High (level) Technical Conference held on 1 April 1935. Of these 'A' and 'B' were discussed principally to compare turbine and combined diesel/turbine propulsion. Finally on 25 May 1935, the ratio of turbine/diesel was accepted at 1:1. On 1 April 1935 the plans for the *Yamato* class were accepted.

In all of Fukuda's designs the displacement was too great, and many further trial designs (J, K, I, F) were suggested (Tables 15 and 16). During this period the advantages and disadvantages of the various designs were compared, and discussions held on gun turret distribution and ship speed. Range was reduced (16kts/7,200nm), and eventually the Navy's design office received the Admiralty staff's approval for the separate turret arrangement, low speed (27-28kts) and restricted range.

The 'F' plan was preferred by the Navy Design office. In this case the vital region was made shorter by the arrangement of the secondary gun turrets above the heavy artillery turrets. Hiraga, on the other hand, was in favour of the 'I' project with 10 guns in two triple and two twin turrets.

TURBINE/DIESEL DRIVE
On 10 September 1935 Fukuda explained the pros and cons of the various designs, after which the basic 'F' design and the specific design F4 was accepted; in this case the waterline length had been increased by 8m. It is no known whether this conference took place within the Navy Design office, or whether it was a High (level) Technical Conference. In contrast with Fujimoto's strategy, this design featured the heavy gun turrets separated fore and aft, but at least it featured mixed turbine/diesel propulsion. This hybrid type of drive was still a feature when the High Technical Conference accepted the plan A 140 F5 on 20 July 1936, which foresaw a standard displacement of 65,200 tons, a speed of 27kts and 9-46cm guns. In the end, Hiraga successfully persuaded the Navy chiefs, including the Navy Minister, to delete all the diesel engines, with the backing of the later Vice-Admiral Ryutaro Shibuya, who at that time was chief of the Fifth (Engine-) Division of the Navy Design office, and was responsible for the design of the engine installation of the *Yamato*. In March 1937 the 100% turbine drive system was accepted. At this time the final design foresaw a trial displacement of 68,200 tons and a speed of 27kts.

TABLE 13: FUKUDA'S BATTLESHIP PLANS, PROPOSED ON 1 APRIL 1935

	A140-A	A140-B	A140-C	A140-D	A140 A1	A2	B1	B2
DIMENSIONS								
Displacement (tons):	68,000	60,000	58,000	55,000	68,000	68,000	60,000	60,000
Length, wl(m):	277	247	247	247	277	277	247	247
Beam, wl(m):	40.4	40.4	40.4	40.4	40.4	40.4	40.4	40.4
Draught, trials (m):	10.4	10.3	10.2	10.1	10.4	10.4	10.3	10.3
MACHINERY								
HP (diesel):	68,000	140,000	105,000	140,000	68,000	68,000	140,000	140,000
HP (turbines):	132,000	–	–	–	132,000	132,000	–	–
HP (total):	200,000	140,000	105,000	140,000	200,000	200,000	140,000	140,000
Speed (kts):	30	28	26	29	30	30	28	28
Endurance (kts/nm):	18/9200	18/9200	18/9200	18/9200	18/9200	18/9200	18/9200	18/9200
Boilers:	8	2 aux	2 aux	2 aux	8	8	2 aux	2 aux
ARMOUR (length-m)								
Aft magazine:	6.5	6.5	6.5	6.5	43	45	42.5	44.5
Engine room:	67.2	53	50	53	67.2	67.2	53	53
For'd mag:	63	63	63	63	39	34	34	32
Total:	136.7	122.5	119.5	122.5	144.2	144.2	129.5	129.5
Total on wl:	142.7	128.5	125.5	128.5	150.2	150.2	135.5	138.5
ARMOUR (height, ft-in)								
Side (at 25°):	17-6	17-6	17-6	15-5	17-6	17-6	17-6	17-6
Side (at 17.5°):	14-0	14-0	14-0	12-5	14-0	14-0	14-0	14-0
ARMOUR (thickness-in)								
Deck:	9-5	9-5	9-5	8-5	9-5	9-5	9-5	9-5
Turret roofs and CT:	23	23	23	18	23	23	23	23
Lower deck fore and aft:	3	3	3	3	3	3	3	3
ARMAMENT								
Main armament arrangement:	3×3 for'd	3×3 for'd	3×3 for'd	3×3 for'd	2×3 for'd, 1×3 aft	2×2 for'd, 2×2 aft	2×3 for'd, 1×3 aft	2×2 for'd 2×2 aft
Main armament:	9-46cm	9-46cm	9-46cm	9-40cm	9-46cm	8-46cm	9-46cm	8-46cm
Secondary armament:	12-15.5cm (4×3) – all designs							
AA armament:	12-12.7cm AA (6×2) – all designs							
AMMUNITIONS STOWAGE (rpg)								
Main:				130				
Secondary:				200/150	all designs			
AA:				200				
STABILITY DATA								
KG(m):				12.5				
GM(m):				2.9				
OG(m):				2.0	all designs			
Angle of maximum stability:				67°				
Rolling period:				16 sec				
WEIGHTS (tons)								
Hull:	18,000	16,100	15,600	14,700	18,000	18,000	16,100	16,100
Fittings:	2150	1900	1850	1750	2150	2150	1900	1900
Intended fittings (fixed) (1)	680	570	520	460	680	680	570	570
Intended provisions (moveable): (2)	820	730	460	555	820	820	730	730
Armour:	24,340	21,300	20,800	18,085	25,340	26,587	22,320	23,547
Guns:	11,900	11,900	11,900	11,900	11,900	11,161.5	11,900	11,161.5
Torpedoes:	60	50	50	50	60	60	50	50
Electrics:	880	700	680	650	880	880	700	700
Aircraft:	90	90	90	90	90	90	90	90
Machinery:	5580	4300	3750	4300	5580	5580	4300	4300
Fuel:	3650	2600	2550	2500	3650	3650	2600	2600
Water:	180	25	25	25	25	180	25	25
Water in hydraulic system:	150	150	150	150	150	150	150	150
Reserve:	200	200	200	200	200	200	200	200
Total:	68,680	60,615	58,800	55,395	69,200	70,188.5	61,635	62,123.5

TABLE 13: FUKUDA'S BATTLESHIP PLANS, PROPOSED ON 1 APRIL 1935

WEIGHT DISTRIBUTION OF GUN TURRETS (tons)

Type:	Triple Turrets in Designs A, B, C, D, A1 & B1	Twin Turrets in Designs A2 & B2
Turrets:	2654.5 × 3 = 7963.5	1869 × 4 = 7426
Ammunition:	753 × 3 = 2259	502 × 4 = 2008
Others:	1677.5	1677.5
Total:	11,900	11,161.6

Notes: (1) Fixtures (proper).
(2) Fixtures (consumable).

TABLE 15: FUKADA'S EXPERIMENTAL PLANS

Designation	Date	Note	Length (ft)	Disp. (tons)	Main Armament (46cm)	Speed (kts)	Immunity Zone (m)	Radius of Action (kts/nm)	Secondary Armament
–	10 March 1935	Displacement too great	900	69,900	L/50, 50° elevation, (3×3)	31	20,000 30,000	18/8000	15.5cm (4×3) or 20cm (4×2)
A	1 April 1935	Displacement still too great	–	65,833 68,000	L/45, 45° elevation, (3×3)	28 39	20,000- 30,000	–	–
GI-A	30 July 1935	Displacement rather low for 18in armament	–	61,000	L/45, 45° elevation, (3×3)	26	20,000- 27,000	16/6600	
K	1 August 1935	Offensive/defensive qualities not satis- factorily balanced	–	50,059	L/45, 45° elevation, (2×3, 1×2)	29	20,000- 27,000 against 16in guns	16/6600	3×3 (1 for'd, 2 aft)
Go-A	19 August 1935	Favoured by Gunreibu (Admiralty Staff)	–	65,450	L/45, 45° elevation, (3×3)	28	20,000- 27,000 against 16in guns	16×7200	–
J	30 July 1935	16in guns	–	52,000	L/53 ×3)	27.5	18,000- 27,000	16/7200	–
J	30 July 1935	16in guns	–	53,000	L/53 (3×3)	28	–	–	–

Notes: L/50 = Length of gun barrel 50 calibres. 45.6cm, L/50 – these guns were not feasible owing to weight and technical problems. Hence 40cm, L/45 Type 94 guns (actual calibre 45.6cm) with elevation angle of 45° were adopted. Weight of double 46cm turret–1934 tons, barrel 183 tons (later 177 tons); weight of triple turret–2585 tons. 40cm L/53; Weight of double turret–1360 tons; barrel 145 tons (later 141 tons); Weight of triple turret 1911 tons. For comparison, *Nagato*'s turrets weighed 1131 tons; barrel 10.25 tons. Design weight was greater than expected, but could still be reduced. If the barrel spacing was reduced, there was a weight saving, but closer than 6.07 calibres was not feasible.

TABLE 16: FUKADA'S EXPERIMENTAL PLANS (POSITION ON 10.9.35) – BATTLESHIPS WITH 18in GUNS

	Design G-A	Design Gz-A	Design Go-A	Design FI	Design I
Standard Displacement (tons):	57,286	58,960	60,824	47,965	60,620
Trials Displacement (tons):	61,600	63,450	65,450	62,450	65,050
Length(m):	245.5	262	268	259.5	268
Beam(m):			38.9		
Draught(m):			10.4	all designs	
Armament:			9–46cm 12–15.5cm 12–12.7cm		
Main Armament Arrangement:	3×3 (for'd)	3×3 (for'd)	3×3 (for'd)	2×3 (for'd) 1×3 (aft)	1×2 (for'd & aft) 1×3 (for d & aft)
Secondary Armament Arrangement:	4×3 (aft)	4×3 (aft)	4×3 (aft)	1×3 (for'd & aft)	1×3 (for'd & aft)
Machinery: *Diesel (bhp)*	55,000	70,000	70,000	70,000	70,000
turbine (shp)	60,000	73,000	75,000	73,000	73,000
Total (hp)	115,000	143,000	175,000	143,000	143,000
Speed:	26	28	28	28	28
Endurance:	16/6600	16/7200	16/6600	16/7200	16/7200
Immunity zone (m):	20,000-27,000	20,000-27,000 (side 18in, deck 8.8in)	20,000-30,000 (deck 9.75in, side 18in (15in))	20,000-30,000	20,000-27,000
Ammunition Stowage (rpg):	–	–	100 (46cm) 150 (15.5cm)	–	–

Profile of forward section of the *Yamato* model.
Jürgen Peters

Originally the plan was to buy the patent for the diesel engines from Germany. However, this plan was later changed in favour of independent development on account of the high price demanded for the licence. In fact, at the time the building of the *Yamato* began, development of the diesel engine was not sufficiently advanced.

It is an ironic fact that the *Yamato* could not be used from Truk, a remote support base of the Combined Fleet where there was a shortage of fuel, in the most critical phase of the battle for Guadalcanal. Instead of this, the seaplane carrier *Nisshin*, which was powered by the diesel engines which had been planned for the *Yamato* and which had a poor reputation, became a most valuable ship, as she was the only high-speed vessel which was able to transport heavy army weapons to Guadalcanal. (The use of diesel propulsion in the *Taigei* proved to be a disappointment, and it was decided not to use diesel propulsion for battleships – see above. However, the seaplane carrier *Nisshin* was selected as a test-bed in order to carry out further studies of this means of propulsion. This experiment later proved to be a considerable success, apart from the problem of smoke. When in autumn 1942 the Navy wanted to force the Americans out of Guadalcanal, all available fast transport ships were mobilised for the transport of soldiers and military equipment. Because the speed of these ships was less than 20kts at that time, and the destroyers could not transport heavy army weapons, *Nisshin* was the only ship which could operate with the destroyers at a speed of 28kts. To sum up, it can be said that the use of diesel propulsion had not presented any disastrous difficulties, and would have been valuable.)

CONCLUSION

The history of Japanese warships has only been written by Hiraga's successors, and the capabilities of the ships have not always been evaluated accurately. The most important thing is to judge by common standards, said the now deceased Admiral Tomioka, one time staff officer in the planning division of the Admiralty staff, in support of Akira Endo, whose material was used as the basis for this essay. He continued: 'Books which are written by shipbuilding specialists do no more than reflect their own standpoints and opinions'. Vice-Admiral Ryutaro Shibuya said to Endo, that 'gigantic complex structures such as warships are not invented by a genius; the *Yamato* was the end product of the work of many over a period of many years,' and he added that 'technology itself does not make progress'. He was the

last chief of the design office of the Navy, and after the war he wrote that the *Yamato* class, had half of their propulsion system consisted of diesel engines, would have been able to take part in the Guadalcanal operation, and that *Shinano*, which was later converted to an aircraft carrier, would not so easily have been sunk.

Yamato was by no means an 'unsinkable' ship. She had only 1147 watertight compartments compared with 1089 in the 40% smaller *Nagato*. She should have had around 1600 in order to achieve the same degree of 'unsinkability' as *Nagato*. In fact she was short of this figure by around 30%. This was the result of Hiraga's excessive reliance on direct armour, because he could not accept Fujimoto's concept of indirect protection.

With the decision to opt for pure turbine propulsion, the last characteristic feature of Fujimoto's strategic planning vanished, and the design of *Yamato* must from this time onward be considered as out-dated. For this reason the Imperial HQ ordered Admiral Takao Kurita to adopt the heavy cruiser *Atago* as his flagship for the 1944 Battle of Leyte instead of the slow *Yamato*. Kurita declined, claiming that his flagship would be sunk, and chose *Yamato* instead, with her higher level of 'unsinkability'. Various historians share the view that Kurita would not have been so enthusiastic about the (useless) attack on the escort carriers, but instead would have headed straight into Leyte Gulf without deviating, if he had been on board a fast cruiser at the time of the Battle of Samar.

It is bound to be a severe shock to a nation to see its ships capsize in a storm, and to break up because of inadequate strength. And yet the measures required to put matters right represented no great technical problem; the real problem was how to overcome the enormous amount of technical work entailed. At that time the Imperial Japanese Navy put great effort into the development of new technologies, in order to prepare itself for the coming international crisis. This was an urgent necessity. Japan was not a wealthy country, and she needed at all costs a long-term strategy. However absurd this may seem, this strategy was the replacement of and the increase in the gun calibre on battleships.

However, the sudden death of Fujimoto nipped all this in the bud, and designers lacking his far sighted strategy took over the planning for the *Yamato*, which subsequently proved to be a useless giant.

The Author would like to thank Mr Jiro Itani for supplying material used in these articles and Mrs Tomoko Rehm-Takahara for translating from the collection of Mr Akira Endo.

Profile of after section of the *Yamato* model.

Jürgen Peters

British Naval Guns 1880~1945 No 10

By NJM Campbell

The cruiser *Blenheim*, and her sister ship *Blake*, carried the same main armament as the *Aurora* class (two 9.2in and ten 6in BL guns).
CPL

6in BL Mk I This gun was Elswick Pattern 'D' and 19 were purchased for the Navy in 1879–80. The construction comprised a steel 'A' tube, into which the breech block screwed, a layer of 3 wrought iron coils and a second layer of 2 wrought iron coils with a forged wrought iron trunnion ring between them. On chase hooping, part of the 'A' tube and the foremost inner coil were removed, and 2 steel hoops, extending to the muzzle, shrunk-on; another steel hoop being added as a new outer layer. Elswick cup obturation was used. Unlike all

The cruiser *Galatea*, of the *Aurora* class, carried a secondary battery ten 6in BL guns, equally disposed along each broadside. These guns were Mk III, IV or VI, the types being interchangeable. She and her sisters were rearmed with 6in QFC guns at the end of the nineteenth century.
CPL

other British 6in guns, the shell was 80 instead of 100lb.

Originally 14 guns were to be mounted in the corvette *Constance*, then her sister *Cordelia* and finally in the rearmed *Rover* on Armstrong Broadside – AB Mk I –mountings with 13° elevation and 8° depression. A note from the second half of 1889 says that *Rovers* were to be chase hooped. Mk I guns were also recorded in the following gunboats for limited periods – *Curlew*, *Landrail*, *Blazer*, *Bulldog* and *Kite*.

6in BL Mk II A Fraser design from Woolwich, of which 143 were made, consisting of a thick steel barrel, taking the screw breech block, and a coiled wrought iron jacket which was welded to the forged trunnion ring. Cup obturation was again used. As would be expected, there were several accidents, with this construction, 5ft of the chase being blown off in the corvette *Active* in November 1884. For some reason only 31 guns were chase hooped. This involved shortening the barrel by 12in, for reasons of balance, and shrinking-on 5 steel hoops from jacket to muzzle. After a gun burst in *Cordelia* in June 1891 the whole lot were demoted to drill purpose only, and were withdrawn by the end of 1892. To increase their usefulness 43 were converted to QF drill guns. Mk IIP indicated a percussion lock and MK IIPA had special breech fittings to suit the corvettes *Heroine* and *Satellite*.

Mk II guns were recorded in the following ships – *Agamemmon*, *Ajax*, *Hotspur*, *Raleigh*, *Boadicea*, *Bacchante*, *Euryalus*, *Volage*, *Active*, *Canada*, *Cordelia*, *Comus*, *Satellite*, *Heroine*, *Hyacinth*, *Royalist*, *Rapid*, *Emerald*, *Dolphin*, *Pelican*, *Wanderer*, *Wild Swan*, *Sphinx*, though it is not certain that all actually received them.

Chase hooped guns were apparently limited to all 10 in both *Volage* and *Active*, 3 of the 10 in *Cordelia* and the 2 in *Ajax*.

Mountings were either AB Mk I, Vavasseur Broadside, VB Mk I, allowing 16° elevation and 6° depression or VCP Mk I or 1* allowing 20° elevation and 7° depression, except that the battleships *Agamemnon* and *Ajax* had Albini CP mountings with the gun recoiling in an arc of a circle, and with 10° depression – 15° elevation.

6in BL Mks III, IV and VI These guns were interchangeable, though Mk III was 0.47 cals shorter than the other two, and mixed batteries were not uncommon. The Navy totals were 112 – Mk III, 326 – Mk IV and 113 – Mk VI; there were also 65 Mk IV and about 88 Mk BVI land service guns used for coast defence, some being semi-mobile siege guns particularly for India.

All guns were of steel construction. The original Mk IIIs were not chase hooped, and had an 'A' tube with a breech piece taking the breech block and a hoop, linked by a two part key ring. Over these were 5 hoops including the trunnion hoop. On chase hooping the first layer comprised the breech piece and 6 hoops to the muzzle, and the second layer 5 hoops and a new trunnion ring interlocking with the breech piece and the hoop next to it, and also with the trunnions 4.4ins nearer the muzzle to restore balance. By July 1888 40 guns were still not chase hooped and 31 of these were afloat in the battle-

PARTICULARS OF 6IN GUNS

	6in Mk I	6in Mk II	6in Mk III, IV, VI	6in QFC
Weight incl BM(tons)	4.065	4.081	4.454 (III)	5.107
Weight chase hooped	4.095	4.435	4.999 (III)	
			5.113 (IV, VI)	
Length oa (in)	165.6	165.5	170.7 (III)	166.55 (orig. III)
Length chase hooped	162.6	153.5	170.7 (III)	
			173.5 (IV, VI)	169.1 (orig. IV, VI)
Length bore (cals)	26.3	26.0	25.53 (III)	26.22 (orig. III)
Length chase hooped	25.53	24.0	25.53 (III)	
			26.0 (IV, VI)	26.64 (orig. IV, VI)
Chamber (cu in)	1155	1364	1364	832
Chamber length (in)	27.4	26.75	26.75	23.65
Projectile (lb)	80	100	100	100
Charge (lb)/type	34/SP	36/EXE	48/EXE	29.75/EXE
			14.75/Cord 20	13.25/Cord 30
Muzzle Velocity (fs)	1880	1672	1960	1913 (2061 Cord)
Range (yds/elevation)	7025/13°	7590/15°	8830/15°	8625/15°
				9275/15° Cord

ships *Rupert* and *Bellerophon*, the cruisers *Leander* and *Phaeton*, corvette *Tourmaline* and gunboat *Bulldog*. In this condition the guns were limited to ¾ charges, and were soon replaced in all but *Bellerophon*.

Mk IV was built with an 'A' tube/breech piece, taking breech block, 'B' tube, 3 hoops to muzzle/jacket in one piece with trunnions, and interlocking with 'B' tube, 1 hoop. Mk VI was the same except that a second 'B' tube replaced the 3 hoops to the muzzle.

These guns were mounted in the following ships – battleships from *Colossus* class to *Victoria* and *Sans Pareil* – large cruisers of *Imperieuse*, *Aurora* and *Blake* classes – other cruisers *Calliope*, *Calypso*, *Leander* class, *Archer* class, *Mersey* class, *Medea* class and all *Apollo* class except *Aeolus*, *Brilliant* and *Iphigenia*. They also replaced Mk IIs in all ships except *Bacchante*, *Euryalus*, *Heroine* and *Wanderer* and were at least for a time in *Achilles*, *Bellerophon*, *Black Prince*, *Northumberland*, *Rupert*, *Champion*, *Cleopatra*, *Curacoa*, *Tourmaline*, *Curlew*, *Landrail* and the school gunboats *Blazer*, *Bulldog*, *Kite* and *Plucky*.

Mountings resembled those for Mk II guns but the Albini CP were replaced by VCP in c1892. New marks included VB Mk II and III allowing an elevation of 16° and depression to 7° and VCP Mk II with 20° elevation to 7° depression. AB mountings, unless strengthened, required ¾ charges.

Land service variants were Mk VIA covering 6 guns adapted for CP Mk I coast defence mountings, and the BLC – breech loading converted – series. These had single motion breech mechanism, a chamber volume of 1530c in and a bore length of 26.58cals. Muzzle velocity rose to 2177fs. BLC Mks I/IV and I/VI were trunnion-less for CP Mk IV coast defence mountings, and were also used as semi-mobile siege guns and as heavy field guns in the First World War. BLC Mk II/VI covered conversion of the 6 – Mk VIA guns and retained trunnions for CP Mk I mountings.

6in QFC The previous BL guns converted to take the the same cartridge cases and charges as the 6in/40cal QF. A total of 73 Mk III, 247 Mk IV and 81 Mk VI were altered and there were 8 different marks, though except in some specialised ordnance literature, they were always referred to as QFC only. The various marks were –

Mk I/IV and I/VI Elswick conversion design. Chamber and short bore liner to start of original rifling, or further if worn. The liner engaged screw threads cut on the breech piece and jacket and a breech ring was shrunk over the rear of the jacket.

Mk II/III, II/IV and II/VI Woolwich conversion design. Liner and breech bush in two parts. The liner was secured by a screw collar at the rear end of the 'A' tube and extended to the start of rifling, half way up the bore or to the muzzle depending on wear. Breech ring added.

Mk III/IV and III/VI Elswick conversion design. Like Mk II but different breech bush, pinned through the jacket and shorter breech ring.

Mk III/III Elswick conversion design – Like Mk II but differences in securing breech ring and liner.

QFC guns were mounted from 1895 in battleships from the *Colossus* class to the *Sans Pareil* (not *Victoria*) and in cruisers of the *Imperieuse*, *Aurora*, *Leander*, *Archer* (not *Serpent*), *Mersey* and *Medea* classes. They were also in the following, sometimes only briefly – *Agamemnon*, *Ajax*, *Rupert*, *Hotspur*, *Raleigh*, *Curlew*, *Landrail*, *Blazer*, *Bulldog*, *Kite*. A few survived to the First World War and were mounted in DAMS, while 2 were in Ft Bedford, Ascension Island.

Mountings were all of Vavasseur type and comprised VB Mk IC (+12°/–6°), VB Mk IIC and IIIC (+16°/–7°), VCP Mk IC (+16½°/–7°) and VCP Mk IIC (+20°/–7°). Fouling of the shot guide limited elevation to the figures in parentheses in VB Mk IC and VCP Mk IC.

6in BL Mk V This mark comprised 10 Elswick Pattern K[1] guns obtained for the defence of Hong Kong. They were of 30.58cal bore length and fired a 100lb shell at 1920fs. A number of identical or similar guns were purchased for the coast defence of Australia and New Zealand and were also mounted in the colonial gunboats *Gayundah*, *Paluma*, *Protector*, and *Albert*. A few Australian coast defence guns were converted to QFC with an MV of 2081fs.

LESSER KNOWN WARSHIPS OF THE KRIEGSMARINE

The Type 43 Minesweepers Part 1
by M J Whitley

Following the end of the First World War, Germany was allowed to retain a number of her wartime built minesweepers of the M16 type in order to clear the large numbers of mines still present in her coastal waters. These ships formed the backbone of the *Reichsmarine* and then the *Kriegsmarine* minesweeping forces between the wars with 25 surviving to see service during the Second World War. By the mid-1930s however, their replacement became imperative and a new design, designated 'Type 35' appeared; basically enlarged and

This photograph was captioned as the launching of *M601*, however, the number of the ship on the next berth is that of a Schichau-Elbing series vessel, it is possible therefore that this is actually *M801*.
Drüppel

modernised versions of the M16 type, the new ships displaced some 700 tons, were oil-fired and armed with two 10.5cm (4.1in) guns.

In design, they were broadly comparable with the contemporary *Halcyon* class minesweepers of the Royal Navy but they retained reciprocating machinery. *M1*, the first ship of the class, was laid down at the Stulcken yard in Hamburg in 1936, being commissioned on 1 September 1938. Thirty further units were authorised before the outbreak of war, construction being shared by four shipyards. Construction proceeded slowly, only one unit a month joining the Fleet, so by September 1939, only 12 ships had been completed.

At war with Britain once more, large contracts were

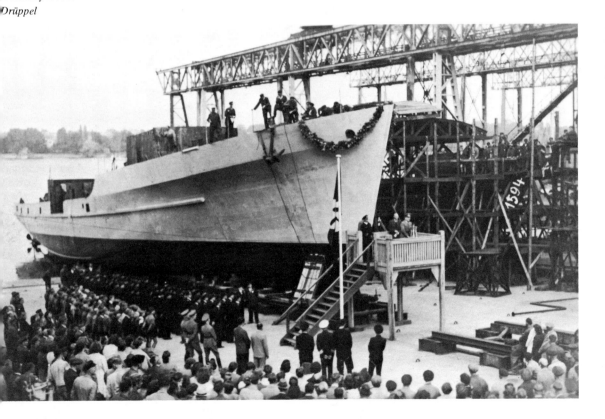

then placed; a total of ten yards being involved. Even so, rate of construction was still very tardy – one per month on average, for material shortages from 1940 caused many units to be suspended for long periods. Fortunately for the *Kriegsmarine*, losses were neglibible; in the first two years of the war only four ships were lost. Construction continued until 1944, the final unit joining the Fleet in May of that year, but after mid-1942 only seven more ships were completed.

This was because the *Kriegsmarine* soon found that it needed more minesweepers quickly and also that it was necessary to conserve oil fuel stocks. As a result a smaller, coal-burning design designated 'Type 40' was adopted, which could do all the tasks of the 'M35' design but displaced only 543 tons. The first ship to complete, *M381* joined the Fleet in August 1941 but deliveries were spasmodic until the last quarter of 1942. To build the new design, 22 yards were given contracts, including 13 Dutch yards. Maximum constructional efficiency was achieved between the last quarter of 1942 and mid-1943, with 73 ships commissioning, 12 in December 1942 alone. The pre-war design (M35) reached no more than 60 units afloat after four years construction, whilst the new design reached almost one hundred units in half that time, and under wartime conditions.

Losses continued to be negligible, but, because of the activities of RAF minelaying aircraft of Bomber Command in the shallow Baltic and continental waters and the desperate need for escort vessels for coastal convoys, there were never enough minesweepers, despite having, by April 1944, a peak of 172 fleet minesweepers afloat (but not necessarily operational). These consisted of 56 Type 35 and 116 Type 40 ships. In 1943 the Naval Design Staff, requiring to speed up production even further, took the M40 design for modification and simplification which resulted in a third design – Type 43. Once this design was complete construction of Type 40 was cut back after the end of 1943, but deliveries continued until as late as March 1945. In all, 69 of the Type 35 and 131 Type 40 ships were completed, almost half of the latter by Dutch yards whilst, up to August 1944, only 29 fleet minesweepers had been lost.

The Type 43 design was intended for multi-purpose use as either minesweepers, torpedo recovery vessels, torpedo armed escorts or anti-submarine vessels. This necessitated a larger hull, so the designed standard displacement rose to 605 tons with an overall length of 68.3m. In appearance, the design closely resembled the Type 40 design except that the forward 10.5cm gun was re-introduced.

MACHINERY

The main machinery was a two shaft installation, steam being provided by two Wagner Marine boilers working at 16.5atmos and 300°. Each boiler, housed in a separate boiler room, weighed 22.5 tons and was equipped with super-heaters and exhaust gas pre-heaters for the feed water, giving fuel savings of some 15%. The main engines were reciprocating triple-expansion units, each with a low pressure, Bauer-Wach, exhaust turbine driving through a Vulcan clutch. Maximum power per shaft

using the turbines was 1200shp (ie 2400shp total) When going astern, the Vulcan clutch was disengaged and the total power on both shafts was only 1600hp ir all. The propulsion unit gave an emergency top speed i 18.5kts and a normal full speed of 17.5kts. Cruising speed was 15.6kts and economical speed 11kts. A already noted, coal-firing was employed, full bunker accommodating 150 tons, extra coal being stowed or deck.

In a separate compartment, the main, minesweeping electrical generator was accommodated on the port side while two four-cylinder 40kW diesel generators wer fitted on the starboard side for the ships domestic sup ply. A 100kW turbo-generator completed the electrica power system giving a total of 180kW.

A steam steering engine aft powered the two stream lined, balanced rudders giving excellent manoeuvrabil ity.

ARMAMENT

The designed armament (as a minesweeper) consisted o two single dual purpose 10.5cm SK C/32 guns, one or the forecastle and one aft on the sweep deck. Both weapons were shielded. Two 3.7cm Mk42 flak guns ir single, shielded mountings were fitted, one forward o the bridge and the second amidships, abaft the funnel. Ir addition, a 2cm *Vierling* was shipped on the shelter dec aft and a two twin 1.5cm Mg 151 weapon on the boa deck. On entering service, a further two twin 2cm gun were fitted in the bridge. When required, 24 mines coul be accommodated, and the torpedo armed units were t be fitted with two single, trainable 53.3cm MZ43 tor pedo tubes on the forecastle. For anti-submarine work four depth-charge throwers were accommodated, tw sided on the boat deck and two more on the sweep deck Up to 92 depth charges could be stowed in the A/S (*L Jäger*) version. Finally, provision was also made fo 7.3cm 'Fohn V2' multiple rocket launchers but it i questionable if these were ever fitted. This weapon con sisted of a 35 round launcher firing a 2.64kg projectil with a range of 4200m at an elevation of 45°, and would had time permitted, supplanted the 2cm guns in all clas ses of ship.

MINESWEEPING GEAR

For their major role, minesweeping, the class was equip ped for dealing with contact, magnetic and acousti mines using wire, explosive wire, electric or hamme sweeps. The standard wire sweep was the *Schan Drachen Gerate (M)* or SDGM using the usual Oropes type float and monoplane otter. This was streamed af using the main minesweeping winch on the sweep deck A heavy boom fitted to the bow at water level was use to steam the 'self protection' sweep (*Otter Raum Gerate* whose two paravanes were stowed on the forecastle Explosive cutters could be fitted to the sweeps.

The magnetic sweep, *Kabel Fern Raum Gerate* (KFRG) was stowed on two reels, under cover in th after shelter deck forward of the winch, being led ou through ports in the after bulkhead. Two extra warpin drums were fitted to the minesweeping winch to worl

The *M612*.
Drüppel

the sweep, which was steamed using wires and floats. Two six cylinder, 88kW/110V diesel engines powered the sweep when steamed with three noise boxes. This sweep, which was similar to the British 'Double O' sweep consisted of two legs of non-buoyant electric cable bound together for a safe distance with the two free ends supported by three floats each. Depending on the field strength, the swept path was about 150m. It could be towed at up to 9kts.

Acoustic mines were dealt with by means of the *Gerauch Boje Trage* (GBT) which was an acoustic hammer. This was either streamed from the bows using the heavy boom forward, or from the stern using float and kite.

Finally, the explosive sweep or *Knall Korper Gerate* (KKG) involved a system of dropping small charges overboard down a tube whilst the sweep was streamed. The KKG was a peculiarly German method of dealing with acoustic mines by what was basically a countermining technique. A metal tube secured to the ship's side approximately amidships was loaded with double ended explosive charges which were dropped in a series of 18–20 charges and fired electrically from the bridge. Differential delays in the charges gave an acoustic effect designed to trigger the mine. Each charge weighed about 1.5kg. The sweep was effective at up to 4000m against deep laid acoustic mines, but premature explosions frequently destroyed the firing tube with the result that sweeping had to be suspended. It was supplemented by

throwing overboard hand grenades and the GBT and ORG was always streamed with it.

EQUIPMENT

As was to be expected, the optical instruments were both numerous and of a high standard. The main armament fire-control system was in the wheel house, as was the D/F set. A gyro compass and several repeaters were also fitted. The radio outfit consisted of a main receiver, two short-wave sets and a transmitter/receiver set. *S Gerate* (German Asdic and NHG (navigational hydrophone) as well as an echo sounder were also provided. Leaders were to be equipped with radar. However, due to the situation in East Prussia by late 1944, most units had to leave the yards without radar and other items of equipment. *M601, M604* and *M610* received FuMO63 sets operating on a 53cm wave length at 556Mh and were also fitted with FuMB10, a crystal receiver ('Borkum'), FuMB28 portable 'Naxos' ZM4 and FuMB30 portable, battery operated 'Cuba'.

CONSTRUCTION

The whole essence of the design was that it was to be mass produced, ie pre-fabricated. The lead yard was to be Schichau at Königsberg with Neptun Werft at Rostock also assembling sections. Schichau would do 40-50% of the work, with the rest being shared by Atlaswerke (Bremen), Rickmerswerk (Wesermünde), Unterwesse (Bremen), Norderweft (Bremen), Nobiskrug (Rendsberg), Lübekermaschinenbau Stettiner Oderwerke and Vulkan (Stettin), The target was 52 ships per year, with each ship being built from seven sections (1 Stern/2 Engine room including motors/3 Boiler room/4 Forecastle/5 Bow/6 Bridge/7 Superstructure).

Some 30,000-40,000 drawings were prepared in the space of only three or four weeks, and a trial ship was begun. By February 1944, the programme called for the completion of 141 ships between May 1944 and December 1945 in four main variations, namely minesweepers (30 at Schichau, Königsberg and 33 at Neptun, Rostock); torpedo recovery vessels (30 at Neptun, Rostock); torpedo armed (24 at Schichau, Königsberg); anti-submarine (12 at Schichau, Königsberg). In addition, 12 more were to be constructed at the Korneuberg Werft in Vienna for service in the Black Sea. However, only nine were numbered (*M1001* to *M1009*) and in view of the situation in the Black Sea, they were later transferred to Deutschewerft (Toulon) in the South of France and finally to Neptun (Rostock) and re-numbered *M667* to *M675*. These particular units were probably planned as the A/S variants but they never received yard numbers.

By the end of 1944, slight changes had been made to the construction programme, with the result that the variants were reallocated as follows: *M601–M610* M/S; *M611–M640* *TRV;* *M641–M662* M/S; *M663–M666* not decided; *M667–M675* not decided; *M801–M811* M/S; *M812–M827* Torpedo; *M828–M839* A/S; *M840–M854* M/S; *M855–M864* *Torpedo;* *M865* & *M866* not decided. The '600' series were for construction by Neptun and the '800' series by Schichau (hull numbers were 535 to 600 for the Neptun ships and 390 to 455 for the Schichau units.)

A starboard quarter view of *M610.*

Drüppel

In addition to the main variations, some units were to be fitted as leaders, some as dan (buoy) layers (*Pozenboot*) and others as flotilla medical boats (*Artzboot*).

BUILDING PROBLEMS

After the construction programme had been put in hand, a number of problems became apparent, of which two two major ones were shrinkage of the welded joints and a shortage of materials. The former was solved by a technical investigation which resulted in a welding manual and an illustrated guide being issued to all firms participating. The material problems were overcome by re-design, which involved reducing the number of bow frames, the removal of a series of bulkheads in the double-bottom tanks and the substitution of a lateral framing system, for a longitudinal one, between bulkheads.

The total time under construction was to be an incredible eight weeks, consisting of 5 weeks to launch, 2 weeks fitting out and 1 week on trials. This target was not fulfilled because, by late 1944, conditions in German industry were no longer conducive to such demands. Nevertheless, the first unit went afloat at the end of August 1944 and by the close of the year, 12 more had left the slips, four of which being commissioned. Building times varied from 6 to 12 weeks between launching and commissioning, but some of the later ships had to be towed westwards for completion in the face of the advancing Red Army and were probably hurriedly commissioned without certain items of equipment. Königsberg was cut off by the Russians at the end of January 1945 and all sea-worthy hulls were hurriedly towed away to Rostock. The town finally fell on 10 April but ship-building obviously came to standstill in the yards long before. Of the Königsberg units, only *M801* to *M806* joined the fleet, while Rostock, being much farther west, managed to complete 12 ships (*M601* to *M612*).

To be continued

THE MAJESTIC PRE DREADNOUGHT
Part 1 by R A Burt

The *Magnificent* in 1898-1899.
Perkins

Towards the end of 1893 Britain's latest battleships, the seven vessels of the *Royal Sovereign* class, were all nearing completion. These ships, with their high freeboard, heavily protected hull and excellent armament, represented a design well in advance of previous battleship construction. The originator of the design, Sir William White, was asked to produce an improved *Royal Sovereign*, if possible, for the 1892-93 estimates, and leaning heavily on his earlier success, set to work on this task. However, he was asked to postpone the advancement of the final layout due to the fact that a new 12in wire-wound gun was being produced and it was hoped that any new battleships would be fitted with this considerably improved weapon. Initially, three ships were laid

down under the 1892 programme, the first two being of the new design – to be named the *Majestic* class – which were finally allowed to proceed under the normal 1893 programme once final layouts were approved. However, the third vessel was redesigned to smaller dimensions; an idea chiefly aimed at providing an economic but strong ship for Eastern waters.

In December 1893, however, following considerable public agitation over the declining state of the strength of the Royal Navy in comparison with the fleets of Russia and France, further building was called for which resulted in an emergency five year battleship construction programme. This being initiated in general by the First Lord (Earl Spencer) it became known as the Spencer Programme. The original amendment called for an additional seven vessels all of which were accepted by Parliament and finally approved in 1894. Although general public satisfaction was thereby guaranteed, the huge

TABLE 1: MAJESTIC CLASS FINAL LEGEND

Load
displacement:	14,820 tons
Freeboard:	25ft forward, 17ft 3in amidships, 18ft 6in aft
IHP	9000
Coal:	900 tons at normal load
Complement:	760
Armour:	9in main belt, with 5ft 6in below waterline and 9ft 6in above in the load condition
Armament:	(see Table 2) 80 rounds of 12in per gun

Weights:	**Legend (tons)**	**Majestic as completed (tons)**
Vertical armour:	1500	1420
Deck:	1230	1200
Wood backing:	180	140
Barbettes:	1180	1210
Conning tower:	85	85
Casemates:	480	480
Hull:	5550	5650
Margin:	175	200
Total:	14,820	14,700
General Equipment	690	699
Side armour:	1420	1517
Machinery:	1320	1356
Armament:	1550	1660
Engineers stores:	55	63
Coal:	900	900

building programme caused much discontent in Government and naval circles; some of the more eminent members of Parliament of both sides threatening to resign over the enormous cost of such a mammoth, and in their opinions unjustified, programme. To smooth things a little, it was agreed that construction could be spread over a five year period in order to minimise the cost in any one particular year.

All nine ships were completed by 1898 and together represented the largest class of battleships ever built. Moreover, in all round qualities, they were among the most efficient warships for their time ever built, the design being greatly admired and widely copied abroad and accepted as the standard battleship type in the Royal Navy for many years (the design's main features being retained in the next twenty ships of the *Canopus, Formidable, London, Duncan* and *Queen* classes laid down during 1896–1901). The design and production of the *Majestic* class was truly the *magnum opus* of Sir William White's long and distinguished career.

DESIGN

The principal innovations of the *Majestic* design, over that of the *Royal Sovereign*s, were as follows:

1 The introduction of the new 12in wire-wound gun, superior to the previous 13.5in in almost everything except weight of projectile.
2 General use of Harvey steel armour in place of compound armour.
3 Fitting of a deeper side armour belt of uniform thickness.
4 Provision of revolving armoured hoods to protect the barbette mounted guns (structures which subsequently became known as turrets).

By taking advantage of the weight economies afforded by the lighter 12in gun and the Harvey armour, together with an improved arrangement of hull protection, it was possible to secure a substantial superiority in offensive and defensive qualities over the *Royal Sovereign* class with a relatively modest increase in displacement.

In addition the secondary armament was increased from 10 to 12 guns, all of which were given the protection of casemates while the anti-torpedo-boat defences were also greatly improved. Maximum designed speed remained the same as in the *Royal Sovereign*s but the steaming radius was increased. The weaker points of the

TABLE 2: PARTICULARS AS COMPLETED

Name	Builder	Laid Down	Launched	Completed
Majestic	Portsmouth Dockyard	5.2.1894	31.1.1895	December 1895
Mars	Cammell Laird	2.6.1894	3.3.1896	June 1897
Prince George	Portsmouth Dockyard	10.9.1894	22.8.1895	November 1896
Magnificent	Chatham Dockyard	18.12.1893	19.12.1894	December 1895
Jupiter	John Brown	24.4.1894	18.11.1895	May 1897
Hannibal	Pembroke Dockyard	1.5.1894	24.4.1896	April 1898
Caesar	Portsmouth Dockyard	25.3.1895	2.9.1896	January 1898
Victorious	Chatham Dockyard	28.5.1894	19.10.1895	November 1896
Illustrious	Chatham Dockyard	11.3.1895	17.9.1896	April 1898

Note: It will be remembered that it was agreed to limit the number of vessels laid down in any one year, but as can be seen, all were laid down in 1894 and 1895, building times being varied to achieve a spread of time of completion.

Displacement:	15,600 tons in the load condition, 16,700 tons at deep load. (see Table 3)
Length:	390ft (pp), 399ft (wl), 421ft (oa)
Beam:	75ft
Draught:	27ft in the load condition, 28ft 8in deep load
Armament:	4–12in, 35cal, Mk VIII, 46-ton BL; 12–6in, 40cal, Mk VII; 16–12pdr 12cwt QF; 12–3pdr QF; 8 machine guns; 5–18in submerged torpedo tubes (2 broadside on each side and 1 aft); 22 torpedoes, plus 6–14in for boats.
Searchlights:	6–24in, one port and starboard on each bridge and one high on each mast. Full complement of searchlights is not always shown in photographs, with considerable variation in arrangements throughout the class although this basic number and distribution of searchlights was used in all later ships up to the *King Edward VII* class of 1903.
Complement:	*Mars* and *Jupiter* (1897) 794. *Caesar* (1905) 735 as flagship. *Majestic* (1895) 672
Ship's Boats:	*Caesar* 1–56ft 3in steam barge; 1–56ft 6in steam pinnace; 1–40ft 1½in steam pinnace; 1–42ft steam launch; 1–36ft steam pinnace; 2–34ft cutters; 1–30ft gig; 1–32ft gig; 1–28ft gig; 2–27ft whalers; 1–24ft gig; 1–13ft 6in balsa raft; 1–16ft skiff dinghy.

The *Majestic* at Spithead in August 1902.

Courtesy R A Burt

design, which were accepted in part to gain some of the above advantages, were:

1 Location of the 6in secondary armament on the main deck with the attendant disadvantages of low command.
2 Reduced stability associated with longitudinal bulkheads without adequate counter-flooding arrangements (150 watertight compartments).

The original design was, of course, based on the *Royal Sovereign*s, although a displacement of 12,500 tons was originally asked for with a board margin of 200 tons. The 18in thick, 250ft long belt of the *Sovereign*s was reduced to 9in thickness and 220ft length, but its height was increased from 8ft 6in to 15ft.

White originally proposed a 6in secondary battery located entirely on the upper deck and this arrangement is shown in a sketch design dated 3 January 1893 and bearing his signature. The sketch also shows one large top, low on each mast, with a small upper top as in the *Royal Sovereign*s, but this was later modified to provide two tops both capable of carrying 6pdr guns.

The design load displacement was only 750 tons more than in the *Royal Sovereign* class while length increased

by 10ft (pp) and the freeboard by 5ft 10in forward and 6in aft (although reduced amidships by 9in) but the beam and nominal mean draughts were retained. The all-round freeboard of the new vessels was never equalled in a pre-dreadnought of any succeeding class. The marked tumble home was rather more than in the previous class, with a marked sheer forward; this tumble home was criticised as it detracted from buoyancy on an already low metacentric height, however, it was considered that the loss of initial stability through action damage was less likely owing to the deeper belt.

ARMAMENT

The *Majestic* class marked a reversion to the 12in calibre gun, which had not been fitted in a British battleship since that mounted in *Collingwood* in 1880. The new gun was the first wire-wound gun in service with the Royal Navy and was such an advance on earlier designs that older guns could not hope to match its qualities. The gun was designed by Messrs Vickers specifically for the *Majestic* class and on trials proved its ballistic superiority to the 13.5in gun of the *Royal Sovereign*s. It was also of superior strength, so much so that Messrs Armstrongs thought that the Admiralty were over worried regarding this feature of the gun and that it was 'over-designed'. There were also considerable improvements in the twin

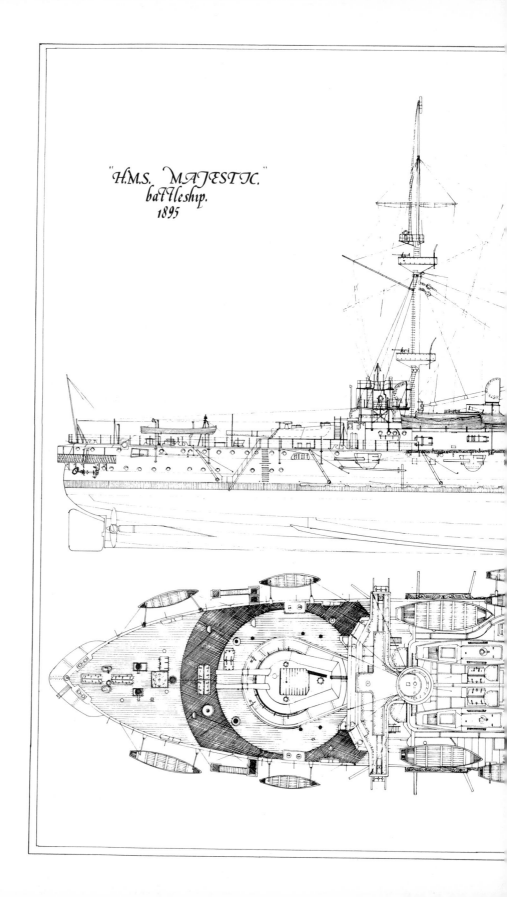

"H.M.S. MAJESTIC."
battleship.
1895

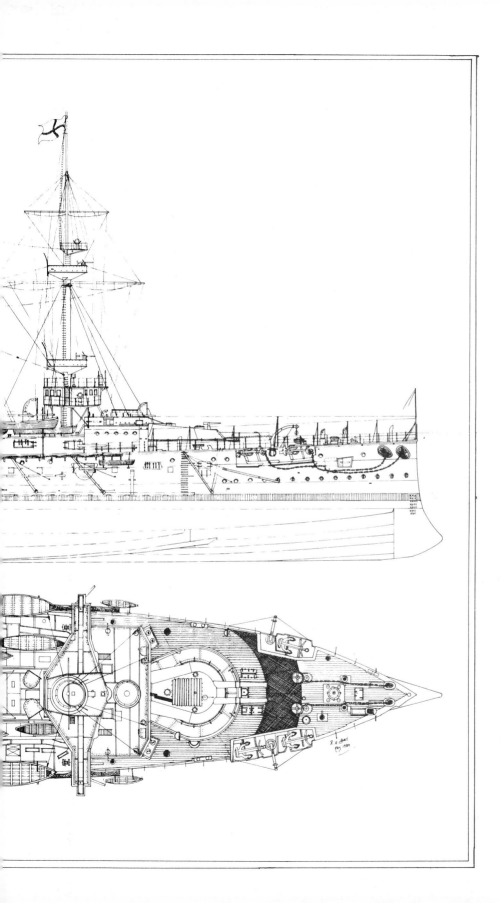

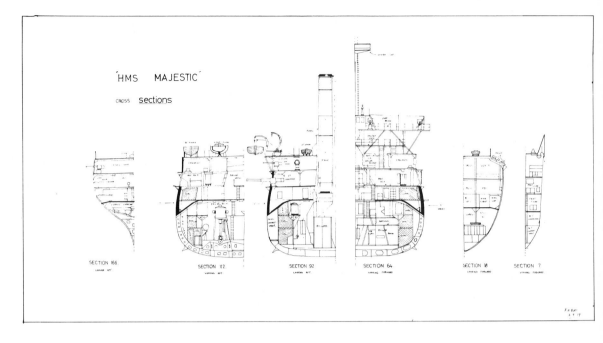

HMS MAJESTIC

CROSS sections

SECTION 166.
LOOKING AFT

SECTION 112
LOOKING AFT

SECTION 92
LOOKING AFT

SECTION 64
LOOKING FORWARD

SECTION 18
LOOKING FORWARD

SECTION 7
LOOKING FORWARD

TABLE 3: STABILITY AND WEIGHT PARTICULARS

Majestic (based on inclining experiments of 16 December 1895)

'A' condition: Fully equipped with 900 tons of coal on board. Draught 27ft mean, Displacement 15,600 tons, GM 3.4ft

'B' condition: As above but with 1900 tons coal on board. Draught 28ft 8in, GM 3.7ft

'C' condition: Ship lightened to a mean draught of 25ft 3in gave a GM of 3.3ft

The angle of maximum stability for the above conditions was 38°-39°

Caesar (based on inclining experiments of 5 September 1898)

'A' condition Fully equipped with 1950 tons coal on board and 66 tons water in the reserve feed tanks (175 tons of fresh water also aboard). Draught 28ft 7in mean, Displacement 15,770 tons. GM 3.7ft.

Displacement sheet for *Magnificent* (December 1895)
15,632 tons deep (draught of 28ft 5½in)
14,982 tons load (draught of 27ft 6in)
13,900 tons experimental condition (draught of 26ft 0⅞in)
13,400 tons light (draught of 25ft 2in)

Total capacity of coal bunkers (tons)

Upper bunkers:	640
Lower bunkers:	900
Wing bunkers:	360
Total:	1900

mountings for the 12in gun compared with those of the 13.5in, these being summarised below:

1 The turntables were balanced at their centre of rotation thus making it possible to employ lighter training engines and allowing the fitting of hand training gear.

2 The mountings were well balanced, even with the guns run-out, allowing for lighter elevating gear and again the use of alternative hand gear.

3 At the fixed loading positions, the rammer was alongside, instead of through, the hoists, thus the cages could be removed whilst the rammers were in motion (the main advantage here was that much time was gained in the loading cycle).

4 The loading trays worked with the rammers and the

TABLE 4: PARTICULARS OF 12in Mk VIII, 35CAL, 46-TON GUN

Construction:	Steel, wire-wound
Weight (less breech):	44 ton 18cwt
Weight of breech:	1 ton 2cwt
Length (bore):	425.15in (35.43cal)
Total length:	445.5in
Chamber dia:	16in (largest); 12.8 (smallest)
Rifling System:	Polygroove modified
Length of rifling:	349.285in
Twist of rifling:	Straight from breech end of rifling to 278.95in from the muzzle, then increasing from 0 to 1 turn in 30 calibres at the muzzle.
Rifling grooves:	48, 1in (straight) 0.8in (twist) deep × 0.62in (straight) 0.607in (twist) wide
Muzzle velocity:	2367fs
Muzzle energy:	33,020ft
Rate of fire:	1 round per 70 seconds until ready use shells are gone, then 1 round per 100 seconds
Shell weight:	850lb
Full charge weight:	200lb cordite MDC 45
Range:	13,900yds
Maximum elevation:	13½°
Penetration:	32in wrought iron at 1000yds; 13in Krupp steel at 3000yds

Notes: The guns were mounted in pear shaped Mk BII barbettes except in *Caesar* and *Illustrious* which were modified for the new Mk BIII circular barbette. The loading system in the BIII was slightly faster than in the BII and incorporated better magazine protection as the hoists were interrupted in the shell chamber instead of having a straight run from magazine to gun house.

entry of the guides of their supply bogies locked the turntable, thus doing away with the need for separate, outside locking bolts.

5 All round loading was provided for from a ready-use supply of 8 shells stowed on the turntable.

6 The turrets, or shields, placed around the two guns had a 10½in armour face, 5½in sides, 4in back and a 2in floor and roof.

The guns were designed for either a right or left hand breech, depending on which position in the mounting they occupied, the barrels were however interchangeable although some of the breech mechanism was different. The firing mechanism was designed for electric or percussion firing with vent sealed tubes and, following

The *Illustrious* in 1903–1904.

Perkins

TABLE 5: PARTICULARS OF 6in Mk VII and VIII GUNS

Length (oa):	279.228in
Length of bore:	269.5in (44.9cal)
Standard chamber:	32.3in
Modified chamber:	32.658in
Length of rifling:	233.6in
Weight of gun:	7 ton 7cwt 2qtr
Weight of breech:	3cwt 8lb
Cordite charge:	20lb Mk I rifling; 23lb Mk I rifling (with modified chamber); 28lb 10oz Mk III rifling (with modified chamber)
Shell weight:	100lb
Burster:	8lb 11oz
Muzzle velocity:	2536fs with Mk I rifling: 2772fs with Mk III rifling
Muzzle energy:	4600ft with Mk I rifling; 5349ft with Mk III rifling
Range:	2500yds with Mk I rifling; 2950yds with Mk III rifling

Starboard quarter view of *Majestic* in 1904.

Perkins

the usual practice of the day, the guns could not be fired until the breech screw was sealed fully home.

Gun trials in the completed ships passed with very little trouble, although in November 1904 there was an accident in *Majestic* whilst she was engaged in prize firing. One of the guns blew-off its muzzle whilst another had lining complications. This latter complaint was due to the inner 'A' tube being out of line with the outer 'A' tube at the first shoulder, near the muzzle, and can be classed as an error in manufacture. The other gun, which had about 13in of the liner blown off, was found upon inspection to have a series of cracks in the inner tube of the gun. Both guns were fired with ¾ charges, made up of one ½ charge of 83¾lb and one quarter charge of 41⅞lb of cordite 50 while the shells in use were solid shot. The accident was noticed as the 7th round was fired and observed to fall 500yds short of the desired range. A crew member also noticed a piece of alien metal flying through the air at the same time, although at the time he

1

2

1 The *Illustrious* c 1905-1906. Note variations in appearance from earlier view; enlarged upper top, removal of searchlights, QF guns and semaphore from masts, lowering of torpedo net shelf, removal of gaff, and fitting of W/T gaff to topmast.

2 *Majestic* in 1909.

Perkins

3 The *Caesar*, c 1905.

thought it might have been a deck fitting which was common.

These accidents led to all the 46-ton 12in guns in use with the Fleet being subjected to close examination with the result that it was concluded that, in their existing state, they were only good for 33 full charge firings before the risk of a similar accident became likely. The problem was 'muzzle choke', caused by the inner tube being contracted and bulged inward around the muzzle opening resulting in restriction and ultimately failure of the bore. Fortunately, because of the great strength of the gun no person was hurt. These faults, in an otherwise excellent gun, were rectified and it was later found, following tests with the damaged guns, that they could still fire to a distance of 10,605yds, with a 200lb cordite charge, at an elevation of 9°.

To be continued

Warship Wings No 6

Grumman F14 Tomcat

By Roger Chesneau

It has long been a goal of jet aircraft designers to combine in one airframe the characteristics that will provide high performance in combat yet endow it with the agility to enable superior attack and evade manoeuvres to be swiftly executed. The problem has been that a wing optimised for high speed (in particular supersonic speed), requiring as it does minimum drag and comparatively little potential for lift, is inherently unsuited to the demands made at the opposite end of the performance regime – indeed, in general, the more suited a configuration is to one end the less appropriate it will be to the other. For naval aircraft there is an added difficulty: the restrictive dimensions of a flight deck (higher speeds equal longer landing runs or alternatively more robust arrester systems). Clearly, then, if a wing could be summoned to offer either low-drag or high lift (and concurrently increased lift) at the whim of the pilot, then it would have a very bright future indeed. This was the drive behind VG, or variable geometry: highly swept wings to lessen the obstacles or high-speed flight, with the option of minimum (or zero) sweep for best low performance.

Varying the configuration of an aircraft's wing is as old as flight itself; wing 'warping', for example, was standard procedure in many early aeroplanes (including the 'Flyer') to assist control, whilst we have already touched on slats and flaps as lift improvement features in these columns. VG, however, is something more radical, affecting as it does both sweepback and hence span, as well as offering varying cross-sectional shapes to the direction of airflow above and below the wing.

Although the advantages conferred by a wing possessing such a capability had been well understood for many years, it was not until the late 1950s that speeds reached the point where serious consideration of VG became warranted. The complexities and compromises involved were daunting. First, if wing sweep were variable so also would be aircraft CG (or, more relevantly, aerodynamic centre, or AC), thus affecting such issues as trim. Second, the hinging mechanism itself both created weight and used up internal volume which would otherwise be given over, perhaps, to fuel. Third, traditional wide-track, wing-mounted undercarriages were clearly out of the question, and fourth, the concept of a wing being a means not only of providing lift and stability but also of carrying offensive loads and significant amounts of external fuel would have to be reviewed.

TFX

'Live' US Navy interest in carrier-borne VG aircraft can be traced back, somewhat tortuously, to the US Air Force's F-105 Thunderchief, which in early 1960 was the subject of a replacement study (SOR 183) at the same time that the Navy was looking towards a successor for its F-4 Phantom, then about to enter service in some considerable numbers. Within twelve months, Defense Secretary Robert S McNamara seized upon both projects and mated them to form the Tactical Fighter Experimental, his object being maximum efficiency and economy at the political level. The outcome was the F-111, the Navy version of which (F-111B) was to be produced by General Dynamics in co-operation with Grumman, who had recently, with Douglas, had their promising F6D missile plane swept away by cancellation. The Navy, however, was not particularly interested in what it saw as an Air Force project, and insisted on impossible design featues; it was to their relief when, with seven airframes built, the F-111B was abandoned.

TOMCAT

With the departure of McNamara the question of an independent Navy air superiority fighter was pushed

hard, and in 1968 a new RFP (Request For Proposals) was issued to US manufacturers. Grumman had meanwhile brought together the useful technology stockpiled from the F6D (Eagle missile) and TFX (Phoenix) projects, and the lead resulted in their winning the production contract.

The F-14 Tomcat was designed around the carriage of six AIM-54 Phoenix missiles and its associated Hughes AWG-9 weapon control system, optimised in addition to handle Sparrow, Sidewinder and the internally mounted cannon, thereby offering a wide combat spectrum and, in the big missile, the ability to engage six targets simultaneously at very long (up to 70nm) range. As for ship compatability, the F-14 has the primary problem of being the largest and heaviest carrier fighter ever to enter service, but its multi-kill capability clearly makes any reduction in on board complement quite palatable, if not totally acceptable. Its VG wing obviates the requirement for wing folding and also aids flight deck take-off and approach in novel fashion, and thus presents a radically different solution to the traditional dilemmas facing carrier aircraft designers.

The F-14 first flew in December 1970 and, after some problems (mainly cost escalation, entered service in October 1972, to be deployed aboard *Enterprise* two years later. The Pratt & Whitney F401-engined F-14B proved to be an abortive programme, but the F-14C is currently under development (upgraded GE F101 plant) and should join the Fleet in FY1984, whilst the F-14D, with improved electronics, a lengthened fuselage (for extra fuel) and the AIM-54C, is due to follow in about five years' time. F-14 production is planned until 1995 for a grand total of 995 aircraft.

Although a fleet air defence fighter, the Tomcat has also been adopted for the tactical reconnaissance role as a successor to the RA-5C Vigilante. A fitment designated TARPS (Tactical Airborne Reconnaissance Pod System) can be carried below the fuselage, although Phoenix carriage is then limited to two weapons (glove pylons).

On 19 August 1981 the Tomcat found itself in the world's first dogfight between VG aircraft. Two F-14s on patrol during US Sixth Fleet exercises in the Gulf of Sirte were attacked by two Libyan Sukhoi 22 VG fighter-bombers and easily shot down their opponents with Sidewinders.

GRUMMAN F-14A SPECIFICATIONS

Overall length:	62ft
Span:	64ft 2in max, 32ft 8in min; 38ft 2in in-flight min.
Max height:	16ft
Wing area:	565ft²
Engine:	2 – Pratt & Whitney TF30-P-412 turbofans, 21,000lb thrust each.
Max speed:	Probably about Mach 2.4
Combat radius:	500nm (2.5-3hrs)
Ceiling:	60,000ft
Weight:	38,000lb (17 tons); 69,000lb (30.8 tons) normal max; 72,000lb (32.1 tons) max gross.
Weapons:	1 – M61A1 20mm Vulcan gun, 6 – AIM-54 Phoenix AAMs, 2 – AIM-9 Sidewinder; options include AIM-9/AIM-7 Sparrow mixtures, or various combinations of AIM-54/AIM-9/AIM-7 missiles.

A VF-84 F-14 (*Nimitz*) shows the low-visibility paint scheme currently applied to US Navy carrier aircraft. The mountings visible below the forward fuselage are the foremost pair of Phoenix missile pallets.

USN

WARSHIP PICTORIAL

America's First Submarines Part 1

By Francis J Allen

In the history of the navies of the world many trends, developments and policies have caused division among those intrusted with the guidance of these services. The challenge of the submarine boat, as perceived by the officers embued with the glory and power of the surface warship, and in particular with the strength of the battleship, was to write a deep chapter in the records of all the great naval services. The United States Navy was no exception, though there was perhaps less determination to hold to a traditional view of naval development and the American navy led the way for the other maritime powers in the development and use of the submarine torpedo boat.

Early development, both in America and Europe, was a haphazard affair at best, with mistakes and successes being repeated in isolation from parallel work. The pioneer work, that solved the problems of angle and depth control, as well as incorporating a reliable power source, was done by John P Holland, whose motive in the early part of his career was to provide a weapon capable of sinking the ships of Queen Victoria's Navy and thus freeing Ireland. However, by the time he had developed a workable submarine this motive was a thing of the past.

The submarine which was given the name *Holland SS-1*, and which was the first operational vessel of her type in the USN, was developed between 1895 and 1897 and launched on 17 May 1897. The launching was recorded for history by the *New York Times* with the following comment '. . . the *Holland*, the little cigar-shaped vessel owned by her inventor, which may or may not play an important part in the navies of the world in years to come, was launched from Lewis Nixon's shipyard this morning.'[1]

The vessel launched from Mr Nixon's shipyard was intended to be a submarine as opposed to a submersible; that is she was designed to perform all of her mission while remaining totally submerged, as opposed to submerging only for making an attack or to remain hidden.

The *Holland SS-1*, incorporated many features which were to become standard in later classes of boats. Her basic dimensions were 53.3ft (oa) length, 10.3ft beam amidships, 63 tons displacement light and 75 tons submerged displacement. The hull form was that of a parabolic spindle. The hull plating was supported by circular frames constructed of angle iron (the largest being 10¼ft diameter) and was strong enough to withstand a pressure of 35lb/sq in. The *Holland* was thus capable of diving to a depth of 75ft, her sinking and trim tanks having a capacity of 10.5 tons. For running on the surface and for charging the batteries she had a 45hp Otto gas engine. This was perhaps the greatest flaw in her design, and in the subsequent early, Holland boats. The gasoline engine was a danger due to its production of poisonous gases in such a confined and poorly vented vessel. In 1899 Holland had anticipated the need for diesel engines in submarines and had negotiated successfully with Adolphus Busch, the American representative of the Diesel Motor Corporation, but these plans bore no actual fruit.[2] In fact diesel engines were not introduced into USN submarines until the building of the 'E' class boats of 1911.[2]

Submerged running was provided by electric motors, which could be run at speeds and power settings anywhere from 10hp to 150hp.[2] The battery stowage area, located amidships, measured 15ft by 6¼ft by 3ft and accommodated 60 cells with a capacity of 1500 ampere hours.[2] To operate the bilge pumps and the air compressor a 10hp electric motor was available, the former being capable of emptying or filling all of the tanks independently and of pumping out the bilge. A ⅛hp electric motor was provided as a means of powering the exhaust pump, used to exhaust air from the boat while submerged. Fresh air was stored in three pairs of reservoirs at a pressure of 50lb/sq in.

A 50lb air tank supplied the whistle, trim tanks, etc, while a 10lb tank was provided for the ballast tanks.

Both the steering and diving engines could be controlled by hand, from the turret or automatically by vanes and diaphragms placed on or near the rudders.[2]

The main armament consisted of three Whitehead 18in torpedoes, two carried on racks inside the submarine and one in the torpedo tube. Those carried in the internal racks were placed aboard through the single torpedo tube[2]. The Holland also carried a pneumatic dynamite gun of 8.425in bore, positioned above the torpedo tube at a fixed elevation of 15°. It fired a 222lb projectile with a charge of from 50lb to 80lb of gun cotton, and had a surface range of 1000yds, or 30yds under water.[2]

The command station, referred to as the turret, was a raised, stationary structure about mid-way along the hull. It was fitted with a 24in diameter hatch with glass windows, 3in × ¾in, arranged for all around vision, while three glass windows, 1in in diameter, were placed in the turret cover, these being used while passing under surface vessels.

The 'A' class submarines which followed the Hollands into service were broadly based upon the *SS-1*. The basic form remained, but the dimensions were altered to give a hull of 11ft 11in in diameter and 63ft 10in long. The gasoline engine, for surface running, was enlarged to one of 160hp and the 70hp electric motor was given storage batteries totalling 60 cells with a capacity of 1900 ampere-hours.[3] The diving and vertical rudders were hand worked because the automatic air-operated system, designed and installed in the *Holland*, was thought to be unreliable.

With the 'A' class boats surfaced and submerged weight rose by 43 tons and 48 tons respectively, while the speed increased to 8.7kts on the surface and 7kts submerged.

The turret of the Holland design was retained for navigational purposes, but it was looked upon as less satisfactory by this time. A periscope was fitted to the *Adder* (A2) during her trials which allowed a field of view of 15 degrees on each bow. It was, obviously, seen as a great improvement in the combat effectiveness of the submarine but the inability of the commander to judge distance correctly was still a disadvantage.[3]

The 'A' class retained the same arrangements for exhausting the air from the engine and battery storage areas. Since the submarine's temperature was controlled by the surrounding water, an electric heater was provided. However, this heater used such an excessive amount of power from the batteries that its use drastically reduced the boat's operational radius.

To be continued

NOTES

1 *New York Times* (18 May 1897).

2 *John P Holland – Inventor of the Modern Submarine,* by Richard K Morris (USNI, Annapolis 1966).

3 *Official Trials of the Submarine Boats Adder and Moccasin'* by William R White, *Journal of the American Society of Naval Engineers*, Vol XV, (1903).

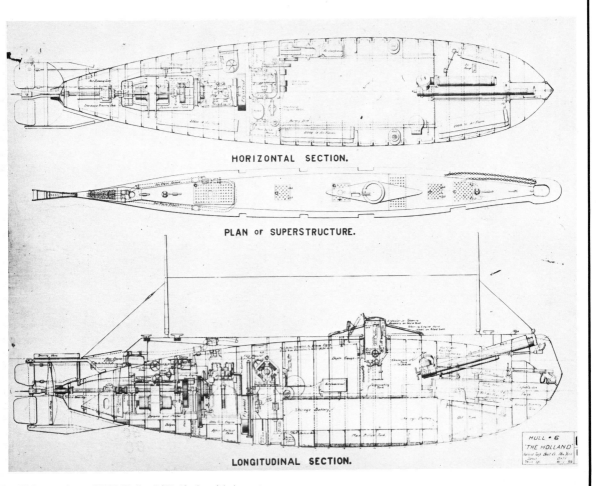

HORIZONTAL SECTION.

PLAN of SUPERSTRUCTURE.

LONGITUDINAL SECTION.

Official drawings of USS *Holland* (SS-1), dated 1 August 1899.

USN

USS *Grampus* (SS-4) and USS *Pike* (SS-6) in the hydraulic lift drydock, at the Union Iron Works, San Francisco, 1903.
USN

USS *Porpoise* (SS-7) and USS *Shark* (SS-8) on cradles for the winter, at the New York Navy Yard, *c* 1905.
USN

USS *Moccasin* (SS-5) launching, at Elizabethport NJ on 20 August 1901.
USN

USS *Adder* (SS-3) in Manila Bay, 1909. View of the interior showing the torpedo tube and torpedoes.
USN

Stereo photograph published *c*1918 by the Keystone View Co, it was taken about 1903, and shows USS *Plunger* (SS-2), with USS *Massachusetts* (BB-2) under refit in the background, at Brooklyn Navy Yard, NY.
USN

USS *Holland* (SS-1) at the New York Navy Yard, October 1901, with the Russian battleship *Retvizan* in the background.
USN

USS *Holland* (SS-1) in the Raritan Dry Dock, Perth Amboy, New Jersey, in the spring of 1898.
USN

USS *Holland* (SS-1) in the Raritan Dry Dock, Perth Amboy NJ in 1898.
USN

USS *Holland* (SS-1) underway on the surface.
USN

USS *Holland* (SS-1) in the shipyard at Morris Heights, New York, during the winter of 1898-99. Her stern has been extensively modified, with the propeller relocated forward of the steering mechanism and diving planes.

USN

USS *Holland* (SS-1) firing her Zalinski Dynamite Gun at Perth Amboy, New Jersey, in the spring of 1898. Note the projectile in flight in the upper right of photo.

USN

GERMAN NAVAL RADAR DETECTORS by Erwin F Sieche

With the introduction of the airborne ASV Mk I (British codename H2S) and Mk II working on a 1,5m wavelength, British aircraft obtained the advantage of being able to detect German naval units – primarily submarines – under all weather conditions. The introduction of the British ASV Mk III working on a 9cm wavelength marked the step to centimetric radar. (German codename for the ASV Mk III was *Rotterdam-Geraet* after a grounded bomber).

German active radar, as described in my earlier article in *Warship* 22, was not developed to the high level of tactical importance and usage as it was by the Allies. However, the passive antennas on German warships became a vital part of their survivability under Allied air attacks. Of course this family of sets and antennas was of the highest importance to German submarines, but was also installed in surface units. The passive antennas were often fitted integrally with or close to the active antennae and were therefore an essential part of German wartime electronic equipment as a whole.

Once again it must be pointed out that this article cannot be considered definitive, as the existing literature on German passive sets and their antennas is not sufficiently complete to compile a full history of the subject. The drawings are largely based on photograph analysis and are not to scale. An exact description of the sets would need a substantial knowledge of electronics and would be outside the field of a magazine of this kind. It therefore makes sense to describe only the significant difference between antennas, their positioning on ships, and to which active sets they were related.

TYPES OF PASSIVE ANTENNAS

The basic German type designation for passive radars was FuMBAnt (*Funkmess-Beobachtungs-Antenne*).

The FuMBAnt 2: codenamed 'Biscay-cross' was a simple wire loop fixed to a wooden cross that had to be rotated by hand. This antenna, the first emergency step towards countering British aircraft using ASV radar to locate German submarines, was due to its technically primitive construction, only used for a short time as a receiving device for the 'Metox' set.

The FuMBAnt 3: codenamed 'Bali', was a round dipole antenna for omni-directional receiving. It could be found in nearly all contemporary submarines, but was also to be found at the mastheads of German surface vessels. Due to its small dimensions it can hardly be seen in photographs of German surface units and is often mistaken for a truck or a block; only a few good pictures show clearly this antenna.

The FuMBAnt 4: codenamed 'Sumatra' is the loop dipole with 45° polarisation which can be found on

nearly all German surface units. There are at least three different forms of this distinctive butterfly-shaped antenna, and it is not known to the author if they had different type-designations (the designation FuMBAnt 5 is missing from the list of types). Probably in its first form, it was completely covered and had parallel sides, in its other two forms it had curved sides and one or two uncovered wire loops. It is also not known to the author if this loop was fixed or could be rotated. On heavy surface units they can be found in fixed positions bearing in four directions, eg on the forward spotting top screen, on the flanks of the armoured spotting top or on special lattice structures. It would be logical to assume that all German surface vessels were equipped with 'Sumatra' dipoles, but photographic evidence is lacking; for example there are no photographs showing them on *Scharnhorst*, *Lützow* or *Admiral Hipper*.

The smaller German surface units, such as destroyers and torpedo-boats, usually had four of them, bearing in four directions, situated around the screen of the forward searchlight platform. As the 'Bali' antenna was developed for omni-directional warning and the 'Sumatra' antenna for exact bearing indication, they were both used to feed the FuMB 4 'Samos' set.

The next, logical, step was from fixed to trainable antennas; the first of the latter being –

The FuMBAnt 6: codenamed 'Palau'. In submarines its double butterfly dipoles were situated on the rear side of the FuMO 30 radar antenna frame (see *Warship* 15, page 165). Surface vessels, being less weight critical, had the larger FuMO 21 frame, and special 'Palau' frames were carried on some destroyers and light cruisers.

The FuMBAnt 7: codenamed 'Timor', consists of eight vertical and four horizontal butterfly-loops of different shape fitted on a huge frame. This device was only fitted in capital ships, situated at the foretop rangefinder cupola. The location changing from front (*Tirpitz*, *Scharnhorst*, *Prinz Eugen*) to rear (*Lützow*. *Admiral Scheer*) as did the layout of the vertical and horizontal loops.

There is a physical similarity between the dimensions of the receiving antennas and the wavelength of the emissions it is intended to receive, so with the introduction of the British Mk III radar and the later centimetric MEDDO-set, the passive antennas became significantly smaller and cannot easily be located in photographs.

The 'Fliege' antenna was a tiny butterfly loop with 45° polarisation and a vertical parabolic reflector. In submarines this small antenna was simply hinged into the circular direction-finder frame of the RDF-set. In surface ships it was situated on a small outrigger on the mainmast and was trainable. The 'Muecke' omni-

TABLE 1: GERMAN PASSIVE RECEIVERS (FuMB)

Type	Last Code Name	Former Code	Frequency (MC)	Wavelength (cm)	Receiving Antenna	Against
–	Metox	R600	–	–	Biscaya-cross	ASV Mk I
FuMB 1	–	R600A	113-560	60-260	FuMBAnt 4	ASVs Mk I, II
FuMB 1	–	R203	60-160	180-500	FuMBAnt 4	ASVs Mk I, II
FuMB 4	Samos	RS1/5UD42	87-470	153-333	FuMBAnt 3 FuMBAnt 7	ASVs Mk I, II
FuMB 7	Naxos I	–	–	9	–	ASV Mk III (H2S) (1)
FuMB 8	Cypern I	Wanz G (2)	–	–	–	ASVs Mk I, II
FuMB 9	Cypern II	Wanz G (2)	156-254	118-192	FuMBAnt 3/7	ASV Mk I, II
		Wanz G (2)	–	150-286		ASV Mk I, II
FuMB 10	Borkum	–	100-400	75-300	FuMBAnt 3 FuMBAnt 4	ASV Mk I, II ASV Mk I, II
FuMB 26	Tunis	Naxos TI	7500-15,000	2-4	Mucke	ASV Mk, III, MEDDO
			1300-3750	8-14	Fliege	ASV Mk III
FuMB 35	Athos	–	–	–	–	–
FuMB 37	Leros	–	–	–	–	–

Notes: (1) German code name: Rotterdam-set

(2) Abbreviation for: *Wellen-Auzeigegeraet,* commonly called *Wanze* (buck); or after the manufacturer *Hanseatische Apparatebau-Gesellschaft Neufeldt & Kuhnke GmbH Kiel*, abbreviation Hagenuk (the Hagenuk-set).

The formula for conversion from frequency to wavelength is: $\dfrac{c}{F} = m$ meaning $\dfrac{\text{velocity of light}}{\text{frequency}} = \text{metres}$

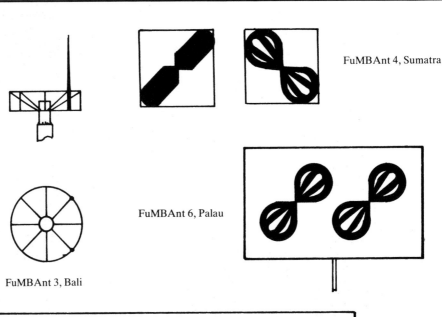

FuMBAnt 4, Sumatra

FuMBAnt 6, Palau

FuMBAnt 3, Bali

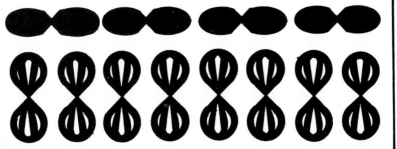

FuMBAnt 7, Timor

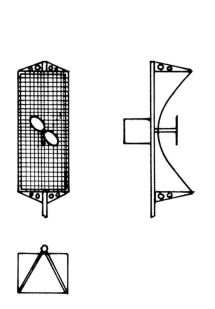

FuMN 26, Tunis

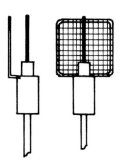

FuME 1, Wespe g

FuME 2, Wespe g (2)

directional antenna was a tiny, round dipole intended to measure Allied centimetric waves and was so small that it could be situated atop a 'Bali' dipole or at the rear side of a 'Fliege' antenna. All these antennas served the various passive receivers as shown in the table.

TYPES OF ACTIVE ANTENNAS

The German types designated FuME (*Funkmess Erkennung*) were the technical forerunners of today's IFF sets. Because they were late in developing this type of friend or foe aircraft recognition/interrogation system only two types of sets were in active service aboard German vessels at the end of the war.

Type FuME 1 'Wespe g' (the letter 'g' referring to the frequency band 335 to 430 MHZ) probably received a return signal activated by the standard German 80cm radar. The antenna was a simple stick aerial with a movable reflector.

Type FuME 2 'Wespe g (2)', was also a simple stick antenna but with a deflecting cone. This cone shows a striking resemblance to the layout of today's British 'candlestick' aerials. The later sets – FuME 4 'Neuling M', FuME 5 'Hohentwiel-Biene' and FuME 6 'Eisenbart' – were in the development stage at the end of the war and not installed in standard shipboard sets.

TABLE 2: GERMAN ACTIVE IFF SETS (FuME)

Type	Code Name	Frequency MC	Notes
FuME 1	Wespe g	361-389	(1)
FuME 2	Wespe g (2)	353-429	(1)
FuME 3	–	–	Navalised FuG 25a 'Erstling'
FuME 4	Neuling M	–	Navalised FuG 226 'Neuling'
FuME 5	Hohentwiel-Biene (2)	–	Navalised FuG 225 'Wobbelbiene' (2)
FuME 6	Eisenbart	–	Development

Notes: (1) probably received return IFF-signal activated by German standard 80cm radar
(2) probably received return IFF-signal activated by German FuMO 63 'Hohentwiel k' (556 MC)

TABLE 3: GERMAN PASSIVE RADAR-RECEIVING ANTENNAS (FuMBAnt)

Type	Code Name	Form
FuMBAnt 2	Biscaya-cross	Wire loop
FuMBAnt 3	Bali	Round dipole
FuMBAnt 4	Sumatra	Loop dipole/butterfly; 45° polarisation
FuMBAnt 5	–	–
FuMBAnt 6	Palau	Two loop dipoles/butterfly; 45° polarisation
FuMBAnt 7	Timor	'Sumatra' and 'Palau' dipoles with vertical and horizontal polarisation
–	Fliege	Loop dipole
–	Mucke	Round dipole

THE US NAVY'S Mk 45 GUN by Antony Preston

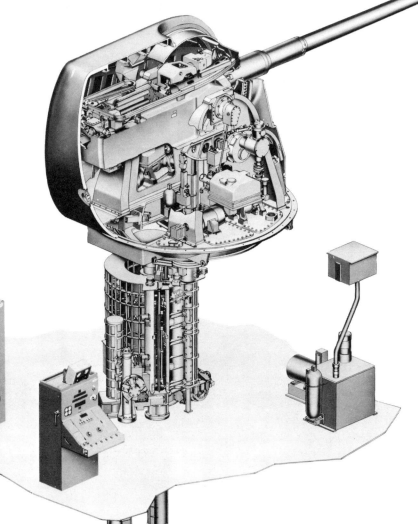

Cut-away drawing of the 5in, Mk 45 gun mounting.

FMC Corporation

The latest medium-calibre gun in the US Navy is the 5in/54cal Mk 45, which replaced the 5in/54cal Mk 42 in the late 1970s. The Mk 45, Mod 0 is now in service in the *Spruance* class destroyers, the *Tarawa* class LHAs and various other surface combatants, providing gunfire support, acting as a back-up to missiles in surface engagements and providing limited anti-aircraft firepower. Compared with previous mountings it is lighter, more reliable and easier to maintain. Rate of fire has been deliberately traded off to achieve these advantages.

The Mk 45 mounting is designed for automatic all-weather operation, with a rate of fire of 20 rounds per minute, although single shots can also be fired. In the Mod 1 version, however, only ten of the new terminally guided projectiles can be fired per minute. The gunhouse is watertight, with zone-temperature controlled anti-icing of the gunport. The loader-drum can be replenished during sustained firing.

The total weight of the mounting is almost 22 tons or 49,064lb (22,226kg), and the optional Mk 6 ammunition hoist weighs a further 2850 to 4765lb (depending on which version is used). The mounting comprises two main groups of components, a lower structure below deck and the upper structure above deck. The components of the lower structure deliver an uninterrupted flow of ammunition to the upper structures, whose components load the ammunition, aim the gun, fire it and eject the empty cartridge cases. The mounting is operated from below by six men; the mount captain, an EP2 panel operator and four ammunition handlers. However, if necessary one man can activate the mounting and fire the 20 rounds of ready-use ammunition.

The Mod 1 version incorporates a major design improvement, enabling the gun to select and fire six different types of ammunition. This facility increases the speed with which the ship's gun-system can respond to different threats. For example, if the ship is involved in a shore bombardment and is suddenly confronted by an air threat, Weapons Control can, at the push of a button, immediately load and fire the type of ammunition needed. In the Mod 0 version changing the ammunition would require special procedures on the part of the gun crew.

The improved system can be started and operated remotely from Weapons Control with an option of any of six ammunition types. The different types are selected from combinations of the following.

PROJECTILES
High Capacity (HC).
White Phosphorus (WP).
Illumination or Star Shell (SS).
Illumination 2 (SS2).
High Fragmentation (HF).
Semi-Active Laser-Guided Projectile (SALGP).
Infra-Red Guided Projectile (IRGP).

FUZES
Mechanical Time (MT).
Control Variable Time (CVT).
Point Detonating (PD).
Point Detonating Delay (PDD).
Infra-Red (IR).
Proximity or Variable Time (VT).
Electronically Settable Fuze (ESF).

A broadside view of the 5in Mk 45 mounting.
USN

PROPELLANT CHARGES
Standard (STD).
Reduced Charge (RCHG).
Super Charge (SPCHG).
Guide Projectile Charge (GPCHG).

The six combinations of projectile, fuze and charge most likely to be used in a given mission are designated Nos 1 to 6, using the assignment switches on the Gun-Mount Control Panel. A display in the magazine also identifies the types of ammunition needed to fulfill the loading-order. Changes required for this improved capability are mainly confined to changes in sensors and logic, the only visible difference between Mod 0 and Mod 1 being a new large single door at the load station.

Other improvements have been made to the Mod 1 mounting. A built-in electronic fuze-setter is now provided. The loading station had to be lowered to allow the loading of the larger guided projectiles. Entirely new microprocessor-based circuitry is provided for control of the mounting, including self-test for detecting faults in the microprocessors. Solid-state optical sensors and a wire-wrapped backplane have improved reliability and safety. A keyboard mounted on the EP 2 panel allows the panel-operator to spot likely failures and to locate the source of the trouble. Even in its unmodified state the mounting is remarkably easy to maintain, required an estimated 2.4 hours' work daily.

The first ship to be fitted with the Mk 5in Mk 45, Mod 1 is the destroyer USS *Briscoe* (DD-977), which shipped the gun for sea trials in February 1980. The rest of the *Spruance* class are to be retrofitted as they are overhauled, starting in 1982.

Reports from *Briscoe* are most enthusiastic. Even without the new naval version of the laser-guided Copperhead projectile, the gun has much greater flexibility than the previous Mk 42. The EP 2 panel allows the operator to see at a glance the type and number of 5in rounds in the load drum; he then merely selects the type of shell, chooses single or continuous fire, and initiates firing. The loader drum rotates to the correct projectile, load and fires. Another improvement is the replacement of the standard photo-cells by infra-red transmitter and receiver units. They require only occasional cleaning, whereas the photo-cells tend to burn out at the wrong moment and require electrical calibration. The addition of a microprocessor creates slightly more complexity but this can be handled with proper training.

The lightweight 5in, 54 cal Mk 45 gun aboard the USS *Norton Sound* (AVM-1), December 1968.
USN

M CLASS From Lt Cdr M R Brady RN, Cosham, Hants. You may care to publish the following Alteration and Additions to the article in *Warship* 25 on the British *M* class submarines.

The alteration is to the published internal arrangement drawing. I based the accompanying drawing on study of the excellent cutaway model in the HMS *Dolphin* Submarine Museum: it shows the stowage for 12in shell and propellant and the loading arrangements. The photograph is one of comparatively few of one of the class firing the 12in gun – I have certainly never seen such a photograph published.

Mr Adams points out that the *M* class were 'monitor submarines' not in the sense of being intended for coastal bombardment (this was considered and dismissed when it was found that nowhere except off Heligoland could a submarine come within 12in gun range of Germany and still submerge), but in the older sense of mounting a large-calibre gun on a small-displacement low freeboard hull. The design was mooted at a time when there was some doubt about the effectiveness of submarine attack with torpedoes – in essence the *M* class were the precursors of those modern submarines which use air-flight missiles as anti-ship weapons rather than torpedoes. Given the technology of the time, however, it was considered that the development of faster torpedoes with heavier warheads was the more promising way forward.

The method of attack with the gun was to approach the target submerged, drive the submarine to the surface (more by putting the planes to 'rise' and going ahead at maximum speed than by blowing the ballast tanks), fire the gun at fairly low elevation (to give the best chance of hitting with a single shot a target whose range would not be known precisely) and then submerge quickly by putting the planes to 'dive'. It is important to remember that the gunhouse was free-flooding – so that the water would drain away as soon as possible the gunhouse floor was of steel girders, with the minimum of plating.

In a trial the gun was kept loaded for a week while on patrol and fired successfully after some hours 100ft down. Time from periscope depth (28ft) to firing was 25 seconds, *vice versa* 15 seconds. Such times could only have been achieved with an already loaded gun fired by remote control either from the loading chamber or the 'sighting hood'.

It is said that the practice was to leave the gun loaded when the boat was submerged, in order to bring it into action sooner. I have my doubts; not only might the chance of misfire be increased, but one also has to consider what might happen if the, supposedly watertight, muzzle tompion allowed water into the barrel and this was not drained away by opening the breech.

The myth that the 12in gun could be fired with only its muzzle and the first sighting periscope protruding above water is an enduring one – first put about in *Jane's Fighting Ships* and perpetuated by H M Le Fleming. In such a case the gun would have been at maximum elevation (giving maximum range) while the height of eye of the 'aimer' (though the short periscope) was at a minimum. The chance of hitting anything with a single shot would be negligible. In addition, I do not believe that the gun could be fired by remote control, nor that it would be safe to fire when the gunhouse was flooded.

The weakness of the concept behind the design of the 'M' Class was that the gun tactics described above would be extremely risky against a warship, and in the 1914–18 War the principal role of our submarines was to attack warships. The chief advantage of submarines is their invisibility; a submarines will only sacrifice invisibility if he has weapons so far-reaching or overwhelming that retaliation is unlikely. Submarine gun tactics were practised subsequently, of course, but were chiefly intended for use against merchant ships.

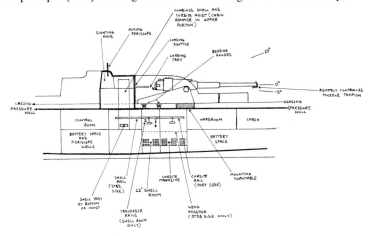

Lt-Commander Brady's sketch of the ammunition stowage and transfer arrangements for the *M* class submarines.

M1 firing her 12in gun at near maximum elevation in 1918.
There is a foresight on the muzzle of the gun and what could
be an aiming periscope forward of the two main periscopes.
The gun was primarily intended as a torpedo substitute – the
submarine could pop up and fire at about a mile range with
less need for calculation and at less cost than a torpedo attack
(12in shells cost £50 and torpedoes £200 even in those days).

PA Vicary

M2 launching a Parnell Peto seaplane from her catapult.
Forward of the conning tower is the water-tight hangar which
replaced her 12in mounting when she was converted during
1928.

CPL

DUTCH 'LEANDERS'
At the time we published Thomas A Adams' article in Warship
23 we had no photograph of a refitted Van Speijk *available.
However, F P Ijsseling has since sent us the accompanying
illustration of* Tjerk Hiddes *following her midlife
modernisation.*

ASKOLD From Hans-Heinrich Merten, West Berlin.
In the article on the Russian cruiser *Askold* in *Warship*
25, one section is sub-headed 'Tsushima' but this ship
did not participate in that battle. The sortie of the 1st
Russian Pacific Squadron from Port Arthur, with the
destination of Vladivostok, and the subsequent battle in
the Yellow Sea, off Shantung, took place on 10 August
1904. *Askold* escaped the pursuing Japanese cruisers,
reached Shanghai on 11 August and was interned there
for the rest of the war. The Battle of Tsushima took place
ten months later on 27/28 May 1905, so the sub-heading
is misleading.

Another action between the Russians and Japanese
took place to the north of Tsushima Island on 14 August
1904 but the author does not mention this encounter:
the so-called Vladivostok Squadron consisting of the
cruisers *Rurik* (flagship of Admiral Jessen), *Gromoboi*
and *Rossija*, ordered to support the sortie by the Port
Arthur squadron, was intercepted by the Japanese
Admiral Kamimura. *Rurik* was heavily damaged and
scuttled, while the other two cruisers returned to Vladivostok damaged.

Incidentally in *Warship* 6 there is a photograph of
Askold, captioned 'The Russian cruiser *Askold*,
interned at Shanghai *after* the Battle of Tsushima'.
*Mr Merten is of course correct in his observations, the
action described in* Warship 25 *was the Battle of the
Yellow Sea. The error was not the author's.*
Editor

ASKOLD'S FUNNELS from G Kodaom, Warsaw.
The statement in *Warship* 25 that *Askold* was the only
five funnelled warship in the world is untrue. The Greek
destroyers of the *Aetos* class (as originally built) and the
French battleships of the *Danton* class also had five
funnels.

*Although this is a correct observation, the author was
referring to the fact that* Askold *was the only five funnelled warship in existence at that time. The* Aetos *class were
launched in 1911 and the* Danton *class in 1909, several
years after the completion of* Askold.
Editor

A SCOUT FOR THE IMPERIAL NAVY

by Adam Śmigielski

At the turn of the century relations between Russia and Britain were not good, and while Russia could not hope to match the strength of the Royal Navy, she could plan for a campaign against British seaborne trade. As early submarines had very limited capabilities, fast and well armed cruisers seemed ideal for this purpose and as a result numerous protected cruisers were built for the Imperial Russian Navy. To this category belonged the ships of *Pallada*, *Varyag*, *Askold* and *Bogatyr* classes.

The battle fleet also required an efficient reconnaissance force, a service which could again be fulfilled by small fast cruisers. Although torpedo boat destroyers were usually the fastest ships available, they were not sufficiently seaworthy, their hulls were too lightly built, their armament too weak and their radius of action insufficient for this function. Reconnaissance is best conducted at speed and in depth, and with such service in mind the Russian Admiralty drew up a specification for a small cruiser with the sea speed of a destroyer, sufficiently armed to fight off escorting destroyers but fast enough to escape from anything larger. The first such ship, *Bojarin*, was built by the Danish shipyard Burmeister & Wain, because the Russians had insufficient experience with the construction of warships of this type and their shipyards were already overloaded with naval construction. Ships were frequently ordered in foreign yards because of the notoriously long building times in home shipyards (the protected cruiser *Avrora* took six years to build). Moreover Russian-built ships were very expensive. A similar cruiser, *Novik*, was built by the German shipyard F Schichau in Danzig (Gdansk). *Novik* reached a speed of 25kts and was the fastest cruiser in the world when completed, but this, at that time considered a fantastic speed, was not sufficient for a battle fleet whose speed was approaching 18kts and more. The 7kt speed margin being too small, especially in rough weather when smaller ships had to work harder than battleships to maintain high speed. These fast ships were built under influence from the ideas of the famous Admiral Stepan O Makarov. This was the situation on the eve of the Russo-Japanese War, when proposals were made for a completely new scout cruiser design, intended to reach the fantastic service speed of 30kts. Such a ship could outrun everything and would be ideal for reconnaissance duty.

MACHINERY

The new 4500-ton cruiser was designed in 1904 by the Russian naval architect Gavrilov. It was not a regular navy project but a speculative work by a dedicated man. The ship however was designed to Russian Navy specifications and the design was so detailed that a cruiser could have been ordered very quickly if only money was available for its construction. The design provided for unusual features and one of these was of course the propelling machinery for a speed of 30kts. She was to be fitted with 18 small-tube destroyer type boilers, contrary to the common practice of fitting larger vessels with the big and heavy large-tube boilers which at the time were more reliable. However, it had already been proved that Thornycroft boilers of the destroyer type gave good service for many years and the small height of such boilers enabled them to be located under the cover of a continuous, low armoured deck. The ship was also to use small high speed destroyer-type reciprocating engines. These engines were to be of the same type as fitted in the US Navy's *Bainbridge* class destroyers. Again, such engines were easy to locate under a low armoured deck and had a good power-to-weight ratio. To attain 30kts the cruiser needed eight engines driving four shafts each fitted with two 2.4m diameter destroyer screws. It is interesting to compare the weight of such a propulsion

KEY: **1** 6 oar whaleboat; **2** 152mm QF gun; **3** compass platform; **4** searchlight; **5** main mast; **6** 14 oar gig; **7** boiler room ventilator; **8** steam launch; **9** uptake; **10** 18 oar launch; **11** 4 oar jolly boat; **12** foremast; **13** conning tower; **14** 76mm QF gun; **15** anchor windlass; **16** Lehoff's chain stopper; **17** staircase; **18** officers' galley; **19** crew's galley; **20** wardroom; **21** engineer's cabin; **22** engine room hatch; **23** communication tube; **24** sick bay; **25** 76mm hoist; **26** 152mm hoist; **27** chain locker; **28** dry room; **29** power and damage control centre; **30** 152mm magazine; **31** 76mm magazine; **32** machine gun ammunition magazine; **33** coal bunker; **34** auxiliary machinery room; **35** boiler; **36** engine room; **37** biler; **38** thrust bearing; **39** condenser; **40** bilge pump; **41** steering engine room; **42** armour protection over steering room; **43** armoured deck; **44** main engine; **45** rudder; **46** inner screws; **47** auxiliary hand steering gear; **48** outer screws; **49** coal scuttle; **50** living quarters; **51** fresh water tank; **52** boiler room No 1; **53** boiler room No 2; **54** boiler room No 3; **55** auxiliary boiler room; **56** boiler room No 4.

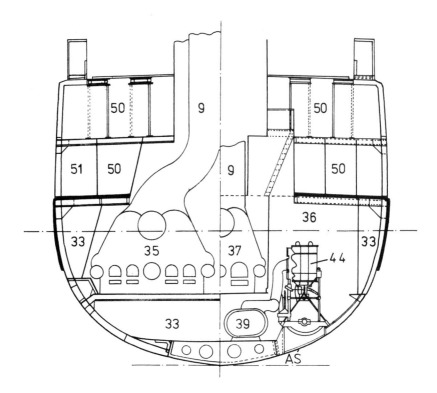

plant of 32,000ihp with a classical cruiser power plant of large tube boilers and large slow engines. That installed in the 7775-ton armoured cruiser *Bayan* produced 16,500ihp and weighed 1390 tons, while that in the new design weighed only 880 tons.

There were, naturally, drawbacks to the lightweight machinery – it required numerous engine and boiler room personnel, which were difficult to accommodate in a relatively small ship. Of a crew of 400, as many as 171 belonged to the 'black gang'. When engines were operating on full power 114 stokers and engine room personnel were required and it was only possible to maintain 30kts for the duration of a watch, ie 4 hours. For a speed of 23-24kts (the maximum for most cruisers of the time) only 57 men were required and the cruiser could steam at this speed for long periods.

In the meantime there appeared new kinds of ship prime movers such as the internal combustion engine and the steam turbine. Turbines were, however, difficult to manufacture and required skilful operation. They also needed men with a higher technical education than reciprocating engines, for these reasons engines well known to Russian personnel were chosen. As a result the power plant was a little bizarre with two engines working in tandem on each shaft (a similar arrangement with four engines on two shafts was tried earlier in the armoured cruiser *Rurik*).

It is doubtful if the scout cruiser described above would have been capable of 30kts in service, with her designed indicated engine power. Displacing 4500 tons normal, she was bigger than, for example, the first 30kt cruiser in the world – the British *Arethusa* built nearly ten years later and fitted with powerful turbine engines. In fact, even the *Arethusa* had a maximum service speed of only 28.5kts. Moreover, the British ship had oil-fired boilers and so fitted could easily keep her high speed for long periods. The Russian ship had a nearly flush deck hull and the characteristic shape of her bow could have been useful during the winter steaming into thin ice. It was a quite different solution to that preferred by most navies, which at that time built their light scout cruisers, and even destroyers, with the obsolete ram shape. Some tried to justify the fitting of a ram by stating that it gave some much needed buoyancy forward facilitating better seakeeping.

After designing this ship, Gavrilov was permitted by the official naval architect Aleksei N Krylov to conduct some model tests in the towing tank in St Petersburg, to provide accurate data on power requirements for the new cruiser. She was compared with other fast ships (cruisers *Askold*, *Novik* and destroyers *Berkut*, *Groznyj* and *Ukraina*) and a second variant of her full form was drawn. The body plan shows that the new hull was longer on the waterline by 6.68m but with other dimensions the same as in the earlier one; strictly speaking only the bow was modified.

The trials showed that the speed of 30kts, computed using Afanasjev formulae, was unattainable with 32,000ihp and the ship would be capable of only 27.5kts. The cruiser in her new form would gain 0.5kts with the same power and on the same displacement. Even then she would be the fastest cruiser afloat. Consideration was given to fitting her with slightly heavier boilers, with stronger watertubes, for 28,000ihp which meant a further reduction in speed of one knot.

ARMAMENT

The armament can be considered as more than adequate in comparison with contemporary scout cruisers, but it was proved beyond doubt during the Russo-Japanese War, and later, that the ship should be rearmed. The designer could have dispensed with the completely useless machine-guns and with the majority of her 76mm (3in) guns, the weight saved being utilised to fit two additional 152mm (6in) guns under the bridge wings forward, or another gun forward and one amidships.

In fact, there was another variant of her armament worked out by Mr Gavrilov, keeping the displacement at the previous 4500 tons. Based on his studies of the lessons of the Russo-Japanese War he considered a new armament of one 152mm (6in) QF gun in the bow, one 203mm (8in) gun aft on the upper deck and six 120mm QF guns so arranged that one stood forward and aft in the superfiring position to the main guns and the remainder were on the upper deck under the bridge (two guns) and abreast the mainmast (two guns). The 203mm gun was to be used to shake off any larger pursuers and the 120mm guns (intended to replace the earlier 76mm) were though to be more useful against destroyers, which were steadily getting larger and better armed. However, a more uniform armament would have been preferable if only with more accurate fire control in view. In addition to the guns the new variant of the armament provided for three above-water 450mm (18in) torpedo tubes fitted one in the stern and two under bridge. Tubes were placed on the armoured deck. The bow torpedo tube was dispensed with because of the dangers of flooding at high speed in a seaway.

The main guns were so placed that they could be worked in almost any kind of weather. However, the placing of the searchlights forward and aft under the upper deck was quite impractical and they would have been useless even in a calm sea during a high speed passage.

No pilot house was provided and it would have been extremely uncomfortable and impractical to con the cruiser from the crowded conning tower during long periods of cruising with the fleet. It is also worth noting that the ship had good armour protection over her vital Her 60mm thick belt, capable of withstanding fire from destroyer guns, was at the time an unusual feature in such a fast vessel – most such ships were small protected cruisers without a belt.

TABLE 1: TECHNICAL CHARACTERISTICS

Displacement:	4500 tons normal, 4900 tons full load
Length:	132.5m (oa), 131.67m (wl), 121.65m (pp)
Beam:	13.41m (wl), 13.57m (max)
Depth:	11.23m
Draught	5.18/5.49m
Armament:	3–152mm L/45, 13–76mm, 22 machine guns of Maxim type
Armour:	belt – 60mm, deck – 29mm, steering engine compartment – 40mm, conning tower – 20mm
Machinery:	four shafts fitted with eight screws; 8 4 cyl vertical triple expansion engines, 4000ihp each (325 rpm, 17.6kG/cm²), total power 32,000ihp = 30kts (natural draught), 34,300ihp (forced draught), 16,000 ihp = 23kts, 10,000ihp = 20kts; 18 Thornycroft small-tube boilers with total heating surface of 6958m² and working pressure of 21kG/cm² (300psi), of these 10 boilers were designed for 2120ihp, 4 for 1910ihp, 2 for 1485ihp and 2 for 1270ihp each
Coal capacity:	600 tons normal, 900 tons maximum
Complement:	400 (16 officers, 9 chief petty officers, 375 petty officers and ratings)
Searchlights:	six 70cm diameter

TABLE 2: LEGEND WEIGHTS OF 4500-TON SCOUT CRUISER

Hull	1750 (tons)	39 (%)
Armour	510	11.3
Machinery	880	19.6
Armament	165	3.7
Anchors, cables, boats, etc	155	3.4
Feed water	50	1.2
Coal	600	13.3
Crew	60	1.3
Auxiliary machinery	110	2.4
Provisions and drinking water	160	3.6
Weight reserve	60	1.3
Normal displacement	4500 tons	100.0 %
Additional coal	300	
Additional feed water	100	
Full load displacement	4900 tons	

ATTACK & DEFENCE No 4

Action Damage to British Warships in the Second World War Part 1

By David Brown RCNC

Most readers will be familiar with the stories of the great disasters – *Hood, Prince of Wales, Ark Royal* – but few are aware of the more numerous examples of ships which survived major damage and were repaired to fight again. This article will concentrate on the survivability of RN ships, though the cause of some losses will also be outlined. No overall comparison with ships of other navies will be attempted as data are too scarce but foreign examples will be used when relevant.

Table 1 sets the scene with some figures on the loss and damage caused by various weapons.

The destroyer *Ivanhoe* showing the damage caused on 1 June 1940 by one hit and two near miss' from 220lb direct-action bombs. The ship was out of action for seven weeks.

MoD

HITTING

Before a ship can be damaged the enemy must get a launching vehicle within range and fire a weapon which must hit. This is not a trivial point; the torpedo, the most lethal anti-ship weapon of the war, did not hit very often. A similar problem faced the bomber, who had to decide on whether to use a large number of small bombs, giving a good chance of a hit, or a single, more lethal weapon which might well miss. In all cases, the launching vehicle had to balance the increased chance of a hit when the range was reduced with the greater probability of being put out of action before launching the weapon.

Even when a hit was scored the weapon had to function properly in order to cause major damage. Delayed action fuzes were and are very difficult to design and

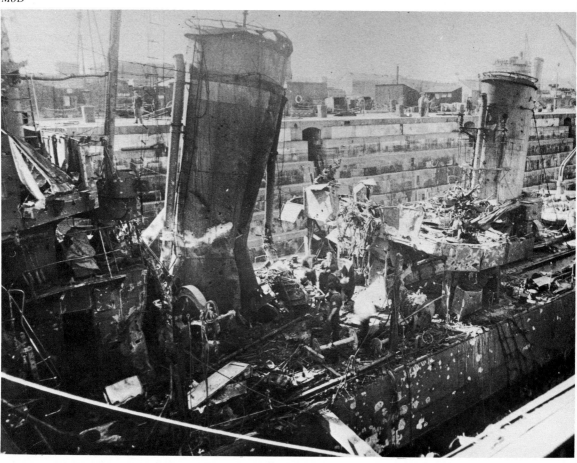

TABLE 1: RN SHIPS LOST AND DAMAGED 1939-1945

Ship type	Gravity of effect	Shell	Bomb	Mine	Torpedo
			TYPE OF WEAPON		
Battleships	Sunk	1	–	–	4
	Serious	2	6	5	5
	Slight	3	11	–	–
Aircraft Carriers	Sunk	1	1	–	5
	Serious	–	10	1	3
	Slight	–	8	–	–
Cruisers	Sunk	3	10	1	13
	Serious	9	42	8	24
	Slight	22	45	2	–
Destroyers	Sunk	13	44	18	53
	Serious	40	81	35	15
	Slight	74	118	4	2
Sloops Frigates Corvettes Minesweepers	Sunk	2	15	17	50
	Serious	2	29	39	19
	Slight	10	33	10	2

many either exploded on impact or failed to explode at all.

THE WEAPONS AND THEIR EFFECTS

Almost all the weapons used carried an explosive charge which detonated on contact or after a short delay or, in the case of underwater weapons, at a distance below the hull. Shells and bombs cause damage both by the force of the explosion and due to the kinetic energy of the striking missile.

Shells have to be very strong to resist the forces imposed on discharge from a gun. In consequence, the charge of a shell is usually fairly small in relation to the overall weight. Typically, a high explosive shell would have a charge weight about 10% of the total and an armour piercing shell would have one of 2%. High explosive shells have a nose fuze which is easily damaged when hitting thick structures. Armour piercing and semi-armour piercing shells (charge weight 4%) have fuzes in the base of the shell.

Gunfire was not particularly accurate and at long range only 1-2% hits were likely. High explosive shells would cause damage mainly by blast but the large number of small splinters could kill or injure exposed personnel and would also set fire to inflammable material. Semi-armour piercing (SAP) shell was effective against unarmoured structure or light protection. The thick walls of this shell broke into a comparatively small number of large splinters which would damage decks and bulkheads allowing flooding to spread. The splinters would be hot enough to start fires if they lodged in inflammable material.

The small explosive charge in an armour piercing shell caused relatively local damage but it was intended to explode in the most vital areas of a ship – magazines, turrets, transmitting stations etc. where the damage could have fatal consequences. Hits below the waterline could lead to flooding which would spread if bulkheads

were pierced by the heavy splinters.

Bombs had somewhat similar effects to shells but because they did not have to be fired from a gun, their cases could be light and the charge weight high. A high capacity bomb could have a charge ratio of 70-80% but such weapons were easily damaged on impact and were rarely used against ships. A 1000lb medium bomb case could have a charge of 500lb and could penetrate about 2ins of non-cemented (NC) deck armour from 3500ft.

Armour piercing bombs required thick cases and hence the charge weights were low (8% or so). A 2000lb AP Bomb could penetrate the following thicknesses of deck armour.

Height of drop (ft)	Penetration (in)
12,000	9
8,000	7
4,000	5

The chance of hitting reduced considerably as the dropping height increased. A bomb hit caused damage of much the same character as that described for shells but, because the charge weight was higher, the damage was much more extensive. Table 1 shows that bombs were the most frequent cause of serious damage to British warships. Near miss bombs could cause serious problems as a burst on the sea surface could cause a shower of splinters which would kill or injure exposed personnel and cause extensive flooding through numerous holes along the water line. Before the war, there were fears that diving bombs, with large charges, could be dropped so that they would explode under the keel causing similar damage to a non-contact torpedo. In practice, the accuracy required of the bomb aimer and the sensitivity of the fuze were such that weapons of this sort proved impractical.

WEAPONS IMPACT – THE DESIGNER'S NIGHTMARE

High Capacity Contact	Effect
1 HE Shell	Blast in air or water
2 HE Bomb	Small volume of high temperature
3 HE Bomb (near miss)	gas (fires).
4 Contact torpedo or mine	Splinter damage to men and light plate.

High Capacity, non contact	
5 Non-contact torpedo, magnetic fuze	Shock wave and gas bubble.
6 Ground mine	Extensive shock damage and whipping. Flooding.

Medium Capacity	
7 Semi-Armour Piercing Shell	Penetrates normal structures and light armour. Very heavy
8 Medium Case Bomb	splinters penetrate bulkheads extending the flooding.

Armour Piercing	
9 AP Shell	Penetrate to vitals – may go
10 AP Bomb	right through a lightly protected ship.

Naval architects are always taught that it is necessary to let water into a ship in order to sink her. Torpedoes and mines, exploding below the waterline were intended to cause such damage and, when they exploded in the right place, were the most effective weapons for sinking a ship.

Most torpedoes of the Second World War ran on a straight course and were aimed to hit the side of the ship with a contact fuze to explode the charge. A very large hole would be blown in the side of the ship and bulkheads rendered non-watertight for a considerable distance either side of the hole. The extensive flooding from a single hit would often sink a small ship. The damage to structure was extensive and a highly stressed ship, such as a destroyer, was quite likely to break in half if hit amidships. There were a few pattern running torpedoes available at the end of the war which if they hit would cause similar damage.

Homing torpedoes of the Second World War sought the propellers, attracted by cavitation noise. They could often be decoyed by noise makers towed astern, particularly if the ship's speed was reduced below that at which propellers cavitated (about 8kts for a Second World War

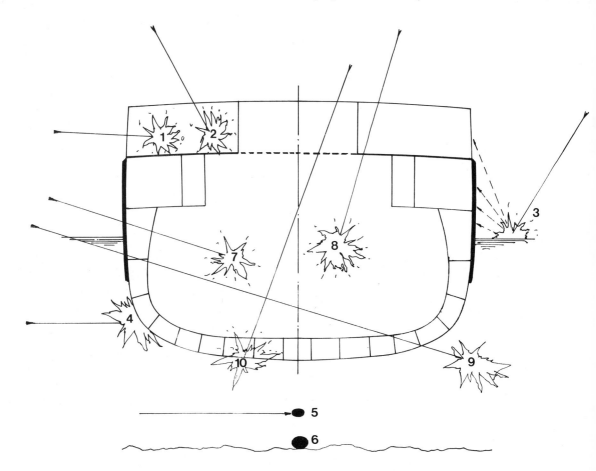

Amidships view of Mountbatten's *Kelly* in drydock at Hawthorn Leslie, showing the damage caused by a torpedo on 9 May 1940. The hole extends from the sheer strake of the upper deck to the keel; she took four days to bring home, a remarkable achievement considering the extent of the damage, which took eight months to repair.

MoD

destroyer with propellers in *good* condition). A hit would usually be at the after end and would put both propeller shafts and the rudder out of action in a destroyer or frigate. Such damage rarely sank a warship but the immobilised vessel was an easy target for a conventional torpedo and would, if brought home, take months to repair (most such casualties were not repaired).

Both Britain and Germany had developed non-contact torpedoes before the war. These had a magnetic pistol which would explode the torpedo well below the keel of the target. The resulting pressure pulses would break any small warship in two (see photograph of *Bruce, Warship* 24). Such pistols also meant that precise depth keeping near the surface, which caused so many problems for torpedo designers, was no longer necessary. However, the sensitivity required from the fuze, particularly when ships were degaussed, meant that tor-

The Tribal class destroyer *Eskimo*, her bows destroyed by a single contact torpedo launched from an enemy destroyer during the Second Battle of Narvik on 13 April 1940. She was under repair for five months.

MoD

pedoes could be accidentally exploded in the earth's magnetic field, or explode too far from a ship without causing damage. Success from non-contact torpedoes was rare.

Some casualties were caused by the old fashioned, moor mine with 'horn' contact fuzes but most of the damage was due to non-contact mines laid on the sea bed. These could be actuated by magnetic, acoustic or pressure signatures of the ship (or by a combination of signatures). Such mines had a very large charge (1000lb, typically) which would change into a very small, very high pressure gas bubble on detonation. This would cause a shock wave to travel through the water at the speed of sound which could shatter plating and fracture machinery seats. The expanding gas bubble, still at very high pressure, would follow at a rather lower velocity and add to the damage. In particular, large under keel explosions would cause a ship to 'whip', ie bend violently in the vertical plane. This would often break the back of small ships and would cause accelerations which would break machinery seats, valves etc unless they were specially designed and flexibly mounted.

A few air launched, guided weapons were used in the war. The German FX 1400 was a rocket assisted, SAP bomb with radio control. It weighed 3100lb, had a charge weight of 620lb and could penetrate about 6ins of armour falling almost vertically. It was these bombs which sank the *Roma* and badly damaged the *Warspite* off Salerno. The HS293 was a rocket assisted bomb with small wings which enabled it to attack on a more nearly horizontal trajectory under radio control from the carrying aircraft. It weighed 1450lb, had a charge of 730lb and could penetrate about 3in of NC plate.

The suicide bomber was a very well guided missile even if rather ineffective.

CONSEQUENCES

The previous section concentrated on the immediate physical effect of the weapon: this section will explore the consequences to the ship. It is most important to note the randomness of weapon damage due to the position in which a weapon hits, the effectiveness with which it detonates, the design of the ship and the skill of the crew in coping with the damage. The examples which follow will show that many hits in non-vital areas might cause minor damage, soon repaired, while one shell in a magazine could destroy the ship.

Torpedo Damage The torpedo was the most effective sinker of ships and must be considered first. A hit amidships caused considerable loss of buoyancy and stability, often with considerable heel, the structure of the ship was gravely weakened, machinery would be out of action and electric lights and power would fail.

At the outbreak of war most countries airborne torpedoes with a warhead of 350-450lb and ship launched torpedoes with a 600-650lb charge. The explosive in 1939 was usually TNT but soon more effective compounds such as Torpex and Hexanite were introduced with about 1½ times the power of TNT (charge weights will usually be quoted in terms of their equivalent in TNT). Since damage radius is proportional to the cube root of the charge weight the difference in effectiveness between airborne and ship size torpedoes and between TNT and Torpex is not as great as might be thought. A 50% increase in power would increase the damage radius by 14% (cube root 1.5 = 1.14). An 18in torpedo had a 50% chance of rupturing a bulkhead 30ft away while a 21in weapon at 35ft would cause the same damage. Since bulkheads are typically spaced about 35ft apart, the best which could be expected from one hit on a small ship would be instantaneous flooding over 70ft length while the worst likely case would be with three bulkheads destroyed and flooding over 140ft. It should be noted that restrictions to these lengths depended on good damage control to minimise the spread of water through minor leaks.

Big ships had underwater side protection systems whose development was described in *Warship* 24. Their success or failure in war illustrates very well the random nature of damage. *Malaya* had an old fashioned external bulge system, improved between the wars, with the main holding bulkhead 13ft from the outer shell. While off West Africa, escorting a convoy, she was hit by a U-boat torpedo (1000lb TNT) on 20 March 1941. There were no casualties and the effect on fighting efficiency was very small once the initial heel of 7° was reduced to ½° by counter flooding bulge compartments in the other side. At the time of the hit the bulge and double bottom tanks were empty and the tank next to the thick bulkead full. The tank behind was about two-thirds full. The bulge was flooded for 100ft and wing protection for 60ft, while all fuel tanks abreast the forward boiler room were flooded.

Repairs to *Malaya* were carried out in the USA and took 13 weeks, fairly typical for a single torpedo hit. The time taken for repairs varied considerably as normal defects would be made good at the same time and new equipment fitted. In particular, work on very badly damaged ships was given low priority and often suspended while more urgent tasks were completed.

Resolution, *Ramillies* and *Barham* were also hit on their bulges by single torpedoes and in each case the effect was much more severe than that described for *Malaya*, mainly because of secondary flood through their aged structure which could not readily be controlled. *Barham* and *Royal Oak* were sunk by multiple torpedo hits.

An interesting and well known incident of a hit on a modern side protection system was that by an Italian aircraft torpedo (700lb TNT equivalent) on *Indomitable* on 16 July 1943. She was unfortunate in that the torpedo hit the lower strake of her 4in cemented side armour. Such armour is rather brittle and fractures under a heavy explosion. Pieces of armour were thrown right through the torpedo protection system and into the port boiler room. *Indomitable* made her way to America where she took 8½ months to repair and refit.

The problem of running uptakes from port and centre boiler rooms under the hangar and across to the funnel on the starboard side of an aircraft carrier was not an easy one and, inevitably, a hazard following damage.

Two views of the destroyer *Javelin* after being torpedoed in both bow and stern on 28 November 1940.
MoD

Raising the uptakes would have meant raising the hangar, flight deck and their protection and the resultant increase in size could not have been accepted under the Treaty limits. The loss of the *Ark Royal* is described in detail in Ref 1. Briefly, the damage from a single submarine torpedo was much more extensive than usual because she was hit below the port bilge while turning. The centre engine and boiler rooms were flooded, mainly through the uptakes. There were numerous electrical problems and as her designer, W A D Forbes, has said, 'the ship could have been saved if the ship's staff had known what were the right things to do . . . (part of the ship's staff) toiled unremittingly and heroically until exhausted doing the wrong things. Even at the last moment *Ark Royal* could have been brought more or less upright by flooding the starboard boiler room and towed the last miles into Gibraltar.

If the old and small cruisers of the C and D classes are omitted, the resistance of cruisers to torpedo attack is seen as good. Twenty one were hit by a single torpedo of which only *Naiad* and *Hermione*, both small, sank (*Manchester* was scuttled later). Repair time varied from $3\frac{1}{2}$ to $13\frac{1}{2}$ months in the extreme with 8 months being reasonably typical.

Five cruisers were hit by two torpedoes of which two sank and three survived. One of the latter (*Edinburgh*) was hit by a third torpedo later and then sank as did *Galatea*, the only cruiser hit by three torpedoes in a single attack.

Adding some American ships, there were 91 destroyers torpedoed and the results can be expressed in a table (Ref 2).

The after end of the frigate *Lagan* showing the damage caused by an acoustic torpedo on 20 September 1943. The ship was not repaired.

MoD

TABLE 2: TORPEDO HITS ON DESTROYERS, 1939–45

	No hit	No sunk
Hit by one torpedo	74	37 (+13*)
Hit by two torpedoes	15	13
Hit by three torpedoes	2	2

* 13 were scuttled by own forces, usually because they were immobilised. It is impossible to say how many of these would have sunk anyway and how many could have been saved.

Of the 37 destroyers sunk directly by a single torpedo, 6 capsized, 7 plunged by bow or stern, 1 sank bodily, 1 blew-up and 22 broke in half. The main concern in pre-war days had been over stability and topweight was controlled as far as was possible. That only 6 capsized went far to confirm the success of this policy.

Breaking in half was the major problem and, while regrettable, need cause little surprise. Destroyers were highly stressed craft and shallow in depth from deck to keel. Submarine commanders would usually aim to hit about amidships and, in fact, hits were reasonably normally distributed about amidships. Something approaching half the strength of the hull would be destroyed by a torpedo, doubling the stresses.

The low freeboard of destroyers arose mainly from the pre-war Staff requirements for them to act as torpedo boats. There was continual pressure to keep the ships low to reduce their visibility (Ref 3). The torpedo armament was heavy and to raise it to forecastle deck level would have required a considerable increase in beam with a loss of speed. The low freeboard aft was probably the main factor in the loss of the seven ships by plunging.

Mainly for this reason destroyers sank very quickly, something like 25% going in under ten minutes. The speed of sinking and the inadequate life saving equipment of the Second World War caused heavy casualties.

Of the destroyers which survived, two of the most outstanding stories came from, the then Captain, Lord

Louis Mountbatten (Ref 1). The *Kelly* was torpedoed in No 1 Boiler room on 9 May 1940 while operating in the North Sea and was saved by the combined skills of her designer, A P Cole RCNC and her captain, Mountbatten. The hole was 47ft long and 14ft deep with damage to the upper deck for 50ft. The ship listed 15° to starboard immediately. The *J* and *K* classes were the first longitudinally framed destroyers. A system introduced by Cole against very strong opposition from the shipbuilders. Longitudinally framed destroyers had a considerably greater resistance to overall collapse by buckling than the older transversely framed ships even when designed to the same nominal stress levels. Of the 17 longitudinally framed destroyers which were torpedoed, two broke in half from a single hit and two more from two hits.

While the *J* and *K* class were being designed, Mountbatten and Cole had many long conversations about damage control and, as a result, a routine had been worked out in advance. As soon as *Kelly* was torpedoed all ten torpedoes and depth charges were jettisoned, the boats were put in the water and all movable gear on the upper deck thrown overboard. Even so she was heeling severely with the starboard gunwhale awash. On the third night Mountbatten noted that the roll was extremely sluggish and 'it seemed to me that our metacentric height was gradually fading away'. He had 212 men (10½ tons) taken off and the ship became a little bit more stable. *Kelly* took 8 months to repair and while

this was being done Mountbatten took over *Javelin*.

On 28 November 1940 this ship was hit simultaneously by two torpedoes. The illustrations show that only 155ft out of her original 365½ft survived. She was brought home to Devonport Dockyard and rebuilt in 13 months. There was an element of luck in *Javelin*'s survival but her designers, builders and crew can still feel proud of their share in her survival.

Most smaller ships hit by torpedoes were sunk or damaged beyond repair. The exceptions which were repaired were usually hit near the bow. The figures in Table 1 are confusing in that many of those marked as seriously damaged were hit by acoustic homing torpedoes in the latter part of the war. The damage was usually extensive and since the shortage of escort vessels was over, no effort was made to repair them. There seem to have been at least 15 such wrecks (including RCN) at the end of the war.

Lagan is a fairly typical example of the damage caused by these homing torpedoes. She was hit in September 1943 near the propellers and about 30ft of the stern was blown off. The next 30ft, up to the after superstructure, was wrecked and blown upwards. There were two buckles, due to whipping, one just forward of the main damage and one amidships, extending right across the decks and down to the waterline. The ship had no rudder, steering gear, tail shafts or propellers. All depth charge equipment had gone and the after gun mount was damaged.

To be continued

Marine – Gestern, Heute

The quarterly journal *Marine – Gestern, Heute* is devoted to the study of the former Austro-Hungarian Navy and merchant fleet. Each 40-page issue is packed with unique information, previously unpublished photographs and a profile of a particular vessel, with a specially-commissioned detailed plan. The articles are written by well known international naval experts and historians, using unpublished material from the Austrian *Kriegsarchiv*, from private collections and other sources. Though the journal is published in German, the ship enthusiast should have no difficulty in gleaning information from it.

SUBSCRIPTION RATES   Europe US $13.00   USA, Canada & Overseas US $17.00, or air mail delivery add US $9.00. Cheques should be sent to: *Marine – Gestern, Heute,* POB 53, A-2130 Mistelbach, Austria.

SELECTED PAPERS ON
BRITISH WARSHIP DESIGN
IN WORLD WAR II

SELECTED PAPERS ON
BRITISH WARSHIP DESIGN
IN WORLD WAR II

From the Transactions of the
Royal Institution of Naval Architects

280 x 220mm (11″ x 8⅝″), 224 pages, 68 photographs, 100 line drawings. ISBN 0 85177 284 6. **£12.50** (plus £1.90 post and packing when ordering direct).

by R Baker, W J Holt, J Lenaghan, A J Sims and A W Watson

Immediately after the Second World War, the wartime experience of British warship designers was summarised in a series of papers which were published in the 1947 Transactions of the Royal Institution of Naval Architects. These papers were first-hand accounts by the people directly responsible for the new ship types and innovative designs produced in response to the pressures of war; by reprinting these papers in a single volume with all the original illustrations this important source material will be available to the layman for the first time.

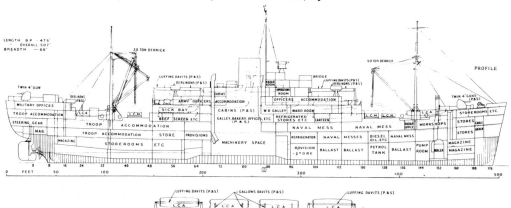

FIG. 1.—"GLEN" CLASS L.S.I.(L).

From your local bookseller or by post from
Conway Maritime Press Limited
24 Bride Lane, Fleet Street, London EC4Y 8DR.

EDITORIAL John Roberts

In peacetime expenditure on defence is, almost without exception, looked upon as a necessary evil. It is always expensive and, except in war, shows little return for the vast sums of money that it absorbs. Under such circumstances any democratic government must be expected to seek ways of reducing the cost of armaments both to increase the finance available for other areas and to satisfy their own and the public's desire to see reductions in taxation. This is a situation of mutual advantage in which the public sees its money, or less of it, well spent, and the government can divert money into projects of social value which both advance its own policies and improve its chances of re-election. There is of course a limit to this in that fears among the public that the defences of the country are weak would have a serious effect on public morale and the status of the government and, on more than one occasion, such fears have generated a substantial increase in defence spending.

In times of recession, such as that that existed in the 1920s and 1930s or that which exists now, the defence departments are continually under pressure to minimise costs and anybody who can produce a reasonably convincing idea to save money will be listened to with sympathy, and often encouragement, by the government. Thus between the wars, the Admiralty were pressurised by circumstances into accepting smaller ships, less sophisticated ships in some cases, and less of them, knowing that they were not completely satisfactory. The inefficiency of the AA systems in British warships at the outbreak of the Second World War was as much, if not more, to do with the fact that the money to develop and produce an efficient fire control system and the weapons to go with it was not available. The Admiralty knew of this situation before the war and any criticism has to be developed in terms of whether or not they had their priorities right in spending money on other projects rather than a simple assumption that they should have known better.

At various times in the 1920s and early 1930s proposals were made both, officially (usually in the hope of international agreement) and unofficially for smaller and hence cheaper battleships, and for the abandonment of battleships, altogether as obsolete. Both these ideas were listened to and encouraged by the governments of the time.

At the present time there is, in Britain, a controversial public debate in progress on what type of ship the Admiralty should build in the future. The argument revolves around whether the Royal Navy should continue with its traditional designs or switch to a short, broad beamed, type claimed to be equally, if not more, efficient and cheaper. On one side is the Admiralty and its design team at Bath which has produced the Type 23 frigate – a traditional vessel in form and cost restricted but nevertheless modern and sophisticated. On the other is a small private company which has used the media and the government to promote its S90, a short, broad beamed design claimed to be cheaper, of high stability and capable of carrying more weapons and equipment than a traditional type of equal or greater displacement. Unfortunately the debate is in the hands of a largely inexpert media who repeat claims without understanding them to a public which is ignorant of the complexities of warship design and can only see the efforts of private enterprise being resisted by civil service bureaucracy.

I have yet to see a reasonable or even partial set of particulars of the S90 so it is difficult to make any sound judgement on the claims made for the design. It is obvious that a broad beamed ship does have a higher level of stability than a narrow beam one and that it can therefore carry more topweight and/or higher topweights, hence the claim to be able to carry more weapons and higher (and hence greater range) radar aerials. However, many questions come to mind and I am still waiting to hear them mentioned in the public debate on the subject. The vessel is claimed as cheaper, and a smaller hull and diesel propulsion would save money but the most expensive items in warships are their weapons and sensors and if more of these are carried the cost goes up again, possibly by more than the saving. At one time claims were made that S90 could reach the same speed as the Type 23 with the same engine power and fuel consumption which, to say the least, is highly dubious. I would guess that a short, broad beamed ship would have a poor motion in any sort of seaway which raises questions of crew and equipment efficiency in rough weather – bearing in mind the Royal Navy's principal areas of operation – the North Sea, Arctic, North Atlantic and now the South Atlantic, this is a very important point. Broad beamed ships, although possessing high stability, heel much more when damaged on one side. What, given that masts are usually placed well apart to reduce mutual interference between radar aerials, will be the radar outfit of S90 which at present has only one tall mast? I mention all this not so much as criticism of the design as to point out that such things are seldom, if at all, mentioned – the debate is much more on the level of 'it's got more guns and it's cheap so it must be better' – I would be much happier, and in a better position to criticise or agree, if more facts and figures were attached to the claims for the S90.

SOME THORNYCROFT DESIGNS

By DJ Lyon

One of the most fascinating aspects of the enormous Thornycroft Collection of plans and associated documents now held in the National Maritime Museum is the vast number of designs for vessels which were never built that it includes. Unfortunately most other shipbuilders' collections of plans only include vessels which were actually built (the smaller and less important, though still interesting, Pollock's Collection is the only other major exception). The interest of the often weird and wonderful designs produced by Thornycroft is added to by the fact that much of the correspondence about them is still surviving. It is hoped to include full details of all surviving designs in the forthcoming 'Thornycroft List' to be published by the Museum, but meanwhile illustrations of some of the most unusual of these projects may interest and amuse other warship enthusiasts as much as they do the writer.

Of course many of the designs are very similar to those used in the building of vessels at Thornycroft's Chiswick, Woolston and Hampton yards, or by subcontractors at other locations. Many represent part of the process of developing the designs of those vessels. There are, however, a few which are totally unlike anything built by Thornycroft's, or indeed anyone else.

Our first example, the 'Design for shallow draft gunboat for the Imperial Russian Government' (Chiswick plan 2089 dated 27 February 1884) is most definitely a case in point. By the 1880s, Thornycroft's, besides being successful builders of steam launches and torpedo boats, had also developed a promising line of river steamers utilising light steel construction, tunnel sterns, and the Thornycroft invention of the 'guide blade screw' or 'turbine propeller', a ducted propeller, to obtain the shallowest possible draft. At this stage they were very much against the cruder and cheaper expedient of using stern paddle wheels to get the same result

Shallow draft gunboat for Russia (Chiswick plan 2089, 27 February 1884). *NMM*

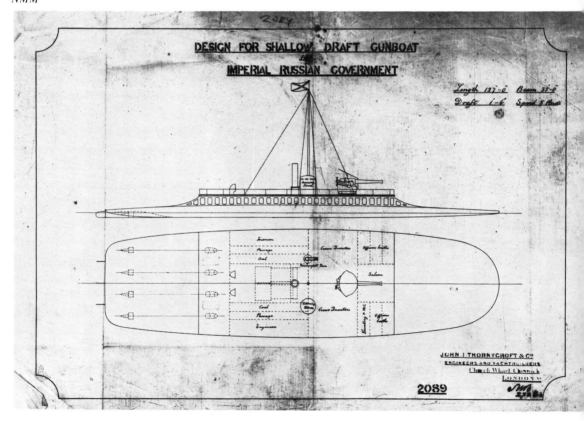

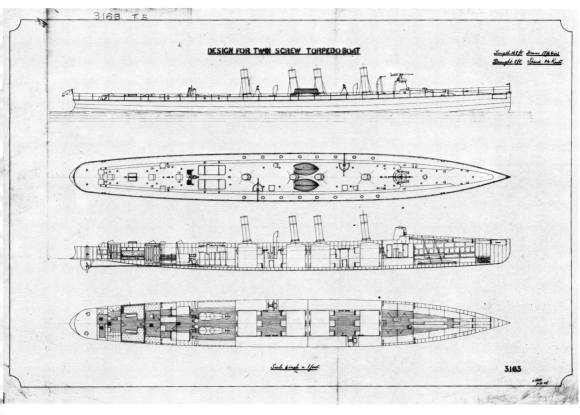

Twin screw torpedo boat (Chiswick plan 3163, December 1886).
NMM

(though they built steamers of this type later). Therefore, when they were asked to submit a design to Russian requirements they utilised four of these propellers, powered by the same type of compound engines used in contemporary second class torpedo boats. The shield for the big 6in gun, and probably the conning tower as well, were of 1½in thick steel. The conning tower was off-centre, as was the 5-barrel 0.45in Nordenfelt machine gun. There is no mention of where this slipper-shaped monster was meant to operate, but the fact that the engines had direct injection instead of surface condensers, and therefore presumably could take advantage of a constant supply of fresh water, probably means she was intended for river use, perhaps in Siberia. She would have cost £20,000 exclusive of armament.

Unfortunately there is no correspondence with the next design, a twin screw torpedo boat (Chiswick plan 3163), but this comes from a time (December 1886) when Thornycroft's were already thinking in terms of bigger and better torpedo boats, a line of development which was soon to result in the torpedo boat destroyer. This vessel, with its four water tube boilers, twin bow torpedo tubes and three quick-firing guns can be seen as a predecessor of the *Daring* and *Decoy*, Thornycroft's first destroyers.

On 25 May 1893 the torpedo cruiser design shown in Chiswick plan 6151 was offered to Captain T Damering of the Royal Norwegian Navy. This was really a cross between a torpedo gunboat and a destroyer. The elevated platforms forward for two 6pdr guns covered the 'heads'. The bigger guns just abaft the funnels were 12 pdrs, whilst the poop mounted two 3pdrs. The 4-barrel machine guns on the bridge were of 1in calibre, whilst the single torpedo tubes offset to port and starboard respectively at the breaks of poop and forecastle were probably for 18in torpedoes. The plan shows how the boilers and machinery were protected by coal bunkers. Six water tube boilers at a pressure of 200lb were to provide steam to the two triple expansion engines, giving a speed of 22 knots with 4400ihp. The crew were to be provided with 24 rifles, 24 cutlasses and 12 revolvers. The price, exclusive of torpedoes and ammunition, was £55,000.

Just before the First World War Thornycroft's produced a whole series of minelayer designs for Turkey, none of which were built, though some river gunboats were supplied. Woolston drawing number 6253 of 1911 shows one of the heaviest-armed designs, a cruiser-type vessel (others were on destroyer lines). The 120 mines stowed on the lower deck aft would be brought up onto the main deck and laid through a single stern port; one would have thought a cumbersome and slow process. The bow and stern guns were 100mm (4in), with two 12pdrs on either side. An alternative version of this design shows two 45cm (18in)

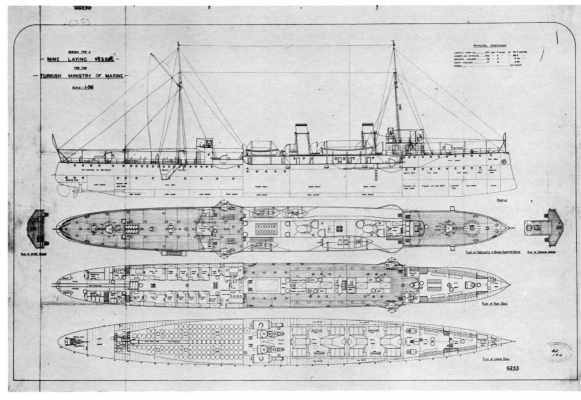

Cruiser minelayer for Turkey (Woolston drawing No 6253, 1 May 1911).
NMM

torpedo tubes on the upper deck. The triple expansion engines were intended to give her a speed of 24 knots. The price was 'say £85,000'.

At much the same time Thornycroft's were producing a series of designs for 'motor torpedo boats', in fact merely versions of steam torpedo boats powered by a couple of diesel engines. A whole series of these were designed for Italy (Thornycroft's had provided many designs of destroyers and torpedo craft for building by Pattinson's of Naples for the Italian Navy), but the design shown in Woolston drawing 6392 was intended for Greece. Two 45cm torpedo tubes are supplemented by a 76mm (3in) gun. The top speed of 26 knots would have made this quite a useful vessel for a small navy.

The 'motor paddle canoe' in the undated plan, Woolston number O/A 235 is probably from late 1914 or early 1915, and may have been intended as a miniature river gunboat for Mesopotamia. Unfortunately, little else is known about it, though the quick-firing gun forward is probably a 3pdr.

The concrete harbour blocking vessel in Head Office plan 16752 is similarly devoid of detailed explanation, but it seems very likely that this 1917 design, with its submarine-shaped hull fitted for rapid flooding was designed for the purpose for which old cruisers were eventually used, the blocking of the German submarine bases at Zeebrugge and Ostend.

In 1930 Thornycroft's were approached by the Dutch to design a very large and powerful flotilla leader, with a specification which eventually developed into the Dutch designed and built *Tromp* class of light cruisers. The flush-decked single funnel design number T548 was produced in 1931, and was one of a series, the others all looking more like the then conventional two-funnelled, forecastle-decked destroyer. There was 1in protective plating on the deck and 1½ on the sides covered the magazine and machinery spaces. Eight 120mm (4.7in) guns, 4–40mm (2pdr) pompoms and two triple 21in torpedo tubes made up the armament.

A seaplane completed the offensive equipment of this powerful small warship. The Dutch were asking for a maximum speed of at least 33 knots. Thornycroft's Dutch agent wrote: 'My impression is that the French Yards will be the most severe competitors in this particular case and therefore we will have to handle the matter of price somewhat diplomatically.' In fact Thornycroft's would have charged £14,000 if the Dutch had decided to use this design for a ship built in Holland.

In the late 1920s, Thornycroft's working in co-operation with Supermarine's, developed a design for a small aircraft carrier to operate flying boat fighters, which were to fly off a flight deck forward using trolleys, and be recovered by taxi-ing up the inclined plane of the stern which extended underwater. By 1932 this design had developed into the form shown in plan T739. This quite elegant small ship was to operate a force of some seven floatplanes by catapulting them off the forecastle, and recovering them either by crane or by a Hein mat which could be towed behind, onto which the aircraft would taxi, and then be winched on board. In practical trials the mat more often resulted in bent aircraft than effective recoveries. The armament of the ship was three 4.7in guns and four AA pom-poms. Destroyer-type machinery would give 28 knots. Thornycroft's prepared quite elaborate brochures on this design, but without any success in selling the idea. An equal lack of success was experienced by a wartime design for a light aircraft carrier to carry fighters on deck, which made the Director of Naval Construction so annoyed about what he considered to be a waste of draughtsman's time that he threatened to take over Thornycroft's design staff for the Admiralty.

One of the more original designs to come out of the Second World War was a small destroyer designed for coastal use as virtually an updating of the First World War 'S' class. Design T1341 shows the basic version of this design primarily intended for anti-E-boat work. The hull lines were specially designed for speed in shallow water (12 to 15 fathoms), and a very large rudder was fitted for quick steering. This type was intended to fill the gap between the steam gunboat and the destroyer proper. The version shown, armed with 2 old 4in guns, a 2pdr bow chaser in a turret, 6 Oerlikons and 4 fixed MTB type 21in torpedo tubes was intended principally for night work. The other anti-E-boat version

was also intended for day work and had a single twin high angle 4in mounting and eight Oerlikons instead of the previous gun armament, though retaining the torpedo tubes. An anti-submarine patrol version was similar to the first version except in adding Asdic and depth charges, whilst a general purpose version was intended to share the same armament as the second version except for having only a single 4in in the high angle mount, and adding a high speed mine-sweep aft. The designed speed in favourable conditions was intended to be 37½ knots.

Amongst Thornycroft's most successful designs during the First World War and for many years later were the coastal motor boats, with stepped hulls and launching a torpedo from a stern trough. Early in the second conflict the growing E-boat menace caused the suggestion to be made of using these well-tried hulls as motor gunboats with an armament of fixed 20mm guns intended to be used like those of a fighter plane by aiming the whole boat. Head Office plan number 23370 shows one of two such surviving designs. The cannon would be supplemented by quadruple Vickers 'K' machine guns mounted on the Scarff ring behind the steering shelter.

The Type 4 'Hunts' *Brecon* and *Brissenden* were very different from the other ships of the 'Hunt' class, and a lot of thought had gone into their design. It is not surprising that Thornycroft's designed improved, enlarged

'Motor paddle canoe' (Woolston drawing no O/A 235, 1914 or 1915).   *NMM*

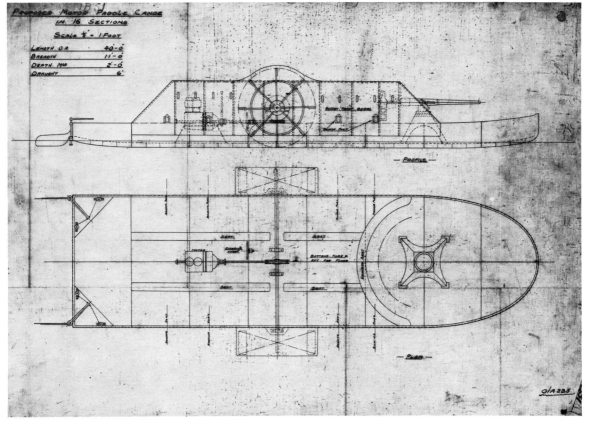

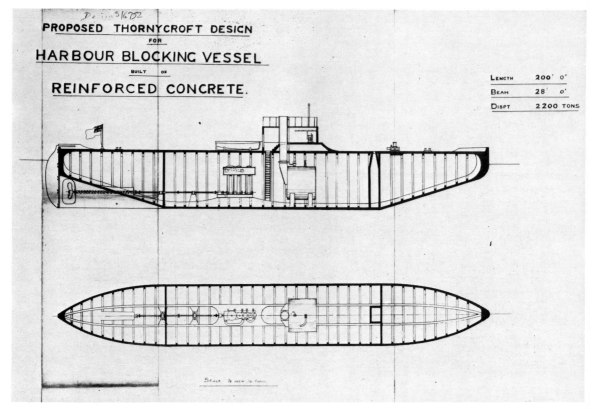

Concrete harbour blocking vessel (Head Office plan 16752, 1917).
NMM

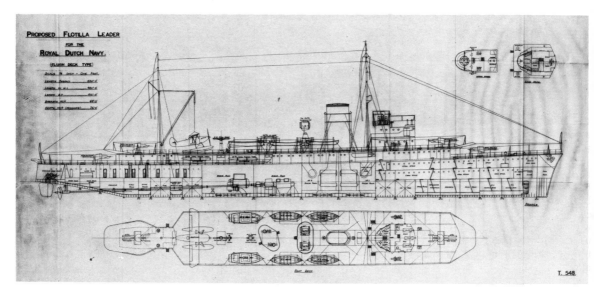

Destroyer Flotilla leader for Royal Dutch Navy (T548, 1931).
NMM

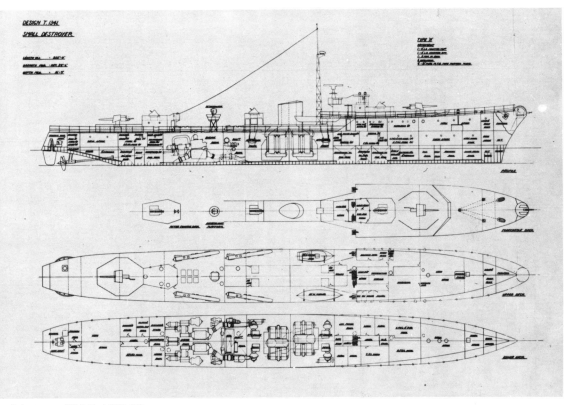

Small destroyer (T1341, 1939-45).
NMM

versions whilst the war was still on, and continued to adapt the design to various sizes and armaments after the war was over. Design TWY 1737 as the initials suggest was a joint tender by Thornycroft's, White's and Yarrow's to the Brazilian Navy in the early 1950s, but its looks betray the fact that it was actually designed by Thornycroft's. The hull is that of an enlarged *Brecon*, the armament that of a *Daring* class destroyer, but with more emphasis on 40mm AA guns, and less on torpedo tubes. The Thornycroft-type funnel is characteristic of a whole series of designs of this period, although in this particular case there was an alternative twin funnel design. Maximum speed was 35 knots. It is perhaps not too fanciful to see in this design the ancestor of today's *Niteroi* class built by Vosper-Thornycroft for Brazil.

NOTE

For further details of Thornycroft history see *A Hundred Years of Specialised Shipbuilding and Engineering* by K C Barnaby (Hutchinson, 1964) and articles by D J Lyon in *Model Shipwright* Nos 17, 18 and 20.

THORNYCROFT DESIGN.

PROPOSED FAST AIRCRAFT CARRIER.

SCALE ⅛″=1 FOOT.

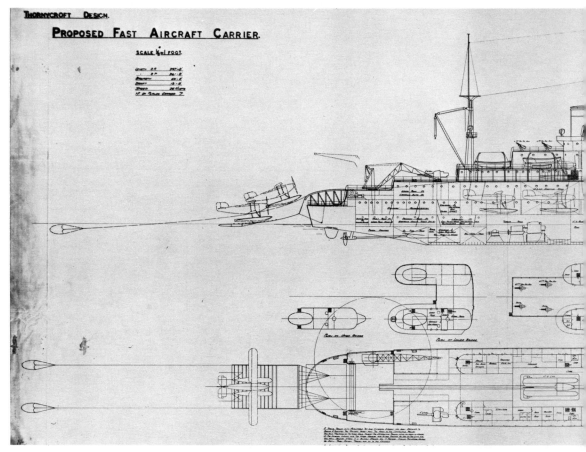

2

T.W.Y. 1737/3

DESIGN FOR A LARGE DESTROYER

FOR THE BRAZILIAN GOVERNMENT

SCALE ¹⁄₄₈ᵗʰ FULL SIZE

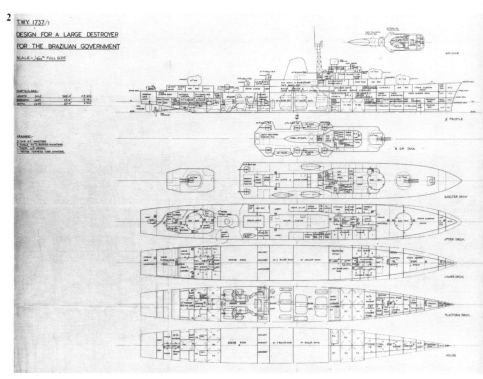

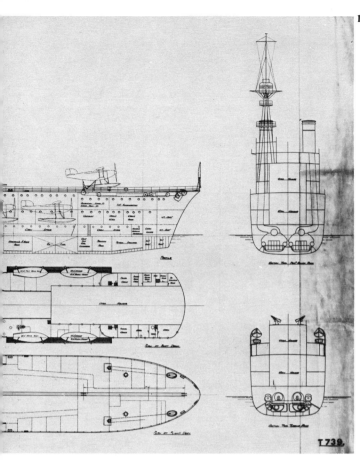

1 Proposed fast aircraft carrier
(T739, 1932).
NMM

2 Large destroyer for Brazil (TWY 1737,
early 1950s).
NMM

3 Fast motor gunboat (Head Office plan
23370, 9 October 1940).
NMM

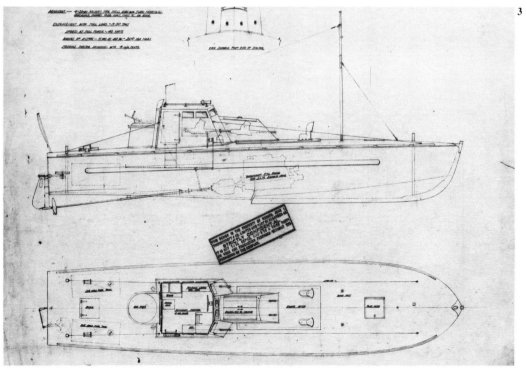

ATTACK & DEFENCE No 4

Action Damage to British Warships in the Second World War Part 2

By David Brown RCNC

BOMBS

There are so many sizes and types of bomb that it is difficult to tell a connected story. In the Second World War, high capacity bombs, exploding in the superstructure, might cause comparatively little damage while medium case bombs, penetrating deep into the ship, would cause severe structural damage as well as flooding and fire.

The great story of survival is that of the carrier *Illustrious* in January 1941, attacked by Ju 87 dive bombers near Malta (Ref 1). On the 10th she was hit by seven bombs and near missed by another, probably all 500kg (1100lb) weapons. The following hits were recorded:

1 On S2 pompom (starboard side). The gun was destroyed but little other damage was caused.
2 Pierced the forward end of the flight deck, went out of the ship and exploded near the waterline causing extensive splinter damage (resulting in some flooding) and a small fire.
3 Hit in the after lift well and severely damaged the lift and its machinery.
4 Penetrated the 3in thick flight deck armour and burst in the hangar, causing serious damage to the forward lift and a bad fire in the hangar. (Some accounts claim that this was a 1000kg/2200lb bomb.) Several aircraft were destroyed in the hangar.
5 Direct hit at the aft end of the after lift.
6 Passed through P1 pompom platform and went into the sea without exploding. Fire started in two mess decks.
7 Hit in the after lift well (possibly a smaller bomb).
8 Near miss off starboard side with slight flooding.

With the steering gear out of action, *Illustrious* returned to Malta steering on her main engines. While she was being repaired she suffered damage from two more 500kg bombs. The first hit the unarmoured after end of the flight deck and exploded above the gallery deck, while the other was a near miss, off the port side, which flooded some of the torpedo protection compartments and caused shock damage to the port boiler and machinery. After all this, HMS *Illustrious* proceeded to Alexandria under her own power at 23kts. Repairs took 6 months in Norfolk Navy Yard, USA. It is interesting to note that the armoured hangar, provided at such great expense, proved of no value. Only one bomb hit the armour and that penetrated the 3in deck (see *Warship* 13). The ship was also lucky in that

several hits were close together so that the later ones added little to the earlier damage. On the other hand, to withstand 8 hits and 2 near misses from 500kg bombs was a great achievement. Her designer, W A D Forbes, Captain Boyd and the crew all had reason for pride in their work.

Bomb hits on thick armour were very few, the best known being on 9 April 1940 when the battleship *Rodney* was hit by a delayed action (DA) bomb, believed to have been a 500kg AP type. After piercing the upper and main decks between the funnel and bridge it broke up while penetrating the 4in armour of the middle deck. There was a partial detonation and minor damage was caused by blast and splinters.

Bombs were a much greater hazard to small ships – Table 1 (see Part 1, *Warship* 27) shows that 44 destroyers were sunk by these weapons and 81 seriously damaged. Even quite small bombs could cause major damage. The destroyer *Vanessa* was hit by a 100kg bomb in June 1941 while operating in the North Sea. It entered through the side at the top of No 1 boiler room and burst near the bottom. The outer bottom was pushed upwards over the whole length of the boiler room and for some distance forward, and a hole 6ft × 9ft blown in the bottom. The upper deck was split and blown upwards, and the forward funnel blown overboard. Both boiler rooms were flooded. Repairs took 9 months including conversion to escort.

GUIDED WEAPONS, ETC

There were comparatively few guided weapons used in the war and their effects were very similar to those of bombs. The sloop *Egret* was hit by an HS 293 glider bomb off Spain on 28 August 1943. The hit was high up on the starboard side near the funnel, she capsized one minute later and sank an hour and a quarter after that. It seems likely that a magazine also exploded. The cruiser *Spartan* was also sunk by this weapon while off Anzio on 29 January 1944. A large hole was blown in the upper deck and a serious fire broke out in the after superstructure and in Y turret. The after engine room was evacuated and the after magazine flooded about ten minutes after the hit. One hour later the ship was abandoned and sank soon after.

Earlier, the battleship *Warspite* survived a hit and a near miss from 1400kg FX 1400 guided bombs (11 September 1943). The hit was on the boat deck, the bomb penetrating to the double bottom before explod-

HMS Cameron capsized in dock following damage from a 250kg (551lb) direct action bomb on 5 December 1940. The ship was out of action for 17 months but this included a 10½ month conversion into an experimental ship.

MoD

ing, producing a a hole some 20ft × 14ft in the outer bottom and wrecking No 4 boiler room. The main bulkheads forward and aft of the boiler room were buckled and torn. The near miss exploded under the bulge abreast No 5 boiler room and flooded No 2, 3, 5 and 6 boiler rooms and other spaces. She was repaired sufficiently to join the Fleet off Normandy in June 1944 but still had a hole in her bottom.

Japanese suicide bombers were a form of guided missile. Hits on the carriers of the British Pacific Fleet are summarised in Table 3.

The County class cruiser *Australia* seemed to have a special attraction for suicidal Japanese. She was hit on 21 October 1944, when serious fires broke out in the bridge area due to burning petrol. She was hit again on 5 January 1945 and remained in action with damage to her AA guns. She was hit again the next day with more

The result of a direct bomb hit on the stern of the destroyer *Acheron* on 24 August 1940. She was also damaged by 3 near misses and was out of action for 13 weeks.

MoD

damage and casualties to the AA guns and crew. On 8 January she was hit by two more aircraft and yet again on the 9th. She was still able to steam at reduced speed and was repaired and refitted in 6½ weeks.

TABLE 3: EFFECTS OF KAMIKAZE ATTACKS

Ship	Date	No of hits	Time out of action	Repair time	Notes
Indefatigable	1 April 1945	1	50mins	1 month	Zeke with 250kg bomb.
Illustrious	6 April 1945	1	–	–	Glancing blow.
Formidable	4 May 1945	1	5 hours	–	Zeke with 250kg bomb, hole in armoured flight deck.
Indomitable	4 May 1945	1	–	–	8 planes lost, 8k, 51w.
Victorious	9 May 1945	2	(Fly off 1 hour) (Fly on 12 hours)	1 month	
Formidable	9 May 1945	1	25 minutes	1 month	9 planes lost, 1k, 8w.

GUNFIRE

Damage from shells is even more variable in extent. The bursting charge is small and serious damage will only occur if a vital space is struck. The damage received by the battleship *Prince of Wales* in action with *Bismarck* and *Prinz Eugen* on 24 May 1941 well illustrates the random nature of damage due to shell hits. The hits and their effects were:

1 A 15in shell which hit the compass platform and passed out without exploding. Damage to the ship was negligible but most of the bridge crew were killed or incapacitated leading to a temporary loss of control.

2 A 15in shell struck the starboard crane and burst just abaft the after funnel causing extensive minor splinter damage. A radar office was put out of action.

3 A 15in shell hit 28ft below the waterline on the starboard side which penetrated the outer torpedo protection and came to rest, without exploding, against the protective bulkhead. There was some minor flooding.

4 An 8in shell (from *Prinz Eugen*) pierced the boat deck, shelter deck and the armoured structure round P3 5.25in turret, bounced off and came to rest without exploding. The gun mount was temporarily out of action.

5 An 8in shell hit the starboard side just below the waterline and partially detonated 11ft inboard. The lower deck was flooded for 60ft and there was minor splinter and blast damage.

6 An 8in shell burst on impact with the side 5ft below the waterline over the steering gear. The armour deck was distorted and there was flooding at lower deck level for 80ft.

7 An 8in shell hit the director support on the bridge, put both HA directors out of action and passed on without exploding.

That only two shells out of seven detonated does not say much for the quality of German fuzes. On the other hand, flooding and minor damage was quite extensive and, had the shells exploded properly, *Prince of Wales* would have been seriously damaged.

The cruiser *Berwick* had an exciting time at the end of 1940. On 27 November she was in action with the Italian Fleet off Cape Spartivento in the Mediterranean and was hit by two 8in shells. The first hit and penetrated the 1in thick support to 'Y' turret and burst in a cabin flat after travelling 21ft. There was only minor structural damage and a small fire. The second shell hit the upper deck, which it penetrated, together with the main and lower decks and burst after a path of 40ft outside 'Y'

turret handing room. The electrical ring main was cut and all lights went out in the after end of the ship. Other than that, damage was slight. *Berwick*'s fighting efficiency was not impaired except that 'Y' turret was out of action.

Temporary repairs took 20 days and, on Christmas Day, she was successfully defending a large troop convoy against the German cruiser *Hipper* off the Azores, suffering four hits from 8in shells. One hit the side of 'X' turret and passed through the floor and support without exploding. The turret was jammed. One hit the side and penetrated the platform deck, bouncing off various sections of structure before coming to rest in a fuel tank without exploding. There was some flooding. The third hit of the engagement was on a 4in AA mounting. The shell was deflected and exploded in a funnel uptake 56ft later, after passing through several bulkheads. Damage was slight. The last hit was on 4½in thick 'C' armour which deflected the shell into the bulge where it exploded. A 40ft length of bulge was flooded.

Damage to the bows of the destroyer *Whitshed* after she struck a contact mine on 30 July 1940; she was out of action for 19 weeks.
MoD

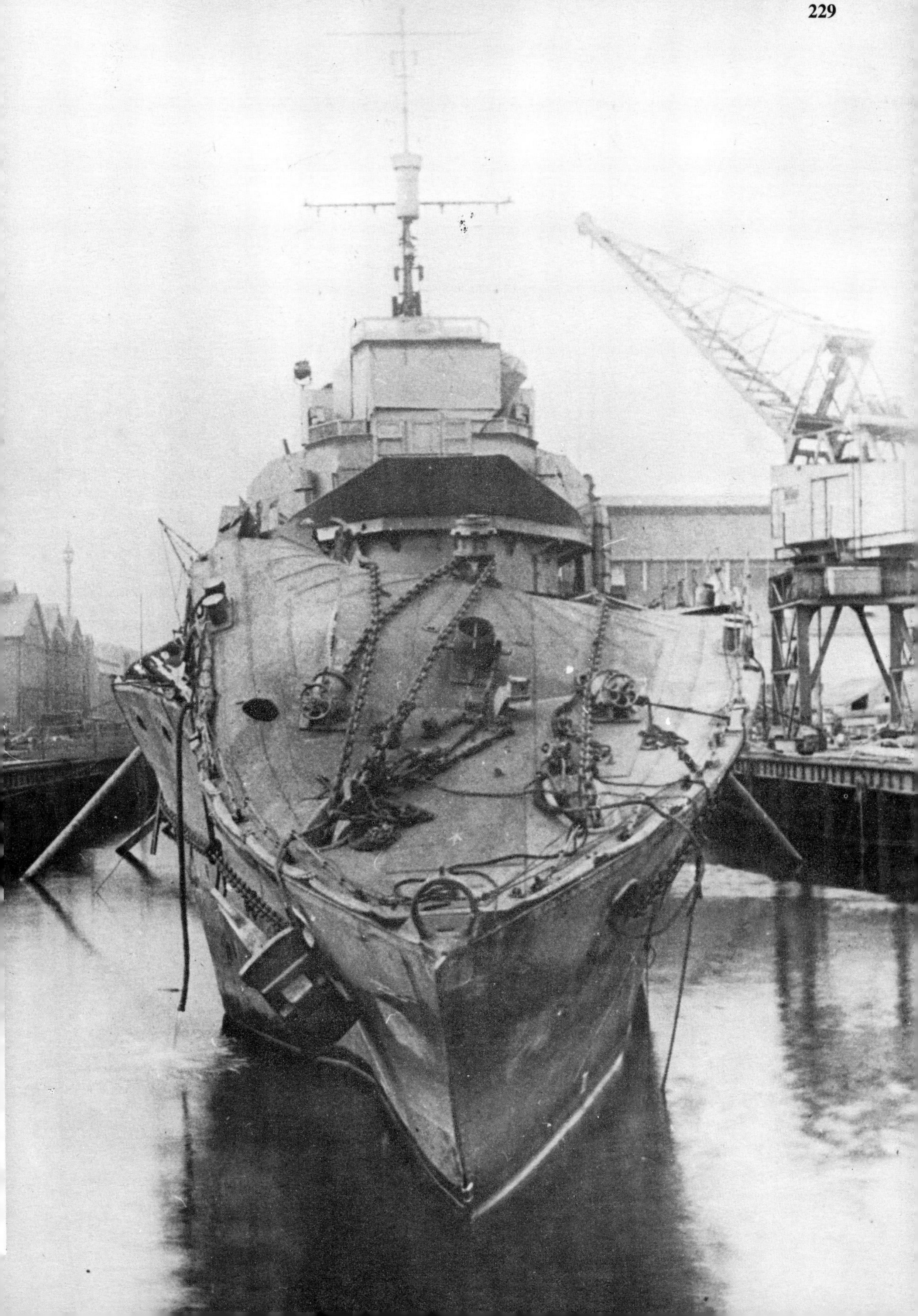

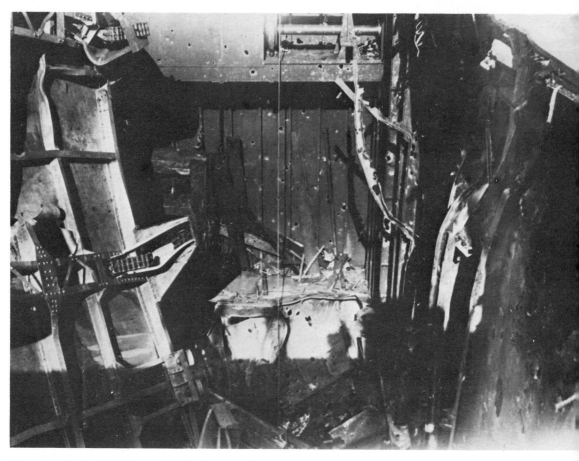

Damage to the after lift of the carrier *Illustrious* caused by a bomb hit on 10 January 1941. The lift platform is on the left!
MoD

Other than the loss of 'X' turret, *Berwick* was in good fighting order. Repairs took 6 months. Once again, poor German fuzes saved her from more serious damage but, even so, she stood up well to shell fire – as indeed did her near sister *Norfolk* when hit by two 11in shells from *Scharnhorst*.

Hipper was in action again in the Barents Sea, 31 December 1942, when she scored three 8in hits on the destroyer *Onslow*. The first hit the funnel and caused very extensive splinter damage – two radars, an Oerlikon and the aerials were wrecked and both boilers damaged. The second shell exploded on the sheer strake between 'A' and 'B' guns, making a hole 6ft × 5ft. Extensive splinter damage was again caused wrecking the main cable runs and 'A' gun barrel, and starting a serious fire. The last hit was on 'B' gun deck making a hole 6ft × 4ft in the superstructure and wrecking 'B' gun. There was also a near miss close to 'B' gun which caused further minor splinter damage. Though the for-

ward guns were both out of action, *Onslow* was still able to steam and use the after guns.

MINES

Contact mines make a big hole similar to that caused by torpedo. In many cases the damage was forward and even when severe the remains could be brought home and repaired.

Damage caused by ground mines was of a very different character. There was shock damage (usually throughout the ship), whipping (which might cause major buckling of the structure) and flooding (through strained seams, ruptured plating or cracked fillings). The cruiser *Belfast* was one of the early victims of a magnetic mine, in the Firth of Forth on 21 November 1939 (Ref 1). The mine exploded 80 – 90ft below the forward engine room causing severe structural damage to the bridge, upper deck and keel – the whole ship was bent upwards through 4½ft.

Despite this damage there was only slight flooding. On the other hand, there was extensive damage to weapons, machinery and electrical equipmemt and all their supporting seats were broken. In most cases, these were of cast iron which is very brittle under shock loading. Repairs to *Belfast* were carried out in Devonport Dockyard at low priority and took two years to complete.

Shock damage had been studied before the war in Job 4 (see *Warship* 24) but the short length of this target did not allow whipping acceleration to develop nor were the charges used as big as those in the mine used against *Belfast*. Improvements were made as quickly as possible with better materials, flexible mounts and equipments designed without overhanging masses. The failure to protect properly against shock was the biggest fault in pre-war warship design – not only in British ships but also in those of all other naval powers. Nearly 5 years after the mining of *Belfast*, the German battleship *Tir-* pitz was similarly immobilised by shock damage caused by the midget submarine attack on her.

CONCLUSION

The study of damage from enemy weapons was taken very seriously by all concerned: the DNC, Sir Stanley Goodall, would usually interview the survivors from major incidents himself. Continual attention to detail in the design of pipe systems, cables and switchgear gradually improved the survivability of ships. The provision of more battery powered emergency lights and of portable pumps helped the crews to control the effects of damage. A damage control school was set up in London in 1942 at which training was given in all aspects of the subject. Flooding, counter-flooding and stability was taught using a large model of the cruiser HMS *London* floating in a big tank.

The fact remains that weapons are meant to cause serious damage and it need cause no surprise that such damage did result. One is inclined to wonder if the massive investment in armour and in torpedo protection

The wrecked stern of the sloop *Pelican* after a direct hit by a 50lb direct action bomb on 22 April 1940. The stern section abaft Y mounting has gone together with the mounting shield. She was also damaged by two 250lb near miss bombs and was out of action for 7 months.

MoD

What is left of the fore end of the destroyer *Express* is almost unrecognisable in this view of the ship after striking a contact mine on 31 August 1940.

systems was justified. Even a Second World War ship had so many vital systems outside the protected area that the ship could be put out of action without the protection being penetrated. Weapon development was so rapid that the protection itself was likely to become inadequate quite quickly.

Many of the incidents of the war could not be fully documented either because the ship sank or because the crew were too busy. Gaps in knowledge were filled after the war when a considerable number of old ships were used for trials of weapon effectiveness before they were broken up (Ref 1).

Both designers and operators learnt much from the hard experience of war and improvements were made to equipment and to training but the Fleet which went to war in 1939 was basically sound.

REFERENCES
1 *A Century of Naval Construction* D K Brown (Conway Maritime Press, 1983.)
2 *US Destroyers* N Friedman, (US Naval Institute Press, 1982.)
3 *British Destroyers* E J March, (Seeley Service & Co, 1966.)

WARSHIP PICTORIAL

America's First Submarines Part 2

By Francis J Allen

Brief Histories of Classes and Ships

With the commissioning of the *Holland* on 12 October 1900 the service career of the submarine designed by John P Holland and built by Lewis Nixon (the designer of the battleships *Oregon, Indiana* and *Massachusetts*) in his Crescent Shipyard began somewhat ignominiously with the boat having to be towed, by the tug *Leyden*, to the Naval Academy at Annapolis, Maryland on 16 October 1900. At Annapolis the *Holland* assumed training duties for the preparation of naval cadets, officers and enlisted men for duty in the fledgling submarine service. *Holland*'s service record was one of experimentation and training. During 8–10 January 1901 she travelled from Annapolis, Maryland to Norfolk, Virginia, a distance of 166 miles, running on the surface; in the process collecting valuable data for use in future submarines. With the exception of a period from 15 June to 1 October 1901, when the *Holland* was stationed at the Naval Torpedo Station at Newport, RI, she remained at the Naval Academy until 17 July 1905 as a training vessel.

Holland's name was struck from the Navy Register of Ships on 21 November 1910 after completing her service career at Norfolk, Virginia. A Henry A Hitner & Sons of Philadelphia purchased her for scrap in June 1913. The sale was made with the understanding that the purchaser was to put up a $5000 bond to guarantee that the ship would be broken up and not used as a warship.

With the advent of the *Adder* Class, later to be redesigned as the A-Class, the submarine fleet of the United States Navy was born. The contract covering these six boats called for their delivery between 1902 and early 1903. The submarines *Adder* (A-2), *Moccasin* (A-4), *Porpoise* (A-6) and *Shark* (A-7) were built by Lewis Nixon at the Crescent Shipyard in Elizabethport, NJ while *Grampus* (A-3), and *Pike* (A-5) were constructed at the Union Iron Works in San Francisco, California. *Plunger* (A-1), ordered under a separate contract, was also built at the Crescent Shipyard. As the boats were completed they were taken to the Holland Torpedo Boat Company's station at Cutchogue Bay for tests and trials. This station at the Goldsmith and Tuttell Yard in New Suffolk soon became a semi-official submarine base for the US Navy. On the West Coast the tests and trials were carried out at the Union Iron Works.

For the most part, the work assigned to these first submarines was concerned with the development of suitable tactics and the training of personnel for these and future boats. All the A-Class were employed in this fashion for the first part of their service careers.

With the exception of *Plunger*, the A-Class boats served their most important duty with the 1st Submarine Division, Asiatic Torpedo Fleet in the waters off Cavite, Luzon, Philippine Islands. The first two of the A-Class, *Porpoise* and *Shark*, arrived aboard *Caesar* (AC-16) and both were in service by November and August 1908 respectively. *Adder* and *Moccasin* were also transported to the Philippine Islands on board *Caesar* and both of these boats were recommissioned by October 1909. The last two A-Class submarines, *Grampus* and *Pike* were operational in March 1915, having arrived on the transport *Hector* (AC-7). They remained in the Philippines through the First World War and for the remainder of their operational careers ending their service as targets and/or being sold for scrap. On 16 January 1922 all of the A-Class boats, with the exception of A-1, were stricken from the Navy List. *Plunger*'s name was stricken on 24 February 1913.

In terms of naval architecture the early submarines and those of today have some strong links. Much experimentation, trial and error has passed over and about them in the intervening years, but the links are still there. The principal link which binds the old boats, considered good only to assist fixed land fortifications in harbour defence, to the modern submarine is the ingenuity and resourcefulness of the men who built, crewed and commanded them.

USS *Ajax* (AC-14) in Manila Bay, PI, after transporting submarines *B2* and *B3* (SS–11 and SS–12) from Norfolk. Taken in late April or early May 1913.
USN

The switchboard and other controls of the *A4* (SS-5) taken at Manila *c*1912.
USN

USS *Grampus* (SS-4) off San Diego, California, 1910.
USN

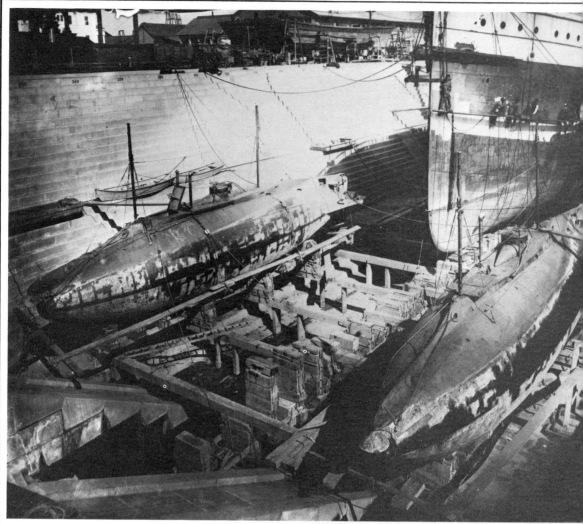

USS *Grampus* (SS-4), USS *Pike* (SS-6) and troop transport
Lawton in drydock at Mare Island Navy Yard, California,
September 1906.

USN

Submarines *A6* (SS-7), *A4* (SS-5) and *A2* (SS-3) in the Dewey
Drydock, Olongapo Naval Station, PI, c1912. The bows of the
submarine tender *Mohican* (1883-1922) are on the left, with
anchor suspended from cathead.

USN

USS *A2* (SS-3) loading a torpedo, at Cavite Navy Yard, PI *c*1912.
USN

Left to right: USS *B1*, USS *A7*, *c*1920, probably in the Philippines.
USN

USS *A7* (SS-8) at the Cavite Navy Yard PI, prior to the First World War.
USN

USS *Adder* (SS-3) running trials, *c*1903.
USN

USS *A2* (SS-3) underway in Manila Bay, *c*1912.
USN

USS *Plunger* (SS-2) *c*1909. The photograph has been signed by the future Admiral Chester W Nimitz, who was her third commanding officer.
USN

British Naval Guns 1880-1945 No 11

By NJM Campbell

6in QF Mks I and II These guns differed in construction only and are listed together in nearly all armament lists. Separate ammunition was fired. Mk I, first ordered in May 1888, was EOC Pattern 'Z' and was of built up construction, the principal components being 'A' tube, breech piece, '1B' and '2B' tubes, 'C' tube and jacket, while Mk II was a Woolwich design with 'A' tube, '1B' tube, 'B' hoop, '2B' tube, wire over the '1B' tube (*c*40% of total length) and jacket. Both had the '2B' tube extending to the muzzle and screw breech blocks with, originally, 3-motion breech mechanism (BM). Most were later converted to single motion BM, indicated by the addition of the letter 'B' to the mark number. One reference has been found to Mk II* which is thought to refer to the addition of a cartridge retaining catch when used as an AA gun.

In the latter part of the First World War, 15 guns of the same general design as the British type, were sent by Japan but they were never mounted afloat. Altogether 137 Mk I and 760 Mk II guns were made of which 133 and 714 respectively were naval and the rest coast defence.

Mks I and II were mounted in the battleships of the *Royal Sovereign* class, *Hood, Renown, Majestic* class, *Canopus* class and rearmed *Nile* class and *Superb*. Of large cruisers they were mounted in the *Edgar* class to the *Diadem* class inclusive, and also as upper deck guns in the rearmed *Blake* class. Smaller cruisers comprised *Aeolus, Brilliant, Iphigenia* and the *Astraea* to the *Highflyer* classes inclusive, as well as the rearmed *Indefatigable, Intrepid* and later *Rainbow* and *Sirius*. In addition they were added to the old battleship *Hercules* and the cruisers *Immortalité* and *Narcissus* and various gunnery school gunboats.

During the First World War they were at one time or another in all the large monitors except *Abercrombie, Havelock, Raglan, Peterborough* and *Picton*, and also in the small monitors *M26, M27* and the *Aphis* class river gunboats as well as in many AMCs and DAMS; 63 Mk II guns were transferred to the Army for conversion to 8in howitzers.

The mountings were CPI and PII allowing 20° and 19° elevation respectively in the upper deck version, and 15° for both in the between deck version. Originally CPI was in the *Royal Sovereign* class and *Hood,* and in the cruisers of the *Blake, Edgar, Crescent,* the 5 *Aeolus* (not *Rainbow, Sirius*) and *Astraea* classes, but there were some changes later. PII* applied to a First World War

EOC conversion with a new cradle allowing 25° elevation, but none of the 40 made were put afloat. Four CPI and 12 PII were adapted by AA use in 1915-16 with up to 53½° elevation, but they were not very successful, though a CPI conversion was fitted in *Roberts* and a PII in the river gunboats *Cicala, Cockchafer, Cricket* and *Glowworm* when stationed on the East Coast as defence against Zeppelins. The remaining mountings were used on land, with the PII on railway trucks.

6in QF Mk III This was a trunnioned version of Mk I, known to EOC as Pattern Z[1], intended for Vavasseur mountings and mounted in VCP Mk IIC or II*, both of which allowed 20° elevation. A total of 53 guns were made and used as the main deck guns in the rearmed *Blake,* and *Apollo* classes except for *Aeolus, Brilliant, Iphigenia, Indefatigable* and *Intrepid* of the latter. About 8 were later in DAMS.

6in BL Mks VII, VIII The only difference between these was that Mk VIII had the breech opening to the left to suit the left hand guns in the twin turrets of the *Kent* class cruisers. The guns were designed by Vickers and became one of the main standbys of both the Navy and Army,

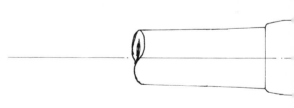

Profile of the PVI mounting for the Mk XI 6in gun, mounted in the *Weymouth* and *Chatham* class cruisers of the First World War.
Drawn by John Roberts

hough originally there was some trouble. They were
uilt with an inner 'A' tube, 'A' tube, wire for about half
ength and 'B' tube to the muzzle, jacket and screwed-on
reech ring. The breech bush taking the Welin screw
lock, was located in the 'A' tube. Mk VIIv comprised
2 Army guns with no 'B' tube, and VII* and VIIv* were
uns relined with a high strength alloy steel inner 'A'
ube to allow heavier charges in the later 45° coast
lefence mountings. Although there were 928 naval
uns; 898 Mk VII, 27 Mk VIII and 3 converted from Mk
/III to VII. The total number of Army guns is not
nown but was probably about 350 with, in addition,
nany transferred from the Navy.

The gun was capable of a much higher performance
han was accepted for reasons of standardisation in
nost, where the muzzle velocity was that required by a
otoriously bad driving band and a coast defence mount-
ng with a cast iron pedestal. Mk VII was mounted in the
attleships of the *Formidable*, *London* and *Duncan* clas-
es, the first 5 *King Edwards*, the *Iron Duke* class and the
attlecruiser *Tiger*, as well as in the rearmed *Barfleur*
lass battleships. Cruisers included the *Cressy*, *Drake*,
Kent, *Hampshire* and *Challenger* classes, and some
earmed ships including *Narcissus*, *Immortalité*,
Undaunted, *Endymion*, *Theseus*, *Edgar*, *Grafton*, *High-
lyer*, *Hyacinth*, *Vindictive*, and all the *Dido* class except
Eclipse, *Astraea*, *Fox*, *Amethyst*, *Adventure* and *Atten-

tive. Other warships comprised the 12in monitors except
Peterborough and *Picton*, the monitor *M27* and the
Humber class, the gunboats of the *Aphis* class except
Ladybird, the leader *Swift* and briefly the destroyer
Viking. It was also in the school gunboats *Bustard*, *Cuc-
koo* and *Drudge*, the 1919 Caspian Force and Siberia
River Flotilla, many AMC and other auxiliary warships
in both World Wars, some DAMS and many DEMS.
Apart from the *Kent* class, Mk VIII was only in the
Drudge and the First World War escort ship *Discoverer*.

On land Mk VII was mainly a coast defence gun
though it was used as a heavy field gun in the First World
War and a few were on railway trucks in the second.

Most naval guns fired charges to give the standard
2562–2573fs muzzle velocity but heavier charges to give
2770–2775fs were used by the 5 *King Edwards*, the *Iron
Duke* class, *Tiger*, the *Hampshire* class and *Swift*. The
gunboats *Aphis*, *Cockchafer* and *Scarab* also had these
heavier charges in the Second World War, as did the
AMCs *Alcantara*, *Carnarvon Castle*, *Cheshire* and *Wor-
cestershire* but with 112lb, 6crh shells and 2640fs MV.
No ship had the charges for 2890fs used in Mk VII* and
VIIv* guns.

The *Kent* class had Mk I (Vickers) or Mk II (EOC)
twin turrets with PIII or PIV single mountings which
were in nearly all other ships, though the *Iron Duke* class
and *Tiger* had PVIII as did some Second World War

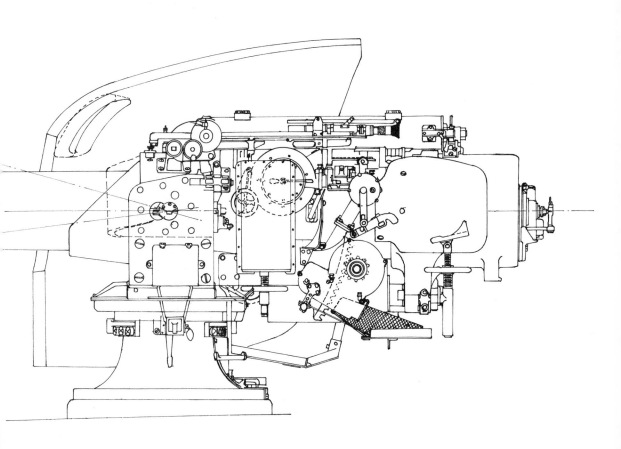

auxiliaries. Elevation was 14° in PVIII and 15° in other mountings, though this was later often increased to 20° in PIII and IV.

6in BL Mks IX, X Only one of each of these 49.8 calibre experimental coast defence guns was made. They were of built up construction differing in the breech blocks, and were respectively EOC Pattern DD¹ and DD², being BL versions of the QF Pattern DD mounted in the Brazilian *Barroso* and US *Albany* and *New Orleans*. With a 100lb shell MV is variously given as 2498 and 2575fs.

6in BL Mk XI Guns of wire wound type with inner 'A' tube, 'A' tube, full length wire, 'B' tube, jacket and screwed on breech ring. The breech bush taking the Welin block, screwed into the 'A' tube. Mk XI* differed in having a thicker inner 'A' with cannelured rings at the two forward shoulders. Of the 177 guns, all naval, 34 were Mk XI, 18 Mk XI* and 124 Mk XI* with a slightly different breech ring to suit PVI mountings, though all would go in PV or PV*. Lastly 'H' XI* was a Coventry ordnance stock gun with Holmstrom BM, eventually linered to an experimental 3in and never mounted afloat. There were slight constructional differences in various guns but with no alteration in mark.

The guns were in PV mountings in the battleships *Africa, Britannia* and *Hibernia*, and the cruisers *Black Prince* and *Duke of Edinburgh*, in PV* in the *Bristol* class cruisers, and in PVI in the *Falmouth* and *Chatham* class cruisers. Subsequently they were in the monitors *Marshal Ney,* the *Protector,* some First World War AMCs and a few other ships including DAMS. In the Second World War they were in Ocean Boarding Vessels and some DEMS. They were also mounted as emergency coast defence guns in the Second World War and to a limited extent in the First, while guns from the Australian ships of the *Chatham* class were installed on land in Australia during the 1930s.

PV and V* mountings allowed 13° elevation, later 20° in some, and PVI 15°. The guns were found heavy to aim manually, particularly in the *Falmouth* class which were lively in a seaway, and hydraulic power gear was added to some in the latter part of the First World War.

PARTICULARS OF 6IN GUNS

	6in QF Mk I, II, III	6in BL Mk VII, VIII	6in BL Mk XI
Weight incl. BM (tons):	6.6 (Mk III 6.75)	7.398	8.588
Length oa (in):	249.25	279.228	309.728
Length bore (cals):	40	44.92	50
Chamber (cu in):	832	1715	2030
Chamber length (in):	23.65	32.74	34.3
Projectile (lb):	100	100	100
Charge (ib/type):	29.75/EXE	20/Cord 20	32.1/MD26
	13.25/Cord 30	23/MD16	33.05/SC 150
	15.94/MD 26	23.13/SC 103	
		28.63/MD 26	
		28.17/SC140	
Muzzle Velocity (fs):	1882 EXE	2536 Cord	2937
	2230 Cord	2562 MD	
	2243 MD	2573	
		2770 MD	
		2775 SC	
Range (yds)/elevation:	10,000/15° (2crh Cord)	14600/20° (4crh SC)	14310/15° (4crh)
		15800/20° (4crh SC)	

Loading practice with a 6in Mk XII aboard a C class cruiser in 1935

MoD

USS KEOKUK

By S Kirby

This, and the other photographs accompanying this article, show the author's excellent model of the *USS Keokuk*.

All photos author's collection

Keokuk was the leader of the Sauk Indian tribe in the early 1800s. His name means 'one who moves about alert' or 'Running Fox'. I wonder what he would have made of the rather useless warship that was to bear his name?

Charles W Whitney was obviously a naval architect with an imaginative mind. His theories were so quite different from those of John Ericsson that the naval authorities must have wondered for some time who was right! Ericsson's main principle was to submerge the main part of the ship almost out of sight, leaving only the turret and pilot house above water level. This resulted in a very small target, but had the great disadvantage of providing very little reserve buoyancy. This small reserve was lost in deep water off Cape Hatteras, below which the *Monitor* still lies!

Whitney gave his vessel *Keokuk*, a much greater reserve buoyancy, but this obviously meant a much

Keokuk viewed from ahead. Note the hull form, ram bow and the grating which formed the roof of the 'fixed' gunhouses.

larger target. The basic design was very advanced, in that the vessel had a central citadel of angled armour with unarmoured, floodable ends. The armour itself is interesting in that it comprised alternate 4in × 4in beams of wood and iron set on edge and running horizontally along the length of the ship. *Keokuk* was armed with two 11in Dahlgren smoothbores.

Whitney submitted the specifications for his design on 22 April 1861. The principal dimensions were to be: length 150ft; beam 30ft; draft 8ft; and displacement 1,497,600lb (668 tons).

For some reason the go-ahead was not given until nearly a year later on 18 March 1862, by which time *Monitor* had been built and had had her rather inconclusive battle with *Virginia*. I am not convinced that the Navy were really happy with *Monitor*, otherwise why did they accept a design that was the complete antithesis of the Ericsson concept? Perhaps due to a shortage of ships the Navy was just making use of an existing design to save time. The cost of $220,000 compared with *Monitor*'s $275,000 must have made *Keokuk* seem fair value for money, bearing in mind they were identically armed. At this stage Whitney's 'Iron Mail' Clad Floating Battery or Steam Gun-Boat was to be called *Moodna* and her keel was laid on 14 April 1862 at J S Underhill's Iron Works, East River, New York.

HULL STRUCTURE

The basic hull structure was of 4in × ¾in iron bar frames at 18in spacing, with five keelsons constructed of 20in deep by ½in thick iron sheet capped with 3½in × 2½in × ⁷⁄₁₆in angle bar. The hull was subdivided by three transverse hulkheads, one each 20ft from the hull extremities and the third just forward of the boilers. The bulkheads were ⅜in sheet stiffened with 3in × 3in × ⅞in angles set vertically and 30in apart.

The hull plating was ⁷⁄₁₆in Best American Boiler plate . . . put on in outside and inside courses[1] . . . up to a line 3ft below the waterline, the rest to be butt-jointed, yielding a smooth surface over which the 'shot-proof mail'[1] or armour would be laid.

The unusual arrangement of this armour was described by Whitney in a letter to Rear Admiral Samuel F DuPont, commanding the blockade of Charleston, on 24 April 1863: 'The apparent thickness of the armour on the sides of *Keokuk* was 5¾in, put on in a peculiar manner, viz: bars of iron 4in wide and 1in thick were placed edgewise over the skin of the ship running fore and aft, 1in apart, and between them were placed strips of wood of the same dimensions; over this were laid two plates of iron each ⅝in thick secured on the edges of the bars by 1⅛in bolts running between them and through the skin and fastened by a nut on the inside of the vessel.'

The captain on his bridge – the roof of the forward gunhouse.

The gun-houses or towers were originally to be diamond shaped, but were later changed to truncated round cones 14ft in diameter on top and 20ft at the base. The tops were covered by a grating for light and ventilation. Each tower had three gun-ports, one on each beam and a third on the centre line bearing either ahead or astern as appropriate to the fore and aft tower. The ports were covered by 4½in thick iron doors or stoppers. Each door was in two parts, these being opened by levers and tackles inside the tower and were designed to close themselves when the gun was fired. This was apparently achieved by letting the split doors rest on the gun barrel when in its 'run-out' position. They then closed themselves as the barrel recoiled into the tower!

The guns were 11in Dahlgren smooth bores mounted on slides, the whole gun and mounting assembly being mounted on a turntable within the tower. The arcs of fire must have been very restricted by the three small ports. The armour on the gun-towers was similar to that on the sides of the ship, but with an extra ½in plate all over.

Whitney's attention to detail led him to realise the danger of the armour-retaining bolts sustaining sheared heads and being driven through into the gun-tower. He overcame this problem by fitting *Keokuk* with 'an inner skin protecting those inside the turrets and pilot house against the flying of the bolts'.

The pilot house was in the form of a bustle on the rear of, and slightly higher than, the forward gun-tower. Slits with sliding shutters on the forward face enabled the helmsman to see ahead.

MACHINERY

The machinery comprised two engines, each of two cylinders with a 23in bore and 20in stroke. The cylinders were vertical and drove the shafts *beside* the cylinders via a system of cranks and links. The result was a complex but compact engine that later proved quite reliable. Each engine drove a four bladed propeller of 7ft 6in diameter and 13ft 6in pitch. Steam was provided by two cylindrical boilers working at 60psi and a total of 400hp was developed. Whitney guaranteed a speed of 10kts, but most references quote 9kts as the speed she finally achieved. Whitney cunningly glossed over this shortfall by proudly stating in his letter to Admiral DuPont 'She was designed to have a speed and she attained it, running out of New York Harbor at the rate of 10 miles an hour' That's almost exactly 9kts to the uninitiated!

The floodable ends of the vessel were filled and emptied by steam driven pumps. The main function is quoted in the specification to be a trimming system to enable the vessel's optimum waterline to be maintained regardless of the amount of coal, ammunition and stores carried. The Captain of the vessel seemed to think that the intention was to fill these reservoirs completely to form 'water armour'. This would undoubtedly have added considerably to *Keokuk*'s displacement, but careful perusal of all available notes has not revealed whether the displacement draft quoted is with the ends full or empty.

Although named *Woodna* when the keel was laid, she had been renamed *Keokuk* by the time Mrs Whitney, the designer's wife, officially launched the vessel on 6 December 1862. The principal dimensions by this time were: length 159½ft (over ram and rudder); beam 36ft; draft 8ft forward, 9ft aft; and displacement around 677 tons.

PREPARATION FOR BATTLE

On 24 February the following year *Keokuk* was commissioned with Cdr Alexander C Rhind in command. On 11 March she left New York to join the South Atlantic Blockading Squadron and arrived at Newport News on the 13th to prepare for a planned attack on Charleston. She left on the 17th and after a short delay to repair a damaged propeller, arrived off South Carolina on 26 March. Rear Admiral DuPont was in command of the squadron at that time but he did not have the confidence that Secretary of the Navy Gideon Welles had that his ships could successfully take on and beat the coastal forts on the approaches to Charleston. Welles strongly urged DuPont to attack and, as this virtually amounted to an order, DuPont had no choice.

So on 4 April he reluctantly issued an order to sail up the main channel towards Charleston and attack Fort Sumter when within easy range. The ships were to shoot from the NE at 600–800yds range and to direct their fire at the central embrasure. They were instructed to take their time to ensure accuracy and not to waste ammunition.

The vessels concerned were the monitor-types *Weehawken*, *Passaic*, *Montauk*, *Patapsco*, *Catskill*, *Nantucket* and *Nahant* along with the gunboat *Keokuk*. DuPont was aboard his flagship *New Ironside*. A follow-up force of wooden gunboats *Canandaigua*, *Housatonic*, *Huron*, *Unadilla* and *Wissahickton* was to join the main squadron in an attack on the Morris Island batteries following the destruction of Fort Sumter.

This basic plan gives some idea of the misplaced optimism of Welles. On the other hand it may have been that DuPont, knowing something of King Canute's activities, put forward this over-ambitious plan to prove it could not be done; like holding back the incoming tide!

The attack was to take place on the morning of 6 April 1863. The squadron formed up off North Edisto Island near Port Royal and reached the Charleston bar late in the morning of 5 April and moored about 6 miles from Fort Sumter. *Keokuk* and *Patapsco* were detailed to mark the bar with buoys and then to stay with them just inside the bar opposite the remainder of the squadron, still outside.

All the crews then settled down for the night except those in *Weehawken* who were preparing an evil contraption invented by Ericsson. This was a 50ft raft for clearing mines and obstructions. It had a large notch into which the bows of the *Weehawken* fitted, to enable it to be pushed. Below the raft hung numerous 700lb charges set to explode on contact with anything. This fearsome device made the handling of the vessel very difficult, quite apart from the danger of it riding up over the bows, or even being caught under the overhang of the armour as the ship and raft pitched at different rates. Capt John

Rodgers feared a collision with a friendly ship and stated that 'He would be more dreaded than an enemy!'

THE ATTACK ON CHARLESTON

Dawn of the 6th broke to reveal dense fog, and although the ships crossed the bar the total lack of any visible landmarks made the trip up the narrow channel too hazardous to attempt. The attack was postponed until the following day.

By the morning of the 7th the fog had cleared, but due to adverse tidal conditions the force had to delay starting until 11.00am. *Weehawken*'s anchor got tangled up with the mine clearing raft and the whole force had to wait whilst it was sorted out. Cdr Rhind of the *Keokuk* decided this would be a good time to flood the ends of his vessel, but the pumps would not work. This was probably a good thing as it turned out!

Eventually, the squadron steamed up the channel towards Charleston led by *Weehawken*. The mine clearing raft had a serious effect on the control of this vessel and, as she meandered about the channel, the rest of the force had great difficulty in following in an orderly manner. They ended up all over the place and several near collisions occurred.

New Ironsides had the deepest draught of all the vessels and as she passed Fort Wagner, the leadsman called out the alarming news that there was barely a foot of water under the keel, so she anchored there and then. Also under the keel was a Confederate mine with electrical firing wires to the shore. However a farm cart had been driven over the wires on the beach and the mine would not work!

As the rest of the force approached the forts, they encountered numerous buoys which they suspected might have explosives attached. At about 2.50pm the first shot was fired at the lead ship *Weehawken* which soon became the target of fire from all directions. To make matters worse, an explosion occurred beneath the *Weehawken*'s bows, giving the vessel quite a shaking. This showed that there were indeed mines around and that Ericsson's ungainly raft was ineffective. *Weehawken* continued to lead the force until she came upon a line of obstructions right across the channel from Fort Sumter to Battery Bee (just NW of Fort Moultrie). Captain Rodgers quickly turned south to avoid running over them as he now had no faith in his raft. This sudden turn threw the rest of the squadron into confusion and the whole lot came to a near standstill under the combined fire of several forts to the north and west.

The attack on Charleston, 6 April 1863.

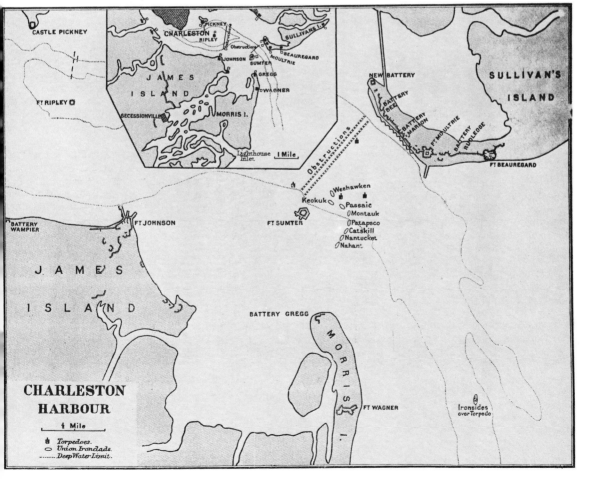

Close-up view of the lifeboat on the port side.

DAMAGE TO THE SQUADRON

The return fire from the ships was very slow, those with 15in guns taking up to 10 minutes to reload. These guns were expected to inflict heavy damage on the forts, but in the event they did no such thing. The main force came to within 1000yds of Fort Sumter. *Keokuk* got closest of all, reportedly within 300yds. She received all the attention one would expect at this distance, receiving 90 hits in 30 mins, 19 of these being on or below the waterline. Her experimental armour was poor and her gun-houses were riddled. The forts were wreaking havoc with all the vessels, *Weehawken* sustaining 50 hits in an hour. *Passaic*'s 15in gun was put out of action when its slide rails were bent. The vessel received 35 hits and the turret which also contained an 11in gun was jammed.

Montauk, a better protected ship sustained 14 hits without serious damage. During violent manoeuvring to avoid a collision, *Patapsco* lay nearly motionless for a few minutes between Forts Moultrie and Sumter, receiving their undivided attention. She stopped 47 shots in all, but suffered only a jammed turret.

This story was similarly repeated throughout the flotilla. *Nantucket* received 51 direct hits, several causing dents in the turret causing the gun port shutters to jam, while 36 hits on *Nahant* jammed her turret and damaged her steering gear.

In all, the attacking flotilla put up a rather poor show discharging a grand total of only 139 rounds. *Keokuk*

Keokuk viewed from astern.

Midships view showing base of funnel; note circular hatch abaft the funnel.

discharged only three rounds in all this time! The forts returned 2220 rounds, representing quite a good rate of fire. Good shooting it was too, representing a success rate of about 17%. Every ship suffered damage, *Keokuk* being by far the worse, her forward gun house was nearly demolished and she was taking water fast by the time she pulled out of action.

As *Keokuk* passed the *Ironsides*, Cdr Rhind signalled to DuPont that his ship was 'riddled like a colander'. Fortunately, her engines and boilers were undamaged and her pumps were just enough to keep her afloat. She limped away to the south of Morris Island, but the sea was rougher there and *Keokuk* sank in shallow water early the following morning. A tug accompanying the squadron stood by and took off all 92 crew of whom only 16 were wounded.

Keokuk's experimental lightweight armour, of which so much was expected, proved to be ineffective. Cdr Rhind felt that had the ship been built at the time she was designed she might have fared better. In a letter of 15 May 1863 he stated 'This vessel was offered to the Department early in 1861 and the contractors agreed to have her ready in 120 days, and if she had been built then she could have cleaned out every battery in the South, but it was not till after the success of the *Monitor* was made that her building was authorised and then the guns had got ahead of her.'

KEOKUK'S GUNS

Keokuk's story does not end there however. The fate of her guns provides an interesting insight into the shortages the Confederates were suffering.

Keokuk sank in about 18ft of water south of Morris Island within sight of Fort Sumter, about 4 miles away. Adm DuPont ordered the wreck to be destroyed and the long-suffering Rodgers of *Weehawken* was given the job. It was intended to push his raft of explosives, used in the battle, up to the wreck but rough seas and shallow water made this impractical and the attempt was abandoned. The Union force withdrew southwards, about 2 miles away.

Almost immediately the Confederates moved in and examined the sunken vessel. They decided to attempt to steal the two guns! The job was entrusted to one Adolphus La Costa, a civilian ordnance engineer, who had overseen the installation of the guns in the forts involved in the battle of only a few days previous. The job was a hard and dangerous one. Imagine having to cut tops out of two armoured gun-houses with saws, chisels and hammers, at night, within sight and gun-range of the Union force. The two guns, each 13½ft long and weighing about 8 tons had to be lifted out of the tops of the gun-houses and carried away. Then in the morning the wreck had to be left with no sign that it had been interferred with.

The forward gunhouse and funnel.

Two weeks of this work saw the gun-house tops cut away and the guns prepared for lifting. The guns had to be detached from their mounts below water-level before they could be lifted.

An old lightship hulk from Charleston was fitted with sheer-legs overhanging the bows by 20ft and around 1500 sandbags were also carried. The hulk was towed to the site at night by the steamer *Etivan*, their movements being concealed from the Union force by the dark background of Morris Island. The lightship hulk was man-oeuvred to bring the sheer-legs over the gun and tackles were fixed. Finally, all the sandbags were brought up to the bows. The slack on the tackles was taken up and the gun lifted as far as possible by the men available. Further lifting was then achieved by moving all the sandbags from the bow to the stern. Sadly this was still not quite enough and just as the tired and disconsolate workers were about to give up, a strong swell lifted the gun clear! The coming of the dawn saw *Etivan* towing the hulk with its precious cargo past the Charleston forts, whose garrisons must have cheered loudly at the sight.

Three days later, on the 6 May, the second gun was successfully recovered. One gun went to Fort Sumter and the other to Battery Bee, the largest guns to be sited in these forts.

SUMMARY

Design submitted:	23 April 1861
Keel laid down:	19 April 1862
Launched:	6 December 1862
Commissioned	24 February 1863
Sunk	8 April 1863

Designed by Charles W Whitney
Built by J S Underhill, New York.
Commanding Officer: Cdr A C Rhind USN

Length:	159ft 6in
Beam:	36ft
Draught (mean)	8ft 6in
Displacement:	677 tons.

DOCUMENTS CONSULTED

1 *Specification of C W Whitney's Iron Mail Clad Floating Battery or Steam Gun Boat* Continental Iron Works, Green Point, Brooklyn. 23 April 1861.
2 Letter from C W Whitney to Rear Adm S F DuPont published in the *New York Times* on 24 April 1863.
3 Letter from Cdr A C Rhind USN to a Professor Soley and dated 15 May 1863.
4 *Plan of Engines for C W Whitney's Mail Clad Battery*
5 *Section of Armor proposed by C W Whitney*
  All the above provided by Timothy K Nenninger, Navy & Old Army Branch, Military Archives Division, National Archives & Records Service, Washington DC 20408.
6 Embellished plan of USS *Keokuk* held by New York Historical Society. Facsimile supplied by: Capt JHB Smith USN, Head Curator Branch, Dept of the Navy, Naval Historical Center, Washington DC 20374
7 *Ironclads in Action* by H W Wilson (Sampson Low, London 1896)
8 *By Sea and by River: A Naval History of the Civil War* by Rear Adm B Anderson (1962)

LESSER KNOWN WARSHIPS OF THE KRIEGSMARINE

The Type 43 Minesweepers Part 2

by M J Whitley

The first ship to complete, *M601*, commissioned on 22 November 1944 but did not join the minesweeping flotillas, being used for development work with the new Construction Trials Command instead. It was not until the 1 December that the first operational flotilla was formed under the command of Kapitanleutnant Reinhart Ostertag. This was the re-formed 12th Flotilla whose previous ships had been lost in France. Three days later, in the forenoon of 3 December, Oberleutnant zur See d R Damerow commissioned his *M801* at Königsberg as the first ship of the flotilla. The designated leader, *M602* did not join the Fleet until noon on 14 December under Ob Ltn z See d R Kroeger but this unit had still not received her radar or *S Gerate* by the end of January 1945 although she was battle-worthy in all other respects.

By the end of January, the flotilla had eight ships: *M602* (Ob Kroeger), *M603* (Kp Lt D R Fremeroy), *M604* (Kpt Lt Anders), *M605* (Ob Lt d R Bellingrodt), *M801* (Ob Damerow), *M802* (Ob Lt d R Leimbach), *M803* (Kpt Lt d R Ahrens) and *M804* (Ob Lt Umbek). This was not its established full strength and the flotilla was attached to the 10th Security Division under the command of MOK (Ost).

The next eight units to complete were to be allocated to the 2nd Flotilla, reforming in Cuxhaven on 1 January 1945. However, of *M606 – M609* and *M805 – M808*, *M807* and *M808* remained incomplete at the end of the war and *M805* had been lost at the beginning of March.

Finally, the last flotilla to be projected was the 6th, scheduled to form on 15 March 1945, but none of its units (*M610, M809* to *M815*) were completed, with the exception of *M610* and that only under Allied supervision some five months after the close of hostilities.

The deteriorating situation on the Eastern Front led to the new ships being quickly deployed to assist in the massive rescue operations to evacuate East Prussia in the face of the Soviet advance. Barely commissioned,

and lacking many items of equipment, *M801, M803* and *M804* were ordered by the OKM to break off work-up and minor repairs and to procede to Königsberg on 23 January 1945 to pick up refugees, where they joined the remainder of their class. Both flotillas remained fully occupied in the task of escorting refugee convoys until the final surrender. Soviet submarines were by now active in the southern Baltic and scored some success against the refugee convoy.

According to some sources, *M801* is credited with the sinking of the Soviet submarine *S4* by depth charges on 23 February but the war diary of Flag Officer (Destroyers) records that the torpedo boat *T3* (sic) rammed and sank a submarine in Danzig Bay on 4 January 1945, damaging her bows in the process and Jürg Meister in *Soviet Warships of the Second World War* (1977) gives the loss date of *S4* as 6 January 1945.

In May 1945, when the Allies entered the north German ports, they found the wrecks of *M802, M804* and *M805* on the bottom at Kiel, and *M804* broken in two at Monkeberg. The three wrecks came under category 'C' of the Tripartite Commission Report, ie those units captured non-operational, wrecked or incomplete and under the terms agreed were to be either destroyed for scrap or scuttled in no less than 100m of water by 15 August 1946. *M802* was partially demolished on 15 December 1945, then completely dispersed by two depth charges on 20 May 1946. *M805*'s wreck was destroyed on 17 August 1946.

POST WAR OPERATIONS

After the German surrender, most of the minesweepers, unlike other German warships, remained operational and were employed on clearing the vast wartime minefields around the continental coasts as part of the German Minesweeping Administration. *M601* to *M612* as well as *M806* took part in this operation. This organisation had been set up in accordance with Article

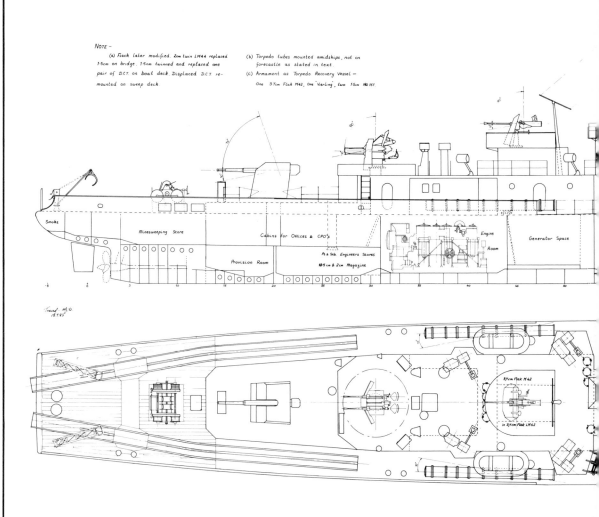

NOTE –

(a) Flack later modified. 2cm twin LM44 replaced 1.5cm on bridge. 1.5cm twinned and replaced one pair of D.C.T. on boat deck. Displaced D.C.T. re-mounted on sweep deck.

(b) Torpedo tubes mounted amidships, not on forecastle as stated in text.

(c) Armament as Torpedo Recovery Vessel – One 3.7cm Flak M42, One 'Vierling', two 1.5cm MG 151.

General arrangement of Type 43 Minesweeper

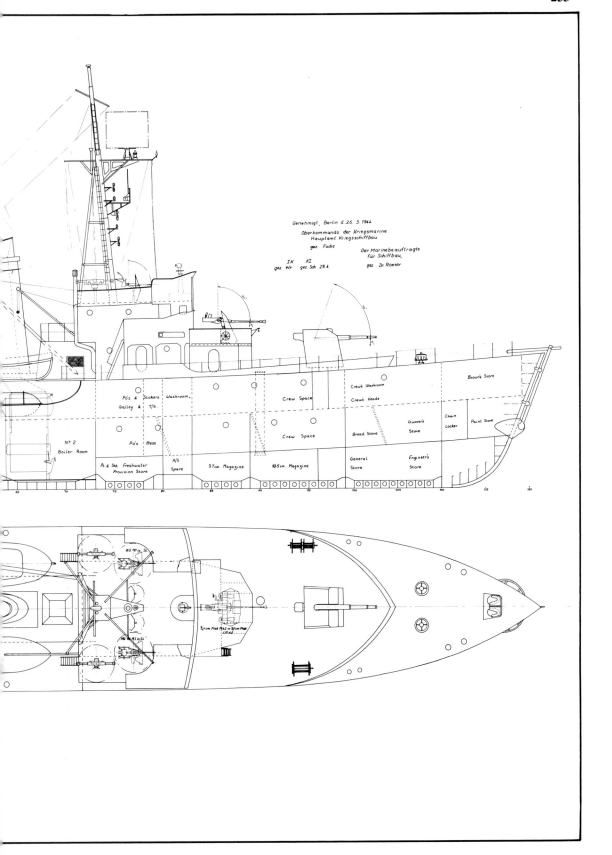

Genehmigt, Berlin d. 26. 5. 1944
Oberkommando der Kriegsmarine
Hauptamt Kriegsschiffbau
gez. Fuchs

Der Marinebeauftragte
für Schiffbau,

IK   KI
gez Wr   gez. Sch 28.4.   gez. Dr. Roeser

Bosun's Store

Po's & Stokers Washroom,   Crew Space   Crew's Washroom
Galley & T/S.   Crew's Heads

Chain   Paint Store
Gunner's   Locker
Store

N° 2   Po's Mess   Crew Space   Bread Store
Boiler Room

Pt & Stb Freshwater   A/S   3·7cm. Magazine   10·5cm. Magazine   General   Engineer's
Provision Store   Space   Store   Store

MG 151 in Sl.

3,7cm Flak M42 in 3,7cm Flak
LM42

MG 151 M2 in SL

7 of the Declaration regarding the defeat of Germany which was signed by the Allied C-in-Cs on 5 June 1945. It was divided into six divisions as follows:

1st Division, Schleswig-Holstein (Kiel)
2nd Division, Western Germany (Cuxhaven)
3rd Division, Denmark
4th Division, Norway
5th Division, Holland
6th Division, US Enclave (Bremen)

The ships were disarmed except for a maximum of two 2cm guns for mine sinking (except those employed in the Baltic where only ground mines were present). Their 10.5cm (4.1in) guns were, in most cases, retained but without breech blocks or ammunition. The personnel were drawn from serving former *Kriegsmarine* officers and men on a compulsory basis, (but no German occupied an operational position above flotilla commander). After the long years of hostilities there was, however, a natural desire by all former combatants to return home to civilian life and the Germans proved no exception. In consequence, desertion was a problem, which in turn caused manning difficulties. Morale was, in general, low, not surprisingly, since those formations stationed in former occupied territories were not allowed shore leave for obvious reasons. Furthermore, men having families in the Soviet Occupation zone or those coming out of those areas to Western areas were continually bombarded with Soviet propaganda extoling the delights of life in the Soviet zone. Under the conditions prevailing, this propaganda had some effect. Then in order to attract men to the service, advertisements were run in German newspapers. This however was frowned upon by the politicians and also attracted a vitriolic diatribe from the Soviets couched in the usual Marxist-Leninist terminology, accusing the Allies of seeking to maintain a disciplined, uniformed Fascist fleet! However, despite all these problems, the operation continued to function.

Its organisation was broadly based upon the flotilla dispositions as of the date of surrender, with some minor alterations. Flotillas were now known as 'German Minesweeper Flotillas' (GMSF). In August 1945, the organisation was as follows:

1st Division (Kiel)
2nd GMSF (*M606 – M611, M801, M371, M373, M374, M388*)
12th GMSF (*M601 – M605, M612, M806*)
23rd GMSF (8 'M40')
29th GMSF (10 'M40')
2nd Division (Cuxhaven)
1st GMSF (10 'M35,)
7th GMSF (7 'M35')
25th GMSF (9 'M40')
27th GMSF (9 'M40')
3rd Division (Denmark)
40th GMSF (3 'M35', 2 'M40', 9 'M16')
4th Division (Norway)
5th GMSF (8 'M35', Stavanger)
9th GMSF (5 'M40' Tromsö)
22nd GMSF (5 'M40', Bergen)
30th GMSF (7 'M40', Stavanger)

In addition, at Lorient, in France, the 24th GMSF had 3 'M40' ships, whilst in reserve or non-operational at St Nazaire, La Pallice and Lorient were a further 9 'M35', 10 'M40', and 1 'M43' (*M803* at La Pallice). Furthermore, there was a huge number of KFK flotillas also engaged on minesweeping.

Minesweeping operations were mainly conducted during the summer months, refits being undertaken during the winter when conditions were in general too rough for minesweeping. Strangely, in this period it was a shortage of coal which impeded, and on occasion halted, operations altogether, whereas oil had been the problem during the war, hence the coal-burning minesweepers (which comprised over 70% of the GMSF).

By 1946, the operation was being reduced as the surrendered warships due to Russia under the Tripartite Agreement began to be delivered. The 1st, 23rd, 29th and 30th Flotilla were handed over completely, with nine more ships from various other flotillas, but none of the modern Type 43 ships were obtained by the Soviets. However, it is believed that the incomplete hulls of *M807* and *M808* were later completed by the Soviet Navy and put into service. Their subsequent fate is not known, although they were probably discarded in the 1950s or 1960s. *M601* to *M605*, *M612* and *M806* were allocated to Britain, whilst *M606* to *M611*, *M801* and *M803* were allocated to the United States.

By 1947, the minesweeping task had been largely completed and the vessels concerned became surplus to requirements. Being coal burners, they were not in great demand for further service by any of the Allied Navies and most of the UK allocation began arriving in breakers yards during March and April 1948. Of the US vessels, three were sold out for commercial use in 1948 and three more sold to the Italian Navy in 1949. *M611*, one of the three sold out commercially in 1948 was later reacquired by the USA and then on 15 August 1956, she was sold to the new German Navy with whom she remained in service as *Seeschlange* until paid off in February 1960 to become an accommodation ship. *M607* and *M608* still remain in commercial service under the Italian and Greek flags.

TABLE 3: CLASS LISTS

No	Launched	Commissioned	Fate
			Neptun Werft (Rostock) Vessels
M601	31.8.44	22.11.44	RN 1945. Arrived Middlesborough for scrapping 20.4.48
M602	21.10.44	14.12.44	RN 1945.
M603	2.11.44	31.12.44	RN 1945
M604	10.11.44	18.1.45	RN 1945. Arrived on Tyne for scrapping 28.3.48.
M605	13.12.44	3.2.45	RN 1945. Arrived on Thames for scrapping 17.3.48.
M606	20.12.45	20.2.45	USN 1945. B/U in Hamburg.
M607	20.12.44	16.3.45	USN 1945. Sold out commercially 1948*
M608	20.1.45	20.3.45	USN 1945. Sold out commercially 1948*
M609	29.1.45	27.3.45	RN 1945. Arrived Newcastle 17.2.48, B/U Dunstan.
M610	27.2.45	5.10.45	USN 1945. B/U Ghent 1950.
M611	12.3.45	12.3.45	USN 1945. Mercantile 1948, USN 1952, W Germany 1956.
M612	23.3.45	11.4.45	RN 1945, Arrived in Thames for B/U 17.3.48.
			Schichau (Königsberg) Vessels
M801	9.9.44	3.12.44	USN 1945. To Italy 20.7.49, *B3 – Gazella*. Discarded 1966.
M802	29.9.44	4.1.45	Sunk by 8th USAAF at Kiel 3.4.45.
M803	19.10.44	17.1.45	USN 1945. To Italy 20.7.49 *B2 – Daino*. Discarded 1966.
M804	1.11.44	23.1.45	Sunk by B24s of 8th USAAF at Kiel 11.3.45.
M805	9.11.44	26.1.45	Sunk by B24s of 8th USAAF at Kiel 11.3.45.
M806	21.11.44	1.45	RN 1945. Scrapped on Tyne 28.3.48.
M807	13.1.45		Completed by USSR.
M808	45		Completed by USSR.

Notes: *M613 – M616, M809 – M813* incomplete at surrender. Scrapped.
M601 – M604 ordered 7.5.43. Remainder 4.12.43.
see below for commercial history.

COMMERCIAL HISTORIES

M607 Sold out 1948 to Hapag and renamed *Hornum*, then in 1950 sold again and renamed *Christian Ivers*, owners not known but managed by Ivers Linie of Kiel. 1953, sold to Kieler Reed Gmbh and in 1954 renamed *Hanne Scarlett*. Then in 1957 she was acquired by a trio of Danish businessmen, J O Jensen, L Jensen and J H J Jensen of Copenhagen but later that same year became owned solely by Jorgen Jensen. Four years later she was resold, this time to Skandinavisk Liniet-rafik AS also of Copenhagen. 1962 saw her renamed *Salvatore Lauro* on her sale to Agostino Lauro of Naples. Finally in 1975, Libera Navigazione Lauro S a S of Hong Kong became her owners, although still registered in Naples, with whom she is still in service.

M608 This ship had a similar career to that of *M607* until 1964, except that she was sucessively renamed *Arum, Harald Ivers* and *Lilli Scarlett*. In 1964, however, she was sold to Christos S Pagoulatos of Athens and renamed *Elena P*. She too, is still in service.

Both ships were re-engined with diesels early in commercial service.

TABLE 1: CLASS TECHNICAL DETAILS

Displacement:	605 tons (standard), 842 tons (full).
Length:	207ft (63.1m) pp, 224ft (68.3m) oa.
Beam:	29.5ft (9.0m).
Draught:	6.5/8.5ft (2.0/2.6m)
Machinery:	2 Wagner Marine Boilers (232 psi, 300° C); 2 sets triple expansion engines with Bauer-Wach exhaust turbines; 2400hp = 17kts maximum; 150 tons coal = 3600 miles at 10kts.
Armament:	2 – 10.5cm SKC/32ge (single mounts) – 210rpg HE, 30rpg star shell; 2 – 3.7cm Mk42 (single shielded mounts) – 1500rpg; 4 – 2cm C/38 (vierling) – 8000 rounds; 2 – 1.5cm Mg151 – 6000 rounds; some 2 – 53.3cm trainable MZ43 torpedo tubes; provision for 24 mines; 1 – 7.3cm 'Fohn' rocket launcher; (TRV's racks for 17 torpedoes in lieu of after 10.5).

TABLE 2: ARMAMENT

10.5cm SKC/30ns	(In 10.5cm centre pivot mounting MPLC/32ge)
Calibre	105mm (4.1in)
Muzzle Velocity:	780m/s (2559fps)
Shell weight:	15.1kg (33lb 4oz)
Shell length:	459mm (18in)
Filling weight:	3.8kg (12lb 7oz)
Complete round:	24kg (53lb)
Max Horiz Range:	15,175m (16,595yds, 8.2nm)
Barrel length:	45 cal/474cm (15.5in)
Liner length:	42 cal/440cm (14.4in)
Constructional Gas Pressure:	2850kg/cm
Barrel life:	4100 rounds
Elevation/Depression:	70°/10°
Armour thickness:	12mm (front)4mm (side and deck)
Armour:	Wsh
Weight of barrel and breech:	1765kg (3891lb)
Weight of cradle and brakes:	655kg (1444lb)
Weight of mounting:	2100kg (4629lb)
Weight of shield:	1670kg (3681lb)
Weight of complete mount:	6750kg (14,880lb, 6.6 tons)

Rocket 'Fohn V2'	
Calibre:	7.3cm (2.8in)
Projectile weight:	2.64kg (5.8lb)
Propellant weight:	0.45kg (1lb)
Explosive charge:	0.3kg (10oz)
Range 0°:	300m (328yds)
Range 45°:	4200m (4593yds)
Range 90°:	2400m (2624yds)
Max trajectory vel:	280 – 300m/sec (918 – 984fs)
Fuze:	Proximity (time of flight 6.5sec) Percussion (RAZ 51)
Firing Rack weight:	600kg (1322lb)
No of launcher trays:	35 (7 horizontal in 5 tiers)
Target area at 1400/1600m:	35 rockets HE in 90m × 120m (98 × 131yds). Fired as one salvo or two halves. Rockets in magazine clips of 7.

Actual warfare concentrates wonderfully the minds of naval aircraft designers, but it also has the effect of sorting the wheat from the chaff, and in our column for this issue we are taking a brief look at an aircraft that was conceived to meet a pressing demand from the Fleet Air Arm but which, for a variety of reasons, was to play no part in the conflict which spawned it.

The wheat in this instance was the Supermarine Seafire, a by and large successful adaptation of the remarkable Spitfire landplane and to which we might return in a future column; the chaff with which we are here concerned was an aircraft expressly designed to fill the role that the Seafire would assume – a single-seat fleet air defence fighter, successor to the Blackburn Skua (but closer in concept to the Sea Gladiator and, as it transpired, the stopgap Fulmar and Martlet) and called Firebrand.

Designed to Specification N11/40 and first flown in February 1942, the new aircraft could hardly have presented a greater contrast in appearance to the machines it was supposed to replace. It was, by the FAA standards of the day, a massive aeroplane: not only did its airframe exceed the dimensions of existing carrier-based fighters, it was also half as heavy again as the RN's Albacore torpedo-bomber; indeed, it surpassed in size the Grumman Tarpon (Avenger) torpedo-bomber then evincing quizzical Admiralty glances from across the Atlantic.

In retrospect, it is not easy to determine just why the Firebrand should have emerged as the bulky aircraft it did; certainly the Napier Sabre powerplant was a hefty piece of machinery, but on the other hand the RAF's Typhoon, which also used the Sabre (and, incidentally, a naval version of which was the Firebrand's defeated competitor for N11/40), weighed only some four tons (empty) as compared with the Blackburn aircraft's five. Additionally, carrier requirements such as wing folding, undercarriage, strengthening and flap mechanisms would account for extra weight, but in general the design seems to have had far less compromise than naval aircraft design in reality demanded.

In fact, both the Sabre engine and the bulk of the aircraft itself, together with the proof that the Seafire was indeed a viable carrier fighter, were the major contributors to the abandonment of development of the Firebrand as a fighter: the Typhoon was accorded top priority for development as the RAF's ground attack fighter and hence Sabre production was concentrated for that purpose; meanwhile the Firebrand's deck-

Warship Wings No7

Blackburn Firebrand

By Roger Chesneau

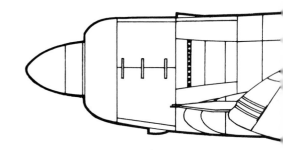

landing characteristics were proving to be something less than ideal.

However, re-engined, the enormous airframe might be put to better use, and with Admiralty encouragement Blackburn started work to reconfigure the project as a torpedo aircraft, retaining the wing-mounted cannon to give the Firebrand a fighter capability as well, something of a change for the FAA since the single seat was to be central to the design. One of the prototypes was rebuilt to undertake trials as such (Firebrand Mk II) and further Mk Is were married to the powerful Bristol Centaurus radial (Firebrand Mk III). The Mk III flew at the end of 1943, but although, somewhat ironically, the re-engined torpedo-fighter variant proved handier and more manoeuvrable in the air than the Mk I fleet air defence fighter, there were still problems in carrier handling, notably approach. The Firebrand was relatively docile at low speeds to be sure, but the view forward, of especial importance to an aircraft whose wingspan amounted to two-thirds the width of a typical flight deck, was virtually non-existent: pilots were reportedly unable to see *any part* of the flight deck during the last few dozen yards of their approach path. How the Firebrand would have faired landing aboard

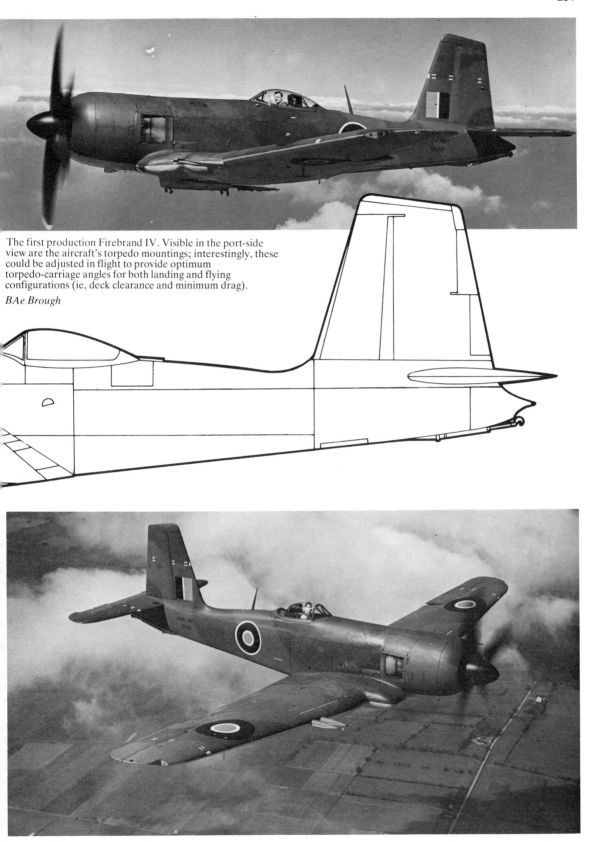

The first production Firebrand IV. Visible in the port-side view are the aircraft's torpedo mountings; interestingly, these could be adjusted in flight to provide optimum torpedo-carriage angles for both landing and flying configurations (ie, deck clearance and minimum drag).

BAe Brough

A Firebrand Mk V rolls aboard *Implacable*. Note the large Fowler-type flaps and the stabilising fins fitted to the torpedo slung below the fuselage. Note also the zero-length rocket rails below the wings: the Firebrand could also operate in the conventional strike role.

Fleet Air Arm Museum

1

3

2

1 The second prototype Firebrand III. The rudder is considerably larger than that first fitted, to counter the torque produced by the propeller.

BAe Brough

2 A production Firebrand IV. The photo gives some indication of the appalling view forward offered to the pilot.

BAe Brough

3 Another Firebrand IV in early postwar colour scheme. The small fairings before the cockpit housed an airspeed indicator, for use by pilots during landing.

BAe Brough

carriers like *Argus* or *Furious*, with no, or at best vestigial, islands, can perhaps be imagined.

As events turned out, the Blackburn torpedo-fighter had no such opportunity, since it was September 1945 before the Mk IV – the production variant and the subject of further design changes – was brought into service. Further small modifications produced the Mks V and VA, and the aircraft went to sea aboard *Illustrious* and *Implacable* during the late 1940s; it also formed part of the initial equipment of the new carrier *Eagle* from March 1952, but within a year or so had been withdrawn in favour of the Westland Wyvern.

BLACKBURN FIREBRAND MK IV – SPECIFICATION

Overall length:	38ft 9in
Span:	51ft 3in (full); 16ft 1in (folded)
Max height:	13ft 3in
Wing area:	383ft²
Engine:	1 – Bristol Centaurus IX piston engine, 2520hp
Max speed:	300kts at 13,000ft
Combat radius:	320nm
Weight:	11,500lb (5.1 tons) empty; 16,700lb (7.4 tons) max
Weapons:	4–20mm Hispano cannon, 1–18in Mk XV/XVII torpedo

THE FINAL ACTION

The Sinking of Bismarck, 27 May 1941

By John Roberts

On the morning of 27 May 1941 the German battleship *Bismarck* was steaming an erratic north westerly course well out in the Atlantic, west of the English Channel. Six days earlier she had sailed from Bergen to raid the

Atlantic convoy routes, a move frustrated by her action of 24 May which, although resulting in the sinking of battlecruiser *Hood*, required an early return to port to repair damage inflicted by the battleship *Prince of Wales*. By circuitous route she headed for Brest but on 26 May Swordfish aircraft from *Ark Royal* hit her with two torpedoes one of which jammed her rudder 20° to

Bismarck as completed.
IWM, courtesy R A Burt

port and damaged her propellers. Attempts to release the rudder failed and steering using only the engines achieved only minimal success. Alone and crippled she could only await the arrival of her pursuers. Away to the north the battleships *King George V*, flying the flag of Admiral Sir John Tovey C-in-C Home Fleet, and *Rodney* approached at a moderate speed with the intention of bringing *Bismarck* to action at dawn.

THE GUN DUEL

As dawn neared *King George V* and *Rodney* began to work up speed as they approached the *Bismarck*'s reported position from the WNW. A Force 6 gale was blowing from the NW generating a heavy swell but dawn showed a clear, overcast day with good visibility. At 0820 the masts of the cruiser *Norfolk* came into view and this ship, which had been shadowing *Bismarck* since 0753, reported the enemy's exact position.

The two British battleships were steering 110° with *Rodney* 1600yds off the flagship's port quarter when, at 0842, *Bismarck* was sighted from *King George V* bearing green (starboard) 7°. One minute later the Air Defence Officer aboard *Rodney* also sighted the German battleship, 25,000yds away (12.3nm), steering directly towards the British ships and listing 3° to 5° to port. For both British ships range-taking conditions were poor, due to the long range and funnel haze, and fire control tables were initially set to estimated ranges (25,000yds in *Rodney* and 24,000yds in *King George V*). However, the flagship's Type 284 gunnery radar obtained a momentary echo at 25,100yds and her table was returned to this range; the Type 284 continued to

Rodney in August 1941.
Perkins, courtesy R A Burt

obtain short echoes until the range dropped below 21,100yds (10.4nm) when they became continuous.

At 0847 *Rodney* opened fire with A and B turrets at a gun range of 23,500yds, followed by *King George V* one minute later at 24,600yds. *Bismarck* replied at 0849, firing on *Rodney* with her forward turrets; her first 4-gun salvo fell 1000yds short; the second 1000yds over; the third (at 0853) straddled, one shell falling only 20yds short just abaft the bridge but causing no casualties and the rest over; the next two salvos fell short, after which there were several overs. Although *Bismarck*'s initial fire was good it was not as accurate as expected and it seems likely she was suffering similar difficulties of observation as the British, combined with her problems of maintaining a steady course. She never did find her target and very soon after the action began damage greatly reduced her fire control capability and armament. Nevertheless, on several occasions her fall of shot came uncomfortably close to the British ships.

Rodney found her target with her second double, fired 0848 (unfortunately not spotted by *Rodney*), *Norfolk* reporting that hits were obtained with one or both of these salvos. At 0850 *Rodney*'s main director rangefinder obtained a plot 2500yds above gun range and, as no range had as yet been obtained from spotting

the fall of shot, her fire control table was tuned to this range. Consequently, *Rodney* was firing 'over' for several minutes and did not regain her target until salvo 18, the 'B' of a down ladder, at about 0859 at a range of 21,000yds. This straddle was seen to produce two hits on *Bismarck*, one on the forecastle and another which sent a sheet of flame up the superstructure. It is probable that this hit on the forecastle put *Bismarck*'s turret out of action. *Rodney* continued to straddle her target until 0902 obtaining several hits.

At 0853 *King George V* signalled for the ships to turn 085° together but *Rodney* was already committed to a port turn to open her 'A' arcs and for a short period the British ships were steaming on diverging courses. At 0853 *Rodney* turned to starboard onto an easterly course, closing the 'A' arcs after 'X' turret had fired in only two salvos (X turret was able to fire in three more salvos 17, 18 and 19 when a small alteration of course was made to avoid enemy fall of shot).

The fall of shot of *King George V*'s first salvo was not seen but the Type 284 reported this as short so an up ladder was fired. However, it was later concluded that the 284 had ranged on *Rodney*'s shell splashes and consequently for a few minutes *King George V*'s salvos fell over. At 0853 the Type 284 obtained a range of 20,500yds and a double, spread 200yds on each side of this (ie 20,300yds and 20,700yds), was fired. The 'A' salvo straddled and produced the first hit actually observed by the flagship. After this *King George V* fired zig-zag salvos using the ranges obtained on the

Type 284 – observing the fall of shot revealed that a correction of 200yds down was required on the radar range, which was in-line with earlier experience in practice firing. Until 0913, when the Type 284 broke down as a result of a heavy shaking from 14in gun blast, at a range of 12,400yds, 14 straddles was observed out of about 34 salvos. Even allowing for spotting errors this was exceptionally good both in terms of fire control and rate of fire – a few salvos fell out of line (ie off the bearing) but the target was only lost twice (on both occasions a regaining ladder was fired) – some salvos were not observed due to cordite smoke.

At 0854 *Norfolk* to the north of *Bismarck* opened fire with her 8in guns and four minutes later *Rodney*'s starboard 6in battery joined in at a range of 21,000yds. By 0900 the fire from *Bismarck* had slackened; 'A' turret was probably out of action, B was firing spasmodically and the after turrets were still unable to bear on the British ships. At 0902 *Bismark*'s foretop fire control post was put out of action and shortly afterwards the lower fire control position on the conning tower, together with both forward turrets, were also put out of action. At 0908 *Norfolk* reported that the guns of 'A' turret were laying depressed as if the elevating gear had gone, while those of 'B' were pointing drunkenly towards the sky. It has been recorded that A or B turret fired a last salvo at 0927 – it is possible that one or more guns were able to fire, perhaps on a fixed bearing, due to the efforts of the turret crews on the other hand it may just be an error of observation.

Just after 0902 *King George V* and *Rodney* turned onto a course of 182°, with *Rodney* well aft, just off the flagship's port quarter. The action was still only 15 minutes old. This southerly course proved difficult for gun control in *Rodney* as the heavy swell on the starboard quarter made the ship yaw badly, and cordite and funnel smoke made ranging difficult. *King George V* employing radar control was much less affected by these conditions although she still, of course, had spotting difficulties. At 0909 *Rodney* altered course 40° to port placing the wind dead astern which improved conditions slightly.

At 0910 *Bismarck*'s after turrets, controlled from the after control post, began firing at *King George V* but three minutes later, after firing only four salvos which were getting progressively closer to their target the director was disabled. Control was transferred to the turrets themselves which continued to fire independently until D turret was put out of action at 0921 (the right gun was wrecked by a premature detonation, two more rounds were fired from the left gun before internal damage brought firing to a stop) and C turret ceased fire at 0931 after the left gun was disabled by a hit. (*Bismarck* had shifted her fire back to *Rodney* at 0920.) Thus, 45 minutes from the start of the action, all of *Bismarck*'s main armament and fire control gear was out of action.

At 0915 *Bismarck* began to draw aft from the British ships and both turned 180° (*Rodney* to starboard and *King George V* to port) bringing them onto a similar course to the enemy. As *King George V* turned A and B

turrets continued to fire while Y turret trained round to pick up the target again at 12,000yds as the A arcs opened on the opposite beam. *Rodney* turned at 0916 after firing her 40th salvo, which straddled, and both main and secondary armament had to check fire while she turned, fire being re-opened by the main armament at 10,000yds at 0918 and shortly afterwards by the starboard 6in battery. Both ships had difficulty spotting on this northerly course because the *Bismarck* was continuously surrounded by shell splashes and the after part of the ship was shrouded in smoke from fires and her funnel. Without radar *King George V*'s performance was reduced but four straddles were spotted between 0913 and 0930 and on three occasions she regained the target by firing a single ladder and once with two ladders. In addition at 0920 she began to experience trouble with breakdowns in her 14in mountings, which so reduced the numbers of guns able to fire that all those still operating were fired together to provide adequate salvos. At 0929 she started using her Type 279 radar to range on *Bismarck* and reverted to firing zig-zag salvos until 0953 when the radar was transferred to its usual function of air search. During this time the *King George V* continually bracketted her target with the 'A' salvos over and the 'B' salvos under but only three straddles and one hit were observed.

Rodney fared much better, with the wind on the port bow-spotting and range taking conditions improved but the swell produced a heavy roll. On her new course she regained the target with three down ladders, obtaining a straddle with the 'A' salvo of the 3rd ladder at 9000yds at 0920. She continued to straddle *Bismarck* for the next eight minutes, only one regaining ladder being necessary. At 0921 she altered course to 021° and at 0926 to 037° which increased the roll and made range taking difficult (no ranges were obtained between 0922 and 0927). At 0928 the target was lost and until 0945 great difficulty was experienced in regaining and holding the target. Hits were obtained at 0929 and 0935 but all other salvos (when observed) were reported 'over' or 'short', due to an error in the TS (Transmitting Station) as well as the difficulties already mentioned.

Rodney's course gradually took her across *Bismarck*'s bows and at 0936 she turned 180° to port and began a pattern of crossing back and forth raking the enemy ship from ahead at range between 4000 and 3000yds. She turned again at 0942. No straddles were obtained on the first leg of this zig-zag course but when fire was reopened at 0945 the fourth salvo obtained hits. Thereafter she continuously hit and straddled the target until cease fire at 1014.

At 0949 she again turned 180° but shortly afterwards the AFCT broke down and fire had to continue under the direct control of the director until, having found the damage to the table could not be repaired, control was rerouted through one of the Vickers AFCC (used normally for the secondary armament). At 0952 full broadsides were ordered, the first was short but the remainder scored hits, as many as five or six being observed in one broadside. At 1003, having altered

King George V on 10 July 1942.
NMM

Bismarck in the Atlantic, May 1941.
IWM, courtesy R A Burt

course 190° to starboard she fired her last broadside at 4000yds and then reverted to salvo firing to avoid waste of ammunition. At 1005 she again altered course as the guns were bearing aft and in her last twelve salvos, between 1008 and 1014 at an average 3800yds range scored several hits. She then turned north to rejoin the *King George V*.

Meanwhile between 0954 and 1009 *King George V* obtained at least three straddles while her zig-zag salvos generally bracketed the target at an average range of 8000yds. From 0955 to 1004 control was transferred to the after DCT while the flagship turned 180° to starboard but 5 minutes later fire had to be checked when she again turned 180° to close the range to 4000yds before opening fire again at 1018. At 1019 a 3-gun salvo was seen to obtain three hits one of which, on B turret, started a fire and caused the back of the turret to be blown out, while the other two hit the base of the forward superstructure and started a large fire which sent flames as far up as the bridge platform – at the time *Bismarck* was head on to *King George V*.

King George V ceased fire at 1021 and, as both British battleships were short of fuel, she joined *Rodney* and steered 027° at 19kts for home. *Bismarck* was a complete wreck, very low in the water and on fire but her flag still flew and she showed no immediate signs of sinking. Admiral Tovey ordered any ships in the area that still had torpedoes to close and sink her. At 1025 the cruiser *Dorsetshire* fired two torpedoes into her starboard side which appeared to have no immediate effect so she steamed around to the other side and fired a third torpedo. Four minutes later *Bismarck* capsized, she sank shortly after in position 48°10′N, 16°12′W.

FIRE CONTROL

In the early stages of the action, until 0913, *King George V* employing her Type 284 radar had an advantage over *Rodney* and obtaining about 14 straddles to *Rodney*'s 8 or 9. It is difficult however, to attribute any particular damage to either ship – it was during this period that *Bismarck*'s A and B turrets and the forward fire control positions were disabled. After 0913 *King George V*'s fire was considerably reduced, initially by the loss of her Type 284 and subsequently by problems with her 14in mountings, and it seems likely that most of the damage done to *Bismarck*, including the disabling of the after control post and turrets, in the period 0915 until 0930 was inflicted by *Rodney*. As the range closed both ships again began to hit consistently, *Rodney* from about 0945 and *King George V* from about 0953.

Spotting for both ships was very difficult due to smoke interference, the heavy swell, *Bismarck*'s continual yaw due to her damaged rudder and the difficulties of distinguishing between the 14in and 16in fall short of shot (further confused by the shell splashes of the secondary armament and the 8in fire of the cruisers *Norfolk* and *Dorsetshire*).

16in GUN MOUNTING PERFORMANCE

Under the circumstances *Rodney*'s 16in Mk I triples performed exceptionally well and there can be little doubt that she did a great deal of damage to *Bismarck*. Her mountings had once given a great deal of trouble and the relative smoothness with which they operated on 27 May 1941 seemed to prove that during her 15 years of service most of the problems had been ironed out. Her performance was all the more creditable when considering that she had only carried out one live firing practice since the previous year and no night firing practice since the outbreak of war. In addition, a week before the action 30 men, mostly leading seamen and petty officers, had left the ship (as she was about to leave for the USA for refit these key personnel could be found more important duties!) resulting in a dilution of the personnel and in particular a reduction in the efficiency of the guns crews.

Nevertheless, the output of her main armament for the first 30 minutes was 90%, at one time firing 3 salvos per minute. In the first hour she achieved 80% with 1.5 salvos per minute. Overall she produced 1.6 salvos per minute during salvo firing and 1.1 broadsides per minute during broadside firing, with outputs of 77% and 62% respectively.

She experienced various minor problems with mechanical failures and drill errors, the worst being with the right gun of A turret. This gun missed 11 salvos due to problems with the slide locking gear and then, at salvo 65, a complete jam occurred in the right shell pusher hoist. As a result of drill errors the top shell was rammed up the hoist and jammed in the gunhouse with its nose against the rangefinder supports. It was not cleared until 12 hours after the action. In addition the centre gun of A missed 2 salvos due to slow drill and all the salvos from 64 to 88 due to mechanical failures, the left gun of A missed 10 salvos and did not fire after salvo 97 due to mechanical failures. B turret's centre gun misfired at salvo 4 and missed 5 or 6 over a period of 7 minutes towards the end of the action due to drill errors. The left gun of B had several delays as a result of drill errors but X turret suffered only two jams which caused only minor delays.

14in GUN MOUNTING PERFORMANCE

King George V's problems were much worse, largely due to the fact that the 14in twin and quadruple mountings were comparatively new and were suffering a considerable number of teething problems. Initially she did well achieving 1.7 salvoes per minute while employing radar control but she began to suffer severe problems from 0920 onward. 'A' turret was completely out of action for 30 minutes, after firing about 23 rounds per gun, due to a jam between the fixed and revolving structure in the shell room and Y turret was out of action for 7 minutes due to drill errors. The left gun of B had several delays as a result of drill errors but X turret suffered only two jams which caused only minor delays. Both guns in B turret, guns 2 and 4 in A turret and gun 2 in Y turret were put out of action by jams and remained so until after the action – 5 guns out of 10! There were a multitude of other problems with mechanical failures and drill errors that caused delays and missed salvoes. There were also some missfires – one gun (3 of A turret) misfired twice and was out of action for 30 minutes before it was considered safe to open the breech.

DAMAGE TO RODNEY

Little of the damage received by *Rodney* was inflicted by *Bismarck*. She did not receive a direct hit but did have slight splinter damage from near misses. Three minor holes were made in the bridge structure one of which cut the control leads to the searchlights. The base of a 5.9in shell penetrated the side of the CPOs' mess and caused some slight damage and another fragment penetrated the side of the HA director and ricocheted about inside. In addition a considerable number of electricity cables were cut and the sluice valve door of the starboard torpedo tube was jammed.

This damage, however, paled into significance compared with the havoc wrought by the blast of her own main armament. The upper deck was depressed to varying depths around the turrets and partition bulkheads, beams and support pillars had been distorted and split between the upper and main decks. Ventilation trunks had been split and blown out. The wooden deck planking had been ripped up and in some places sections were missing, many of the deck fittings had been broken and distorted. The watertight hatch over the sick bay was blown open and the area below completely wrecked.

In the *Rodney*'s torpedo flat the entire complement of torpedoes were fired without success but not without considerable difficulty. Vibration from the main armament and near misses started the rivets in the fresh tanks immediately over the torpedo body room and water began to seep down into the flat. In addition all the lamps were shattered and light had to be provided by portable lamps and torches. When the starboard sluice valve door jammed it was twice opened with difficulty but after that seized up solid and all torpedoes had to be fired from the port tube. With only two torpedoes left the deck head began to sag, the depression of the deck forward caused by the gun blast having transmitted itself to the lower and the beam on which the torpedo traversing trolley ran dropped 1in. Both the remaining torpedoes were on the starboard side and to fire them it was necessary to transfer them to the port tube with this traversing trolley. The torpedoes, however, would not clear the loading rack and it was necessary to bump them over.

DAMAGE TO BISMARCK

The full effect of the British shellfire on the *Bismarck* is, apart from the damage to the armament and upperworks, difficult to evaluate. Two points of controversy have clouded this issue, the statements by survivors that the main belt was not pierced and that scuttling charges were used to sink her. However, there were no survivors from the fore end of the ship, so such statements can only be accepted with certainty as applying to the after part of the ship. No evidence exists, to prove or disprove that *Bismarck* was penetrated below the armoured main deck but the two decks above it, both from the evidence of survivors and observation by British ships were subject to considerable damage. This at the very least required the penetration of either the 50mm (2in) upper deck – at long range – or the 145mm (5.6in) upper belt. However, the most direct evidence

Bismarck early in May 1941, viewed from *Prinz Eugen*.
Drüppel, courtesy R A Burt

of armour penetration comes from *King George V* which obtained one or possibly two hits on *Bismarck*'s B turret at a range of 4000yds. These appeared to go through the armour and blow out the back of the turret throwing part of the armour plate over the side. These shells were fired from nearly right ahead, so probably went through the turret's side which was 220mm (9in forward and 150mm (6in) rear thick, unless the turret was trained ahead (the face plates were 380mm – 15in thick). At such short range they certainly would not have penetrated the sloping roof plates. Some deliberate waterline shots were fired by both *Rodney* and *King George V* at close range in the latter part of the action but *Bismarck* was low in the water and listing to port (the engaged side) so much if not all of the thickest belt armour was probably submerged.

Damage to the upperworks and higher decks was considerable and severely disrupted the communication systems (which were mainly above the main armoured deck). Some British shells passed through the ship and exploded on the starboard (disengaged side) while others, hitting the superstructure, passed right through without exploding (a 1in mild steel plate, hit at the normal was required to initiate the 159 fuze fitted to 16in and 14in APC). *Rodney* estimated that she obtained 40 16in hits, those achieved by *King George V* are not known but one would assume a similar number. Although these would seem sufficient to cause the *Bismarck* to sink, the majority would have caused damage above water, particularly those fired at close range (from which the majority of hits were obtained) and, as it is necessary to admit water to a ship to sink her, it is not perhaps surprising that she appeared to be foundering very slowly.

Survivors state that orders were given to scuttle the ship just after 1000, however, this does not indicate a well organised system of laying scuttling charges around the ship. First, only those stations still in communication with whoever gave the order would have been able to carry out that order, and communications had been severely disrupted; second, the scuttling order related more to the opening of seacocks, valves, watertight doors and so on than the blowing holes in the bottom of the ship (survivors have said they saw not evidence of damage to the ship's hull when she capsized). Two of the ship's three engine rooms and the after damage control post received the order to scuttle (and possibly others) in each case steps were taken to flood the compartments concerned the only charges mentioned being those fitted to the sea intakes of the condensers in the engine room. The only clue that these steps had an effect is in the fact that she sank stern first when most of the shellfire damage was forward. On the other hand it is hardly fair to assume that the gunfire and *Dorsetshire*'s torpedoes had a minimal effect on the speed with which she sank particularly as she capsized to port – the engaged side – which survivors could not have seen. Personally I am of the opinion that *Bismarck* would have sunk and that any scuttling measures were only partial and served only to hasten that end.

TABLE 1: HMS RODNEY RECORD OF 16in SALVOS

Time	Salvo	Correction	Range (yds)	Fall of Shot	Notes
0847	1A	Spread for	23,500	R	
	2B	deflection		L & R	
0848	3A	Spread for		None in	Hits observed
	4B	deflection		line	from *Norfolk* from 3 or 4 or both
0850	5A	Spread for		R	
	6B	deflection at new range		R	
0851	7A	L1		Over	
	8B	L2		Over	
0852	9A	Down ladder		L	
	10B			L	
0854	11A	R		Over	
	12B	R		Over	
0855	13A	Down ladder		L	
	14B			L	
0856	15A	R4		Over	
0856	16B	R2		Over	
0858	17A	Down ladder	21,000	Over	
	18B			Straddle	
0900	19A	Zig-zag		Straddle	
	20B	group		Straddle	
0901	21A	None		Straddle	
	22B	None		Over	
0902	23A	Down ladder		Over	
	24B			Straddle	
0904	25	None		Over	
	26	D400		Over & L	
0905	27	D400, R2		Straddle	
	28	None		Not clearly seen	
	29	D400		?	
0905	30	U400		R	
0908	31A	L2		Not clearly	One of 31 or 32
	32B	L1		seen	obtained hits
0911	33A	Zig-zag		Not seen	
	34B	group		Not seen	
	35A	None		Short	
	36B	U400		Over	
0914	37A	D200		Over	
	38B	D400		Over	Correction error
0915	39A	Down ladder		Over	
0916	40B			Straddle	
0918	41A	New course	10,000	Over	
	42B	(spread for line)		Over	
	43A	Down ladder		Over	
	44B			Over	
0920	45A	Down ladder	9000	Straddle	
	46B			Short	
0922	47A	Zig-zag		Straddle	
	48B	group		Straddle	
	49A	Zig-zag		Over	
	50B	group		Over	
	51A	Down ladder		Over	
	52B			Straddle	
	53A	None		Straddle	
	54B	None		Straddle	
	55A	Zig-zag		Straddle	
	56B	group		Straddle	
	57A	None		Straddle	
	58B	None		Straddle	
0928	59A	1st salvo of zig-zag		Short	

	60	U400	Over	
0929	61A	D200	Short	
	62B	Zig-zag group	Short	
	63A	U400	Straddle	Hits observed
	64B	U400	Mostly over	
	65	D200	Over	
	66A	D400	Over	
	67B	D400	Over	
0932	68A	D800	Short	Correction error
	69B	U400		
Over	70A	D200	Short	
	71B	U400	Over	
	72A	D400	Short	
	73B	U200	Straddle	Hits observed
	74	None	Straddle	Hits observed
	75	None	Straddle	Hits observed
0938	76	Fired on mean of RF ranges	Over	
	77	Fired on mean of RF ranges	Over	
	78A	Down ladder	Short	
	79B		Short	
	80	U800	Over	
	81	D400	Over	
	82A	Down ladder	Short	
	83B		Short	
	84		Over	
0945	85		Short	
	86	U400	Over	
	87	D400	Over	
0945	88-89		Straddles	Hits observed
	90-92		?	AFCT broke down
0952	93	Broadside	Short	
	94	U400, broadside		Hits observed
	95-97	None, broadsides		Hits observed
	98	D200, broadside		Attempt at hits on waterline
1003	99	Last broadside	4000	
	100-101	Salvos		
1008-1014	102-113	Salvos	3800 (mean)	Several hits obtained

Notes: L = left; R = right; corrections for bearing (ie L1, L2 is left one unit, left 2 units). U = up; D = down; corrections for range (ie U400 = up 400yds, D200 = down 200yds); A and B indicate 'A' and 'B' salvos of ladders or zig-zag groups; ladders, fired up or down, consisted on two salvos fired in succession without waiting to spot the fall of the first salvo (ie if a fall of shot was spotted over, a down ladder would be fired the 'A' salvo being 400yds down on the previous salvo, and the 'B' salvo a further 400yds down on that – 200yd and 800yd steps were also used depending on circumstances), the next correction would be based on the spotting of both salvos. When the target was found a zig-zag group was fired to give a spread of shells over the target's position.

TABLE 2: 16in AMMUNITION EXPENDITURE IN RODNEY

Turret	Gun	Rounds fired
A	L	36
A	C	46
A	R	22
B	L	45
B	C	44
B	R	52
X	L	44
X	C	42
X	R	44
	TOTAL	375

TABLE 3: 14in AMMUNITION EXPENDITURE IN KING GEORGE V

Turret	Gun	Rounds fired
A	1	22
A	2	27
A	3	30
A	4	32
B	1	36
B	2	40
Y	1	21
Y	2	45
Y	3	37
Y	4	49
	TOTAL	339

TABLE 4: BRITISH AMMUNITION EXPENDITURE

Ship	Gun Calibre	Ammunition	Rounds Fired
King George V	14in	APC Mk VIIB	339
King George V	5.25in	SAP MkIC (Fuze 501)	660
Rodney	16in	APC MkIB (Fuze 159)	375
Rodney	6in	CPBC Mk XXVB (Fuze 480)	716
Norfolk	8in	–	527
Dorsetshire	8in	–	254

Notes: Rodney fired 150 salvos from her starboard 6in battery (5 salvos/min) and 98 salvos from her port 6in battery (3.9 salvos/min). During the first 9 minutes at close range the 6in achieved 5.9 rounds per minute and an output of nearly 100%. In King George V the starboard 5.25in battery fired approximately 70 rounds per gun (except S4 left gun which misfired after 12 rounds) and the port battery about 29 rounds per gun.

THE MAJESTIC PRE DREADNOUGHT Part 2 by RA Burt

Launch of the *Prince George* on 22 August 1895. The photograph shows clearly the recess for the 9in belt, which covered 220ft of the ship's side.
IWM

The armour layout of the *Majestic* was designed to give maximum protection against the ever developing threat of attack from medium calibre guns and HE shells, the main belt was reduced in thickness to increase its area and give improved protection to the middle side, above which the majority of hits were expected in any action. The principal improvements in armour layout were:

1 General use of Harvey armour for the vertical main belts, in place of Nickel or Compound armour or plain steel.

2 Adoption of a much wider belt, made possible by the reduction of thickness over previous classes, backed by a sloping deck (instead of a flat deck placed on top of the main armour strake as before). Again this helped in reducing thickness without excessive loss of protection.

3 Provision of closed armoured shields (turrets) over the barbettes which afforded much protection for the guns and guns crews.

The sloping deck employed in the Royal Navy for many years and extensively copied abroad, originated in a desire to provide deck protected cruisers with a degree of vertical armour and first appearing in the cruiser *Leander* of 1880. This in association with the wide belt, previously proposed by William White for both the *Royal Sovereign* and *Centurion* classes, allowed the main strake to be reduced in thickness (the Admiralty Board would not approve any reduction in protective qualities until the coming of Harvey armour which proved to be much more resistant than any compound plates). The Harvey process consisted of taking an all-steel plate and covering with animal charcoal, another plate (to be given a similar treatment) was then placed on top of this to form a sandwich. The plates were then surrounded with bricks, the whole assembly placed in a large furnace and heated for around 2-3 weeks. After this the plates were removed and left to cool for 6 or 7 days. This treatment greatly increased the carbon content of the surface of the plates; a high carbon steel face was thus combined with a standard steel alloy back. The change from one to the other being gradual and without a joint (as in compound armour). Both plates were re-heated in the furnace again and on withdrawal were doused in cold

Victorious at anchor in Beirut in 1900.

Author's collection

water the rapid cooling causing the high carbon steel to become extremely hard thus producing the ideal armour requirement of a super hard face and a soft (resilient) back in one piece. Any forming of the armour plates was done prior to the hardening process.

The deck protection consisted of three thicknesses of plates, two of 1½in and one of 1in, all sloping at an angle of 40° to the ship's side, which was estimated to represent a deflecting resistance equal to about 8in of vertical armour. The wide belt along the waterline provided a constant 9in thickness to a height of 9ft 6in above the waterline compared with only 5in the the *Royal Sovereign*s at a height of 3ft 6in. This protection in *Majestic* was considered sufficient to burst any HE shells, in which case the armoured deck would afford effective splinter protection. Armour piercing shells would have needed to pierce both the 9in side armour and the 4in sloped deck to reach the vitals of the vessel and this was seen as a great improvement over the older methods of armour distribution.

The edges of the flat section of the protective deck were extended right across the ship to the sides by shell plating, the triangular spaces thus formed between the flat and the slope providing watertight flats on each side which could be filled with coal or water; this arrangement was retained in all later battleships with sloping deck protection. As in the *Royal Sovereign* class the protection to the extremities, outside the citadel, were confined to an underwater deck with a cellular layer of watertight compartments above this rising to the middle deck level which was about 3ft 6in above the waterline. These unarmoured ends were a point of criticism owing to the loss of the battleship *Victoria* in June 1893 after being accidentally rammed by the battleship *Camperdown*, the construction of the *Majestic* and *Magnificent* was delayed pending a special investigation into this

TABLE 6: Armour Protection	
Main belt:	9in Harvey steel, 220ft long by 15ft wide
Bulkheads:	14in forward, 12in aft
Barbettes:	14in above armoured deck, 7in below
Turrets:	10½in face, 5½in Harvey sides (see gunnery notes)
Casemates:	6in face, 2in side
Protective deck:	3in flat, 4in (40°) slope
Lower deck outside citadel:	2½in forward, 2½in aft, both sloping
Conning tower:	14in face with 8in tube descending to the protective deck. Rear of CT was 12in
Aft conning position:	3in
6in ammunition hoist:	2in

Notes: 4in teak backing to armour. There were 78 watertight compartments outside the armoured citadel and 72 inside. A double bottom was provided from 8ft 9in past the citadel at both ends. Coal bunkers were 11ft and 8ft inboard respectively, behind the armoured belt above the middle deck, and abreast engine and boiler rooms below this.

incident but it was established, after a board of enquiry, that the absence of an armoured belt forward was not responsible for her loss.

MACHINERY

The *Majestic*s were given the same basic machinery as that fitted in the *Royal Sovereign* class, although an extra 1000shp was made available in the former. This gave the same speed but the ships were able to reach their speeds more easily. The new class had improved radius of action, coal stowage being increased to 1900 tons maximum, and 1100 tons at normal load, the latter raised from 900 tons owing to the fact that the board margin was not used up.

It was discovered during the first trials of *Royal Sovereign* in 1892 that the high level of forced draught caused her boilers to leak badly and the steam pressure to fall off so rapidly that she was in danger of complete boiler failure. To avoid this problem the *Majestic* class

The Channel Fleet at anchor, c1900. Units of the Flying Squadron (*Royal Sovereign* class) and *Majestic* class.

Author's collection

were not forced to the same extent but nevertheless they achieved the same speed, due mainly to the fact that the new vessels had much finer hull lines. The *Illustrious* and *Magnificent* were fitted with induced instead of forced draught, although the results obtained were slightly less than in the rest of the class. The system was accepted as giving better reliability and safety.

The nominal speed of the *Majestic* class was approximately 1kt faster than in the *Royal Sovereign*s with natural draught and about the same with forced draught although the latter was reached with 1000shp less.

The class had little trouble with their machinery, although there were small problems, one such was the thrust blocks becoming over heated in the *Prince George* whilst running at high power, this was found to be a condenser fault, one of which had perforated. Similar troubles were experienced in *Illustrious* with leaking glands and valves, and some ships suffering from vibration; in general however, other than minor mechanical faults the vessels performed well. In 1903–4 two of the boilers in *Hannibal* and four in *Magnificent*, *Majestic* and *Mars* were converted to burn oil and coal simultaneously. Each boiler was fitted with 8 sprayers giving a total output of 880lb of oil per boiler per hour at a pressure of 150psi. The radius of action using oil was increased from 6260nm at 10kts to approximately 7000nm, and from 3490nm at 14.6kts to 4420nm at the same speed.

TABLE 7: MACHINERY

Engines:	2 sets of 3 cylinder, vertical, inverted triple expansion engines driving 2 4-bladed improved Griffith propellers.
Cylinders:	40in – 59in – 88in with a stroke of 51in
Boilers:	8 cylindrical single ended, with 4 furnaces each. Water in boilers when full to working height: 120 tons. Heating surface: 24,400sq ft. Revolution of screws: 100–107 (see trials). Working pressure of boilers: 155lb psi.
Weight of machinery as fitted:	*Majestic* 1356 tons, *Mars* 1328 tons, *Jupiter* 1315 tons.
Fuel stowage:	900 tons coal in normal load condition, 1900 tons maximum. The coal stowage was later reduced by 200 tons and 400 to 500 tons oil added in those ships converted in 1903–4.
Radius of action:	With oil sprayers: 7000nm at 10kts. 4420nm at 14.6kts.
Coal consumption:	At full power: 250 tons coal per 24 hours. At ⅜ths power: 140 tons per 24 hours. At economical speed (8kts): 50 tons per 24 hours.
Ships engined by:	*Magnificent* Penn. *Majestic* Vickers. *Hannibal* Harland and Wolff. *Mars* Lairds. *Jupiter* Clydebank. *Illustrious* Penn. *Prince George* Humphreys. *Caesar* Maudsley. *Victorious* Hawthorn Leslie.

The *Majestic*, being the first of the class to complete, was put through a lengthy series of trials. It was during these trials that the Vice-Admiral commanding the Channel Squadron, Lord Kerr, made the following statement whilst watching the vessel perform and having taken many notes with great care:

'I am thoroughly satisfied with the ship, and I think the result is most creditable to the designers and fitters out. We went through manoeuvres and target practice as though we had been in commission for a year already,

*Mars c*1904 in all grey paint scheme, with early funnel bands, WT gaff on mainmast and with shields removed from her 3pdr guns. Note the torpedo net shelf at main deck level, she was the only unit of the class so fitted before 1903-04.

Author's collection

but everything went without a hitch. The new ship steers well, and is quicker off the helm than the *Royal Sovereign*'.

APPEARANCE CHANGES

Well proportioned and handsome ships, they were considered by many to be better looking than the *Royal Sovereign*s mainly due to the closer spacing of the funnels and the pronounced sheer at the bows. The masts, each with two large military tops, gave a rather impressive profile, whilst the modified arrangement of the forebridge and conning tower introduced in the first six ships gave them a unique appearance. In this latter arrangement the bridge was built up around the pole foremast, leaving the conning tower clear of obstruction, a departure from previous practice in which the bridge

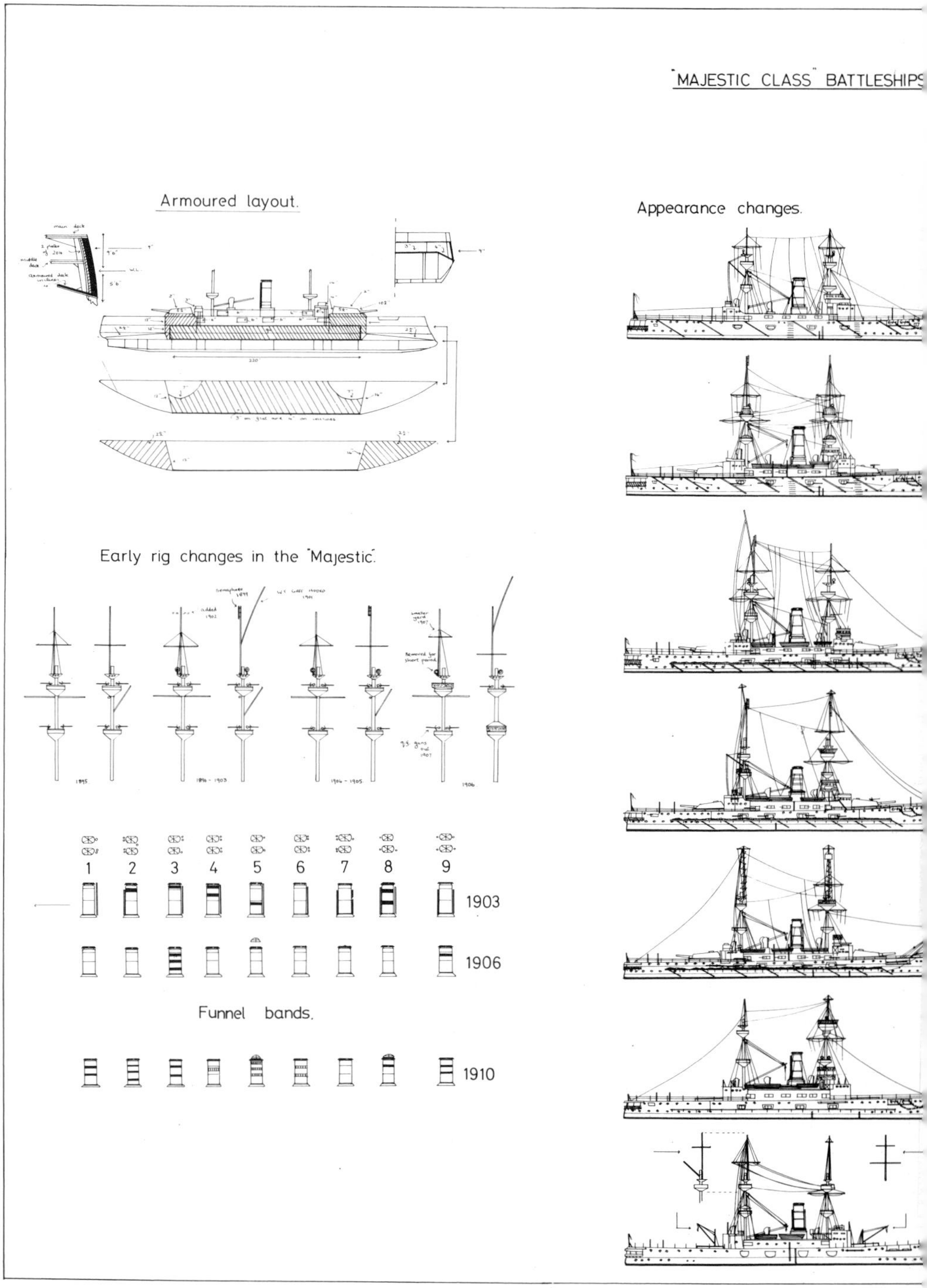
"MAJESTIC CLASS" BATTLESHIPS
Armoured layout.
Appearance changes.
Early rig changes in the "Majestic".
1 2 3 4 5 6 7 8 9
1903
1906
Funnel bands.
1910

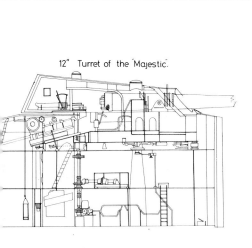

12" Turret of the 'Majestic'.

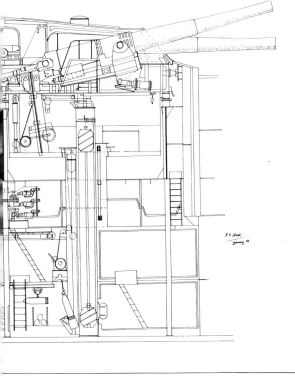

12" Turret of the 'Cæsar' and 'Illustrious'.

APPEARANCE CHANGES

1 *Jupiter* 1897 as on trials

2 *Majestic* 1899

3 *Illustrious* 1907

4 *Jupiter* 1910

5 *Prince George* 1915

6 *Magnificent* 1916 as depot ship

7 *Prince George* 1918

FUNNEL BANDS

1 *Majestic*

2 *Mars*

3 *Magnificent*

4 *Hannibal*

5 *Jupiter*

6 *Illustrious*

7 *Caesar*

8 *Prince George*

9 *Victorious*

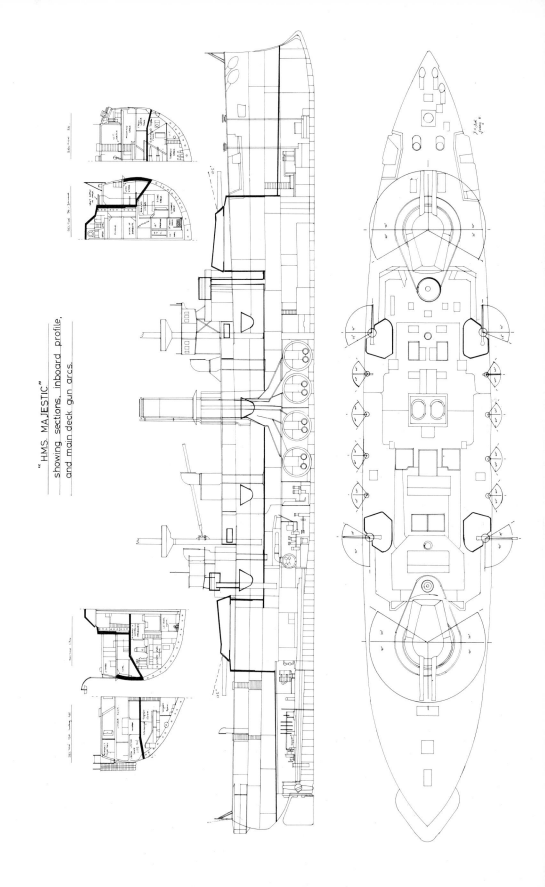

"H.M.S. MAJESTIC"
showing sections, inboard profile,
and main deck gun arcs.

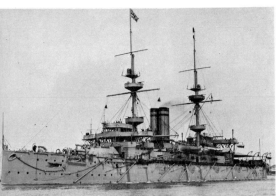

1 *Hannibal*, with early funnel bands (2 black on each), seen entering Portsmouth Harbour in about 1903/4. Although not evident in this photograph she is painted in an experimental light green/brown colour.

Author's collection

2 *Hannibal* leaving Portsmouth about 1910. Note rangefinder drums on the fore and mainmasts, standard funnel bands, no 3pdr in tops, searchlight redistribution and tall WT topgallant mast to main.

Author's collection

3 *Prince George* in 1905-06. Note the searchlight on the lower foremast, the early funnel bands and 3pdr removed from the tops.

NMM, Perkins collection

3

TABLE 8: STEAM TRIALS OF MAJESTIC 19–20 OCTOBER 1895

Conditions:	Bottom clean, Sea smooth, Wind Force 1.
Propellers:	4 bladed, 17ft ¾in dia with a pitch of 19ft 8⅝in.

30 HOUR TRIAL

Displacement:	13,181 tons.
Revolutions:	85.5 per minute.
IHP:	6075.
Speed:	14.67kts logged.
Coal Consumption:	1.84lb/hp/hour.

8 HOUR TRIAL

Displacement:	13,360 tons.
Revolutions:	100.6
IHP:	10,453.
Speed:	16.9kts.

4 HOUR TRIAL

Displacement:	13,225 tons.
Revolutions:	107.2.
IHP:	12,554.
Speed:	17.8kts.

COLLECTIVE TRIALS of class whilst in Channel Fleet 1904 (8 hour trial).

	IHP	Revs	Speed (kts)
Illustrious	10,073	92.7	15.2
Magnificent	10,365	92.9	15.4
Majestic	9,315	95.9	15.2
Mars	10,025	90.3	15
Hannibal	10,209	95.4	16
Jupiter	10,539	?	16.2
Victorious	10,189	100	16.6
Caesar	10,740	93.7	16.1

As above at ⅗ths power and normal draught,

Illustrious	6,521	84.1	13.6
Magnificent	6,519	80.1	13.1
Majestic	6,765	87.5	14.4
Mars	6,976	84.2	13.97
Hannibal	6,291	84.1	14.03
Jupiter	7,047	?	14.45
Victorious	6,416	88	14.50
Caesar	6,608	83	14.17

was built above the conning tower. The advantages of this arrangement were the increased all-round view from the conning tower and the elimination of the risk of it being obstructed by the collapse of the bridge or parts of it in the event of action damage, and the increased distance between bridge personnel and the blast of the forward 12in gun turret when being fired abeam or abaft that position.

In the last three ships (*Caesar*, *Hannibal* and *Illustrious*) the earlier system of fitting the bridge over the conning tower was reverted to and this remained a feature of British battleships until the later Dreadnought type *Orion* class in 1909. In William White's January 1893 sketch, the bridge is shown over the conning tower indicating that this had been the original plan for the class.

A flying bridge was fitted in all upon completion, with the exception of the *Magnificent* although she received hers shortly after this. Accommodation was slightly inferior to the *Royal Sovereign* vessels with the cabin arrangements on the whole being more cramped. The

bow scroll was abandoned in this class on the grounds of possible interference with the anti-torpedo nets.

As completed the ships are extremely difficult to tell apart, although there were some differences, in particular the following: bridge differences as already noted above.

Jupiter had striking topmasts, a large starfish below the searchlight platforms, an upper yard high on the foremast, tall steampipes abaft the funnels, heavy close fitting funnel caps and small brackets on the inner side of the funnels.

Magnificent had fixed topmasts, charthouse on after flying bridge added in 1896, starfishes, upper yard and funnel caps as in *Jupiter*.

Majestic had light starfish below the searchlight platforms, an upper yard low on the foremast, tall steampipes abaft the funnel and light funnel caps clear of the casing. Topmasts and charthouse as in *Magnificent*.

Mars had topmasts and starfishes as in *Majestic*, two widely spaced steampipes before each funnel and one abaft on the inner side of each funnel (all short), main deck net shelf (only ship so fitted prior to 1903–4).

Prince George had striking topmasts, large starfishes, short steampipes before and abaft each funnel (one only before each funnel) and small light funnel caps clear of casing.

Victorious had topmasts and starfishes as in *Prince George*, steampipes as in *Prince George* except in having two before each funnel and heavy close fitting funnel caps.

Caesar had short steampipes before and abaft the funnels and the upper stay rim on the funnels well below the top.

Hannibal had steampipes abaft the funnels only and to the same height as the funnels and lighter, solid points to the starfish below the searchlight platform.

Illustrious had steampipes abaft the funnels only (but shorter than the funnels) and larger perforated points to the starfish.

Alterations after completion:

1898: Fixed topmasts in *Mars* replaced by striking topmasts stepped forward.

1899: Shields began to be removed from 3pdrs and the number of guns carried in tops were reduced. The guns being relocated on board ship in various positions. Shields removed from all guns by 1902.

1901–2: Wireless Telegraphy fitted with W/T gaff on main topmast.

1902–3: Electric hoists fitted to 6in guns in addition to the hand gear. Experimental oil sprayers fitted in *Hannibal* and *Mars* late in 1902 with the work being completed by February 1903. These two were the first British battleships to be fitted with oil burning gear.

Hannibal, *Magnificent* and *Majestic* used in experiments with 'Invisible painting' to determine colour to paint ships to replace Victorian colours. *Hannibal* painted greenish brown at first and then black hull and light green upper works. *Magnificent* painted grey and black. *Majestic* black hull and grey upper works. The light green in *Hannibal* proved to be the most difficult to see

Majestic c 1906 with temporary, red funnel bands.
Author's collection

in some conditions. Final result was an overall grey slightly darker than that which had been used by the German Navy for some time.

1903–4: Net shelf in some ships lowered to main deck level. Fixed topmasts in *Jupiter, Magnificent* and *Majestic* replaced by striking topmasts. Victorian paint replaced by all grey scheme.

1903–4: Funnel bands painted up in some ships. Black top to each funnel with single band below in *Hannibal, Magnificent* and *Majestic*. These bands being used for identification of ships in different squadrons whilst in the Channel Fleet and not for individual ship recognition as with those bands painted up in 1909 (see funnel bands).

Magnificent in late 1908 with an enlarged fore top and a yard fitted to her WT gaff.

NMM – Perkins collection

1905–9: Fire control and rangefinder equipment fitted, the *Magnificent* was given a new oval top fitted in place of the searchlight platform in the foremast. In others original upper fighting top covered in and roofed over being adapted for rangefinder gear although not in *Victorious*. These modifications were all effected from 1905/6 in all except *Majestic* and *Victorious* who were fitted in 1907/8.

In one or two of the first ships fitted, the fire control for the secondary armament was not fitted until as late as 1909. 12pdr guns were removed from the main deck in 1905/6. Some were remounted in various positions, others removed altogether.

Searchlights removed from masts in all ships except *Majestic* (1905/9) but remounted over forward 6in casemates. A great deal of experimental work was carried out in some of the class with regard to the arrangements of the searchlight positions. 2 extra 24in lamps were added in some vessels. Masthead semaphore removed 1906/7. W/T gaff triced up 1907.

1909–14: Small rangefinder mounted in lower foretop in some of the ships (1909–10). Minor changes in the location of 3pdr guns with no more than 4 per ship carried by 1914. Reported in 1912 that 6in and 12pdr were to be replaced in *Magnificent* (then gunnery training ship at Devonport) with 4in quick firing guns although nothing came of this. Nets removed in *Illustrious* and *Magnificent* and more than likely in some of the others from 1912/13. Still in *Hannibal* and *Victorious* by 1913. W/T gaff replaced by tall W/T topgallant mast in all except *Majestic* (1909/10). *Majestic* still had triced gaff in 1913. Heavy yards removed from mainmast in some. Standard funnel bands painted up in 1909.

1914: Funnel bands painted out.

1915: *Majestic* and *Prince George* modified for service in the Dardanelles Campaign. A small howitzer mounted on roof of each 12in turret to engage shore battery at close range, although found to be of little use in practice and removed by April 1915. Nets fitted and minesweep-

ing gear fitted over the bows. After flying bridge and charthouse removed from *Prince George*. Stockless anchors fitted in this ship. Topgallant fitted to each mast in *Majestic*. Small spotting top at head of fore topmast fitted in both ships and rangefinder baffles fitted around masts but this proved to be of little value and was removed.

Jupiter modified for Suez Canal Patrol in 1915. 12pdr field gun on HA mounting added on fore turret in September 1915 for AA defence. Searchlights reduced to 4. Torpedo nets fitted, after flying bridge removed, and maintopmast reduced to stump.

1915–16: *Hannibal*, *Magnificent* and *Mars* were disarmed except for 4 upper deck 6in and a few smaller guns, the 12in guns were used to arm the *Earl of Peterborough* class monitors. All three were used as depot ships of some sort.

Magnificent used as troopship September 1915 although it is most likely that *Majestic*, *Hannibal* and *Mars* were used the same way.

Hannibal reduced to harbour subsidiary service in November 1915 and then the same for *Magnificent* and *Mars* in March 1916.

Victorious disarmed and converted for subsidiary service with the Grand Fleet from September 1915 until February 1916.

Illustrious disarmed and converted as others in November 1915.

1917: *Jupiter* paid off with all 6in and lighter guns removed.

1918: *Prince George* disarmed and converted to depot ship May to September 1918.

Caesar refitted at Malta from September to October 1918 for service as depot ship for the British light forces in the Adriatic.

Main deck 6in removed and small AA gun mounted on after 12in turret, the possibility of a similar fitting forward cannot be ruled out although details are uncertain. Casemate and boat deck searchlights removed, two being remounted on the after flying bridge. Torpedo nets fitted but removed altogether shortly afterwards. Repair shops fitted together with recreation and reading rooms, etc for personnel of the Otranto Barrage patrol craft. Topgallant to mainmast only with full topmast to each mast.

At the end of the war the *Caesar* was the only unit of the class with any armament on board, she retained her four 12in as well as four 6in, all at upper deck level. She had two 36in and four 24in searchlights.

FATES

Majestic Sunk in the Dardanelles 27 May 1915 by *U21*.
Magnificent Scrapped at Inverkeithing from 1921.
Mars Scrapped at Briton Ferry from 1921.
Hannibal Scrapped in Italy from 1921.
Jupiter Scrapped at Blyth from March 1920.
Victorious Scrapped at Dover from 1923.
Prince George Wrecked off Holland and scrapped there (1922).
Caesar Scrapped from July 1922
Illustrious Scrapped at Barrow from 1920.

Jupiter on manoeuvres in 1909, with units of the *Canopus* class following.

Author's collection

TABLE 9: FUNNEL BANDS

As already mentioned the funnel bands in use throughout the period from 1903 to 1904 were for Fleet recognition only and were prone to constant change, they are therefore very unreliable for individual ship indentification. The bands seen in photographs for this period are as follows:

Caesar	None.
Hannibal	Black top with thin black band lower.
Illustrious	None.
Jupiter	One low black band.
Magnificent	Narrow black band on top.
Majestic	None.
Mars	One red band.
Prince George	Two widely spaced black bands.
Victorious	None.

Other markings seen in this period:

Majestic	seen with two red bands.
Magnificent	seen with three dark bands, colour uncertain.
Illustrious	with three dark bands.
Victorious	with a narrow black band.

In 1906 these bands were still being carried but again they are unreliable and changed a great deal:

1906 Bands:

Caesar	None.
Hannibal	None.
Jupiter	None.
Illustrious	None.
Magnificent	Three red bands.
Majestic	None.
Prince George	None.
Victorious	One red band.
Mars	None.

1909–10 saw the introduction of the standard funnel band system which identified individual vessels:

1909–10 funnel bands:

Caesar	None
Majestic	Two red bands.
Magnificent	One red band.
Mars	Three red bands.
Illustrious	Two white bands.
Jupiter	Three white bands.
Prince George	One black band.
Hannibal	One white band.
Victorious	Two black bands.

1 *Jupiter* at anchor in Malta during the Dardanelles campaign, Spring 1915.

Author's collection

2 *Prince George* laid up at Sheerness 1919/20 awaiting scrapping.

Author's collection

3 *Illustrious* partially dismantled at Barrow-in-Furness October 1920.

T W Ward

BOOK REVIEWS

'A CENTURY OF NAVAL CONSTRUCTION – The History of the Royal Corps of Naval Constructors'
by D K Brown RCNC. Published by Conway Maritime Press, March 1983
384pp, 92 photographs, 20 line drawings, glossary, index. ISBN 0 85177 282 X. £20.00

The Royal Corps of Naval Constructors (RCNC) was founded in 1883, and there could be no better tribute to its centenary than this book with its foreword by HRH The Duke of Edinburgh. Nor could there be a better person to write it than D K Brown. Not only is he an Assistant Director of Naval Construction with 30 years' experience in the RCNC (and a deserved mention in the book in his own right for his work on propellers), but, as regular buyers of *Warship* will know, he also has a profound knowledge of the past 150 years of British warship design and a very readable style.

For your money you get a history of the methods, organisation and major personalities of the RCNC, as well as an informed and informative work on the design and development of RN ships from the introduction of iron and steam. Either would be worth the price: together, they represent amazing value. Extensive contributions from senior members of the RCNC past and present have been skilfully worked into the story and add considerably to the reader's understanding.

In order to illustrate the work of modern members of the RCNC, the book starts with a fascinating account of the 'hows and whys' of the design of the postwar *Tribal* class frigates as experienced by a young Constructor, and of *Renown*'s late 1970s refit at Rosyth as seen by the Project Manager. After a full account of the situation in the early and mid-nineteenth century, the main part of the book consists of a chronological account of the work and major personalities of the RCNC. Each chapter deals with the rule of successive Directors of Naval Construction (there is even a section dealing with the inexcusable treatment of Sir William Smith by Winston Churchill) and their successors up to and including the present day and the Type 2400 SSK submarines. The final part consists of individual chapters on the Royal Dockyards, research and development (many fascinating snippets here), education and training, and the wide range of activities undertaken by members of the RCNC, though some of this – particularly the fearsomely difficult training – is also touched on in earlier chapters. It ends with an all too short postscript on the Falklands War.

Although there are clear signs of official reticence in the final chapters, this is not an official history, and it is all the better for that. The author is able to illuminate the book with his personal insights and opinions, for example describing Sir Stanley Goodall as 'probably the most outstanding warship designer of all time', and explaining with admirable clarity why the 1905 battleship *Dreadnought* needed particular care taking over her hull form, and why the cancelled aircraft carrier *CVA-01* would not have been satisfactory had she been built.

D K Brown has a passionate (and justified) pride in the RCNC, and he quite rightly demonstrates how wrong much contemporary and modern criticism of their work has been. In so far as there is a villain in the book it is the Naval Staff, whose demands give rise to some of the most heartfelt (and humorous) quotations from his contributors. This is fair enough, if only because the RCNC has had to suffer much ignorant criticism in the past from naval officers, oversensitive to minor failings in British ships and apparently totally unaware of major flaws in some prominent designs in other navies. However, though D K Brown freely acknowledges mistakes made by the RCNC, I feel that he is overly charitable in his treatment of them. I would also question whether, under the circumstances existing at the time, it was wrong to close the first two schools of naval architecture. The groundwork of naval architecture has not yet been firmly established, and the schools' failings were more significant than their virtues.

These are minor quibbles, though, compared with the sheer volume of excellent work contained within its covers. The book is all the more impressive because so little has been written at this level on either the RCNC itself, its members, or on the designs they produced. As the author says, this book was written about a technical subject by engineers, but it is impossible to write sensibly about ships without any technicalities. There is nothing that a layman cannot understand with the aid of a simple introduction to naval architecture, and the only reason that you need even this is because of the totally inadequate glossary. There is no excuse for this, because the publishers have wasted so much space in the index that there would have been more than enough room to explain everything twice over. Do not let this put you off. If you have any interest in the RCNC, modern warship design, or the Royal Navy, this is a book you must have in your library.

One final point. The frontispiece consists of a photograph of *Dreadnought* on trials in October 1906, signed by the major figures in her design, construction and trials. Some are identified underneath, but some are not. Most of those not identified are in fact from private shipyards, A (Not N) Noble for example being Sir Andrew Noble, then managing director of Armstrong Whitworth. This further illustrates one of the themes of the book, the close relationship between private industry and the Navy in general and the RCNC in particular.

Hugh Lyon

OTHER BOOKS RECEIVED

Red Navy at Sea: Soviet Naval Operations on The High Seas 1956–1980, Cdr Bruce W Watson, USN (Arms & Armour Press/RUSI and Westview Press, October 1982) 245pp, 10 maps, 25 tables, 29 photographs, bibliography, index. An impressive and highly statistical operational survey of the first 25 years of the Gorshkov era.

The Complete Encyclopedia of Battleships and Battlecruisers: A technical directory of all the world's capital ships from 1860 to the present day, Tony Gibbons (Salamander Books, July 1983) 272pp, index, £11.95. Full colour Salamander chronological treatment for

324 classes with line drawings by John Roberts. A full review will be given in *Warship*.

United States Navy Destroyers of World War II John C Reilly Jr. (Blandford Press, May 1983) 160pp, 250 photographs, bibliography, index, £8.95. To be reviewed in *Warship*.

The New Observer's Book of Warships, Hugh W Cowin (Frederick Warne, May 1983) 192pp, index, £1.95. Handy pocket reference in the new large 'Observer' paperback format for 165 of today's classes usefully grouped by general category. Many gaps but at the bargain price a useful primer to avoid going to weightier tomes.

On His Majesty's Service: Observations of the British Home Fleet from the Diary, Reports and Letters of Joseph H Wellings, Assistant US Naval Attaché London 1940–41 edited by John B Hattendorf (US Naval War College Press, Newport RI, 1983) 258pp, 11 photographs, indexes. Free from the publishers (zip code 02841) No 5 in the college's historical monograph series. To be reviewed space permitting.

Soviet Warships: The Soviet Surface Fleet 1960 to the present, John Jordan (Arms & Armour Press, June 1983) 128pp, over 150 illustrations, bibliography, index, £12.95. To be reviewed.

THE IMPERIAL RUSSIAN NAVY
THE IMPERIAL JAPANESE NAVY
by Fred T Jane

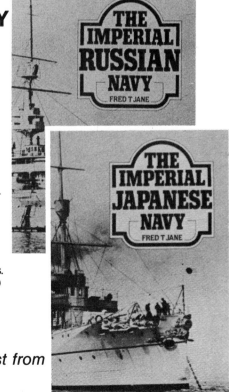

Although Jane is best known for his annual review of the world's fighting ships, he also published a number of more detailed works of naval reference. His complementary studies of the navies of Russia and Japan, written in 1904, are among his best, offering authoritative reviews of two navies which were largely unknown to the West at that time. Jane secured the close co-operation of both services and as a result, much of his detailed information – on ships, weapons, personnel, shipbuilding, dockyards and less visible factors such as

organisation, training and morale – has never been surpassed.

The Imperial Russian Navy: 234 x 156mm (9¼" x 6⅛"), 736 pages, 71 photographs, 109 line drawings. ISBN 0 85177 295 1. **£18.00** (plus £1.80 post and packing when ordering direct). Published in September.

The Imperial Japanese Navy: 234 x 156mm (9¼" x 6⅛"), 432 pages, 56 photographs, 34 line drawings. ISBN 0 85177 296 X. **£15.00** (plus £1.50 post and packing when ordering direct). Published in February 1984.

From your local bookseller or by post from
Conway Maritime Press Ltd.
24 Bride Lane, Fleet Street, London EC4Y 8DR.

CONWAY'S ALL THE WORLD'S FIGHTING SHIPS 1947-1982

The publication of this second part completes the postwar volume of Conway's four volume history of iron and steel warships. Since the war there has been a veritable revolution in naval affairs; not only has the balance of power shifted dramatically away from the traditional Western naval powers, but warships themselves have changed beyond rcognition. An authoritative survey of the period is long overdue and *Conway's All the World's Fighting Ships 1947-1982* fulfils this need by providing a clear but comprehensive picture of postwar naval affairs from the largest issue to the minute technicalities of warship design. This second part contains the navies of the Warsaw Pact, non-aligned countries and minor navies and includes the most up-to-date analysis of the Soviet and Communist Chinese navies currently available.

Part II: The Warsaw Pact and Non-Aligned Nations

310 x 216mm (12¼" x 8¼"),
256 pages, 250 photographs,
240 line drawings.
ISBN 0 85177 278 1.
£25.00 (plus £2.50 post and packing when ordering direct).
Published in October.

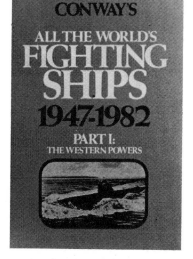

From your local bookseller or by post from
Conway Maritime Press Limited
24 Bride Lane, Fleet Street, London EC4Y 8DR

Naval Books

onway Maritime offer an unrivalled range of
uthoritative and well-illustrated titles on naval
ubjects. A free catalogue is available, but some of
he leading titles are listed below:

NAVAL WEAPONS
Norman Friedman
is exhaustive study by an acknowledged
pert on the subject discusses the
velopment and function of every weapon
stem employed by the US Navy from the
th of the 'New Navy' in 1883 to the
esent day.
¼" x 8½", 288 pages, 200 photos, 150
e drawings. ISBN 0 85177 240 4. £18.00
us £1.80 p + p)

AVAL RADAR*
Norman Friedman
ayman's guide to the theory, functions
d performance of seaborne radar
stems, from their introduction just before
Second World War to the present day,
luding a catalogue of every major piece
radar equipment to have seen service
h the world's navies.
" x 8½", 240 pages, 200 photos, 100 line
awings. ISBN 0 85177 238 2. £18.00
us £1.80 p + p)

ARRIER AIR POWER
Norman Friedman
penetrating analysis of how carrier
rfare operates, with extensive data on
ships and their aircraft.
" x 9", 192 pages, 187 photos, 32 line
awings. ISBN 0 85177 216 1. £12.50 net
us £2.00 p + p)

NATOMY OF THE SHIP: THE
ATTLECRUISER HOOD*
John Roberts
e first volume of this new series. Every
pect of the Hood is covered in a degree
detail never previously attempted for a
cent capital ship, and the standard of line
awings has been highly praised.
" x 10" landscape, 128 pages, 24
otos, 320 line drawings. ISBN 0 85177
0 1. £8.50 (plus £1.50 p + p)

NATOMY OF THE SHIP: THE
RCRAFT CARRIER INTREPID
John Roberts
e second in this new series, this volume
vers the Essex class aircraft carrier
ich is now being refurbished in New
rk as a floating Air-Sea-Space museum.
" x 10" landscape, 96 pages, 20 photos,
0 line drawings. ISBN 0 85177 251 X.
50 (plus £1.50 p + p)

CAMERA AT SEA 1939-1945*
edited by the staff of Warship
"A unique collection of some of the best
photographs of World War II at sea" – Sea
Power
12¼" x 8½", 192 pages, 250 photos, 24
colour plates. ISBN 0 85177 124 6. £12.00
(plus £1.50 p + p)

SUBMARINE BOATS
The Beginnings of Underwater
Warfare
by Richard Compton-Hall
"Cdr. Compton-Hall has produced a
book whose research and many rare
photographs and drawings will delight
both the technically-minded and the
general reader." — Daily Telegraph
9½" x 7¼", 192 pages, 173 photos
and drawings. ISBN 85177 288 9.
£10.50 (plus £1.55 p + p)

CONWAY'S ALL THE WORLD'S
FIGHTING SHIPS 1922-1946
The second in this highly acclaimed series,
the 1922-1946 volume covers all
significant warships built between the
Washington Treaty and the end of the
wartime construction programmes. With
over 1000 illustrations, it is the ultimate
reference book on the navies of World War
II.
12¼" x 8½", 464 pages, 506 photos, 530
line drawings. ISBN 0 85177 146 7. £30.00
(plus £2.00 p + p)

CONWAY'S ALL THE WORLD'S
FIGHTING SHIPS 1860-1905
The first complete listing of all warships
between the first ironclad and the
Dreadnought. " . . . must rank with the all-
time great naval reference works . . ." – The
Navy. ". . . all the thoroughness and
attention to detail we have come to expect
from Conway Maritime . . . excellent value".
– Ships Monthly
12¼" x 8½", 448 pages, 471 photos, 506
line drawings. ISBN 0 85177 133 5. £24.00
(plus £2.00 p + p)

A CENTURY OF NAVAL
CONSTRUCTION: The History of
the Royal Corps of Naval
Constructors
by D K Brown R C N C
This behind-the scenes history of the Royal
Navy's designers offers a new insight into
the factors governing British warship
design from the nineteenth century to the
Falklands conflict.
9½" x 6", 384 pages, 92 photos, 20 line
drawings. ISBN 0 85177 282 X. £20.00
(plus £1.00 p + p)

DESTROYER WEAPONS OF
WORLD WAR 2*
by Peter Hodges and Norman Friedman
A detailed comparison between British and
US destroyer weapons, including
mountings, directors and electronics. ". . .
one of the greatest possible additions to
the . . . range of naval books . . ." – The Navy
9½" x 7¼", 192 pages, 150 photos, 73 line
drawings. ISBN 0 85177 137 8. £7.50 (plus
£1.25 p + p)

BATTLESHIP DESIGN AND
DEVELOPMENT 1905-1945
by Norman Friedman
The first layman's guide to the design
process and the factors governing the
development of capital ships. ". . . an eye-
opening study of an extremely complex
business . . ." – Nautical Magazine.
10" x 8", 176 pages, 200 photos, plans and
line drawings. ISBN 0 85177 135 1. £8.50
(plus £1.25 p + p)

MODERN WARSHIP DESIGN AND
DEVELOPMENT
by Norman Friedman
". . . never before have the problems and
parameters of modern warship design
been set out so comprehensively,
informatively and clearly . . . the book
should be read by everyone with a concern
for the modern naval scene, professional or
amateur, uniformed or civilian." – Journal of
the Royal United Services Institute
10" x 8", 192 pages, 167 photos, 65 line
drawings. ISBN 0 85177 147 5. £9.50 (plus
£1.25 p + p)

AIRCRAFT CARRIERS OF THE US
NAVY
by Stefan Terzibaschitsch
". . . a definitive history of the US carrier
fleet from 1920 until the present day . . ." –
Journal of the Institute of Marine Engineers
11¾" x 8¼", 320 pages, 322 photos, 94
plans and line drawings. ISBN 0 85177
159 9. £15.00 (plus £1.50 p + p)

CONWAY
MARITIME PRESS

hese titles are available in North America from the Naval Institute Press, Annapolis, Md 21402.

rom your Local Bookseller or by post from

onway Maritime Press Limited
Bride Lane, Fleet Street, London EC4Y 8DR
hen ordering direct please add the posting and packing charge noted after the price)

BOOKS FROM
NAVAL INSTITUTE PRESS

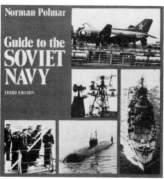

GUIDE TO THE SOVIET NAVY, 3rd edn

Norman Polmar

This superb reference work is the only contemporary English-language publication to present the full depth and scope of Soviet Navy ships and aircraft and their weapons and electronics suites. Organization, mission, tactics, personnel and support activities are all covered in this latest, completely revised and updated edition, which is also a companion volume to the highly successful **Ships and Aircraft of the US Fleet**. It carefully examines the newer ships, such as the **Kirov** battle cruisers, the **Sovremenny** and **Udaloy** destroyer classes, the Typhoon, Oscar, Alfa, Kilo and Lima submarines, and even previews its upcoming series of warships. This is a work which well deserves its worldwide reputation as the most reliable source available on the Soviet Navy.

9½" x 9½"; 576 pages; 413 illustrations; **£27.95** + £1.45 *postage and packing.*

NAVAL OFFICER'S GUIDE, 9th edn
Vice-Admiral William P. Mack and Captain Thomas K. Paulsen

This entirely new edition provides all the information essential to officers preparing for their first assignments after commissioning, as well as offering advice to those already serving. Completely revised and updated, the guide includes information on military law, the code of conduct, the US defense department, and other topics of general interest to naval officers. It will be a vital part of every young officer's professional library.

7½" x 5¼"; 440 pages; **£9.95** + £1.20 *for postage and packing.*

CONFLICT OF DUTY
The US Navy's
Intelligence Dilemma,
1919-1945
Jeffery M. Dorwart

Many sensational events never revealed before are brought to light in this fascinating history of the US Office of Naval Intelligence during its most crucial years. Written by a noted military historian, it analyses the dilemma faced by naval intelligence officers as they attempted to reconcile the contradictions of their legal responsibilities and the 'extralegal' activities they were calle on to carry out by government officials as high as the President himself. The book reveals the astonishing facts of how ONI spied on fellow Americans for political purpos and how it became involved in the internal affairs of other nations.

9" x 6"; 320 pages; 25 illustrations; **£13.95** + £1.20 *for postage and packing.*

ASSAULT FROM THE SEA

Essays on the History of Amphibious Warfare
Lt. Col. Merrill
L. Bartlett

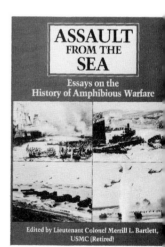

This great collection of over 50 articles from the world's leading publications brings together for the first time a history of amphibious landings throughout the ages – from Marathon in 490 BC up to the 1982 Falklands War. The book is divided into four sections dealing with amphibious warfare in the age of sail, the age of Mahan, World War II and the nuclear age. This is an invaluable reference work for all those concerned with the current debate on the future of amphibious forces, and the tactical maps included will be of special value to wargamers a historians.

10" x 7"; 312 pages; 40 illustrations; **£18.95** + £1.45 *postage and packing.*

a& ap Arms & Armour Press, 2-6 Hampstead High Street London NW3 1QQ Telephone: 01-794 7868 (24 hours)

If ordering by post, please add 35p each additional book to a maximum of £2.50, for postage & packing.